The New Edinburgh History of Scotland

VOLUME 9

Industry, Reform and Empire

The New Edinburgh History of Scotland

General editor: Roger Mason, *University of St Andrews*

Advisory editors: Dauvit Broun, *University of Glasgow*; Iain Hutchison, *University of Stirling*; Norman Macdougall, *University of St Andrews*; Nicholas Phillipson, *University of Edinburgh*

1 From Caledonia to Pictland to 795
   James Fraser, *University of Edinburgh*

2 From Pictland to Alba 789–1070
   Alex Woolf, *University of St Andrews*

3 Domination and Lordship 1070–1230
   Richard Oram, *University of Stirling*

4 The Wars of Scotland 1214–1371
   Michael Brown, *University of St Andrews*

5 The First Stewart Dynasty 1371–1488
   Steve Boardman, *University of Edinburgh*

6 Scotland Re-formed 1488–1587
   Jane Dawson, *University of Edinburgh*

7 Empire, Union and Reform 1587–1690
   Roger Mason, *University of St Andrews*

8 Nation, State, Province, Empire 1690–1790
   Ned Landsman, *State University of New York, Stony Brook*

9 Industry, Reform and Empire: Scotland, 1790–1880
   I. G. C. Hutchison, *University of Stirling*

10 Impaled Upon a Thistle: Scotland since 1880
   Ewen A. Cameron, *University of Edinburgh*

edinburghuniversitypress.com/series/nehs

Industry, Reform and Empire
Scotland, 1790–1880

I. G. C. Hutchison

EDINBURGH
University Press

To Rose and Patrick, the Future

Edinburgh University Press is one of the leading university presses in the UK. We publish academic books and journals in our selected subject areas across the humanities and social sciences, combining cutting-edge scholarship with high editorial and production values to produce academic works of lasting importance. For more information visit our website: edinburghuniversitypress.com

© I. G. C. Hutchison, 2020

Edinburgh University Press Ltd
The Tun – Holyrood Road
12 (2f) Jackson's Entry
Edinburgh EH8 8PJ

Typeset in 11/13 Ehrhardt MT by
IDSUK (DataConnection) Ltd

A CIP record for this book is available from the British Library

ISBN 978 0 7486 1512 4 (hardback)
ISBN 978 0 7486 1513 1 (paperback)
ISBN 978 0 7486 2848 3 (webready PDF)
ISBN 978 1 4744 6294 5 (epub)

The right of I. G. C. Hutchison to be identified as author of this work has been asserted in accordance with the Copyright, Designs and Patents Act 1988 and the Copyright and Related Rights Regulations 2003 (SI No. 2498).

Contents

Tables and Illustrations	vi
Acknowledgements	vii
Abbreviations	viii
General Editor's Preface	ix
Introduction	1
Chapter 1 The Agrarian Economy and Society	7
Chapter 2 The Manufacturing Economy	37
Chapter 3 Urban Society	64
Chapter 4 Urban Social Conditions	95
Chapter 5 The Presbyterian Churches	122
Chapter 6 Assimilation and Acculturation	148
Chapter 7 Politics in the Era of Revolutions, c. 1780–1815	183
Chapter 8 Politics in the Last Years of the Unreformed System, 1815–32	212
Chapter 9 Politics in the Age of the First Reform Act, 1832–c. 1865	237
Chapter 10 Inching towards Democracy: Politics, c. 1865–80	267
Conclusion: Approaching Niagara?	297
Guide to Further Reading	300
Bibliography	305
Index	334

Tables and Illustrations

Table 4.1	Death rates per 1,000 living, 1861 and 1881	96
Table 4.2	Scottish housing stock by room size, 1861–1901	99
Table 4.3	Population in house sizes, 1861–1901	99
Table 4.4	Overcrowding in Scottish houses, 1861–1901	99
Table 7.1	General Election results, England and Scotland, 1784–1812	190
Table 9.1	Conservative MPs, Scotland and England, 1832–59	241
Table 10.1	Scottish and English Conservative MPs, 1865–80	287
Figure 1.1	Farm workers at Phantassie Farm	17
Figure 2.1	Camperdown Jute Works	40
Figure 3.1	Furnacemen at Dalmellington Iron Works	82
Figure 4.1	Close no. 80, High Street, Glasgow	98
Figure 5.1	Rev. Thomas Chalmers	127
Figure 6.1	A Premonstratensian priest with schoolchildren, Whithorn	150
Figure 7.1	Henry Dundas, 1st Viscount Melville	202
Figure 8.1	Francis Jeffrey	217
Figure 9.1	Kirriemuir weavers' banner celebrating the repeal of the Corn Laws, 1846	248
Figure 10.1	West Calder reception committee for Gladstone, 1879	285

Acknowledgements

I am indebted to the British Academy, the Carnegie Trust for the Universities of Scotland, the Strathmartine Trust and Stirling University Faculty of Arts for generous financial support of the research for this book. I wish to thank the following owners of manuscripts who kindly gave me permission to quote from their papers: Mr K. Adam (Blair Adam MSS), Mr J. H. Crawford (Naughton House MSS), Lord Mansfield (Mansfield MSS), Sir Robert Clerk (Clerk of Penicuik MSS) and Mrs P. MacNeil (Kennedy of Dunure MSS). The staff at the National Register of Archives (Scotland) are thanked for their efficiency and courtesy in dealing with my requests for permission to consult manuscripts held in private hands. Staff at various university, national and local government archives were invariably helpful and friendly. David Lonergan and Sarah Foyle at Edinburgh University Press supported and advised me with great tolerance. Professor R. A. Mason and an anonymous reader read my draft chapters, and their comments greatly improved the final version. I am, of course, responsible for all errors of fact and oddities of opinion that remain. My wife Pat has patiently borne the interminable gestation of this book, for which I owe her an incalculable debt of gratitude.

Abbreviations

BL	British Library
CSU	Complete Suffrage Union
GCA	Glasgow City Archives
IRSS	*International Review of Scottish Studies*
JSHS	*Journal of Scottish Historical Studies*
MOH	Medical Officer of Health
NAVSR	National Association for the Vindication of Scottish Rights
NLS	National Library of Scotland
NRS	National Records of Scotland
NSA	*New Statistical Account*
NSWS	National Society for Women's Suffrage
NYRO	North Yorkshire Record Office
PP	*Parliamentary Papers*
RSCHS	*Records of the Scottish Church History Society*
Scot. Trad.	Scottish Tradition
SCRAN	Scottish Cultural Resources Network
SESH	*Scottish Economic & Social History*
SGM	*Scottish Geographical Magazine*
SHR	*Scottish Historical Review*
SLHSJ	*Scottish Labour History Society Journal*
SPBA	Scottish Permissive Bill Association
SWTA	Scottish Women's Temperance Association
UFC	United Free Church
UP(C)	United Presbyterian (Church)
USC	United Secession Church

General Editor's Preface

The purpose of the New Edinburgh History of Scotland is to provide up-to-date and accessible narrative accounts of the Scottish past. Its authors will make full use of the explosion of scholarly research that has taken place over the last three decades, and do so in a way that is sensitive to Scotland's regional diversity as well as to the British, European and transoceanic worlds of which Scotland has always been an integral part.

Chronology is fundamental to understanding change over time and Scotland's political development will provide the backbone of the narrative and the focus of analysis and explanation. The New Edinburgh History will tell the story of Scotland as a political entity, but will be sensitive to broader social, cultural and religious change and informed by a richly textured understanding of the totality and diversity of the Scots' historical experience. Yet to talk of the Scots – or the Scottish nation – is often misleading. Local loyalty and regional diversity have more frequently characterised Scotland than any perceived sense of 'national' solidarity. Scottish identity has seldom been focused primarily, let alone exclusively, on the 'nation'. The modern discourse of nationhood offers what is often an inadequate and inappropriate vocabulary in which to couch Scotland's history. The authors in this series will show that there are other and more revealing ways of capturing the distinctiveness of Scottish experience.

The astonishingly rapid and wide-ranging changes that Scotland experienced in the century after 1790 were not only without precedent, but transformed the country beyond all recognition. What was in the late eighteenth century a relatively under-populated rural society was by the 1880s densely populated, highly urbanised and heavily industrialised. The first part of Iain Hutchison's compelling study of these decades charts the demographic, economic and social changes that lay at the heart of these seismic developments, capturing the experience of Scots of all backgrounds – Lowlanders and Highlanders, landowners, tenants, artisans and entrepreneurs – as they were buffeted by the revolutionary changes that were taking place around them, and analysing the high social costs that so often accompanied them. As with the New Edinburgh History of Scotland in general, however, the politics of the period – broadly conceived – lies at the heart of the volume. Thus issues of political identity within an expanding imperial framework come under the author's close and insightful scrutiny, while the extension of the franchise and the emergence of class politics, the great schism in the established kirk known as the Disruption and the impact of Catholic emancipation all fall under his purview. Covering an era that witnessed the rise of revolutionary nationalism across Europe, this volume engages with Scotland's self-perceptions as at once a historic nation and a 'partner' in British imperial expansion in ways that are as nuanced as they are enlightening. One could ask for no richer or more satisfying introduction to a transformative century of Scottish history.

Introduction

ON THE EVE: SCOTLAND, C. 1750–C. 1780

Population statistics offer a striking manifestation of the extent of the changes which Scotland underwent in the period of this study. In 1755, there were 1,265,380 people in Scotland, and the first official census, taken in 1801, recorded a total of 1,608,420. By 1881, the population had leapt to 3,735,573. Moreover, in 1755, the great preponderance of the population was not urbanised, with around 9 per cent living in towns with 10,000 or more inhabitants, placing Scotland well down the table of European urbanisation, while England was at the top, with 17 per cent.

The demographic data underline the fragile economic condition of Scotland in three decades after 1750. Low population growth in part reflected an agricultural system which struggled to do more than, at best, provide basic foodstuffs, and indeed was frequently afflicted by dearth. Compared to England, there were few signs of proto-industrialisation before the 1780s, apart from the manufacture of linen, whose output value by the 1770s was four times greater than in the later 1720s. There were in the 1760s around 20,000 men and women engaged on a full-time basis in the sector, all in domestic production mode. The success of linen signposted a key element of Scotland's economic strength in the nineteenth century, namely, foreign trade: by the start of the 1770s, linen constituted 40–50 per cent of Scotland's total exports, with North America and the West Indies the main markets. Another instance of overseas trade was tobacco: in 1760, 40 per cent of the total UK trade was funnelled through Scotland, much of which was exported to France and the Netherlands.

Linked to this, the tradition of Scots seeking to better themselves by moving overseas was solidly established by the third quarter of the eighteenth century. Scots swarmed over the West Indies, some owning or managing the sugar and cotton plantations which exploited slave labour, and others providing ancillary support, such as medical and legal services. Many Scots settled in both the future United States and also in Canada, while India was another major target for Scotsmen on the make; as early as 1750, they comprised about 30 per cent of the East India Company's workforce in Bengal.

The social structure of the country around the accession of George III remained quite traditional. Ownership of land was more concentrated than in England, and the dominance of the great proprietors in political and social affairs was virtually unchallenged. In towns, many tradespeople and professionals depended on the neighbouring gentry for custom and trade. Urban craftsmen were protected from competition by the monopoly powers of their trade incorporations, but this protection was creaking in several occupations, notably in tailoring and handloom weaving, where it was easy to pick up the basic skills and demand for these products was growing.

The overwhelming defeat of Jacobitism in 1746 entrenched the commanding position of Presbyterianism, for both Episcopalianism and Roman Catholicism were tainted with pro-Stuart sympathies. From the 1760s, the Moderates were the dominant grouping in the Church of Scotland. They were theologically liberal and relaxed about religious diversity, but quite conservative in social and political affairs. The Moderates were intimately involved in the Scottish Enlightenment, the great intellectual and cultural phenomenon of the third quarter of the eighteenth century. The Enlightenment stressed the centrality of reason and science, and highlighted the importance of the civic responsibilities of engaged townspeople and the desirability of both economic and moral improvement, as well as of progression towards social stability and the optimisation of human potential.

After the collapse at Culloden of the Jacobite rising, the challenge for Scottish politics was to establish a firm commitment to the Hanoverian dynasty. From 1746 until his death in 1761, Lord Ilay, later the third duke of Argyll, maintained the dominant influence which the political faction centred on his family, known as the Argathelians, had exercised from the 1720s. Ilay used the power of his political bloc to induce the government to promote Scottish interests, such as the linen trade, fishing and the building of Edinburgh New Town. He also ensured that the best talents were appointed to the judiciary and avoided perpetuating the rancid divide which Jacobitism had created, by eschewing any vindictive persecution of erstwhile supporters of the Stuart cause. But for the fifteen or so years following his death, there was no clear overall manager of Scottish politics, until the emergence of Henry Dundas in the 1780s.

OUTLINE OF CONTENTS

The core objective of the series of studies which comprise the New Edinburgh History of Scotland is to pay special attention to the political developments occurring in the relevant time span, and this volume follows this prescription.

The first six chapters, however, seek to outline the complex set of social, economic and cultural contexts which shaped the politics of the era, while the last four consist of a survey of the political developments.

Chapter 1 examines the diverging experiences of agricultural change in the Lowlands and the Highlands. In the former, there was a remarkable transformation, as the area moved from a rather static mode of subsistence farming to becoming one of the most highly advanced regions in the United Kingdom. Although the initial impetus for improvement stemmed from landowners, motivated in part by Enlightenment ideals of economic and social advancement and in part (for some) by financial pressures, the forward momentum was quite soon taken up by tenant-farmers, who became a prosperous, sturdily independent class. The Highlands, in contrast, failed to achieve such a positive outcome, and instead endured serious economic, demographic and social dislocation, which scarred the region for generations.

Chapter 2 charts the process by which Scotland became a significant industrial power. Initially, this took place in textiles, and then in the last third of the period, the country established a major world presence in heavy industry. The key aspects of the later phase included the international dominance of the Clyde in shipbuilding, along with several engineering specialisms, and the associated exponential growth in the production of coal and iron. The reasons for these achievements are discussed in both material and cultural terms, but it is also noted that many people were still engaged in traditional occupations, and that most firms employed only a handful of workers.

The changes in social structure flowing from developments in industry and commerce are analysed in Chapter 3. The solid middle classes – the professions and businesspeople – expanded greatly, and these cadres were self-confident and assertive of the values of competitiveness, laissez-faire and meritocracy. As such, they assumed virtually full control of the social institutions of towns, and shaped them in order to fulfil the goals of social status and good order. The lower middle classes, mostly shopkeepers and master craftsmen, were less assured than these comfortable middle-class people. Their economic circumstances were much more precarious, and their social activities were more circumscribed. The new economic order presented challenges to many of the working classes, for several established occupations were swept away, de-skilling was imposed, and employers' control of the workplace was entrenched. On the other hand, new skills and job opportunities were forged, especially in the heavy industries. One upshot of these forces was the formation of a gulf between those in skilled and those in semi- or unskilled occupations, which was evidenced in income levels, employment prospects and social differentiation.

The consequences of the processes outlined in Chapters 2 and 3 are examined in Chapter 4, mostly as they impacted on urban areas. In places like Glasgow, health standards fell from about 1820, and did not return to that level in the succeeding sixty years. Urban housing conditions were easily the worst in Britain; two-thirds of properties in the 1860s consisted of one- or two-roomed houses. Sanitary provision was quite inadequate, and there was severe air and water pollution. The prevailing doctrine of laissez-faire meant that no serious attempt to interfere with market conditions occurred until the very last decades of the period. The operation of the Poor Laws was similarly shaped in conformity to unfettered free market principles, which were applied more stringently than in England. Because all of these problems were interlinked, institutional efforts to reduce their extent were largely vitiated.

Chapter 5 surveys the turbulent trajectory of the Presbyterian churches. The rise of Evangelicalism gravely challenged the Church of Scotland's dominant Moderate wing in two respects. Firstly, from the later eighteenth century, there were substantial secessions from the established church, and secondly, from the early 1830s there was a bitter tussle within the state church which resulted in over a third of its clergy and laity breaking away to form the Free Church in 1843. This rift affected not just the different Presbyterian denominations, for it carried important social and political implications, which ramified for the rest of the period.

In Chapter 6, the varieties of identities in Scotland are outlined; the gradual assimilation of Highlanders into mainstream Scottish society is explored, as is the integration of Scots into a British identity, where the role of empire played a prominent part. The obstacles which Irish Roman Catholic immigrants encountered in blending into the host community included a marked guardedness by the latter about absorbing these newcomers. But also, there was a strong impulse among the incomers to adhere to their faith, which required withdrawing engagement with public agencies that they regarded as deeply permeated with Presbyterian values. In place of these bodies, the Irish Catholic community established parallel institutions, but in the case of education, this involved providing a significantly lower standard of instruction, thereby rendering the goal of social mobility harder to achieve.

Chapters 7 to 10 cover the political history of the period in chronological segments, with the underlying theme being the gradual erosion of the dominance of the Tory party and the establishment after the 1832 Reform Act of an unassailable Liberal hegemony. The latter party won all twelve general elections in Scotland held between 1832 and 1880, whereas in England, the Conservatives won five times. Chapter 7 explains the unreformed electoral system and charts responses to the French Revolution, which included the break-up of the opposition Whigs and the consequent consolidation of the Tories' grip on Scottish politics under the masterful direction of Henry Dundas. The eclipse of the emerging reform currents under the stress of events in the 1790s was mirrored by the sizeable volume of loyalist opinion across a broad social spectrum. Chapter 8 studies the last years of the unreformed system, covering the challenges of working-class radical movements in the immediate period after the end in 1815 of the wars with France; the continuing Tory grip on power; and the emergence of a new generation of Whigs. These last were influenced by the economic and social ideals of the Scottish Enlightenment, which they expounded in the *Edinburgh Review*. By the later 1820s, there had emerged a rising tide of support for parliamentary reform, yoking together solid bourgeois progressives, working-class radicals and the rejuvenated Whigs. This alliance cohered around demands to reduce taxes, to end obstacles to free trade, pre-eminently the Corn Laws, and to reform local government.

Chapter 9 looks at the new electoral dispensation and its impact. The Reform Act largely enfranchised middle-class men, with few workingmen qualifying. The initial post-Reform Act euphoria of Whigs and Radicals was derailed by the Disruption of 1843, which resulted in internal faction-fighting among the Whigs until a degree of unity was restored in the later 1850s under Palmerston's premiership. The Whigs were greatly assisted by the problems dogging the Tories, who were tarnished by their implacable resistance before 1832 to every proposed measure of reform. This reactionary image was reinforced by Tory opposition to the abolition of the Corn Laws, a widely supported demand in Scotland – even among farmers. The party was further contaminated by the Disruption, which occurred during a Conservative administration that declined to accede to Free Church demands.

Chapter 10 discusses the evolving political landscape under the impact of a much broader electorate created by the Second Reform Act of 1868, which in many burgh constituencies meant that a majority of voters were drawn from the artisanal working class. Although there was an initial degree of harmony in the Liberal party between the new electors and the more middle-class adherents, this came under strain in the early 1870s. Middle-class Evangelicals pressed for morality-grounded social reforms, such as teetotalism. Working-class Liberals, however, focused on reform of labour legislation, but middle-class Liberals resisted such demands as being in conflict with pure laissez-faire principles. Fractious disagreements between the two camps grew, until Gladstone suppressed them in his Midlothian election campaign late in 1879 by dint of focusing almost exclusively on the mistakes of the Conservative government. Thus, the Liberal triumph in the 1880 general election revealed a reunited party. For the Tories, the years between 1868 and 1880 offered few comforts. The alliance of the Free Church and Seceder Presbyterians ensured that barely any burgh seats went over to the party, unlike in England. But Scottish Tories faced a further challenge. The party essentially relied on county seats to return the great preponderance of its MPs, but from 1865 tenant-farmers revolted against the power exercised over them by landowners. This protest movement resulted in several Tory seats being lost at successive general elections, and it persisted until remedial legislation was passed in 1880. But six years later, the mould of Scottish Victorian politics was irreparably shattered by the Irish Home Rule question.

CHAPTER I

The Agrarian Economy and Society

I. THE LOWLANDS

THE IMPROVING PROCESS

A profound modernising process occurred in Lowland farming between the last decades of the eighteenth century and the middle of the next century, a change neatly summarised by the parish minister of Alford, writing in the mid-1830s, who marvelled at the sweep of changes which 'have transformed the rude and unproductive husbandry of 1796 into our present skilful and productive one'.[1]

The traditional system of agriculture in the Lowlands contained many or all of the following features, with local variations always present. Most farms were leased on a joint-tenancy basis, as at Canonbie in Dumfriesshire, where in 1775 there were 149 tenants in 48 farms. Leases were normally granted for only one year – or at most a few years. Also present were cottars, who provided additional labour at points of pressure in the agricultural calendar for the farmers, and at other times worked either as labourers or as rural craftsmen, for instance, weavers and tailors. Cottars had no formal leases, but held a small plot of ground for growing vegetables. The arable fields – the infield – were divided into strips randomly apportioned between the joint tenants, with high ridges of earth separating the portions – i.e. the runrig system. To ensure fairness between the joint farmers, the allocation of strips changed every year. There was usually a three- or four-year arable rotation system. Livestock was kept on the area of pasture – the outfield – which was worked on a communal basis. There were normally also scrubland areas, used by cottars for fuel.

The limitations of this set-up were numerous. The ridges wasted large areas of the fields, so reducing yields, and the communal working of the fields meant that more efficient tenants could be detrimentally affected by less able men, notably with weeds drifting and stones not being cleared. Moreover, the annual circulation of strips was a disincentive to long-term improvement efforts by any tenant. The soil quality of the arable fields was poor, because of over-cropping and inadequate manuring, and so yields were generally low and uncertain. This meant that nearly all produce was consumed by the humans, therefore animals were killed or sold on in autumn as they could not be over-wintered, and thus stock improvement was impossible. Productivity was also inhibited by the distribution of houses and steadings, which was utterly haphazard and meant that much working time was consumed simply in getting to and from fields. Additionally, implements and machinery were very basic and labour-intensive: wooden ploughs struggled with poor soil, and it required four men operating in pairs with up to eight oxen (horses being a rarity, and lacking in strength) to work a single plough. Winnowing and harvesting was done by hand, with flails and sickles. In this context of a highly precarious agricultural regime, famine was an ever-present prospect, and as late as 1782–3 a very severe food crisis occurred across large parts of the Lowlands. This was, then, a subsistence agrarian economy, with no regular surplus to sell in the marketplace, which in any case the lack of a dependable transport network prohibited. For much of the eighteenth century, roads were of a very poor standard, and in wet weather were virtually impassable.

In the middle of the eighteenth century, therefore, Lowland agricultural performance contrasted dismally with the more dynamic English sector, as observers on both sides of the border commented. But the pace of change in Scotland then accelerated, and by the second quarter of the nineteenth century, it was England which now looked admiringly at Lowland farming. In 1832, William Cobbett, normally a curmudgeonly commentator where anything Scottish was concerned, lavishly praised developments in Lowland farming. In East Lothian, he reported, 'the land is the finest that ever I saw in my life . . . there are, in almost every half mile, from fifty to a hundred acres [twenty to forty hectares] of turnips in one piece, . . . all in rows as straight as a line, and without a weed ever to be seen in any of these beautiful fields'.[2] Landowners in England now imported Scottish 'bailiffs' to instruct their tenants in best farming practices; in 1806, James Grant of Rothiemurchus brought down a grieve from Scotland in order to improve his Hertfordshire estate.

At the core of the reconfiguration of Lowland agriculture lay several profound innovations. Joint-tenancy agreements were replaced by leases granting one individual sole control of a farm. This had been initiated on a sporadic basis in the first half of the century, but was embarked on systematically from the 1770s and 1780s, being applied as old leases fell in: on the duke of Hamilton's Lanarkshire estate, joint tenancies fell by almost 50 per cent in the second half of the eighteenth century. The significance of single tenancy was that considerable surpluses of produce could be generated, in contrast to the scratching subsistence level of the older arrangement. The consolidation of farm units was enhanced by a systematic drive, which was particularly rapid and extensive between 1760 and 1815, to enclose common ground, and this process was abetted by the Scottish legal system, which did not recognise unwritten customary rights. Hence, there was no need for the cumbersome procedure of seeking parliamentary legislative consent, whereas in England, 1,800 enclosure bills were drawn up between 1760 and 1800. Instead, the local sheriff had the power to decide the apportionment of such areas.

Further changes served to orient the new tenantry towards the demands of the market, which were growing rapidly thanks to accelerating urbanisation and rising real wages – plus supplying provisions for the armed forces during the twenty years of war with France, beginning in 1793 – which all resulted in significantly higher prices for produce. Importantly, the foodstuff needs of townspeople were now regular and predictable, and to supply this guaranteed market bold innovation in farming practices was encouraged. Moreover, urban requirements were not confined to feeding humans. Horses, vital for town transport, required large quantities of straw and hay for bedding and fodder. Businesses such as shoemakers, glue manufacturers and soap- and candlemakers all relied wholly on farms to supply, respectively, leather hides, animal bones and tallow. There was thus forged a beneficial symbiosis between town and countryside, whereby agriculture modernised to expand its output, and the consequent shedding of surplus rural labour supplied a workforce for the rising urban manufacturing sector, which in turn augmented demand for farm produce.

Three crucial innovations transformed Lowland agricultural practice in the last third of the eighteenth century. Firstly, leases were now given on a long-term basis, normally nineteen or twenty-one years in localities with a high arable content, but in places with difficult soil conditions, this was sometimes extended to as many as twenty-six years. In grazing areas, where there was less need both for long-term working of the soil and for large capital inputs, as in Ayrshire, leases of ten years were more common. Nineteen-year leases were much longer than the conventional length given in England, and their significance was that they allowed the tenant to experiment, in the expectation that over the period improved returns would justify the long view adopted. Furthermore, tenant-farmers had limited capital resources to start with, so the accumulation of the necessary funding took a considerable time. Secondly, by the 1770s, payment of rent was steadily being moved from kind to cash, and by the 1790s, money rents were almost universal, thus adding to the incentive to enter the market economy. Thirdly, rents were raised very significantly: between 1770 and the early 1800s, across a spectrum of Lowland estates, landowners set rents at up to three or four times higher than previous levels. Thus, between 1767 and 1812, the annual rental revenue of the Buccleuch estates rose from £19,000 to £50,000. This was, of course, intended to drive tenants to substantially improve their productivity and output levels to meet these demands.

The response of tenants to these challenges focused both on extending the area of productive land and on improving soil quality, in order to maximise production of crops, along with raising the standard of livestock and using labour as efficiently as possible. The removal of field ridges at once greatly expanded workable land and regularised the shape of fields, which could now be worked by machinery such as ploughs in a more efficient manner. Reclamation of waste land was another means of expansion, and this could only be carried out over several years, which of course the extended lease facilitated. Draining wet and boggy land – of which Scotland had a superabundance – became a major preoccupation, and the clearing of the Kincardine Moss in west Stirlingshire provided a model of what could be achieved. Here, in 1766, Lord Kames began a project to remove layers of peat between two and three metres deep from a bogland area of 450 hectares. Beneath the peat lay rich alluvial soil, on which by 1811 some 150 small farms had been established. The benefits of effective draining were considerable: ploughing could take place earlier in the year, allowing a longer growing season for crops; the need for fallowing was obviated; and machinery could be used more freely over drier ground. Drainage tiles were laid on a mammoth scale, 75 centimetres deep and in rows 45 centimetres apart, and at Fenton Barns in East Lothian, £2,500 was spent on drainage.

Heavy fertilisation was another characteristic of the improved farming agenda: 75,000 to 100,000 kilograms of manure per hectare was the standard application for growing potatoes. Hitherto, only manure produced on the farm had been used, and with no overwintering of stock, this was in short supply. With the new practices, more livestock was kept and, crucially, it was no longer necessary to kill beasts in autumn, as winter fodder was now grown. This of course greatly increased the amount of farm manure, but additional outside sourcing was universal. Guano, the droppings of seabirds around the coast of Latin America, became available from 1841, and demand seemed insatiable: in 1842, some 31 million kilograms were spread across Scottish fields, but by 1872, this had surged to over 85 million kilograms. The growth of urban centres proved an invaluable boon. Obviously, horse dung was available on a monumental scale, but human manure was another major supply. Night soil, as it was euphemistically called, was gathered in large middens for removal by farmers, but in practice, only farms within eight miles of a town could haul town manure with ease. A significant innovation was the addition from the later 1830s of bone-meal, a slow release plant feed, especially beneficial for root crops such as turnips. Other imaginative sources of fertiliser were taken up. Shoddy, the waste from woollen textile manufacture, was used, as was soot, of which there must have been vast amounts, and waste grain from breweries and distilleries was another source. In coastal areas, crushed seashells and seaweed were applied. Over-use of manure, however, could turn the soil sour, so reducing crop yields. This problem was particularly common in heavy soils, which were widespread in Scotland, and the remedy was the application of lime, often in large quantities. Lord Elgin's limeworks on the Firth of Forth produced between eight and nine million kilograms per annum, and the revenue in 1816 – £3,263 – amounted to one-half of the of the estate's rental income.

Improved quality and quantity of crops were sought by way of sophisticated crop rotation programmes, with a full cycle typically lasting from five to eight years. The aim was to revive the land after a greedy crop, such as grain and roots, by using techniques of self-sufficient agriculture, rather than overdosing on bought-in fertilisers, while simultaneously avoiding soil and plant diseases and also avoiding spreading the risks presented by monoculture. In order to refresh the soil with nutrients, especially nitrogen, clover or other sown grass was put down for one or two years, and two years of legumes (e.g. peas, beans and lentils) were frequently also included in the rotation. Sown grasses additionally suppressed weeds and provided hay for winter feeding.

Two contributory factors in improving farming output were, firstly, better machinery and implements, and, secondly, rationalisation of the layout and structure of buildings. A range of mechanised aids were introduced, initially concentrated in harvesting, draining and threshing. Threshing machines marked a significant advance, and the pioneering innovator in Scotland was Andrew Meikle, who started their manufacture in 1784. Some were water-powered, but the larger farms mostly installed steam power, and by 1860, portable steam machines extended the benefits of reliability and speed to smaller farmers as well. Other machines included turnip cutters, cake crushers, butter churns, potato lifters, steel harrows and seed drills. These all economised on labour and gave a more uniform standard of outcome. Harvesting machines, especially reapers, only arrived after about 1850, with Bell's reaper the most favoured. Probably the most influential development, not just in its agricultural but also in its social impact, was the replacement of the pre-improvement wooden plough with the metal swing plough devised in the later eighteenth century by James Small. The new plough was immensely superior: it was lighter and so could be worked by one man in charge of two horses – one-quarter of both the humans and animals required under the old dispensation. Its greater manoeuvrability meant it performed tasks much more speedily and precisely. It cut deeper into the ground than its predecessor, and was less prone to damage from stones and boulders, so that it was immeasurably more effective in land reclamation work. The efficacy of these advances in machinery and implements was to a large extent conditional on the creation of large, regular-shaped fields with no obstacles, so that they could operate at optimum levels.

The higgledy-piggledy scatterings of buildings prevalent in the older system were seen as barriers to improvement. Of course, with the removal of the cottar class and joint farmers, the number of structures was much reduced. But now the layout of the buildings was planned to ensure the greatest efficiency of movement between buildings and the land. From the early 1800s, the courtyard or square format became the norm. The farmer's house, usually a substantial building, was the hub, situated alongside integrated outhouses, in order to cut down on needless waste of time and effort. Covered byres for cattle were constructed, and manure no longer sat in an exposed midden, open to the degradation of nutrients through rain and snow, but was now housed in a shed. This was sited adjacent to the byre, and had wide doors at the rear leading to a farm track, so allowing horse-driven carts to convey dung speedily to the fields. Equally, the new machinery and tools required protection from the elements to prolong their lifespan. Crops were stored in a position equally central for feeding to livestock or for taking to market for sale. As a core part of this new regard for the quality of buildings, materials with a long lifetime were used: slate replaced thatch as roofing, and stone walls ousted wattle or wood.

The fruits of this slew of improvements were reflected in farm produce. On the whole, Scottish Lowland farmers tended to opt for a broadly mixed system, although the predominant weighting varied regionally. In the Borders, sheep were the main product, but in the south-west, it was dairy cattle. The Lothians, Fife and Easter Ross focused more on grains, and the north-east concentrated on beef cattle. Among grain crops, wheat was less grown than in England, as weather and soil conditions were not suitable in many areas, especially in western parts. Therefore, oats tended to be the main cereal crop, and output rose threefold over the period. In regions where there was a distilling industry, such as Speyside, barley was the preferred grain. Root crops, especially potatoes and turnips, were vital for the success of improved farming, as they provided winter feed for livestock and consumption of turnips increased the amount of animal dung for fertiliser. In the north-east in 1855, 50,000 hectares were used for turnips, and 7,200 hectares for potatoes.

The boom in cattle derived from the benefits of better breeding and feeding, with the latter the result of the improvements in soil quality outlined earlier. Intensive breeding by Hugh Watson of Keillor produced the prizewinning Angus variety, and William MacCombie of Tillyfour took this further by establishing the Aberdeen Angus breed, with an average of five calves per annum born to each cow. In the case of sheep, the Cheviot was widespread across Scotland, usually crossbred with the Blackface variety for the fattening trade. The advantage of the Cheviot was that it was less labour-intensive than other breeds, especially as the fleeces could be sheared, while other varieties required plucking. A major breakthrough came with the arrival at Kelso mart in 1802 of 2,000 Leicester tups for breeding in Scotland. Leicesters in the Borders were larger than in England, and when crossbred, they gave more meat and better-quality wool. An additional benefit of bigger livestock was that more manure was produced.

The role of transport was central to the transformation of Lowland agriculture, both in giving access to wider markets, and in facilitating the importation of essential materials to increase production. The construction of turnpike roads immensely improved the quality of roads which both permitted year-round transport and also made previously remote places quite accessible. For instance, between 1790 and 1810, 246 miles of turnpike roads were built in Aberdeenshire, and by the 1830s the network had reached Corgarff, the county's *Ultima Thule*.

The advent of the railways and steamboats proved even more galvanising for farmers. Trains allowed the south-west dairy specialisation to take off, as fresh milk could be brought daily to the large urban concentrations in Renfrewshire and Lanarkshire. Further south, where milk tended to sour before reaching the Glasgow area, butter was churned, and beyond that, cheese prevailed. By 1820, there were 20,000 dairy cattle in Cunninghame district, each cow producing its own weight in cheese and half its weight in butter annually. The beef cattle trade in Aberdeen was taken to astonishing levels, firstly by steamboats, then by rail. A steamboat service from Aberdeen to London began in 1828, and by 1850, 16,000 animals were shipped south annually. The advent of the rail system from mid-century proved even more advantageous. The journey time was much shorter; moreover it was more reliable, being largely unaffected by adverse weather and, perhaps more importantly, there was no risk of cattle being harmed by a rough sea passage. By the 1850s, 12,000 cows went annually by train from Aberdeen to the capital. Steamboats were still important for conveying cattle, especially dead meat, which obviously was not affected by travel conditions. By the 1860s, the equivalent of 33,800 cattle, alive and dead, were sent annually from Aberdeen to London by both boat and rail. The railway system also let north-east farmers supply the meat trade in the urban west of Scotland, which previously had not been very accessible.

But the coming of new transport facilities was not in every respect beneficial. Rural craftspeople found themselves undercut in price and outstripped in quality by products made in specialist regions which could now penetrate hitherto protected markets. Local textile activity was very much damaged by this: stocking-makers in Aberdeenshire were virtually obliterated by English manufacturers, and south-western weavers likewise collapsed in the face of competition. Other sectors at risk included brickmaking, metal crafts and wooden shipbuilding. The response was to develop specialisms in which the region could establish primacy in a national marketplace: so, the north-east focused on meat-packing and granite-quarrying.

THE MOTIVES UNDERLYING IMPROVEMENT

The initial impetus for improvement essentially emanated from the landowners. In considerable part, they were inspired by several of the key ideas of the Scottish Enlightenment. These they would pick up sometimes by contact with the thinkers themselves, as the social worlds of Edinburgh, Glasgow and Aberdeen were small and intimate, with gentry often members of local clubs and learned societies. Perhaps the most striking instance of this process was the employment in 1764 of Adam Smith as tutor to the third duke of Buccleuch, then aged seventeen. The youthful peer was profoundly influenced by Smith's argument that agriculture occupied a central role in increasing the wealth of the nation, and therefore it should be the recipient of heavy capital investment. Accordingly, from 1770, Buccleuch switched the direction of his estate management from mere expansion to sustained improvement. Another fulcrum for the spread of these improving concepts was through land agents, many of whom had been educated at the universities where the scholars of the Enlightenment taught. Most landowners relied heavily on these individuals for guidance on estate improvement; as an indicator of their contribution, the factor on the Seafield estate was paid the remarkable annual salary of £600. William Kerr served as overseer for nearly forty years on the vast Buccleuch estates, and became the main driver of change from 1778 until 1810, as the duke increasingly concentrated on public affairs.

There were two strands in Enlightenment thinking which struck home with landowners. The first was the movement's programme of economic and social advancement, which stressed the formation of a market-oriented agricultural sector as a core prerequisite for moving to the next developmental stage, namely, industrialisation. One aspect of this analysis was the importance of eliminating the peasant – or, in Scotland, the cottar – class from farming. The second theme to resonate was the concept of moral virtue manifested in civic patriotism, which Scottish landowners should embrace by seeking to emulate England as a progressive, modern society, especially by promoting economic and social change. This was linked to the argument that culture was evidence of civilisation, and hence untamed nature was no longer acceptable; instead there should be order and control. Thus, in agriculture, rationality should replace tradition and custom.

But less elevated motives also lay behind the landowners' interest in reforming agriculture. A good number were in a precarious financial position, as the costs of maintaining an upper-class lifestyle imposed heavy burdens on estate revenues. These included supporting the members of the family, especially unmarried and widowed relatives, and even burial costs – the funeral expenses of the penultimate duke of Gordon ran to around £3,600. Interest charges on inherited debts consumed large portions of annual income, while the laws of entail, stricter than in England (although progressively relaxed from 1770), made it very difficult to release funds by selling off parts of the estate. Successive earls of Elgin struggled with severe financial pressures: in 1812, net indebtedness came to £103,000, and in 1861 it was £170,000. Elsewhere, in 1825, the earl of Galloway's estate was £303,000 in the red. But these sums were modest compared to the financial depredations bequeathed by the fourth duke of Gordon, who died in 1827, leaving debts exceeding half-a-million pounds to his heirs.

Therefore, at the outset of the moves to improved agriculture, the landowners had a significant role. They authorised the changes in leasing policy to single occupancy of farms, and they increased the number of specific stipulations in the contract about such matters as rotation: whereas in the early eighteenth century, a normal lease might run to two or three pages, by the end of the century it would typically contain twelve to fifteen pages. However, from the early years of the nineteenth century, the landed class became less important in the improving surge as the initiative in progress and innovation shifted decisively to the tenant-farmers. The contribution of landowners was now more directed to improving the infrastructure and the broader environment. The construction of turnpike roads and the erection of bridges became a major focus of activity, facilitating the development of farming for the market: for example, the duke of Buccleuch spent £7,000 on building turnpikes. Harbours were also built by landowners, such as Port Gordon. Trees were planted on a grand scale in order to afford protection to farms on exposed sites: Lord Fife alone was responsible for creating 5,600 hectares of woodland on his Banffshire estate. Rivers had their banks reinforced and built up to reduce the risk of fields being flooded: 200 hectares were reclaimed by such operations on the rivers Isla and Ericht in Angus.

The tenant-farmers emerged as entrepreneurs just as able and original as the more widely acclaimed Scottish industrialists. As we have seen, they explored every market opportunity, strove to minimise costs and maximise output, and embraced new technology with gusto. Their organisation of the layout of farm buildings, for instance, carefully planned to guarantee a smooth work flow with no waste of time or unnecessary use of labour, mirrored the preoccupation of textile manufacturers to position machinery and integrate production stages so as to optimise labour productivity. Most of the farmers were recruited from those joint tenants deemed by landowners as the most likely to succeed. In Aberdeenshire, however, men from the Lothians were brought in to set examples to the native farmers. As we have seen, the locals soon matched their tutors in achievement.

Farmers learned in good measure from experience, especially from observing their neighbours, whether prospering or failing. But they also read widely about agriculture. There were several Scottish publications in the later eighteenth century which advocated a scientific and rational basis to farming, such as books by Lords Kames (1776) and Dundonald (1795). In 1800, the *Farmer's Magazine* was launched in Edinburgh, reporting on theoretical and practical improvements, and it was avidly read by tenant-farmers. Interest in agricultural progress was, significantly, not narrowly confined to the farming community: 40 per cent of the members of Selkirk Subscription Library, founded in 1772, borrowed at least one work on farming. Academics made an important contribution; thus, the first chair of agriculture in a British university was established at Edinburgh in 1790. Before then, Professors Joseph Black and William Cullen used their expertise in chemistry to give advice on enhancing soil quality, for example. Both men occupied chairs initially at Glasgow University, then at Edinburgh University. Thus, there was a broad spectrum of sources of advice which were accessible to all ranks of improvers.

Another very important source of information was the Farmers' Clubs, which spread across the Lowlands – by 1834 there were 136 local bodies. At their meetings, experiments and new developments were reported and discussed. The clubs held annual shows and organised competitions in order to encourage emulation of the best practices. The Ardrossan Agricultural Society, founded in 1775 and embracing nine Ayrshire parishes, awarded annual prizes for the best local crops and livestock, while ploughing matches began in Alloa in 1784. These societies also made arrangements to improve stock; even in a small and not particularly prominent farming area, the Clackmannanshire Farmers' Club organised the delivery from Ireland of a stallion to mate with local mares, in a bid to raise the quality of draught horses in the county. At the national level, the Highland and Agricultural Society made a major contribution to sponsoring the culture of improvement. Formed in 1784–5, with 39 founding members, by 1800 the membership was 700, and in 20 years it had doubled to 1,400. The society promoted information to agriculturalists about new technology and innovative techniques, such as harrowing machines and water meadows.

THE AGRICULTURAL LABOUR FORCE

The improved agricultural regime imposed major changes in the structure and nature of the labour force, although no uniform pattern emerged, because of regional differences in farming systems. But the broad trend was clear, and

THE AGRARIAN ECONOMY AND SOCIETY 17

Figure 1.1 Farm workers at Phantassie Farm, East Lothian, c. 1870s–80s. The preponderance of women is striking. © National Museum of Scotland. Licensor: www.scran.ac.uk

differed significantly from the English pattern. The practice of mixed farming meant that labour was required all the year round, partly because of the importance of root crops for the success of the whole process. Additionally, unlike the previous system, specialised labour – above all, ploughing – was now a crucial component, particularly as the new plough required great skill and delicacy to operate properly. Ploughing would take place on around 200 days a year on an average farm; turnip and potato fields, for example, required regular weeding and dunging.

In the Lothians and the Merse, the characteristic farmworker was the married ploughman, locally termed a hind. He was given a cottage and a patch for growing vegetables. Payment was primarily in kind – up to 80 per cent of the total – and this served as a hedge against price fluctuations, so limiting discontent. In the north-east, unmarried farmworkers were the norm; in 1851, three-quarters of the 15,000 agricultural labourers in Aberdeenshire were unmarried. Most were sons of the small crofters in upper Aberdeenshire, obliged to seek work elsewhere as the croft could not support resident adult children. These workers were paid in both cash and kind, mainly oats, plus accommodation. The last was not, in the north-east, a bothy, but a 'chaumer', a room above the stables housing their horses. The ploughmen were relatively young: four-fifths were under thirty years old, whereas the average age of their employer was around fifty-five years. They were able to save perhaps £40 to £50 while working, which provided a nest egg for their marriage, which usually marked their departure from paid farmwork. After quitting, they found work in different spheres: a good number returned to the family croft, to take over from elderly parents, some found employment in towns as carters, while others, like Chris Guthrie's brother in *Sunset Song*, Lewis Grassic Gibbon's classic regional novel, emigrated – in his case to South America.

Day labourers were relatively scarce in Scotland – certainly compared to England. One reason was that no poor relief was given to the able-bodied, nor was there housing available in farming areas for seasonal workers. Additionally, with a layer of skilled farmworkers above them, and virtually no smallholdings (outside the upland areas in the north-east), there were few prospects of upward mobility for this group. Although wages for day labourers rose by about 50 per cent between 1800 and 1843, pay levels and job opportunities, especially for other family members, were more attractive in urban areas. Male day labourers seem to have been mainly drawn from the ranks of ex-cottars and from former ploughmen too old to continue in that line of work. But many of the additional workers required at seasonal points of pressure, such as harvesting, were women.

This reliance on female labour marked out the Scottish agricultural sector as yet again quite different from the English, where the numbers of women declined steadily through the nineteenth century. In 1851, just over one in five Scottish farmworkers were female, as against one in ten in England, but by 1881, the numbers for England had fallen to 6 per cent, whereas in Scotland the drop was to only just under 20 per cent. In the Lothians and the Merse, women comprised between one-quarter and one-third of the total agricultural labour force. In this area, the work was seasonal, particularly at harvest-time. The farm's hind was obliged to provide these women, who were often his wife and daughters, but sometimes he had to bring in other women. These were the bondagers, who attracted much attention, in part because of their striking clothing and hats. There was also an influx from mid-summer until early autumn of women harvesters from both Ireland and the Highlands, who progressed through the Lowland farming areas. Additional seasonal female labour came in some areas from adjacent mining and textile villages. The employment of women on a seasonal basis began to decline from the 1860s. This was in part because the sickle, which could be used by women, was gradually replaced from the 1840s by the scythe, which tended to be worked by men only. Another factor was that alternative employment increasingly became available for women, notably domestic service, a job which had a higher social cachet among young women and their parents, and certainly seemed less laborious than fieldwork.

The dairying area in the south-west differed from elsewhere in that women were employed on a permanent footing. Milking the cattle and subsequently making butter or cheese were tasks undertaken virtually exclusively by females, in part because it was believed women had a gentler touch when handling the cows. One woman could milk about twenty cows, and with herd sizes up to eighty, this frequently meant that four women were employed on a farm, while only a couple of men were needed to do the rest of the tasks.

THE ANCILLARY LABOUR SECTOR

As noted, one result of this shift from generalised, part-time farmwork to full-time skilled labour was that the cottar class, so crucial to the old regime, had no obvious role. The contribution of the cottars was further diminished by, firstly, the improvement in roads, which meant that less service labour was needed on poor-quality parochial roads, and, secondly, the growing reliance on coal as the main fuel in place of peat, which had required long periods of labour from cottars. Although considerable numbers of them moved from the countryside to towns, others remained active in the rural economy and society. As discussed earlier, some shifted to becoming day labourers. Others, however, followed a different route to survival in the countryside, since the agricultural revolution had created jobs even as it destroyed the cottars' economic livelihood. The new machines needed repairing, ditchers and drainers were in high demand, as were vermin trappers, while the construction of farm buildings led to an increase in building tradesmen; in addition, the transport infrastructure had to be maintained and patched up. Farmers increasingly had more disposable income, and as they normally lived at a distance from towns, they patronised small villages for their regular needs. Hence bakers, butchers, dairymen and grocers could make a living, as did innkeepers, drapers, tailors and shoemakers.

The demand for these tradespeople was heightened by the creation of planned villages, of which some 450 were founded in the century down to 1850. Most were in the Lowlands and the more advanced farming portions of the eastern Highlands, with only a smattering in the western Highlands and islands. Many of them commemorate in their names the estate owner who oversaw their building, for example, Archieston in Moray was founded by Sir Archibald Grant. Landowners undertook building these communities in part because they were reluctant to lose people from their estate. Moreover, the inhabitants provided a local source of seasonal labour when needed on the farms. It was also hoped that small-scale manufacturing linked to agriculture might develop, such as brewing, tanning and textiles. The villages were normally placed on land of low agricultural value, so the rents and feu-duties received from the residents boosted estate revenues.

The emergence of a sizeable sector of specialised traders and craftsmen added to the complexity of the rural social structure, and constituted an intermediate class between tenant-farmers and farmworkers. In Perthshire in 1851, nearly a quarter of the rural workforce was included in this category, most working on their own account and sometimes employing one or two staff.

LABOUR RELATIONS IN LOWLAND AGRICULTURE

Lowland agrarian society was differentiated from its counterparts in both the Highlands and England in that there was relatively little militant opposition to the wave of reforms which affected most of those who lost out in the new disposition. The 'Captain Swing' protest movement created panic amidst English landowners in 1831–2, as acts of agrarian terrorism, such as maiming livestock and burning crops, swept through a broad swathe of the countryside. These incidents were carried out by landless labourers protesting against the introduction of threshing machines, which imperilled their livelihood, yet in Scotland, the contemporaneous arrival of these machines provoked no significant resistance. Again, the 'Revolt of the Field', an upsurge in trade union organisation which spread across rural England in the 1870s, was not mirrored in the Lowlands. There were several reasons for the more muted Scottish response in both episodes. As discussed above, in contrast to England, there was no pool of underemployed labour in the countryside. Equally crucially, the transition from the old to the new system was in most instances a slow, protracted process, taking place across two or three generations. Hence solidarity and a sense of an endangered community were difficult to evoke, in contrast to the Highlands. An extra factor was the absence of external leadership and a coherent ideology of resistance. Unlike England, for instance, there was no clerical support for protest, as the testimony of the *Old* and *New Statistical Accounts* exemplifies: virtually universal approbation for the improvement agenda prevailed among the ministers who compiled the parish surveys.

In the new set-up, trade union organisation was stymied by a variety of factors. The Master and Servant Act, for instance, bore severely upon farmworkers who sought to break their employment contract. In general, too, the six-monthly feeing system of employment that was almost universal in Lowland Scotland made it straightforward for disgruntled workers to move speedily away from an unsatisfactory job. These factors tended to eliminate most sources of friction between farmer and ploughman. The ever-present attraction of urban work, with higher pay and better living conditions, also impelled farmers to offer reasonable pay and conditions. The bargaining power of employees was considerably enhanced by the status of ploughing as a highly skilled job, so that the threat of withdrawal of labour posed a serious challenge to farmers.

> **Feeing fairs**
>
> Recruitment of Lowland farm servants (apart from the hinds in the Lothians) in this period was normally carried out at feeing fairs, which were held twice yearly, usually at Whitsuntide and Martinmas. These events were often part of a local country fair, but elsewhere, the labour market was the sole focus of concern, and large numbers turned up for these events: at Turriff in 1882, over 3,000 jobseekers and employers together crowded into the town centre. At the hiring market, those looking for employment frequently indicated their status with a blade of corn on their jacket, or a straw in the mouth. An oral deal between worker and employer was settled by a handshake, a dram bought by the farmer and the payment of arles money – a silver crown (25p) or a half-crown (13p) – to the new hand. The merits and demerits of these half-yearly occurrences were regularly debated. Some farmworkers enjoyed the social aspect, meeting old acquaintances and exchanging gossip, while the benefit of picking up information about good and bad prospective employers was inestimable. Others, however, felt that the system was reminiscent of a slave market, with farmers physically examining men to test their strength. While some contended that word-of-mouth reputations impelled employers to offer better working and living conditions, farmers were widely perceived to have the upper hand in negotiations, as they could delay offering a job until late in the day, when fear of unemployment would drive an applicant to accept less generous terms. Additionally, guardians of morality were exercised by the excesses of drink and sexual immorality associated with the fairs, the epitome of which was Aikey Brae, held in Old Deer. Hence, by the 1870s, increasing numbers of workers were recruited through advertisements in the press or by private communication, but feeing fairs lingered on in some places into the inter-war period.

The varied circumstances of the labour force also militated against a sense of intolerable injustice. In the Lothians, as noted earlier, the bulk of the hind's payment took the form of kind, which acted as insulation against inflation. In the Borders, shepherds were treated generously. As well as an annual allowance in kind worth about £60, they were permitted to have their own small flock of between 50 and 150 sheep, which they worked alongside their employer's herd. Their pay was frequently set above that of a schoolteacher, and, like ploughmen, they possessed unique skills. In the dairying country of the south-west, the prospect for the hired hands to become tenant-farmers was higher than anywhere else in the country, in part because farm sizes were quite small, so large amounts of finance were not required, and because the bowing system prevalent in the region promoted the accumulation of reserves by the employee. Under this practice, the farmer supplied both the fixed and the working capital, such as summer pasture and winter feedstuff, while the bower contracted to supply a specific volume of cheese or butter at an agreed price, leaving all surplus produce to be sold by the latter. In the north-east, a major safety valve was that, as discussed above, very few farmworkers stayed after their early to mid-thirties, when they looked for employment elsewhere. Hence, they had no long-term commitment to a career in farming, and this normally acted against a union mentality.

The farmworkers, however, were not quiescent, whatever the low level of organised activism may suggest. Deference, a pervading presence in English rural communities, was markedly less evident in the Lowlands, primarily because there was little scope for landowners to indulge in the paternalistic gestures widely obtaining in England. It is significant that after the passage of the Third Reform Act in 1884–5, agricultural workers in Scotland, as distinct from England, voted overwhelmingly for the Liberal party, so that the Tories' electoral hold in shire seats was gravely endangered. The Liberals' victory at the 1885 election in East Lothian, the ultimate county for High Farming prowess in Scotland, and safely Tory since 1837, was attributed by both parties to the support of radical ploughboys.

II. THE HIGHLANDS

THE DEMOGRAPHIC TREND

The prosperity and self-confidence of Lowland agrarian society was not replicated in the Highlands. One graphic illustration of the latter's travails was demographic: in 1801, 15.2 per cent of the Scottish population lived in the four counties of Sutherland, Ross and Cromarty, Inverness, and Argyll, but by 1881, only 7.7 per cent did so, and 1841 marked the peak population point for the region. But these overall data cover complex factors. Firstly, rural depopulation was not solely a Highland phenomenon, for it also characterised many Lowland counties. In mid-Ayrshire, it was reported in the later 1830s that '[s]everal parts of the parish, which were known as separate farms of considerable extent, are at present without a single dwelling on them'.[3] Perthshire, the most populous county in 1801, achieved its maximum population as early as 1831. The total population of the three south-western counties of Dumfries, Kirkcudbright and Wigtown fell from 6.6 per cent of the 1801 Scottish total to 4.2 per cent in 1881, with an absolute decline setting in from

1851. Secondly, there were growth pockets in the Highlands: towns such as Oban and Stornoway expanded in size over the period, and there was a steady increase in the population of Lewis and Harris after 1861 for the rest of the nineteenth century.

The responsibility for the difficulties in the Highlands is frequently assigned either to the landowners, blamed for greed, short-sightedness and inhumanity, or (less often) to the tenants, for their implacable resistance to change. Dr John Mackenzie, who administered the Gairloch estate during the minority of his nephew Kenneth, the thirteenth baronet, contrived to apportion culpability equally. In 1849, he met Sir Robert Peel, who contrasted the responses by Highland lairds to the potato famine favourably with their Irish counterparts. Mackenzie retorted that the main priority of Scottish landowners was not concern for the plight of the tenantry, but rather to maximise rental income.[4] Nevertheless, not all landowners were self-seeking, and several endangered their own financial stability in trying to shelter their tenants from the harsh winds of adversity – including Mackenzie's brother, Francis.

But Dr Mackenzie also bemoaned the reluctance of the leaders of townships to strive to improve crofting agriculture, and indeed the Highland peasantry were frequently charged with blind conservatism as their default position when confronted by change; this allegation constituted the standard claim of outside commentators and estate factors, such as Patrick Sellar. This is rather misleading, however, as Highlanders often responded positively to new options. The speedy adoption of the potato as the staple crop is the most obvious, but people also flocked to the coast to work at kelping during the wars with France. The large numbers who migrated to the Lowlands for seasonal work throughout the nineteenth century also testify to a widespread spirit of adaptation.

Beyond these human failings, however, there lay an inexorable economic context. It was the great misfortune of the Highlands to be adjacent to and permeable by the two most advanced industrial regions of the time, namely the Scottish Lowlands and England. As happened subsequently to underdeveloped economies and societies across the globe, the superior efficiency and price competitiveness of industrialised production irreparably weakened the prospects for the establishment in the Highlands of a stable and prosperous economy. From the 1830s, regional products were undercut in quality and price by southern competitors; for instance, by 1840 in Durness, the most remote settlement in mainland Scotland, cloth made in Glasgow was cheaper than that produced locally. The only Highland commodity for which there was a high level of demand in industrialising Britain was wool, and the prevailing economic ideology of the age required that sheep should flourish without the impediment of the small peasantry competing for land use.

The term Clearances covers a range of depopulation processes which operated at different times and places, rather than being one uniform system. Four broad categories may be identified. The most benign in terms of its application was voluntary emigration by the tenantry of a community departing wholly or partly en bloc, frequently organised and led by the local tacksmen.[5] Between 1790 and 1815 almost 100 boats carried over 11,500 emigrants from the Highlands to Canada, many of whom were part of this phase. Indeed, so many were leaving that, in 1803, Highland landowners persuaded parliament to pass an act which raised the cost of emigration by 250 per cent. This did staunch the outflow, but the tradition persisted. Thus, in 1852–3 numerous inhabitants of St Kilda petitioned their landlord, MacLeod of Harris, to let them emigrate to Australia, which he very reluctantly acceded to, and about one-third of the population departed.

A second form of depopulation was closely approximated to the Lowland agricultural pattern, namely, a gradual leakage, usually on an individual or family basis. This was quite routine in areas within easy reach of the Lowlands, and in many instances, there was a tradition of such movement dating back to at least the middle of the eighteenth century. It further resembled the Lowland experience in that the consolidation of holdings and a shift to commercial agriculture was occurring, as in south-east Inverness-shire and west Stirlingshire. Mainland Argyllshire in particular experienced a continuous haemorrhaging of people throughout this period, hence its population fell in more decades than any other Highland county. Consequently, in most western Lowland towns in 1851, Argyllshire natives constituted the largest number of Highland-born immigrants.

THE SUTHERLAND EXPERIMENT

The third category of population movement was a planned relocation of the peasantry – but not necessarily their removal outwith the estate – with the objective of directing them towards commercially productive activities, while redeploying the land they had vacated for more efficient agricultural purposes. The main exemplar of this strategy was the Sutherland estate development project. When the eponymous countess married the future marquess of Stafford in 1785, her estate was a byword for backwardness, even by the lax standards of the Highlands, and remained so for about twenty years. In 1803, Stafford somewhat unexpectedly inherited half of the vast fortune accumulated by his uncle, the duke of Bridgewater, then the wealthiest individual in Britain. With financial resources in abundance, the modernisation of the estate could be undertaken. In this project, the Sutherlands were guided by a series of Lowland improvers, particularly Patrick Sellar and William Young, to be followed by James Loch.

Sellar and Young's strategy was grounded in Smithian economics, particularly the centrality of the division of labour in promoting growth and development. Applied to Sutherland, this concept estimated that the current rental yielded a bare one-quarter of the potential value of the land. The attainment of the maximum revenue, however, required the removal of the small tenantry from the straths and glens of the interior, where their agricultural practices were deemed unsatisfactory. The peasantry had virtually no implements or working animals and yields were very poor, so that localised famines still occurred very frequently, whereas in Lowland Scotland they had been absent since the early 1780s. Since the tenants lived on the uttermost edge of economic margins, high rent arrears were a permanent feature. They were to be replaced by large-scale capitalist sheep-farmers, since sheep were the only item that the area could produce which would compete in the national marketplace, where demand for wool had ballooned with industrialisation in Yorkshire, the Scottish borders and Clackmannanshire. Only men from the Lowlands had the capital and skills to run flocks numbering in the thousands, and they would be given an untrammelled run of the interior, using the lower ground in the straths for overwintering and growing foodstuffs for their sheep. It was estimated in 1806 that the revenue from sheep-farming could yield £20,000 a year, while the current estate rental was just below £6,000.

The peasantry were to be removed to the coastline to undertake various forms of paid work. On the east coast at places like Helmsdale, they would engage in fishing, as herring were abundant. While most men caught fish, women were to work as gutters and packers, and other men would do the coopering for the barrels, making nets and repairing fishing boats. At Brora, where coal had been found, miners, imported from the south, would instruct the Highlanders in the art of winning coal, to be used for making glass and bricks, with the extensive sandy beaches of the area providing the essential ingredient for these. Brewing was to be carried on with barley grown in east Sutherland, and cotton manufacture would be located at Spinningdale, the site of a failed factory experiment in the 1790s, where women from the interior, accustomed to spinning, could find work. On the west coast, where those cleared from Assynt were settled at Lochinver and at Bettyhill on the north, fishing was to be the prime source of employment.

The grand plan began to be implemented in 1812, with removals from inland Assynt going smoothly, but evictions at Kildonan and Strathnaver in 1813–14 were stoutly resisted by the tenantry, and Sellar's violent conduct at the latter led to a court case, in which he was acquitted of charges of destroying property and the culpable homicide of five individuals. Despite the notoriety of this episode, the scheme was continued, although Sellar was removed from any subsequent managerial involvement. His successor, James Loch, adopted a less confrontational approach – for instance, relocating tenants no more than twenty miles from their settlements. By 1819, some 5,500 people had been taken from the interior, of whom two-thirds had been re-sited within the boundaries of the estate, while nearly 30 per cent were living in adjacent estates and counties and a mere 2 per cent had emigrated from the region.

Patrick Sellar after Strathnaver

Following Sellar's removal in 1817 from his managerial role on the Sutherland estate, he devoted his energies to building up his farming concern. He expanded his lands in Strathnaver, and became the leading sheep-farmer in the Highlands, thanks to his great efficiency, especially in breeding high-quality stock. By 1830, he was the biggest tenant-farmer on the Sutherland estate, where he kept 10,000 sheep and employed 10 adults and 35 youths on a full-time basis, along with between 60 and 80 seasonal workers. His annual rental payment came to £1,700. Sellar played a key role in developing an association of larger tenants to promote the marketing of wool from the Highlands. Despite this successful business career, Sellar remained prickly about perceived infringements of his rights, and continued to express grievances in aggressive language and actions. He quarrelled on several occasions with his ducal landlords and their factors over interpretations of leases.

In 1838, Sellar rose in social status from being a tenant-farmer to entering the lairdly class when he purchased the 1,500-hectare Acharn estate in the Morvern region of north Argyll for £11,250. In 1844, he acquired the nearby Ardtornish estate, which ran to 2,500 hectares, for £11,000. In Morvern, he resumed – after a twenty-year interlude – the practice of clearing small tenants and cottars from his property, and he removed more people than he evicted in Sutherland in 1814. His standing as a solid member of the landowning class was underlined by, firstly, the careers of his children, and secondly, the distinguished visitors who frequently stayed at Ardtornish. One son, William, was professor of humanity (i.e. Latin) at Edinburgh University for twenty-seven years. Another son, Alexander, was educated at Rugby and Oxford University, became a barrister and entered parliament in 1882 as a Liberal MP, holding a junior ministerial office. In 1853, Alfred, Lord Tennyson stayed at Ardtornish, accompanied by Francis Turner Palgrave, the compiler of *The Golden Treasury of Lyrical Poetry*. Yet, even in this exalted state, traces of the old Adam flared up in Patrick Sellar. He had a bitter falling-out over access rights with the owner of an adjacent estate, and they did not speak for some years. This rift was all the more difficult since his son, Alexander, was married to that laird's daughter. In the last two years of his life he conducted a vigorous dispute with the Sutherland estate concerning shooting rights over his farms. Sellar died in 1851, and 1859–60 his family sold the Morvern properties, so that the Sellars had been cleared from the Highlands.

The Sutherlands ploughed vast amounts of money into their plan: between 1802 and 1817, some £211,500 was spent on the project, and from 1811 to 1843 £80,000 was invested in road-building alone. Yet the whole scheme was an abject failure, whether by the yardsticks of human well-being, social progress, economic development or sound accountancy. Only the sheep-farming aspect proved satisfactory, at least from the factor's viewpoint: by 1850, 120 farmers were rearing 127,000 sheep, paying a total rental of over £25,000 and establishing the county as a major player in the sector. But none of the industrial ventures were successful, for the manufacture of glass, bricks, tiles and textiles all quickly succumbed to the ruthless pressure of advanced industrialism: for instance, bricks made in Bathgate were at once cheaper and of better quality than the local product. Similarly, the efforts of Sutherland men to secure a foothold in deep-sea fishing quickly collapsed; in the face of the more efficient and experienced fishermen from the north-east coast, the undercapitalised Highlanders were unable to flourish. The dislocation of being torn away from a centuries-old rural social, economic and cultural environment, together with the distress caused by the pressures of being dependent on income wholly earned in a market economy, resulted in many people moving away from the county in the decades after 1820. For the estate, the book-keeping costs were unwaveringly negative, and in the years between 1811 and 1833, it was asserted by the estate manager that no net income was generated.

After the death of the first duke in 1833, the improvement plan was abandoned, and for the rest of the period to 1880, his successors studiously avoided mass evictions in a bid to restore the family's reputation. The consequences of the failure of the Sutherland experiment were profound. Other landowners tried, albeit on a much smaller scale, to emulate it, such as Lord MacDonald at Sleat in Skye, but, as in Sutherland, the outcome of these experiments was invariably unsuccessful. The inability of the richest family in Britain to effect the transformation of their estate may very well have fuelled pessimism among other Highland landowners as to the likelihood of finding a viable solution to the region's social and economic problems.

LANDOWNERS' FINANCIAL STRATAGEMS AND THE SOCIAL CONSEQUENCES

Indeed, for many traditional landlords, their financial position was light years removed from the ample cushioning afforded to the Sutherlands by their English-derived wealth, with varying levels of indebtedness instead the norm; in 1800, Mackenzie of Seaforth's debts amounted to £100,000. The efforts by these landowners to establish a sound financial footing dominated their estate policy from the later eighteenth century until around 1850, as they desperately strove to avoid bankruptcy and to retain ownership of their lands. Their approach can be characterised as combination of short-termism, incompetence and bouts of frivolity and extravagance, with the inevitable consequence that most failed to achieve their goal. As their problems mounted and grew more complex from the start of the 1820s, some owners moved to implement the fourth mode of clearance, usually identified as the classic form, namely, mass removals at extremely short notice.

These financially fraught landlords sought to remedy their plight in part by looking to augment estate income from outside sources, but few of these proved fruitful. A major goal was to become an army officer, the attraction of which was a blend of income, economy and social aspiration. The service paid its officers well, with a pension after retiring. For parents, it was cheaper to put sons to military service at thirteen years of age, rather than spend money on an expensive education, especially at an English public school. Possessing an officer's rank bestowed status and glamour, and the title was retained after leaving the service. In the second half of the eighteenth century, one-quarter to one-third of army officers were Scottish and 50 per cent of Highland lairdly families provided at least one officer, against 40 per cent for all Scottish gentry.

But the drawbacks of such a career were considerable. The expensive lifestyle associated with the officer class was a constant problem for cash-strapped Highland gentry: the cost of items such as clothes, housing, horses and entertainment could soon overwhelm an officer's salary. Death was of course an occupational hazard, and it could plunge the family's estate into crisis, especially if there were dependants to be maintained. The trend to opt for a military career had another disadvantage, since in the middle decades of the eighteenth century, it had become common for sons of Highland lairds to take up a business partnership with city merchants in places like Glasgow or Edinburgh. These were not only lucrative occupations, but gave experience in business-like approaches and established useful links for both financial assistance and professional advice. But by the end of the century, such occupations had lost out in popularity to posts in the armed forces, with long-term deleterious implications for the Highland gentry's business competence.

Others sought livelihoods in law, mostly in Edinburgh as advocates or, like John Peter Grant of Rothiemurchus, at the London Bar. But here again, obstacles arose: it took many years to establish a successful career, and in the interim the high costs of living in capital cities added to the burdens on the estate. For yet others, a seat in parliament promised to be the key to a well-paid official position, or to receiving profitable government contracts. But the expenses of being an MP were high, not least the cost of acquiring and retaining a seat; Grant of Rothiemurchus, according to his daughter, spent in the region of

£20,000 in an unsuccessful contest for Morayshire in 1807, in which a grand total of eleven electors voted.⁶

A significant consequence of the search for gainful employment away from the estate was the fraying of contact with both the tenantry and Highland customs. This was reinforced by the tendency for the sons of gentry to marry women from the Lowlands or from England, who had little connection with Gaelic culture or Highland mores. Many did not carry out the traditional wifely farming duties, instead opting to live much of the year in the Lowlands, and they expected their spouses to stay with them. The Highland estate would now be visited for a short spell in summer, no more. In a further attenuation of the Highland influence, most landlords had their children (especially sons) educated in Lowland Scotland or in English public schools.

In trying to reorder the finances of their estates, lairds sought to make money wherever possible, with very little consideration of the long-run consequences. One instance was military recruitment. This yielded useful rewards for landowners who exploited the warrior tradition of the Highlanders, already established by the Black Watch. Between 1790 and 1815, between 37,000 and 48,000 Highland soldiers were enrolled, out of a total regional population of around 250,000; Lord Breadalbane raised 3,500 soldiers from his estate alone. In all of Scotland, one in eighty-three adult males joined up, but in the Highlands, it was one in twenty-four, with six of the ten parishes with the greatest recruitment located in the region. The monetary rewards were great: by 1800, the earl of Seaforth drew as much income from recruitment as from the combined rental of two of his sizeable mainland estates. For the lesser gentry, it made a crucial contribution, providing between 20 and 40 per cent of their entire income. One benefit to cash-strapped lairds of having half-pay officers settled on their property was that rental payments were virtually guaranteed. But the downside was that most of these men had no interest in or need to drive forward farming improvements, instead settling for a quiet life of retirement.

The ordinary recruits were mostly drawn from the cottar or landless categories, especially as tenants who did not want to leave their farms often paid them to serve as substitutes. The promise of land at the end was immensely appealing to these landless men, as pressure for small farms was intense. But the allocation of plots to volunteers acted in the longer perspective as a brake on agricultural progress. The commitment to offer smallholdings to volunteers necessitated the subdivision of existing larger farms; in the 1790s, between five and seven crofting units were carved out of one Glengarry farm.

The end to the exploitation of the opportunities presented by military recruitment came firstly in 1800, when the army high command stopped the creation of proprietary regiments, and secondly in 1811, when the practice of repaying recruits with land at the end of their service was abandoned. The military top brass wished to establish a more professional ethos, and to end the proliferation of, at best, semi-competent officers. Landowners were left with a long-term obstacle to agricultural improvement while simultaneously experiencing dwindling revenues. After seven years, the normal period of lease granted to recruits, a programme of evictions was launched on many estates, such as Lord Breadalbane's extensive property in Argyll and Perthshire.

THE WARTIME BOOM AND SUBSEQUENT COLLAPSE

A second case study in short-sightedness, greed and social irresponsibility began with the imposition of a high tariff on imports of Spanish barilla during the wars with France, which began in 1793. Barilla was used in the production of alkali, a vital component in manufacturing bleach and ammonia, which were consumed in massive volumes by the textile and soap industries, among others. The search for a domestic substitute resulted in a surge in demand for alkali produced from kelp, a variety of seaweed found in abundance on the coastlines of the western Highlands and islands. It was extremely cheap to manufacture: in summer, the kelp was gathered manually along the tide line and brought to local kilns to be burnt, with the ashes providing the in-demand chemical. Kelp was a modern alchemy for landowners: prices rose tenfold between 1750 and 1810, with the bulk of the growth in the later twenty years; Seaforth's profit in 1809 came to £5,770, whereas in 1794 it was £1,104. In a bid to maximise profits, landowners devised an ingenious method of compelling the peasantry to work at kelp-gathering: rents were raised above the price fetched by the sale of cattle (the normal means of funding rent payments). This hike at once obliged the small tenant to gather kelp to bridge the cash gap, and it reduced the net cost of wages, while additionally rendering the payment of rents safer. At its apogee, kelping employed between 25,000 and 40,000 individuals, out of a population in the relevant area of around 170,000.

But this interlude of high profitability contained the seeds of a profound demographic, social and agricultural crisis. The high demand for labour encouraged population growth and in-migration, so that subdivision of plots took place with the consent – or connivance – of landowners, who were anxious to have a large kelping workforce. Thus, a holding in Coll, which initially had two or three families living on it, by 1811 contained twenty-two families. But the concomitant subdivision made improved farming quite impracticable, and created a potentially highly vulnerable class should kelping decline. This catastrophe duly occurred. The abolition of salt duty in 1825 meant that the new Leblanc process produced substantially cheaper alkali than kelp. The main market for kelp alkaline, the Liverpool soap manufacturers, was lost by 1827, when the price of kelp, which had been £17 per 1,000 kilograms in 1817 – itself well below its peak – had fallen to £4. The collapse was cataclysmic for proprietors: MacNeil of Barra saw his kelp revenue plummet from £2,535 in 1817 to £180 in 1828. Not only did landowners face a drastic slump in income, but the consequent impact on the workers, namely high unemployment levels, added to the estate owners' plight. The heavy costs of poor relief to support the unfortunate kelpers had to come from the shrunken coffers of the landowners, with the result that throughout the later 1820s and the 1830s, financial jeopardy was an ever-growing threat.

The deterioration in the economic circumstances of the peasantry in the 1820s was deepened by the loss of various ancillary sources of income which for up to about thirty years had afforded a measure of added financial resilience. The end in 1815 of the long wars with France steeply reduced the demand for beef for the military, and the consequent fall in the price of cattle – the main supply of cash for the Highland tenantry – rendered rental payments more difficult. Also, military demobilisation after 1815 presented two problems. Firstly, payments to serving soldiers dried up, a serious challenge for people living on precarious margins; and the return of the soldiers meant that food and money had to be spread more thinly within families. An era of public works, such as bridge, road, canal and harbour construction in the Highlands, which had generated employment in the region from the 1780s, dried up in the era of post-war austerity. Work in the Lowlands also fell away in the 1820s, as demobilisation there flooded the labour market. Herring, which had been in abundant supply from the 1780s, thereby at once creating jobs and offering an extra supply of food, became much less numerous. The disappearance of these additional cushions against hardship which had encouraged headlong population growth served to intensify the deprivation experienced after 1815.

Over and above the landlords' failure to adopt a long-term perspective on the development of their estates, incompetence and folly compounded their predicament. Few had a firm policy and a clear prioritisation of economic and social desiderata. The Seaforth family clung on to parts of the estate partly for sentimental reasons, and partly to sustain their political influence, even though these objectives dragged down their financial position to an almost fatal extent. Again, an absence of commercial nous was all too prevalent. Seaforth decided to buy back the ancestral home at Brahan, but paid considerably over the market value. After his death, his heirs had to sell most of the mainland estate to keep afloat financially. Akin to this problem was the propensity of landowners to squander scarce funds on grandiose self-serving projects which inevitably resulted in the weakening of the overall position of the estate, sometimes terminally. MacLeod of MacLeod's foray into a parliamentary career in the 1796 election cost him over £5,000, yet his annual income from the estate only amounted to £15,000. The desire to indulge in conspicuous consumption was a besetting sin: Sir Duncan Campbell of

Barcaldine, always teetering on the verge of ruin, contributed massively to the eventual sale of the estate by commissioning the addition of a library to the family house in 1830. At Brahan castle, in 1811 Lord Seaforth employed twenty-two gardeners.

THE NEW CADRE OF LANDOWNERS

Accordingly, from the mid-1820s, the landlords' downward financial spiral took on a greater velocity. The dilemma was acute: on the one hand, not to remove at least some of the impoverished tenantry could plunge the estate into bankruptcy, and its consequent sale, but on the other hand, maintaining the status quo appeared equally fatal. Estates flowed on to the market throughout the forty years after 1815, and by 1850, 60 per cent of the western Highlands and Islands – about 500,000 hectares – lay in new hands: the Clanranald properties went between 1818 and 1830; MacDonnell's estates of Glengarry, Glenquoich and Knoydart were sold off in, respectively, 1836, 1840 and 1854. The new owners were predominantly non-Highlanders, and frequently proved more ruthless than the traditional chiefs in applying strict financial criteria to their estates, and so had little compunction in removing tenants deemed economically unproductive. Perhaps the most rigorous exponent of this approach was Colonel John Gordon of Cluny, who acquired most of the southern parts of the Outer Hebrides in the 1840s and evicted large numbers of small tenants and cottars. On the other hand, the Glenquoich tenantry preferred the policies applied by Edward Ellice, an English businessman, to those of their departed clan chief, MacDonnell of Glengarry.

The climacteric in this fourth mode of clearance came with the Great Highland Famine, which was contemporaneous with the Irish Famine, beginning in 1846, and shared the same cause, namely, the fungal disease which almost completely destroyed the region's potato crop for several years; thus, in a part of Harris, the yield shrank by five-sixths between 1846 and 1849. Without a winter feed of potatoes, the number of cattle in the western Highlands fell by one-third over five years from 1846. The consequences were dire, as in many communities the staple diet for humans was potatoes, which could make up four-fifths of the total food consumption, as in Glenelg. Moreover, the combination of additional cash income sources had led to subdivision of holdings to an extreme extent – in Glenelg 86 per cent of tenants held under half a hectare of land – so that there was no scope to expand production or to diversify.

Nevertheless, the crisis in the Highlands was markedly less acute than in Ireland. In Scotland, only a handful died directly of starvation; the authoritative study suggests fewer than ten such deaths.[7] Outside of the western Highlands and islands, there was less suffering, as the agrarian economy in the rest of the region was appreciably less dependent on potato cultivation, and there was alternative work for agricultural labourers in arable and livestock farming. In contrast to the stereotyping of Irish landowners as broadly indifferent to the suffering of their tenantry, many Scottish proprietors actively strove to support local populations with financial assistance. The duke of Sutherland spent £18,000 on the relief of his dependent population, while between 1846 and 1848 assistance to his Lewis tenants cost Sir James Matheson £30,000. Overall, it would appear that only 10 to 15 per cent of the population in the famine-affected region endured indifference on the part of their landowners.

Moreover, there was a large-scale charitable campaign in the Lowlands to relieve the distressed Highland areas, with the Free Church especially active in supporting co-religionists in the north-west. A propitious geographical factor meant that relief supplies could be delivered quickly and accurately to points of need. The vast preponderance of localities experiencing severe hardship were easily accessed by sea from Glasgow or Greenock, being almost invariably situated on the islands or the western mainland seaboard. In Ireland, however, many crisis centres were in the interior, with poor overland communications systems, while the west of the country was quite remote from major ports.

Although in relative terms the famine was far less devastating in Scotland than in Ireland, the consequences were still very severe. The cost of relief laid a heavy burden on estate finances: for example, in Barra, 90 per cent of the population qualified for Poor Law support. Yet simultaneously, the acute impoverishment of the tenantry resulted in steepling rent arrears: in northwest Sutherland, they soared from 12 per cent of the total rental in 1846 to 63 per cent in 1848. Consequently, the bulk of the landlord class determined to act to avert a repetition of these circumstances. This, they concluded, could best be achieved by the removal on a large scale of those groups deemed to be agriculturally marginal and accordingly highly vulnerable to any adverse conditions. Cottars, squatters and crofters with extremely small holdings were all considered to be negative factors in securing the sound long-run financial footing of an estate, and therefore should be removed forthwith. The population of Tiree had grown from 2,800 in 1801 to 5,000 in 1841, by which time over one-half were sub-tenants, but between 1847 and 1853, one-third of the people had departed, 70 per cent of whom were cottars. This was in accordance with the duke of Argyll's instructions that those in the most precarious situation should be the primary candidates for removal. The restructuring on the island meant that by 1861, 5 per cent of tenants occupied holdings of less than two hectares, against 24 per cent in 1847, and the total rental had risen from £700 in 1847 to £2,200. In sum, in these western outliers, there was a population decline of about one-third between 1845 and 1849, followed by a further fall of one-quarter from 1850 to 1854, so that perhaps one-third of the overall population decline over the years between 1801 and 1891 occurred in the twenty years between 1841 and 1861.

1850–80: STABILISATION?

From the middle of the 1850s, after the upheavals of the preceding period, a phase of relative stability ensued, lasting until the 1870s. The incidence of mass evictions declined, although the occasional deployment of writs and warrants probably intimidated crofters. But from the start of the 1870s, significant changes began, and they escalated in the next decade. After some fifty years of high profitability, sheep-farming ran into difficulties. Sheep from the Antipodes now arrived in Britain, with profound consequences. Australian wool was of higher quality than Highland wool, and the growing food preference in the Lowlands was for lamb, which, thanks to refrigeration in steamships, New Zealand and Australia could supply, while the Highlands still mainly produced mutton. Between 1850 and 1880, Highland wool and meat prices dropped by between one-quarter and one-third. As leases fell in for renewal in the 1870s, many sheep-farmers quit, but landlords found a ready and more profitable alternative by turning the sheep farms into sporting estates. The growth in wealth among aristocrats and businessmen meant that abundant cash was available, and the cult of Queen Victoria at Balmoral made owning a Highland property very prestigious. Deer forests grew exponentially: in 1839, there were 28; by 1870, they numbered 73; and in 1883, some 800,000 hectares were contained in 120 Highland deer forests. The resulting shift in landowners' policies towards crofters rapidly led to the confrontations of the 1880s.

RESISTANCE AND ACQUIESCENCE

The jarring disruptions embodied in mass evictions elicited resistance on a sporadic but frequent nature. Between 1800 and 1855 at least forty mass protests are known to have occurred, and there were almost certainly numerous other unrecorded incidents. These incidents had a range of characteristic features. Many took place in Easter Ross and Sutherland, locations less prominent in the agitation of the 1880s. The most common form of demonstration was the petty humiliation of the officers trying to carry out the clearance. But violence sometimes accompanied the protests, notably at Coigach in 1852–3, and at Culrain in 1820, where a crowd of about 600 forcibly opposed evictions for 14 days. While on occasion the tenants created the disorder, the enforcers of clearances also rioted: for example, at the Kildonan and Strathnaver removals in the 1810s and at Coigach. Interestingly, there was, however, little of the agrarian outrages – burning crops and maiming livestock – which typified similar protests in rural England, although some of Sellar's sheep had their throats slit. Another peculiarity of the Highlands was that women – and occasionally men disguised as women – were often in the forefront of the protest, and participated fully in violent incidents.

Yet the significant point is that these demonstrations had no direct impact: nearly all the evictions were quite quickly implemented. In part, the initial success of protests was because the local forces of law and order were usually very small in number, and reluctant to act for fear of retaliation. But once reinforcements were procured by the landowners – at Coigach, police from Glasgow; elsewhere, soldiers – the will of the proprietors inevitably prevailed. The contrast with the 'Crofters' War' of the 1880s is instructive. In the earlier period, there was limited press or other outside coverage of the bulk of these localised incidents, whereas in the 1880s newspapers, both Highland and Lowland, were highly influential. There were very few means of communication across the Highland area in the first half of the century, so outbreaks of resistance remained local, sparking no chain of imitative acts of solidarity. In 1820–1 at Culrain, violent mass protests against evictions were only contained by the military after prolonged resistance, but there were no copycat actions in the adjacent Sutherland estate, even though very large clearances were being carried out there. By the onset of the 1880s, a network of exiled Highlanders, both in an individual capacity and organised into urban Celtic societies, existed throughout the Lowlands – and further afield – ready to articulate a wider perspective and give practical assistance.

Perhaps the most telling weaknesses of these early outbreaks were that they had no effective leadership cadre, and there was no ideological framework to offer a realistic alternative to mere resistance. There was almost no middle class to speak – and write – for the peasants. The tacksmen had largely been eliminated, and pretty well all that might be found were a handful of teachers, half-pay officers and small traders. Above all, the clergy, the most influential men in the community, insistently stressed that there should be no opposition to the evictions. This, of course, was different in the 1880s, when Free Church ministers not just condoned but actually led the revolt of the crofters in their parishes. These earlier ministers did not preach acquiescence because, as some have claimed, they were Church of Scotland Moderates, cravenly submissive to the landowner-patron.[8] Indeed, most Highland clergy joined the Free Church in 1843, including the minister of Farr parish, who at the time of the Strathnaver evictions had urged his parishioners not to defy the wishes of the proprietor. This doctrine of obedience derived from the emphasis of evangelical Presbyterianism on individual salvation, not community action. Ministers were on occasion critical of evictions, but usually on pragmatic, not theological grounds. The minister at Farr objected that the clearances there would not work, but did not condemn them as unchristian. And in the 1830s, the clergy who compiled the parochial reports for the *New Statistical Account*, even if uneasy about evictions, tended to argue that emigration was the only viable answer. The shift in clerical thinking came as the Free Church experienced landowners' hostility to releasing land for building its churches. This antipathy meshed with the perceived failure of the proprietors during the Highland Famine to support the crofters, while the Free Church had been most active in relief work. By the end of the 1870s a theology of resistance had become widespread among the Highland Free Church ministry, which helped fuel the crofters' struggle in the succeeding decade.

The pre-1880 resistance also lacked a coherent ideology to challenge the rights of private landownership, and sought only to restore the traditional set-up; even in the 1850s and 1860s the crofters did not dispute the duke of Sutherland's position as proprietor, but instead opposed social and economic changes because they threatened the status quo. The doctrine of an historic claim by the peasantry to the land they occupied was not explicitly formulated until the late 1870s. This ideology drew much on the revival of Celtic culture and history which had sprung up during that decade, and its viability was greatly enhanced by the activities of the Irish Land League. The Crofters' War of the 1880s thus marked a major shift in Highland political, social and economic attitudes.

NOTES

1. *New Statistical Account* [*NSA*], Vol. XII, 507 (Alford).
2. W. Cobbett, *Cobbett's Tour in Scotland; and in the Four Northern Counties of England in the Autumn of the Year 1832* (1833), 102–3.
3. *NSA*, Vol. IV, 392; cf. Cobbett, *Cobbett's Tour*, 93–4, 107 on East Lothian.
4. C. B. Shaw (ed.), *Pigeon Holes of Memory: The Life and Times of Dr John Mackenzie (1803–1886)* (1988), 253.
5. Tacksmen were an intermediate class between landowners and tenants, who acted as leaders of local communities. They were frequently quite close kinsmen of the landowner.
6. E. Grant, *Memoirs of a Highland Lady* (1988), ed. A. Tod, Vol. I, 71–3.
7. T. M. Devine, *The Great Highland Famine: Hunger, Emigration and the Scottish Highlands in the Nineteenth Century* (1988), 59–63.
8. D. Paton, *The Clergy and the Clearances: The Church and the Highland Crisis, 1790–1850* (2006), 1–8 and ch. 4, gives a good overview of these negative verdicts.

CHAPTER 2

The Manufacturing Economy

Initially, Scotland followed England's path to an industrial economy, with textiles the first sector to move from domestic to factory production. But subsequently the composition of Scotland's advanced industrial sector deviated somewhat, as specialisations in heavy industry emerged which tended more to complement than rival England.

TEXTILES AND INDUSTRIALISATION

Cotton was the path-breaker; the first spinning factory was established at Penicuik in 1778. By 1796, there were thirty-nine mills, mostly sited in a crescent of locations which formed an arc through the western and central Lowlands, running from New Lanark to Stanley, by way of factories in Ayrshire, Bute, Renfrewshire and Stirlingshire. Partly this was to utilise water power, but proximity to a potential supply of labour from immigrant Highlanders was also a calculation – even New Lanark, rather remote from the Highlands, employed a considerable number of Gaels in the formative phase. Beginning, however, in the early 1800s, the geography of cotton mills altered as Glasgow and Paisley became the centres of cotton manufacturing, so that by 1839, 175 out of a total of 192 factories were sited in Renfrewshire and Lanarkshire, and places outwith these two counties declined in importance. A major reason for relocation was that the preferred source of power for factories switched from water to steam, which was more reliable and easier to control. Few of the early mills were near a supply of coal, whereas Glasgow and Paisley were adjacent to major coalfields. An additional draw of these cities was their geographical benefits. The Clyde made both the supply of raw cotton and the shipping out of the finished goods quite straightforward and cheap. As the huge preponderance of cotton was exported from Scotland – in 1825, only 5 per cent of cotton products went to the home market – these savings were important. Glasgow and Paisley also had a pool of engineers to service machinery and these men formed centres for both experimentation with and modification of machinery. Moreover, towns offered a readily available pool of cheap labour, whereas rural mills had to organise recruits from various sources, and the extra capital cost of building accommodation for workers and their families was obviated in an urban setting.

The industry took off in spectacular fashion during the first half of the nineteenth century. In 1812, there were 120 mills with 1,560 looms, employing 20,000 workers, but in 1861, 163 mills had 30,110 looms, and employed over 40,000. Output increased steeply; between 1785 and 1835 exports grew by 900 per cent. In the 1820s and 1830s, Glasgow was seen by many trade commentators as a serious rival to Manchester for the title of 'Cottonopolis', and in 1835 Scotland contributed 13 per cent of the total British output. Not surprisingly, the industry was, for the successful businessmen, highly profitable. Robert Owen's New Lanark mill yielded a total profit of £400,000 between 1799 and 1828, while for a quarter-century after 1850, J. & P. Coats's annual profit margins ranged between 18 and 26 per cent, averaging about 20 per cent.

There were several key reasons for the success of the Scottish cotton industry. The transition from linen manufacture was relatively straightforward, and the labour force was already acquainted with spinning and weaving cloth. Most of the cottonmasters had been involved beforehand in linen production, and had acquired a good knowledge of overseas markets, financial arrangements and shipping practice. An important ingredient in Scotland's growth was that it was the second country to move to factory production, so it was possible to learn from the positive breakthroughs notched up in England while simultaneously avoiding the pitfalls encountered by the southern pioneers. Indeed, the connection between the two countries was made physical by the presence in Scotland of experienced cottonmasters coming up from England to give advice and to run mills themselves. The most obvious exemplar of this trend was Robert Owen, who came north to work for his father-in-law, David Dale. Richard Arkwright, the inventor of the spinning frame, visited Scotland in 1784 and gave technical briefings to local manufacturers and investors, such as George Dempster, Kirkman Finlay and James Monteith.

Where cotton led, wool and linen followed, with locational concentration of factories a shared key feature. Wool production became focused in two areas, namely, the Borders, which by mid-century contributed 80 per cent of total Scottish output, and the Hillfoots district in Clackmannanshire. The former specialised initially in hosiery, but from the 1830s moved into tweeds, while the latter's expertise included fine shawls, fancy tartan dresses and hosiery. Spinning factories in the Borders and the Hillfoots were set up after cotton had established the advantages of machinery. There had been 85 woollen mills in Scotland in 1830, employing 3,500 hands, but by 1850, there were between

8,000 and 9,000 workers in 182 mills, and Alva alone had nine mills by mid-century. The expansion occurred partly because technological advances made weaving by machine at least as good as handwoven material, and so the transition of the weaving side to factory production accelerated in the 1840s. Additionally, the coming of the railways to the Borders in the late 1840s made steam power much cheaper, by substantially reducing the cost of coal. In Hawick in 1846, 1,000 kilograms of coal cost £1.71; six years later, the price was 54p, and the volume of coal sales had more than doubled. While other textiles were disrupted by the civil war in the United States in the first half of the 1860s, wool was much less affected, and it continued to grow as the demand for woollen clothing expanded with rising living standards.

Linen, although ousted by cotton in the west, continued to prevail and prosper in the east. Some 13 million metres were produced in all of Scotland in 1770, and 50 years later, output had more than doubled to 27 million metres. The growth in population (up by two-thirds between 1755 and 1820), accompanied by rising living standards and changing tastes, meant that domestic demand for linen products such as tablecloths and clothing increased steadily. Mechanisation began at the end of the eighteenth century, so that in 1800 there were twenty-five spinning mills, and by 1830 production of coarse linen was almost entirely carried out in factories, although finer-quality material was slower to follow suit, and the weaving side principally remained in the hands of domestic producers until the 1840s. One important benefit of machinery was that the cost of making the finished cloth was about 25 per cent cheaper. Just as importantly, the material turned out by factories was of a uniform standard, whereas the quality of handloom-spun linen was quite variable. As with cotton and wool, production became geographically highly concentrated, in this instance in Fife and Angus, and by 1838 these two counties were responsible for 95 per cent of the total Scottish output. Again, urban dominance occurred, as Dunfermline and Dundee became the centres for factories. The former specialised in high-quality products, whereas the latter manufactured coarser material, such as sheeting, sailcloth and osnaburgs (which provided low-quality clothing widely used in slave-owning areas). Dundee's attractions included the consequences of twenty years' worth of dock improvements, begun in 1815, which offered easy access to supplies of coal and flax, along with minimal transport costs in exporting finished goods. By 1830, steam power produced 70 per cent of the horsepower used in Dundee's factories. Additionally, the city had a pool of skilled engineering firms, and a well-developed banking and financial framework. Hence, in 1822 the Baxter company moved to Dundee from its original premises in rural Angus. As a result, the number of mills in Dundee surged from four in 1811 to thirty in 1832. In 1845, Dundee consumed one-third of all the raw flax produced and imported in the United Kingdom.

Dundee extended its textile repertoire in the 1850s as jute manufacture became established, and quickly the city became the world centre of production. In its natural state, the raw material was extremely hard to work with, but the breakthrough came with the serendipitous discovery that the application of whale oil softened it, so that it became supple and pliable. Dundee, the major whaling port in Scotland, was ideally placed to exploit the potential of this development, and jute became the preferred material for bagging, tarpaulins, matting, backing for carpets and other low-quality products. The emergence of the mass-produced linoleum industry in Kirkcaldy from mid-century generated huge demand for jute. The raw material was much cheaper than flax; in 1835 the former cost £12–14 per 1,000 kilograms, whereas the price for the latter was £40–54, and this attraction was enhanced by the removal in 1832 of the long-standing state subsidy awarded to the manufacture of linen. Moreover, jute used the same techniques and technology as linen, so the transition to the new industry was relatively straightforward.

The main company engaged in manufacturing jute, Cox Brothers, which had been a long-established force in linen, switched to the new product in 1840, and success was almost instantaneous. Output of jute in Dundee in 1841 came to 2,600,000 kilograms, but a decade later it had risen tenfold. Great

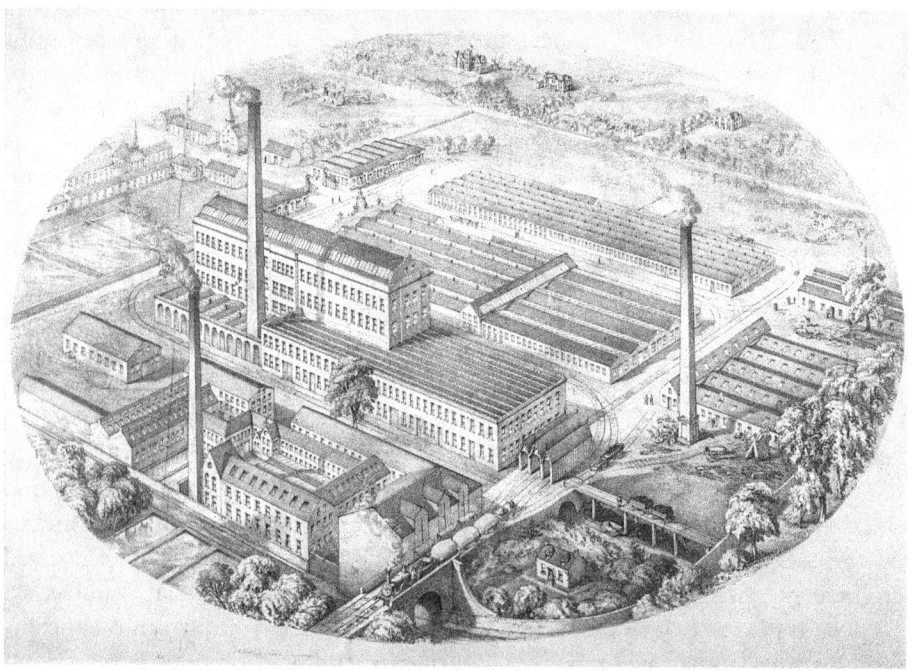

Figure 2.1 Camperdown Jute Works, Dundee, 1866. At the time, it was the largest jute factory in Britain. © Dundee Central Library. Licensor: www.scran.ac.uk

advances were achieved during the Crimean War, when the British army and navy used massive quantities of jute, and in the following decade, the American Civil War further boosted the industry's sales. Growth was substantially boosted by the removal in 1860 of the tariff on imported raw jute, as imports leapt from 37 million kilograms in 1860 to 103 million in 1870. In 1881, a remarkable 49 per cent of the city's labour force was employed in manufacturing jute. By then, Cox's Camperdown works was the largest jute factory in the world: there were over 5,000 employees, who were accommodated in a complex of buildings on a seven-hectare site, with a floored area measuring 45,000 square metres.

THE RISE OF IRON AND COAL

The next significant modernising industry was iron. Until the later eighteenth century, most iron furnaces were in the Highlands, as charcoal was used in the smelting process and wood was far more abundant there. The first iron factory in Lanarkshire was founded in 1779, and several others soon followed, especially after the discovery in 1801 of extensive iron-ore supplies in the blackband seam in the vicinity of Mushet. But for several decades, costs were substantially above English levels, mainly because of poor transport facilities and the low quality of coal, so that growth in output before 1830 was very limited. In 1825, Scotland produced about 25 million kilograms of pig-iron, which was just over 6 per cent of the British total. The prospects of the industry in Scotland were transformed in 1828 by J. B. Neilson's innovation of the hot-blast system. Hitherto, iron ore had been extracted by applying cold air, an expensive system which necessitated the application of large volumes of coal. Neilson's discovery, which involved passing hot air into the furnace, sharply reduced the amount of coal required to produce a ton of pig-iron. Whereas the traditional method required the coal to be converted to coke before carrying out the cold-blast process, this was not needed when using the hot-blast system. As an example, Clyde Iron Works in 1829 used 8,100 kilograms of coal to make 1,000 kilograms of iron, but in 1833, after adopting the hot-blast system, this had fallen steeply to 2,900 kilograms.[1] Additionally, the process was much quicker than the cold-blast method, which meant that the volume of iron produced per furnace soared. According to one calculation, in 1823, average weekly output per furnace was about 22,000 kilograms, and in 1846, it was just under 112,000.[2]

The overall result was that production costs fell by as much as a remarkable 66 per cent, as in the case of Cadder Iron Company, where in 1829 it cost £6.90 to make 1,000 kilograms of pig-iron, but after the application of Neilson's innovation, this was reduced to £2.50 in 1834. The combination of lower cost and greater output meant that the Shotts Iron Company increased its volume of iron manufactured by 60 per cent, and its profits rose by 34 per cent. The upshot was that Scottish pig-iron became cheaper than that produced in all other British regions, even after carriage costs were included. By 1833, the price of 1,000 kilograms of Scottish pig-iron on the Liverpool market (the main British trading centre for the metal) was £4.75, while that for Staffordshire iron, hitherto the market leader, was £6. Consequently, a flood of new furnaces was constructed to maximise earnings; in 1796, there were seven furnaces, by 1830, 27, and in 1850 there were 144, the expansion coming mostly after 1842, when Neilson's patent right (which had earned him £30,000 p.a.) expired.

The centre of the industry was in the Monklands district of Lanarkshire, and particularly Coatbridge, which grew from having seven furnaces in 1830 to sixty in 1849. The town was the home of the Gartsherrie works, owned by William Baird & Company, which was the second biggest iron manufactory in Britain, employing 3,200 men in 1866. In 1830, the firm's share of total Scottish output was barely 5 per cent, but from 1850 onwards it regularly produced between 15 and 25 per cent. The discovery that the blackband iron seam extended into north-east Ayrshire, together with the arrival of the railway in the county, led to the development of the iron industry there in the 1840s, especially as landowners' royalties were appreciably lower than in Lanarkshire. In 1830, Ayrshire had only four furnaces; in 1843, it had twelve; and ten years later, forty-one. The county's output surged from seven million kilograms in 1830 to 250 million in 1854, which represented one-third of the Scottish total. Overall, Scotland's share of total UK production spiralled from 7 per cent in 1830 to 22 per cent in 1850, and for the next thirty years, Scottish furnaces consistently rolled out between 20 and 25 per cent. Employment also expanded, going from a little over 13,000 in 1850 to more than 38,000 in 1880.

The expansion of the coal industry was likewise highly impressive. The growth in output was enormous, rising by a factor of eight between 1775 and 1880, when it reached 20,000 million kilograms. But these overall figures rather obscure the great leap forward which occurred after 1830, when output came to 3,000 million kilograms, slightly up on the 1770 figure of 2,500 million. Scotland was the only British region to record an increase in output in every decade from 1830 to 1880, and it became the third biggest region, as its share of total UK output moved up from 9.8 per cent in 1830 to 12.9 per cent in 1870. Employment in the industry also soared; in 1801 there were perhaps 9,000 workers in mining, and by 1881, there were nearly 54,000, about a third of all those in the Scottish heavy industry category, working in some 500 collieries. The rise in the volume of coal extracted was boosted by the use of steam power, particularly in winding and pumping machinery. Steam pumps improved drainage dramatically, permitting the depths which could be worked to move from between 13 and 18 metres in 1810 to 270 metres by mid-century. Steam-powered winding speeded up the transfer of hewn coal from the seam face to the surface.

The wellsprings of this performance were manifold. One of the most significant growth points was the boom in iron production after the application of the hot-blast process, even though the key feature of Neilson's innovation was the reduction of coal usage. For the rest of the period, the iron industry consumed one-third of the total Scottish coal output. There were, however, other industrial sources of the rising demand for coal. Steam engines in factories played a prominent part, as the number of plants using them expanded. In Glasgow alone, these rose from 98 in 1839 to 196 in 1850, and the steady growth in textile factories, the great majority using steam power, was a prominent part of this process. In addition, the heating, cooking and lighting needs generated by the relentless march of urbanisation created an insatiable demand for coal for domestic usage and for conversion to gas, which arrived in Glasgow in 1817 and in Edinburgh in the following year. As discussed below, the advent of the railways enormously increased the market for coal, allowing it to reach most of mainland Scotland and simultaneously cutting the cost to the consumer, industrial and domestic alike. It is instructive that in 1852, 80 per cent of railway tracks was situated in the coalfields. Additionally, the export trade grew exponentially, so that by the end of the century, Methil, whose sole export was coal, was one of the busiest east-coast ports in Britain, while one-third of Ayrshire's output was sent via Ardrossan and other Clyde ports to Ireland.

The emergence of these new market forces not only increased the overall scale of coalmining activity, but also the geographical balance of the sector was tilted decisively westward, as part of the wider process of the formation of west-central Scotland as the heartland of Scottish manufacturing. The shift is illustrated by the declining role of the Lothian coalfields. In 1800, the pits in the three Lothian counties contributed one-eighth of the total Scottish output, but in 1864, although the region produced three times as much coal, its overall share had fallen to barely one-twentieth. Lanarkshire and Ayrshire emerged as the dominant areas, to the extent that by 1874 they together produced 80 per cent of the Scottish total output (12,000 million out of 15,000 million kilograms) and employed almost 75 per cent (34,700 out of 47,000) of all miners. For the western pits, iron was the decisive ingredient in growth, because the hot-blast furnaces required splint coal, and the seams containing this type were almost uniquely found in Lanarkshire and Ayrshire.

THE EMERGENCE OF HEAVY ENGINEERING IN THE WEST OF SCOTLAND

Heavy engineering rose after 1850 to become the most important contributor to economic growth and employment, and in this respect Scotland diverged from England, where the sector was never so dominant. The most dynamic branch in Scotland was shipbuilding and marine engineering, as almost all the significant innovations in the field in this period were either made or adopted first on the Clyde. In the early years of the nineteenth century, the Clyde shipyards had not been in the forefront, and before 1830 they built only 5 per cent of total British output, with English centres, notably London, dominating the market. But even so, the river had established an emergent pre-eminence in the construction of steamboats and the use of iron, for in the 1820s, the river's share of steam and iron vessels came to 14 per cent. Thereafter, with Robert Napier's yard as the pioneer and the training ground for the next generation of shipbuilders, the Clyde steadily assumed the ascendancy as the most advanced and technically proficient region, not just in Britain, but in the world – a status it maintained at least until the First World War.

In 1834, Tod & MacGregor became the first shipyard on the river exclusively dedicated to building iron boats. Then, in 1843, the Royal Navy commissioned from Robert Napier's yard its first iron ships, thereby confirming Napier's contention that these would have a longer life, greater capacity – between a quarter and a half more – and achieve optimum use of steam power. In 1856, Napier launched an iron paddle steamer, which was acclaimed as the harbinger of a new era in mercantile shipbuilding. At the very end of our period, the first steel ocean-going ships were also built on the Clyde, beginning with the *Rotomohama*, launched at Denny's Dumbarton yard in 1879. A particular merit of building with steel was that it provided 15 per cent extra capacity.

The benefits in speed and size which iron and then steel brought were incalculable, but they were matched by equally crucial marine engineering innovations which improved energy efficiency and cut fuel costs. A stream of these emanated from Clyde shipbuilding firms, beginning with John Elder's pioneering development of the compound engine between 1853 and 1857. Elder's breakthrough yielded fuel savings of 50 per cent, thus demonstrating the superiority of steam over sail in long-distance shipping, and justifying the Clyde's commitment to iron in the face of criticism from conventional experts. Subsequent engine improvements included the Scotch (*sic*) boiler, devised in 1862 by James Howden, which addressed the problem of maintaining the high boiler pressure levels required for compound engines. Next, in 1874, A. C. Kirk's triple-expansion engine more fully exploited the potential of steam power for engine efficiency.

The upshot of these factors was that the yards lining the river from Glasgow to Greenock on the south bank and to Dumbarton on the north – by 1870 there were over forty companies – became the first resort for any ship-owner seeking high-quality boats equipped with state-of-the-art technology. For instance, between 1863 and 1883, the contracts for twenty-one of twenty-eight ships commissioned by the Cunard line were placed with J. & G. Thomson, and by 1870, the Clyde constructed 70 per cent of all iron ships and two-thirds of steamship tonnage built in Britain. In 1876, more ships made of iron were built on the river than in all the rest of the world. Indeed, until the 1880s, US and German ship-owners routinely placed orders for large vessels with Clyde builders. A vivid indication of the river's stellar position in the galaxy of shipbuilding regions was the confidence bestowed on it by the Admiralty. The first commissions to shipbuilders outwith the navy's own dockyards for the construction of naval warships were almost automatically given to Clyde yards. One-fifth of all warship and engine contracts were won by shipbuilders along the river in the decade from 1869. As a consequence of the Clyde's leading role, the number of shipbuilding workers doubled from 11,000 in 1852 to 21,000 in 1877.

Heavy engineering was, however, not restricted to shipbuilding. Ancillary and supportive sectors formed constellations around shipbuilding, as machine tool-makers, boiler-makers, brass-founders and crane and hoisting apparatus manufacturers spread along the banks of the Clyde. Locomotive building developed in the later 1850s, when two firms opened large works in Glasgow. Walter Neilson (the son of the pioneer of the hot-blast) had set up a general engineering firm in the 1840s, but from 1855 he concentrated solely on building locomotives, operating as the North British Locomotive Company, sited at Hydepark in Springburn, in north Glasgow. A few years later, his assistant, Henry Dubs, established his own works, the Glasgow Locomotive Company, at Polmadie on the city's south side. Both soon established a reputation for excellent craftsmanship and technical skill; at Hydepark in the later 1860s, it was reported that over 5,416 separate pieces of metal were involved in building a single engine.[3] By the 1870s, each employed over 1,000 men, with Dubs's works the second biggest of its kind in Britain, and in 1876, they jointly manufactured 230 engines. Some 80 per cent of the world's output of sugar-making machinery was made in Scotland, where the leading firm – Mirrlees, Watson & Co. – constructed almost 4,000 pieces of equipment between 1851 and 1876. Structural engineering was another Scottish strength, and William Arrol's firm became renowned for erecting steel bridges in difficult technical conditions. Arrol suffered a demoralising blow when his Tay Rail Bridge collapsed in 1879, and the construction by him of the Forth Rail Bridge in 1890 was intended as a riposte to derogatory commentators on the Tay fiasco.

Iron foundries and forges also formed an expanding branch of heavy industry. Carron Company, established near Falkirk in 1759 and specialising in stoves, grates, domestic utensils and cannonades, was for a long time the main manufacturer of iron products, and in 1814 it was the largest ironworks in Europe. New entrants emerged, especially in the aftermath of the hot-blast revolution, and by the 1860s Falkirk had at least seven more foundries, with a total workforce of 1,500 – in addition to 2,000 at Carron. Physically, the biggest forges were located in William Beardmore & Co.'s two factories in Glasgow, at Parkhead and Lancefield. By 1867, there were nine huge steam hammers in each of the plants, which employed well over 600 men apiece. No job appeared impossible for Beardmore; so, in 1858, Lancefield supplied the castings for the shafts on Isambard Brunel's gigantic ill-fated vessel, the *Great Eastern*, when it had been believed that no firm could meet the specifications.

But impressive as this broad swathe of radical changes was, it is important to place it in perspective. The so-called modern industries – i.e. those using steam-powered machinery and factory production methods – remained but a lesser part of the overall economy at least until 1850, so that it was effectively only in the concluding thirty years that the extent of the changes became fully apparent. The 1851 census showed that more people were employed in traditional than in new occupations: shoemakers and tailors were as numerous as woolworkers, and rope-making works had more hands than chemical plants. Moreover, three-quarters of urban firms employed fewer than ten people, while only 10 per cent of businesses had more than fifty workers on their payroll, and factories with more than a hundred employees made up a mere 3 per cent of the total. The growth of heavy engineering works in the post-1850 era marked a significant transition: in 1870, five Clyde yards employed between 2,000 and 3,000 men, and Elder's had a workforce of 7,000. Hence, the existence of a mass factory workforce, usually seen as typical of industrialisation, was only at an embryonic stage before 1880. This configuration of the labour force may help to account for their political behaviour in this period.

THE CONTRIBUTION OF ADVANCES IN TRANSPORT

Better transport provision bestowed several broad benefits for economic development. Consumer prices fell, as local monopolies were broken; labour mobility was encouraged; national integration grew; knowledge was spread by personal visits. The reduction in costs facilitated regional specialisation, like the Alloa brewing industry, as new markets beyond the immediate local area became accessible. In England, the role of transport was vital for industrialisation, but, arguably, it made a lesser contribution in Scotland to economic modernisation. Almost all the crucial developments in Scottish industrialisation occurred within a very constricted space across the central belt, so that little long-distance transport was required.

By 1850, England boasted 4,023 miles of canal waterways – double the 2,091 which had existed in 1780 – whereas Scotland had a mere 260 miles. Moreover, a quarter of the Scottish total – sixty-nine miles – was accounted for by the Caledonian and Crinan canals, which contributed virtually nothing to industrial growth. Essentially, four canals, namely, the Forth and Clyde, Monkland, Paisley and Union, amounting to ninety-eight miles in all, were central to providing the crucial arteries for moving heavy goods such as coal and iron around the industrial heartland of Scotland. Thus, the Union canal brought between

80 and 110 million kilograms of coal each year to Edinburgh. Canals were less labour-intensive than roads for shifting heavy bulk goods, but their slow pace limited their utility to journeys of twenty-five miles or so.

From the later eighteenth century, the Scottish road system improved both in quality and in quantity. The use of superior materials, notably tarmacadam, better engineering and the construction of high-grade bridges together meant that roads were smoother, faster and much less affected by bad weather. Additionally, more efficient vehicles were built and horses were bred to be fitter and stronger. The introduction of turnpike roads stood at the forefront of these developments. These were built to a superior standard and laid out in a more direct route than the normal roads, so that they were ideal for long-distance journeys, such as the route between Perth and Inverness. By 1830, Scotland had around 11,000 miles of turnpike roads. These advances undoubtedly helped improve communications, but it seems that in Scotland the main benefits fell to agriculture rather than to industry, as is suggested in Chapter 1. With the advent of the railways, roads suffered a steep decline in goods traffic; between 1834 and 1838, turnpike revenues fell by 162 per cent, and journeys made by carters from Aberdeen city to surrounding localities plummeted from 660 per week in 1838 to 231 in 1851.

The railways, however, were not an absolutely indispensable component of industrialisation. Opened in 1826, the first line ran for ten miles between Kirkintilloch and Old Monkland. Initially, growth was sluggish; in 1840, the route mileage totalled only 137, and there was no coherent network system. Almost all the earliest routes were designed to convey freight, the only exception being the Dundee to Newtyle route. Increasingly, however, passenger traffic appeared in the 1830s to be a lucrative proposition, and this became the determining factor in the huge expansion of the 1840s, so that in 1842, nine million passengers were conveyed by train. Edinburgh and Glasgow were not linked until 1842, and lines to London from Edinburgh and Glasgow only began in 1848, raising the total route mileage to 872. Expansion beyond the central belt developed thereafter, so that in 1879, Scotland had 2,864 route miles, double the 1859 figure of 1,418.

The railways did not in themselves create very much direct demand for Scottish industrial goods until after mid-century. The iron used to make the permanent way was overwhelmingly sourced from England, partly because Scottish pig-iron was too brittle to make efficient track lines and partly because the Scottish malleable iron industry – in the 1840s, essentially a couple of firms – was quite inadequate to meet the rigorous requirements of the railway contractors. Therefore, only between 7 and 10 per cent of the output of the Scottish iron industry was used in constructing the country's rail system. Also, since, as we have seen, locomotive works only developed in Scotland in the mid-1850s, the rolling stock in the first thirty years was mostly provided by English manufacturers. Even the demand generated by the railways for coal was a rather insignificant share of Scottish output: in 1854, it came to a bare 2 per cent of that year's total volume product, whereas the iron industry took 32 per cent. Twenty years later, the rail network still took only 4 per cent – 5 per cent of Scottish coal sales. The impact of the trains on employment was slight; the permanent workforce, once the railways were operating, was no more than 8,000 in 1851.

The secondary benefits brought by the railways were, however, very considerable. Coal now reached a much wider range of places. At the same time, the price of coal fell substantially, as happened in Forfar in 1837, when the advent of the railway immediately cut the cost by 20 per cent. More coal could be delivered by rail to towns: in 1854, two-thirds of the coal supplied to Edinburgh was transported by rail. The great surge in demand from urban areas for domestic coal encouraged the development of mines in relatively remote areas, for instance, the Slammanan pit was opened in response to Edinburgh's seemingly insatiable appetite. By 1859, the Lothian coalfields, which before 1830 had a monopoly of supplying the capital's coal, were matched by the contributions from Stirlingshire and Lanarkshire. Beside the growth in domestic use of coal, the railways permitted steam power to be introduced to places where it had hitherto been too expensive, as its sweeping march through the Borders wool industry after 1850, referred to earlier, shows.

Trains also influenced society and the economy at a more diffuse level. The provision of faster communications between regions and towns which the railways brought facilitated businessmen's access to new markets and supplies. Additionally, the acceleration in the delivery of mail permitted the more efficient transaction of business and official matters, as well as enhancing social solidarity and well-being by improving contact between far-flung family members and acquaintances. The major advantage of travelling by train was not so much comfort or cost as the saving of time. The journey between Greenock and Glasgow by rail took one hour, in contrast to two-and-a-half hours by boat, and travelling from Edinburgh to London shrivelled from forty-five hours by coach to thirteen hours by train. Moreover, trains were reliable and more impervious to bad weather, and conveyed passengers directly to town centres. If there was a hold-up on one line, there was often the opportunity to switch to a rival's service. The coming of the railways had a substantial impact on the urban morphology. As stations were sited in town centres, this inevitably involved the wholesale demolition of buildings and entire streets, which in larger places frequently meant a slum-clearance programme, since compensation for that type of property was the least expensive. Train traffic afforded opportunities for new business services to flourish, including hotels, restaurant, shops and taxis; in 1873, there were some 10,500,000 departures and arrivals in Glasgow's four main rail termini. Indeed, the fortunes of whole towns could hinge on the advent of the railway. Crieff offers a good example of this, as the coming of trains made it the market town for west Perthshire, and also attracted holidaymakers to the area. The spread of the rail network also facilitated the growth of suburban and commuter villages, as noted in the next chapter.

There were, however, aspects of the burgeoning railway system which adversely affected certain parts of society. Local businesses could reach wider markets, but they could also be undercut by more efficient outside producers, and this is part of the reason why small-scale textile manufacturers in outlying locations went into decline, a process which reached from Galloway to rural Aberdeenshire. In larger towns, individual retailers and artisan craftworkers often struggled to cope with the challenge posed by the rise of department stores, which used the freight system to bring in goods cheaply, as discussed in Chapter 3. Also, it is possible that the money invested in constructing the railroad system in the 1840s diverted capital which might have been more usefully devoted to social infrastructure projects, such as providing working-class housing of a decent standard. This argument gains force when linked to the proposition that Scotland was over-provided with railways. The fierce rivalry between train companies, notably the North British and the Caledonian, meant a needless duplication of routes, stations and permanent ways. In a country which offered a relatively small market for railway business, and which had limited capital resources, it might have been more beneficial for all sides if there had been more co-operation instead of intense competition.

With the arrival of steam power, coastal shipping proved to be highly efficient, and cheaper than most overland transport for long-distance bulk. Thus, iron produced in Lanarkshire and Ayrshire was easily taken to ports along the Clyde and transported to Liverpool, the centre of the trade in iron. Advances in river deepening and dock construction boosted the attractions of coastwise traffic. Glasgow's dock frontage rose from 1,600 metres in 1840 to 5,500 in 1870, with designated quays to handle different goods, such as cattle, while custom-designed vessels were used for specific materials, and specialist shipping companies provided an efficient service. This all meant that turn-rounds were greatly speeded up. Additionally, the Clyde was progressively deepened throughout the century, which permitted larger ships of up to 500,000 kilograms to come all the way upriver to Glasgow. Similarly, the construction in the 1860s of a wet dock at Dundee opened that port to bigger boats.

THE FINANCIAL SINEWS

Claims have been made that Scottish banking played an important role in the country's advance to industrialisation, because it had certain superior aspects when contrasted with England.[4] The provincial banks are particularly singled out for praise. They sprang up across Lowland Scotland from the middle of the eighteenth century; between 1747 and 1836, over forty were established, and several had branches in nearby localities. They innovated in banking practices which subsequently became widespread, such as paying interest on deposit accounts, giving credit to businesses, and offering overdrafts, which were frequently secured on the borrower's buildings and equipment. Their strength was that the directors were local men who had an informed awareness of the reliability of clients and the viability of business ventures. Under Scots law, there was no limitation on the number of partners, and it was not uncommon for there to be fifty to sixty partners. This was not the case in England, where the legal limit for equivalent banks – the country banks – was six partners. The advantage of the Scottish system was that risks were spread widely, and a broad range of knowledge and expertise was available in decision-making; for instance, in 1803 the Aberdeen Banking Company had 116 partners, drawn from merchants, landowners, public officials, tradesmen, university professors, lawyers and doctors. Moreover, unlike their English cousins, they could issue their own notes and currency, and most provincial banks accepted these on a reciprocal basis. This greatly aided business transactions across Scotland, as well as eliminating the problem of coinage and small note famine often prevalent in England. The mutual support that provincial banks provided helped to avert major business failures. When a town was hit by trade difficulties, these banks could act to sustain the business community until recovery took place, as happened in Dundee during a crisis in the textile industry in 1826. The solidity of the Scottish institutions was highlighted by the severe banking crisis of 1825–6, in which 20 per cent of English banks, but only 5 per cent of Scottish banks, failed.

The contribution of the provincial banks to economic development was much more in the nature of furnishing working capital to enterprises, so enabling their day-to-day financial needs to be handled, rather than in providing loans to meet major long-term capital investment. There were two reasons for this. Firstly, until the advent of ironworks and heavy engineering, where large-scale plant and machinery were involved, and spacious buildings were needed to accommodate them, fixed capital was not necessarily required on an extensive scale. The total fixed capital in the cotton industry has been put at £1.4 million in 1812, and £4 million in 1840,[5] and most coal mines were, compared to England, not very large outfits. Secondly, it seems that most entrepreneurs financed fixed capital projects either by ploughing back past profits, which were often exceptionally high, or by receiving loans and gifts from relations and acquaintances, often themselves in business. Examples of the first include Bairds of Gartsherrie and Coats, the Paisley thread manufacturers. Bairds reaped massive gains from the introduction of the hot-blast – between 1833 and 1840, profits totalled £250,000 – which were mostly put back into the business. At least 50 per cent of Coats's annual profits were regularly reinvested in the business, rather than distributed to partners. As an instance of the second approach, David Colville built his path-breaking steel plant with a loan of £33,000 from a business associate, a Glasgow iron merchant, while the Hawick wool manufacturers, Dick & Laing, relied on family loans to establish the firm.

The role of provincial banks was eclipsed from the 1820s by the rise of joint stock banks, and their numbers plunged from twenty-five in 1820 to three in 1845. Provincial banks often lacked the resources to survive straitened economic circumstances; one-third failed between 1747 and 1834, and their average lifespan was thirty-two years. Joint stock banks circumvented these problems in several ways. They had deeper reserves, as the number of shareholders was far higher than provincial bank partners. The National Bank of Scotland, founded in 1825, had 1,300 stockholders, and the Commercial Bank, launched in 1810, had 673. They also built up extensive branch networks to expand their business, and by 1850 the Glasgow-based Western Bank had seventy-two branches, the largest number of any bank in the world. As part of this strategy, joint stock banks gobbled up much of the business previously going to the provincial banks. Sometimes they absorbed older banks to expand rapidly, and between 1829 and 1844, twelve – i.e. one-half – of the functioning provincial banks were swallowed by joint stock concerns, with the Union Bank alone taking in four. The numbers of branches made the conduct of financial transactions much more straightforward across the country; for instance, the Clydesdale Bank's branch network ran from Campbeltown to St Andrews. The joint stock banks continued the innovative policies pioneered by the provincial banks, namely, paying interest on deposits, lending on discounted bills, and providing overdrafts, such as one of £55,000 advanced to the Monkland Iron Company.

The success of these new banks compared to English banks is clearly delineated in statistics. In 1845, the Scottish joint stock banks had one branch for every 7,200 individuals in the country; their English counterparts had one per 15,000. Bank assets per capita gave the same picture. In 1800, the English figure was £5.97, and the Scottish was £7.40, yet by 1850, the figure for England was £9.50, while for Scotland, it was £18.05. The dynamic nature of Scottish joint stock banks is further illustrated by the data for 1825 and 1850. The number of bank branches increased from 173 to 407; bank deposits rose from £4.6 million to £35 million; and advances rose from £17.6 million to £36.5 million. Part of the reason for this growth was that the banks moved to increase their efficiency by professionalising their staff. Full-time employees were used in lieu of the previous reliance on local solicitors, and regular inspections from head office were carried out on branches. But these banks also posed serious threats to stability, since a failure could have a much wider negative impact than the foundering of a provincial bank, as was illustrated by the collapses of the Western Bank in 1857 and of the City of Glasgow Bank in 1878.

The failures of the Western Bank (1857) and the City of Glasgow Bank (1878)

These were two very large outfits with branches in many towns; the Western had the most branches of any bank in the world, and the City Bank was the largest in Britain. There were similarities between the two collapses. Firstly, the liabilities were considerable: for the Western they ran to £9,000,000, and with the City, they amounted to £12,750,000. Secondly, both had lent heavily to a highly restricted number of clients. Six firms together owed £1,600,000 to the Western, and eight companies owed the City of Glasgow £6,000,000 – almost one-half of the total loans advanced by the bank. This rendered the banks highly vulnerable if these large debtors ran into trouble, as happened to the Western when three firms owing £1,200,000 failed in 1857, as a recession hit the textile trade. Moreover, both banks had not ensured that adequate collateral securities were in place. Thirdly, the two banks had invested heavily in highly speculative ventures overseas, notably in the United States, Australasia and India. These investments were overvalued, and many proved worthless, as the City of Glasgow discovered was the case with holdings in US infrastructure ventures nominally valued at £1,000,000. Fourthly, neither bank had built up adequate reserves – the value of advances made by the City Bank came to 133 per cent of deposits; moreover, these reserves were not held in financially safe locations, such as government securities. The City of Glasgow Bank compounded this catalogue of reckless banking practice by illegal activities. The bank's accounts had been fraudulent for several years, at least from the early 1870s, with bad debts not written off, but rather treated as good, while investments and assets were greatly overvalued. In addition, the directors had a very limited investment stake in the bank, as in total they held only 1 per cent of the stock, whereas in several other banks, the directors owned 7 per cent or more. A small inner ring of directors took decisions which were not disclosed to the whole board. Eight directors and senior managers were prosecuted and received jail sentences – the only such occasion in Scottish banking history, so far.

The consequences of the two banks' failures rippled widely. In the case of the Western, the cotton sector in the Glasgow region suffered a setback, as several muslin manufacturers were clients, and the trade was plunged into an irreversible decline. In addition, four other banks were dragged into closure, either directly or indirectly, by the demise of the Western. The bank's shareholders lost their investments completely, and had to make an average contribution of £1,090 to meet the deficit. The impact of the City of Glasgow Bank's collapse was still more profound. There were 1,819 shareholders, and they were required to meet an average call on them of £12,705 in order to meet the bank's deficit. The aftermath was that of the 1,335 individuals who owned shares, only 129 – under 10 per cent – escaped bankruptcy, while of the 484 trustees (mainly lawyers) holding shares, 339 (around two-thirds) were likewise bankrupted. The consequence was a serious downturn in the economic life of the west of Scotland, with thousands of workers out of work for many months: a survey of 180 large Glasgow workplaces undertaken a year after the bank's failure found a 13 per cent fall in employment numbers. At the peak of the unemployment crisis, 30,000 individuals in Glasgow were receiving charitable relief, and emigration figures rose steeply.

THE SOURCES OF ECONOMIC MODERNISATION

There is an assumption that there were exceptional factors to explain the entrepreneurship exhibited by the Scottish business class.[6] The contribution of human capital to the process of industrial transformation is perhaps not as straightforward as might appear at first sight. Scotland had an education system which appeared to be immensely superior to England, as Scots never ceased to point out: every parish had a school supported by local ratepayers, and in 1800 it boasted five universities, against England's meagre two. Moreover, both schools and universities laid stress on practical knowledge, while the latter also emphasised the need to blend the practical and the theoretical by linking technical solutions with rational explanations of the answers. University teachers were perfectly willing to offer scientific advice to businesses and agriculturalists. Additionally, the Andersonian Institute in Glasgow specialised in training in the applied sciences: J. B. Neilson and William Beardmore junior attended classes there while apprentices in their fathers' firms.

Yet the origins of industrialisation did not occur in Scotland, and except for James Watt, the great inventors and innovators during the first stage were English. Further, the earliest advances required only very limited technical knowledge, and were often the products of artisans' experimentations, rather than stemming from any profound academic knowledge. Even among the major chemical manufacturers, where perhaps scientific training at university level might be thought a useful acquisition, the record is indistinct, possibly in part because Scottish universities focused on inorganic, and not practical, chemistry. Charles Macintosh, a partner in the Tennant chemical firm and the pioneer of waterproof clothing, attended Edinburgh University, where he was taught by Joseph Black. However, the first Charles Tennant (1768–1838), the driving force in the establishment of the great chemical dynasty, had only a limited education: the child of a small tenant-farmer in Ayrshire, he was educated at Ochiltree parish school, and then was apprenticed to a master handloom weaver in Kilbarchan, after which he started a bleachfield business near Paisley. Likewise, the Baird brothers of Gartsherrie, among the mightiest British ironmasters, were the sons of a farmer and received a basic schooling locally, yet became pre-eminent in their chosen industry. A detailed survey of successful nineteenth-century first-generation Scottish businessmen concluded that two-thirds were not educated beyond school level, but thereafter became in-house apprentices.[7]

In the later phase of industrial growth, however, scientific and technical expertise did become ever more important, especially in the field of engineering. So, Glasgow University's professor of civil engineering and mechanics from 1855 to 1872, W. J. M. Rankine, became the go-to boffin for shipbuilders seeking to improve the energy efficiency of ships, and he was linked at the university with one of the greatest British scientists of the second half of the century, William Thomson, Lord Kelvin. Rankine and Kelvin, with their assistants and students, formed a collaborative circle with shipbuilders and engineers, along with ship-owners such as George Burns, one of the founders of the Cunard line, to formulate theoretical solutions to marine engineering roadblocks and then to conduct practical tests to verify the solutions proffered. This collaborative relationship was formalised in 1857 with the formation of the Glasgow-based Institution of Engineers and Shipbuilders in Scotland.

For some commentators, Calvinism made a significant contribution to the Scottish entrepreneurial spirit, notably by suggesting that worldly success was an intimation of God's favour and the promise of eternal life. It also stressed the ethical responsibility to work hard, and to eschew indulgent self-gratification.[8] This gave businessmen self-confidence, as they were carrying out God's will, and assured them that there were no theological concerns about profit and economic growth. Additionally, it may explain why engineering became such a pronounced feature of Scottish industry, in that the austere character of Scottish Presbyterian worship and its disapproval of most forms of artistic expression led to engagement in an industry which combined utility with the pleasing aestheticism of good clean design, whether in ships or bridges. While there may be some validity in these suppositions, it is not always compelling: after all, the most intensely Calvinist parts of the country were the Highlands, not an area abuzz with business vitality. Furthermore, many leading businessmen took a keen interest in artistic and cultural pursuits, acquiring paintings from all periods, past and present, and attending musical and theatrical performances, while others were avid collectors of rare books. As an example, the second Charles Tennant (1823–1906) built up a library of 5,000 books, and amassed an extensive fine art collection, including works by Turner, Reynolds, Hogarth, Stubbs and Gainsborough.

This suggests that a wider cultural and social context beyond religion counted. The percolation of Enlightenment concepts, diffused through universities, public lectures, printed material and social intercourse, spread the beneficial ideals of improvement and progress. The key aspects were the emphasis on modernising values, lauding a mix of rationality, self-interest and achievement, which created an open, competitive society to replace a prescriptive, hierarchical system. The application of scientific and rational modes of analysis held the key to such advances, with experimentation the best way to achieve improvements. Crucially, these developments were at once possible and desirable, demonstrating that useful knowledge bestowed power over nature. These concepts were at the core of the arguments espoused by the leading figures in the Scottish Enlightenment. The ideas reached a wide circle of Scots, some through personal acquaintance with the literati, as the latter were well-known figures in the public arenas of Aberdeen, Edinburgh and Glasgow. A second circle of influence embraced the broad span of individuals who attended university classes or public lectures given by these thinkers. The most celebrated exponent of Enlightenment values was Dugald Stewart of Edinburgh University, but Glasgow and Aberdeen universities also had their advocates of the cause. A still broader audience was reached by print media, above all the *Edinburgh Review*, which circulated widely throughout Scotland.

In addition, many advances came about not through the stereotypical medium of a lone individual heroically making the critical breakthrough; instead they came by micro-innovations, that is, by gradual refinements and tweaking of existing machinery, as for instance in textiles, iron and marine engineering. Research and development rendered the initial scientific discovery practical and valuable, for instance, the steam condenser in marine engineering. This indicates a social aspect of collective innovation, with men watching what others had done, and then working to produce a better piece of equipment, as happened in the Dundee linen and Paisley cotton sectors. In the former, the modifications to machinery regularly implemented by Peter Carmichael, the engineering expert at Baxters, kept the firm at the technological forefront of the trade. James Baird filled the role of technical director at the family's iron firm, and he was constantly striving to improve and refine. He redesigned the shape of the furnaces to make them more efficient, and made important improvements to Neilson's hot-blast process. As he remarked, '[i]t was always my endeavour to find out the defects of the various apparatus with which I had to work'.[9] Again, while J. B. Neilson is customarily credited with making the innovation of the hot-blast process, several other individuals played a significant role in what was in reality a wholly collaborative enterprise. For instance, the vital perception that the hot-blast process should use raw coal, rather than coke, thereby greatly reducing the production cost, was first made by the coalmaster William Dixon, and not by Neilson. Additionally, John Condie, an artisan, made an indispensable contribution to the project.

Another version of social innovation was the practice of collaborating in networks. Contacts were made between academic specialists and businessmen anxious to improve their goods or to innovate new production techniques. The outstanding example of such fruitful interchanges was, as already discussed, the circle linking engineering dons at Glasgow University with the leading Clyde shipbuilders. There were also more informal institutions where knowledge was shared, and innovations and new patents were discussed. These sometimes occurred on a regional basis, such as a network in Angus and Fife of linen and jute manufacturers, and another in Edinburgh and Midlothian comprised paper manufacturers and book publishers. Towns were vital for small and middling concerns, which could enjoy the benefits of economies of agglomeration by sharing knowledge and technical information. Urban life also conferred important psychological and material benefits, in that a good reputation could be established, and thereby trust between businessmen was made easier.

THE QUALITY OF SCOTTISH ENTREPRENEURSHIP

The overall quality of entrepreneurship is also ambiguous, as, after early success, many sectors seemed to lack staying power and the ability to adjust to new circumstances and adapt to fresh challenges. Whereas in the 1820s and 1830s Glasgow had been a contender with Manchester for supremacy in British cotton production, the Scottish industry entered unsettled conditions in the 1840s, and although Glasgow managed to stagger on as a cotton centre until the 1870s, the sense of being on the wane was unmissable some twenty years earlier. In 1861, there were around 100 spinning firms in Scotland, but 25 years later, a mere 15 remained. Scottish cotton production suffered because manufacturers were unwilling to invest in up-to-date machinery; for example, Lancashire began installing highly efficient spinning mules in the early 1820s, but in Scotland, this only started in 1837. Scottish millowners opted for the cheap labour cost advantage which employing women offered, but Lancashire, in contrast, prospered by employing men, who were deemed capable of working more looms. As a result, in 1867 it was calculated that productivity per operative in Lancashire was 50 per cent higher than in Scotland. It is illustrative of the Scottish cottonmasters' indifference to improving production standards that they had little involvement with the Glasgow Weaving College, established in 1877.

Moreover, flawed management decisions about industrial relations policy rendered it well-nigh impossible in Scotland to raise output per worker by paying higher wages. Lancashire achieved this by firstly negotiating joint agreements between firms, which established a united strategy on wages and other labour issues, and this was intimately linked to accepting the role of trade unions, which could direct and discipline the workforce on these matters. In Scotland, there was no organisational unity among employers, and hence no consensus on labour questions; instead each firm pursued an individual route. In the not too long run, this strategy of undercapitalisation and a low-wage, low-productivity regime was a recipe for failure, as emergent industrialising countries could undercut Scotland in low-cost production. When in the 1860s, overseas competition drove the Lancashire manufacturers to withdraw from coarser cotton products, they turned to making finer-quality goods, in direct rivalry to Scotland. With superior productivity levels and up-to-date machinery, they were able to beat most Scottish firms in both price and quality. The main survivors in Scotland from this onslaught were the highly specialist manufacturers, such as the Paisley thread companies, J. & P. Coats and J. & J. Clark. In other words, specialisation was more likely to guarantee survival as a niche producer than the generalist route mostly taken in Scotland.

Jute, too, seemed to be on a shoogly peg. In the 1880s, the importation of raw material from the Indian subcontinent to Dundee was challenged by a not unreasonable decision that jute could equally easily be manufactured in its country of origin. Kolkata mounted a vigorous challenge in hessian products, and by 1890 it had ousted Dundee from markets in North and South America, Europe and Australasia. This instance of the empire striking back was greatly boosted by the opening of the Suez Canal in 1869, which removed the geographical protection enjoyed by Dundee jute's European trade. Quite quickly, therefore, Dundee's prosperity was imperilled, although it limped on for a considerable period. The city's other staple, linen, was in no better condition. Baxter & Co. was the sole firm to survive through the entire nineteenth century. A major factor was that the size of linen factories (apart from Baxters) was markedly smaller than the city's arch-rival, Leeds, so that the Yorkshire firms reaped greater economies of scale. The same issue of size applied to woollen firms: in 1835, the average workforce in a Scottish factory was thirty-five; in England, it was sixty-six.

Again, in iron, entrepreneurship seemed to wilt. Scotland remained committed to the production of the basic level of pig-iron. There was only a limited interest in entering the higher stages, such as malleable iron, which was mostly carried out in England, and although some places, such as Falkirk and Glasgow, did have several foundries, all but a handful were quite small by English standards. Thus, in 1871, Scotland produced 17.5 per cent of British pig-iron, but only 4.9 per cent of puddled iron. The vulnerability of this high dependence on pig-iron, which relied on local supplies to maintain competitiveness, was highlighted by the middle of the 1870s, as the Scottish blackband deposits became exhausted, so that production could only be kept going through imports, whether from England or elsewhere. Once the cheaper cost benefit brought by native sourcing was lost, inevitably it became harder to compete with other regions. The level of output attained in 1870 – 1,250 million kilograms – was not matched in the rest of the period. In 1880, while overall British tonnage had grown, the Scottish figure had fallen by 16 per cent over the decade, so that it contributed 13 per cent of the grand total, against 20 per cent in 1870 – and by 1890, output was just one-half of the peak performance.

The problems presented by this short-term perspective were intensified by two further failures. As local supplies dried up, it was logical to relocate ironworks to sites nearer the coastal ports, in order to minimise the costs both of bringing in bulky raw materials and of sending the pig-iron elsewhere for processing and refining, but no firm made such a move. The insistence on staying in inland plants left the Scottish iron industry with a long-run disadvantage, which became increasingly evident in subsequent decades. This precarious situation was aggravated by problems uniquely presented by the Scottish furnaces. They were designed to function only with splint coal – which was widespread in Lanarkshire and Ayrshire – but these seams were running dry. Furthermore, the size of furnaces was proving too small and inefficient for modern needs, so that output per unit lagged well behind England, thereby intensifying the uncompetitiveness of the Scottish sector.

The second blind spot was the reluctance of ironmasters to move into steel production. It is true that there were metallurgical obstacles to adopting the first processes for converting Scottish pig-iron into steel, but by the 1870s alternative methods made it possible to produce good-quality steel. It is revealing that the first steel plant in Scotland was set up in 1872 by the chemical manufacturer, Charles Tennant, who saw steel manufacture as a means of deploying waste iron oxide residues from his Spanish copper mining concern. The most important steel company to emerge in Scotland was created at the end of the period by David Colville, whose background was atypical of the majority of iron manufacturers. He had come to Glasgow from Campbeltown, where his father ran a shipping company and a distillery. After establishing himself as a tea and coffee merchant, he set up an ironworks in 1861, and nearly twenty years later, in his mid-sixties, he moved to steel manufacture. The more established ironmasters stood inert on the fringes of this new metal industry; instead they considered the solution, at least in the case of William Baird & Company, to be to move backwards to get control of the coal mines which supplied fuel.

Coal, too, faced similar obstacles. The average size of a Scottish coal pit was appreciably smaller than in the rest of Britain; the norm for a Yorkshire pit in the 1870s was about 400 miners, whereas in West Lothian, the average was 137, and a good number of Scottish collieries employed fewer than 20 workers – including half of Ayrshire mines. Thus, the majority of Scottish mines were not able to reap the same economies of scale enjoyed by their competitors south of the border. This disadvantage was compounded by the problems posed by the industry's ownership structure. Three-quarters of coal companies owned just a single colliery and only four ran more than ten pits, so that administrative and financial costs could not be spread, while the quality of management was likely to be low-grade in many instances. The firms in the industry suffered from in-built and systemic instability. In Lanarkshire, for instance, the average working life of a colliery was twenty-one years, and between 1854 and 1874, only 40 per cent of companies operating at the outset lasted the full two decades. This combination of a splintered ownership structure and a volatile existence rendered it virtually impossible to act collaboratively to restrict output and thus raise prices; instead there was a drive by each pit to maximise production with low profit margins. This cut-throat competition led to under-capitalisation, so that it was only in the 1870s that coal-cutting machinery was brought in to the Lothian coalfields. An added hazard which emerged in the western mining fields, and whose consequences ramified widely across industries heavily reliant on coal, was the exhaustion of the coal seams. This had begun in Ayrshire, where, by the early 1870s, total output had stalled. In Lanarkshire, the same decade marked the relocation of core mining activity away from its previous heart in the Monklands to the more southerly areas of Hamilton and Lesmahagow.

Even shipbuilding, the leader in entrepreneurial innovation from mid-century, was not immune from signs of stress. Engineering breakthroughs were very impressive, but they were brought forward without much regard to cost. For instance, between 1866 and 1879, J. & G. Thomson (later renowned as John Brown & Co.) made no profit on at least two-thirds of the ships they built, so that accumulated losses from 1871 to 1879 ran to £64,749. These deficits arose because of lax pricing procedures and no proper control of costs. A second frailty was that several shipyards became too closely tied to a single shipping line in order to maintain a full order-book, and this over-dependence could create problems if the customer switched to another shipbuilder. By the 1880s, several shipyards were in a parlous financial position: J. & G. Thomson was on the verge of bankruptcy after Cunard moved its contracts elsewhere. Fairfield, one of the most illustrious yards, set up by John Elder, Robert Napier's ablest assistant, was also very near to collapse in that decade. The generous costings allowed in Admiralty contracts became irresistible in the 1880s to Clyde shipbuilders, who used the generous profits to sustain the wafer-thin margins obtained on mercantile ships; this was the case with J. & G. Thomson. So, while ingenuity in engineering reveals one aspect of entrepreneurial competence, it is also important to remember that the iron laws of accountancy will eventually prevail.

But beside these frailties, two indicators of deep-rooted problems were looming. Firstly, the closing two decades of the century intimated that the river's pre-eminence in technological innovation was ebbing. Although several middle-ranking innovations of the period did originate on the river, the main engineering development was the steam-turbine, pioneered in 1884 by C. A. Parsons in England, while the start of the crucial shift in fuel from coal to diesel took place with no engagement by the Clyde. Secondly, the shipyard owners had consciously adopted a strategy of fragmenting production into highly discrete manual crafts, rather than investing in high-tech machinery, still less in technical or scientific education and training, which would have promoted significant long-term benefits. This approach had the advantage of offering a quick, flexible response to the regular cyclical downturns which the industry endured every five to seven years, as men could be laid off at far less cost than having expensive equipment lying idle for a prolonged period. But over time, this dependence on a differentiated skilled workforce promoted the growth of demarcation disputes between crafts, and consolidated the power of sectional trade unions, two processes which severely eroded the power of the owners to execute their managerial strategies successfully.

Two general points arise from a survey of the range of Scottish industries. One is the over-reliance on family members to run a firm's business. In some cases, such as Carron, Coats, Baird and Cox, the combined talents of siblings and other kin were highly effective and sustained over the generations, but elsewhere, the wellsprings of enterprise seemed to dry up rather too promptly. For second and third generations of the original owners, distractions and diversions occupied too much of their time and energy, whether these took the guise of politics, cultural activities or plain indolence. There was also a pronounced absence of the emergence of a professional managerial cadre in many branches of industry and commerce, except for banking. Perhaps linked to this, a second feature was the volatility and brevity of many concerns. In Hawick, of the thirty-eight woollen firms existing in 1838, only seven were still active in 1846; and similarly, only one-third of Glasgow cotton manufacturers operating in 1830 were still in business in 1860. As noted, coal companies also experienced high levels of churn. These failings have to be set in a highly favourable context, since, as is fully explored in the following chapter, trade unions were weaker than in England, and Scottish wage levels were anything between 10 and 20 per cent lower. These may be pointers to weaknesses in Scottish entrepreneurship which are sometimes obscured by focusing on the success stories.

To a much greater extent than in England, the emergent Scottish industrial configuration was heavily dependent on international trade, with the domestic market much less significant. Mainly, this was because of the nature of the heavy industries which Scotland specialised in, but in addition, home demand was weaker than in England. Firstly, the population was quite small, and moreover, it grew at a slower pace than in England. The Scottish population rose from two million in 1821 to three-and-three-quarter million in 1881, which meant that while it was 20 per cent of England's population in 1821, sixty years later, it had slipped to 15 per cent. Secondly, over the period, incomes in Scotland were not high enough to generate vibrant levels of domestic demand. The solid middle class was the prime home consumption market, because this sector had markedly greater incomes than other categories. But, in 1851, they comprised 10.9 per cent of adult males, against 12.9 per cent in England, a differential of almost one-fifth, and only Edinburgh approached the English average.

The success of Scottish businessmen in seeking out markets outside the country was remarkable, with exports penetrating most European states, North and Latin America, the Indian subcontinent and China, plus British colonies. The main products were textiles, iron, coal and heavy engineering, notably ships and locomotives. In the Scottish cotton industry's high-tide years, the overwhelming preponderance of production went outside the country. The two Paisley thread manufacturers, Coats and J. & J. Clark, exported 75 per cent of their output to the United States from the 1840s, but China and India took cheaper cloth and clothing. For linen also, overseas trade was pre-eminent. Dundee, which focused on making coarser goods, sent much of its output to clothe slaves in the West Indies until the era of emancipation in the 1830s, whereafter it shifted to the United States, where 'the peculiar institution' still flourished. But in the 1840s, the city's manufacturers added South America and Australasia to its export outlets, as demand for heavy linen items such as sailcloth and sheeting increased. Dunfermline, the centre in Scotland for high-quality linen, also depended on the United States, which took half of its products. Jute was sold in North and South America, Europe, Australia, New Zealand and much of Asia as a cheap and sturdy all-purpose material.

In the heyday of iron manufacture, at least two-thirds was sold outside the country, the bulk going to England, since Liverpool was the main iron trading centre in Britain, but a considerable amount also went further afield. Bairds sold 60 per cent of their iron beyond Scotland, of which the United States and Europe each took roughly one-fifth. Export sales of coal formed a much smaller share of total output, averaging around 10 per cent per annum between 1831 and 1881, but this was still a sizeable volume, as it exceeded 1,500 million kilograms in the latter year. The fortunes of shipbuilding depended on world traffic in goods and people, as the proportion of output on the Clyde contributed by coastal shipping was very slight. The rise of the Scottish locomotive engine-building sector was heavily reliant on foreign demand, as the rail mileage inside the country could not possibly sustain the levels of output. Furthermore, the health of both coal and iron in turn were closely tied to the demands of shipbuilders.

The volume of traffic created by this focus on foreign markets contributed to the rise of large-scale Scottish-based shipping lines, and by 1891, 15 per cent of the total British shipping tonnage was registered in Glasgow. Most shipowning concerns tended to operate in particular areas. The Allan line, the world's seventh largest shipping company by 1880, concentrated primarily on Canadian business, while Donaldson dealt with South America, and William MacKinnon's massive conglomerate traded in India, the Far East and the Antipodes. One somewhat immodest Scottish shipping agent claimed to 'control a splendid connection through China, Burmah [sic], India, South Africa, South America and the West Indies, in each of which territories able correspondents are employed'.[10]

But there were drawbacks to this impressive display of entrepreneurial verve, for the high reliance on world economic performance rendered Scotland profoundly vulnerable to several grave threats. The frequent but unpredictable recessions which swept across international trade had a serious impact, as many Scottish industries were highly interlinked in this field. The absence of any robust and sizeable home demand sector meant there was no cushion to withstand the cold blasts of global downturns. This exposure to extreme volatility in employment and growth no doubt played a part in the fluctuating trends in emigration from Scotland, which was particularly marked in skilled workers. Another difficulty starting to emerge was that exporting to places which were initially under- or, at best, semi-developed carried a risk that as industrial modernisation inevitably occurred in these countries, domestic production was likely to undercut the price of goods made in Scotland. As discussed, Dundee's stranglehold on jute production was steadily eroded by the rise in manufacturing of the textile on the Indian subcontinent. A further challenge was presented by the drift to protectionism, as several countries opted to build tariff walls in order to allow their home industry to expand without the competition from established producers elsewhere. Several European states, along with the United States, began to flirt with this policy, which of course posed a major threat to a wide range of Scottish products. This protectionist trend, linked to the dwindling availability of domestically sourced raw materials, notably iron and coal, began to erode the cost-competitive advantage hitherto enjoyed by Scotland, with grave long-term consequences.

NOTES

1. R. D. Corrins, 'The Great Hot-Blast Affair', *Industrial Archaeology*, 6 (1970), 233–4.
2. C. A. Whatley, 'The Process of Industrialisation in Ayrshire, 1707–1871', Strathclyde University PhD Thesis (1975), 222–4.
3. D. Bremner, *The Industries of Scotland: Their Rise, Progress and Present Position* (1869), 101.
4. R. Cameron, 'Banking and Industrialisation in Britain in the Nineteenth Century', in A. Slaven and D. H. Aldcroft (eds), *Business, Banking and Industrial History* (1982), 102–7.
5. J. Butt, 'The Scottish Cotton Industry and the Industrial Revolution', in L. M. Cullen and T. C. Smout (eds), *Comparative Aspects of Scottish and Irish Economic and Social History* (1978), 120–2.
6. E.g. R. H. Campbell, *The Rise and Fall of Scottish Industry, 1707–1939* (1980), 36–55. See also A. Slaven, 'Entrepreneurs and Business Success and Business Failure in Scotland', in D. H. Aldcroft and A. Slaven (eds), *Enterprise and Management: Essays in Honour of Peter L. Payne* (1995), 59–92; C. A. Whatley, *The Industrial Revolution in Scotland* (1997), 38–63.
7. Slaven, 'Entrepreneurs', 59–62.
8. Campbell, *Rise and Fall*, 27–9; cf. K. Kinninmonth, 'Weber's Protestant Work Ethic: A Case Study of Scottish Entrepreneurs, the Coats Family of Paisley', *Business History*, 58 (2016), 1236–61.
9. A. McGeorge, *The Bairds of Gartsherrie* (1875), 65.
10. Stratten & Stratten, *Glasgow and Its Environs: Literary, Commercial and Social* (1891), 124.

CHAPTER 3

Urban Society

The inrush of new social forces forged by the changing nature of manufacturing and trading impacted hugely on the social structure of non-agrarian Scotland. These processes profoundly affected both the middle and working classes.

THE MIDDLE CLASSES

As a proportion of town populations, the middle classes grew from about 10–15 per cent in 1800 to perhaps 25 per cent by 1861 in places with a pronounced manufacturing base, such as Dundee and Glasgow, but somewhat higher in those where the service sector was more pronounced, like Aberdeen and Edinburgh. But this was never a homogeneous body, as it contained significant differences in occupation, income, lifestyle and values. Hence, conflict could arise between segments of the broad class grouping, notably where issues of power or of status collided.

One significant area of tension centred on the friction between the established urban elite and the new businessmen. At the start of the nineteenth century, the former – mainly merchants and professionals, such as lawyers – frequently had close business links with neighbouring lairds, and indeed often acquired small estates and married into lesser landed families. So, William McCombie, a snuff manufacturer in Aberdeen, bought estates in Skene and Leochel Cushnie. They tended to share the views of the gentry class on public affairs, particularly hostility to political reform and to free trade. The new middle class, however, was antipathetic to the landed interest for social, political and economic reasons, as discussed more fully in Chapters 7, 8 and 9.

Conflict within burghs arose from the tight control exercised by the old upper stratum over key institutions which conferred both power and prestige. These men formed a close-knit group, often inter-married and conjoined in business partnerships, dominating alike the self-elected town councils, the burgh's guilds and incorporations, and most other public bodies, including the established church's Kirk Sessions. Aberdeen provides a good instance of this narrow elite, as the brothers John and Gavin Hadden exercised virtually unchallenged leadership of the city council in the first quarter of the nineteenth century. Both served several terms as provost, while numerous councillors were tied to them by kinship and business connections. The *arriviste* middle classes resented this exclusive caste's stranglehold for two broad reasons. Firstly, they were effectively denied positions which would publicly acknowledge their wealth and their contribution to the material well-being of the burgh. Secondly, in their own towns they discerned, writ small, many of the abuses which they objected to at the national level; namely, a lack of democracy and transparency, cronyism and corruption in public institutions and the retention of monopolistic practices and outmoded customs. The struggle for reform within towns was a long-running feature of this period, as is outlined in Chapters 7 and 8.

THE PROFESSIONS

The composition of the nineteenth-century urban middle class was tripartite: about 75 per cent were businesspeople, 15 per cent were professionals and perhaps 10 per cent were rentiers, many of the last category being retired. Growth was marked in the professions, partly because the existing occupations, primarily lawyers, university professors, clergymen and doctors, expanded. For instance, the Disruption of 1843 and the steady expansion in Voluntaryism, along with the need to cater for a larger population, doubled the number of Scottish clergymen between 1801 and 1851, while in England the rate of increase was one-third. Additionally, new professions, closely tied to business and commerce, for example, accountants, actuaries, civil engineers and stockbrokers, came into being, and increased rapidly as economic development, urbanisation, the greater complexity of social organisation and continual advances in knowledge all heightened the demand to meet the needs of an expanding middle-class population. Additionally, the growth in the scale and scope of local government resulted in the emergence of occupations such as sanitary engineers, Poor Law administrators and office managers.

Most of the older professions gradually changed their training and practice towards a more disciplined and codified system. In the first half of the period, they largely operated through patronage, and offered only informal training to entrants. In the second half, they moved to making appointments on the more meritocratic grounds of knowledge and skills, as tested by examination, and a prescribed programme of formal education became a prerequisite for admission to the professional body. Before the 1830s, university chairs were often awarded on political or sectarian, and not academic, grounds, an approach vividly illuminated during the Leslie case in 1805. John Leslie, the successful candidate in that year for Edinburgh University's chair of mathematics, was supported by local Whigs and Church of Scotland Evangelicals. He was strenuously opposed by a candidate backed by the Moderate party and, at least by implication, Dundas and the governing Tories. Leslie's appointment was heralded as a turning point in the fortunes of contending political and ecclesiastical parties, with little regard paid to the academic merits of the applicants. Professors regarded their posts as a form of property, bequeathing it to their offspring or a favourite ex-student, with minimal regard to aptitude or competence. Frequently, professors neglected their teaching duties; in 1824, no Aberdeen professor in divinity, law and medicine delivered lectures, instead farming these out to subordinates. One reason, apart from sloth, was that more income was generated from university endowments at their disposal than from lecture fees. Research was an optional extra which most chair-holders declined to take up, as it yielded no guaranteed revenue stream. An act of 1858 largely eliminated these customs, as university courts, which included non-academic businessmen and professionals, were created and given full oversight of finance and of teaching staff. Research increasingly became a central focus of academic activity, and consequently appointments based on nepotism faded away.

The cases of law and medicine exemplify the inadequacies of formalised teaching in the earlier period. Until 1854, entry to the Faculty of Advocates in Edinburgh did not require even the completion of a course of lectures, and qualifying examinations were introduced only in 1865. In the case of solicitors, practical learning in legal offices was the norm until the second half of the nineteenth century, and legal training was not standardised until 1873. Before then, control of entry and regulation of the conduct of solicitors were vested in local bodies, for example, the Society of Writers in Paisley. Law degrees were introduced at universities in 1862, and Edinburgh was the sole university to offer a full range of courses, yet ten years later, a mere twenty-four individuals had graduated in Law there. For medicine, a similar set-up obtained. Local institutions had the power to confer the title of doctor or surgeon without candidates having acquired formal academic knowledge – indeed at the turn of the century, St Andrews and Aberdeen universities sold medical degrees, and waived even the flimsiest attendance requirement. The powers of these provincial medical societies were effectively curbed by the Medical Act of 1858, and universities became the sole route to practising medicine.

There were several characteristics which most of the emerging business-associated professions displayed. Sometimes, the first generation had only a very limited advanced education in their chosen field: for instance, Thomas Telford had a rather rudimentary education. But subsequent cadres mostly attended universities or technical institutions, acquiring formal academic qualifications. Many of the bodies established to represent and regulate new professions were purely Scottish, rather than British-wide. Moreover, given that England's industrialisation comfortably preceded that in Scotland, a surprising number of bodies were first formed in the latter. Thus, the Scottish Institute of Engineers and Shipbuilders (1857) was the first in Britain, and the Institute of Bankers in Scotland (1875) also preceded England. Another pioneer was the Institute of Chartered Accountants in Scotland, founded by a merger of local societies in Aberdeen, Edinburgh and Glasgow in 1867, thirteen years ahead of its English counterpart. The Educational Institute of Scotland was launched in 1847, nearly a quarter of a century before its English equivalent, as a cross between a trade union and a monitoring body for schoolteachers. In 1865 the Institute advocated that only university-trained teachers should be appointed, a classic instance of a professional closed-shop mentality.

The cohesion and self-confidence of this sub-class was due to several factors. A sense of shared identity within each profession was promoted by the spread of national organisations. The rise of professional societies and clubs, and the publication of specialist journals – in both of which medical practitioners were very active – added greatly both to the spread of knowledge and social collegiality. These bodies increased their influence by acting as a vocal pressure group, and the Institute of Chartered Accountants, for example, commented regularly on legislative proposals affecting its members.

These professional qualifying occupations enjoyed high public esteem and wielded considerable influence. They were perceived as dignified, dispassionate and independent, while they derived great authority because of their highly specialised knowledge and skill, which few members of the general public could challenge. Their insistence on the maintenance by members of high standards reinforced their reputation. The Edinburgh Institute of Chartered Accountants expelled members for professional misconduct, and at the same time the Institute took great care to ensure that only qualified chartered accountants could use that name. The strong ethos of disinterested public service which motivated many enhanced their aura of impartiality, notably in questions of health and environmental policy, where Doctors Henry Littlejohn and John Burn Russell were quickly established as virtual demi-gods in the eyes of the citizens of, respectively, Edinburgh and Glasgow, where they were the cities' Medical Officers of Health. The reputation of professionals for stability and solidity was augmented because they were relatively sheltered from the frequent economic fluctuations which impacted unpredictably on businessmen's fortunes. Hence, the incomes of professional people tended to be much more stable from year to year than those of businessmen, and it is significant that they were more likely to retire in comfortable circumstances than those in manufacturing and trade.

THE UPPER-MIDDLE-CLASS BUSINESSPEOPLE

It has been estimated that one-third of the broad category of businesspeople might be termed the solid middle class, and two-thirds the lower middle class.[1] At the apex of the former were those who possessed great wealth generated by the industrial revolution. Based on estates at death, west central Scotland was the British region, outside of London, which had the greatest number of millionaires and half-millionaires in the period before the First World War. Most very rich Scottish businessmen did not acquire large landed estates, unlike the trend in England. Although in the 1850s, five Baird brothers bought rural estates from Ayrshire via Fife to Knoydart and Kincardineshire, few others followed. Most sought a small country estate within perhaps one hour's travelling distance (i.e. up to forty miles or so) from their business headquarters – William Baxter lived at Kincaldrum, some ten miles outside Dundee. Often a country house was purchased, but accompanied by only a very small acreage. The second Charles Tennant bought The Glen in Peeblesshire in 1853, along with a mere 1,600 hectares. Many still lived in the locality of their business premises, or moved to suburban villages within a short journey. The Cox family, despite their clichéd description as 'jute barons', stayed not in feudal edifices, but rather in comfortable houses around Dundee, and indeed one lived in a property adjacent to the factory.

There were two reasons for this approach. Firstly, the economics of landownership were not very attractive, because the returns on land were rather poor compared to other investment opportunities. Additionally, the convention of primogeniture prevalent in landed society ran counter to businessmen's general preference for bequeathing their estate equally among all heirs, regardless of sex. Secondly, for most rich businessmen, their uneasy status as brash newcomers among snobbish country gentry meant that greater esteem and eminence flowed from association with their places of business. The rewards of urban locality were arguably more considerable. There was the opportunity as a civic grandee to meet distinguished visitors – monarchs, government ministers, military heroes, foreign dignitaries and leading cultural figures from Dickens to Verdi – and few landed gentry outside the magic inner circle of the great nobility could expect to mix with such VIPs. Recognition for their contribution to town life was also given to these wealthy men by their fellow citizens. The gift of public amenities was commemorated, as in Baxter Park in Dundee. Leadership of the local community was regularly bestowed on these men: they frequently served as provosts, and a good number were returned as MPs for the local constituency – in Edinburgh, Duncan Maclaren and the publisher Adam Black held both offices.

THE SOLID BOURGEOISIE: LIFESTYLE

Below this select elite lay the core middle class, which included manufacturers, merchants, professionals and leading figures in the financial and service sectors. By mid-century, an annual income of at least £100 would qualify for inclusion, although around £300 ensured full membership. These people increasingly became a distinct social stratum, defined by differences in lifestyle and by engagement in civic affairs. The rising bourgeoisie preferred privacy in social life and retreated from mixing with other townspeople, except when necessary. The leading citizens before the 1830s tended to reside in town centres: in Aberdeen, most lived in the Denburn area. The old guard also maintained a visible presence in the daily life of the burgh, often promenading in public places and holding large social events; in Aberdeen, grand dinners attended by 60 to 120 guests were not unusual, and in many places, gala balls were regularly held in the town's assembly halls.

Until the development of a speedy public urban transport system and a passenger railway network, which only became effective in the 1850s, the constraints of horse-carriage traffic meant that almost all businesspeople needed to live near their workplaces. But from mid-century, the trend among the more affluent was to move out to commuter towns or to city suburbs. In a thirty-odd mile radius around larger burghs there grew up villages and small towns mainly populated by the city's business and professional classes, ranging geographically from Troon to Cults. Prosperous middle-class districts developed in most sizeable towns, such as Kelvinside, Morningside and Rubislaw in, respectively, Glasgow, Edinburgh and Aberdeen. The population of Glasgow's west end suburban quarter, fanning out from Hillhead, grew from 1,350 in 1850 to 20,000 forty years later, as the arrival of bus, tram and suburban rail services afforded easy access to the city centre. The occupancy of a large self-contained suburban house appealed to the mid-Victorian bourgeoisie because it provided greater comfort and privacy than a tenement flat, however spacious. Feu charters for Kelvinside properties had strict clauses prohibiting most forms of commercial activity, so the blight of industry was not a threat, and social exclusivity was guaranteed, since there was no risk of any working-class presence in the area (except, of course, domestic staff).

The increasing insulation of the middle class from the rest of the citizenry was reinforced by the provision of many amenities in, or adjacent to, the suburbs. These included high-quality schools, like Kelvinside Academy, while parks, such as Glasgow's Botanic Gardens, were patronised virtually solely by middle-class families. Theatres and concert halls likewise became tailored to a bourgeois audience. The rowdy, disreputable theatres of the Georgian era were abandoned by respectable citizens, and instead they turned to newly built ones which were lavishly furnished, charged high prices and presented plays palatable to middle-class tastes. In Aberdeen, Her Majesty's Theatre, erected in 1872, epitomised this transition, as it replaced the more demotic Theatre Royal, and was sited nearer the growing suburban areas than the latter's Marischal Street venue. Social segregation was reinforced by the very high percentage of new churches erected in suburbs and dormitory towns from the 1860s.

This physical divorce between business and domestic lives meant that the home became the main focus for social interaction, but a blend of other influences heightened this process. Entertaining now took place in the intimacy of the home, and involved small numbers, unlike the large semi-public dinners of previous generations. Houses flaunted the occupants' wealth and status through furniture, paintings, interior decoration and tableware, while the fall in food prices from mid-century encouraged lavish meals. In these ways, the modernity of the suburban inhabitants was emphasised in contrast to the old elites. The texture of middle-class cohesion was given depth by house visitors who were mainly connected by business or family ties, and marriages were often based on one or the other of these bonds.

The impact of evangelicalism played an important part in this shift. Men were exhorted to spend their free time at home, rather than in places of public entertainment, which were deemed too raffish. The benefits of devoting oneself to the domestic ambience were compelling. The duty to imbue children with high moral values was a – if not the – primary requirement of parents, and both should be involved. A stable household setting also helped to secure the family psychologically against the uncertainties of economic fluctuations. The ideal format to sustain these qualities was held to be a household which consisted of a 'pure' nuclear family, i.e. two married parents and their children. However, there were a surprising number of deviations from this model stereotype. One close study indicates that in a mid-Victorian Glasgow quarter, one-third of these bourgeois homes contained extended families, mostly composed not of grandparents and/or grandchildren also living in the house, but rather unmarried siblings co-residing. Additionally, nearly 20 per cent of families were headed by a sole parent, for the most part widows or widowers.[2]

THE SOLID MIDDLE CLASS AND CIVIC ENGAGEMENT

Despite the great stress placed on domesticity and seclusion in private life, the core bourgeoisie provided the backbone of civic urban Scotland in the nineteenth century. Their commitment to striving to secure the betterment of urban conditions, moral and physical, stemmed from two main sources. One was the impact of the Scottish Enlightenment, particularly the writings of Adam Ferguson, who stressed the importance of civic responsibility and engagement in active citizenship. Ferguson argued that it was the duty of men of property to act to protect the interests of the community over a wide range of matters through involvement in running the affairs of their burgh. Many middle-class men would have encountered these ideas as part of their university courses, while the spread of libraries and quarterly periodical literature – most importantly, the *Edinburgh Review* – diffused these concepts to a wider audience. A second wellspring was supplied by evangelicalism, deeply imbued with the strategies propounded by Thomas Chalmers. Chalmers called on ardent Christians actively to promote the godly commonwealth by steering people away from immorality towards virtuous behaviour, but he also stressed that a first stage to moral regeneration was the transformation of the environment in which the individual was situated.[3]

There were two broad agencies through which these aspirations were modulated in practice, namely voluntary associations and police commissions. Since only very limited state action, central or local, was applied to addressing social issues, it fell to voluntary associations to meet most of the social, moral and cultural needs of the locality. For these middle-class activists, voluntary associations served a dual function. On the one hand, they promoted the spread of desirable values and the suppression of dangerous tendencies, as defined by their supporters. Some organisations focused on moral reform, such as temperance bodies, Magdalene institutions (to rehabilitate prostitutes) and agencies to deal with neglected children, whereas others aspired to soften the rigours of the Poor Law by providing material support, for instance, coal or clothing, to the deserving poor, while medical provision was directed through hospitals and dispensaries. In tandem with these associations, which addressed identifiable problem areas, a plethora of religious bodies were established in a bid to implement a deeper change throughout society. As is outlined fully in Chapter 5, these included bible distribution agencies, domestic missionary societies and organisations catering for classes of people deemed at potential risk, for example, young men and women newly arrived in town.

The core middle class supplied the bulk of the individuals who ran these bodies, in part because they had more spare time than most other townspeople to devote to such work, and in part because they often had specialist knowledge, for example, lawyers and accountants. But an important attraction was that by administering the voluntary associations, the bourgeoisie could at once determine who would be the beneficiaries and dictate the conditions on which support should be granted. In carrying out these philanthropic services, a culture of a collective obligation to address critical social problems and to provide a badly needed measure of stability in an era of rapid change fostered a sense of greater cohesion and shared outlook among middle-class people, even as they asserted their authority within the community and defended their values.

In addition, by their methodology of addressing urban problems, the middle-class civic society activists clearly delineated the shift to modernity that they represented, in contrast to pre-existing approaches. They advanced their cause by accumulating statistical data and expounding their arguments in a rational discourse, rather than relying on generalisations and emotionalism. This objective, scientific style stressed that a formal, institution-based system was necessary to tackle the more complex and extensive challenges of urban conditions, which the individual-centred paternalism customarily obtaining in rural society could not address. Instead of the scatter-gun techniques used in the past, a carefully targeted focus on specific sub-categories would be more effective. The organisational structure of urban charities further underscored the new direction being taken. They were subscriber democracies, working within a constitutional framework, who gained legitimacy and acceptance by virtue of their adherence to clear procedures.

As well as these external goals of voluntary associations, there were other attributes which were directed towards fostering closer integration of the varied strands of middle-class sub-groups. The membership of these bodies in most cases transcended political and religious differences, so creating a sense of unity in civic action. This cohesion was also promoted by the second form of voluntary associations, which sought to integrate new arrivals into the social and cultural bourgeois mindset, and in the main had no explicit moral overtones. One type, found in most larger places, was of associations formed for migrants from a county or region, where they could meet earlier incomers from their native area and be initiated into urban society. Thus, Stirling people living in Glasgow could join the poetically named Sons of the Rock Society. Other organisations focused mainly on scientific and artistic activities. Archaeological, scientific and philosophical societies proliferated – indeed, Paisley had two ornithological societies. For cultural interests, book clubs, literary societies and subscription libraries were popular, and Greenock had all three. Musical societies, whether choral or orchestral, were extremely well-supported; Paisley boasted a Glee Club, a Musical Association and a Tonic Sol-fa Institute. These associations served to demonstrate the superior cultural and intellectual appetites of the urban middle classes, as compared to the landed class, who were regarded as more interested in culture-free rural pursuits, such as fishing and hunting.

The second mode by which this cadre sought to exercise control over much of urban life and conditions was through police commissions. Originating in the last quarter of the eighteenth century, these were established to fill the gaps in the provision of burgh amenities. A wide range of activities were permitted, which could include street lighting, paving, refuse removal, as well, of course, as authorising the establishment of a police force. Thus, police commissions in Scotland had a wider, more European sense of policing than in England, where it was conceived in narrower terms of law and order. The commissions were given fiscal powers, usually with an upper level of taxation stipulated. Very significantly, the appointment of commissioners was by popular election, with the franchise customarily set at £10 ratepayers, although it was sometimes £5, as in Aberdeen, Dundee and Paisley. Moreover, in several burghs, including Glasgow, it was accepted that women who met the property criterion were entitled to vote, although after 1843 this right was for the most part removed.

The creation of police commissions was a blend of practical and ideological factors. A prime impetus was that, as explained in Chapters 7 and 8, unreformed burgh councils, whether through incompetence or lack of resources, appeared unable to address the growing range of urban problems, which were exacerbated by Scotland experiencing the fastest rate of urbanisation in Europe. In Aberdeen and Edinburgh, the bankruptcies of the councils prompted the formation of police commissions. But there was also a belief that the ideas of the Scottish Enlightenment should be applied to modern society. The older custom of townspeople voluntarily assuming responsibility for keeping the burgh clean and well-run was no longer applicable as urban centres grew in population, so the device of civic leaders elected to tend the needs of the community was an obvious solution. The police commissions also conveyed a vivid statement about the difference between the values of the rising business and professional men, who dominated the commissions, and the old established elite which until 1833 still controlled town councils. Not only were the commissioners elected on a wide franchise, but they held their meetings in public, with the proceedings reported extensively in the local press. The commissions' financial accounts were independently audited and made available for inspection. These practices were all a radical departure from the unreformed councils' preference for operating in a highly secretive mode.

As well as demonstrating the qualities of democratic transparency and accountability, the commissions addressed town problems vigorously; by 1833, the Glasgow commission employed 318 staff. Here again, the bourgeoisie were able to shape the urban environment in accordance with their own criteria: nuisance removal and cleansing, installing sewers, pavements, lighting, water and gas supply were the primary foci for action.

From the 1850s, enthusiasm among the solid middle class for police commissions in larger towns rather lost momentum, and mergers with the burgh councils were carried through, so that by 1871 all four big cities no longer had separate commissions. Partly this was because the new middle class had mostly ousted the old guard from control of burgh councils, and the old problems of corruption, nepotism and secrecy had largely disappeared. But it was also because of the growing presence on the commissions of lower-middle-class elements, who were treated with reservations because some were very radical, as in Glasgow.

THE ROLE OF WOMEN IN THE COMFORTABLE MIDDLE CLASSES

Despite the emphasis placed by the core middle class on domesticity, women did not always conform to the stereotype of retiring, house-centred females, as work and involvement in public life were not unusual. The number of women in this class who worked was sometimes under-reported in the census; in 1871, most wives were deemed to have no occupation. But they often did work, albeit unpaid, from home, especially where professionals such as doctors and dentists conducted their business from their residences. Women also ran businesses, and Glasgow valuation records show that in 1861 some 600 were owned by women, including about 24 shops in the city's two high-prestige retail thoroughfares, Buchanan and Sauchiehall Streets. Twenty years later, the city had 1,500 businesses managed by women.

Before the 1840s, there was only very limited scope for single middle-class women to obtain paid employment, but opportunities steadily widened thereafter. School teaching increasingly offered attractive career prospects: in 1838, females made up around 20 per cent of the profession; by 1870, they constituted 38 per cent and a decade later, 50 per cent. The demand for women teachers was boosted by the sharp increase in the number of girl pupils after the 1872 Education Act. But the rise of women in teaching was not completely or unmitigatedly progressive. They were normally confined to taking infant and early primary classes, while men taught the older children. Partly this was because it was claimed that women's nature made them better suited to teach young children, and it was feared that they would not be able to maintain discipline at more advanced levels. But it was also argued that the high national esteem in which Scottish education was held would be irreparably damaged if women, who could not attend university, taught older pupils. The Scottish tradition of teaching girls and boys together militated against women becoming head teachers, whereas the English preference for same-sex education opened the door for headmistresses in all-girl schools. Furthermore, the income differential between men and women teachers widened significantly; in 1865, women's pay was about 75 per cent of men's, but by 1878 this had shrunk to 55 per cent, and by 1900 it had fallen to 45 per cent.

Beginning in the 1820s, women steadily increased their participation in voluntary associations, both because of a wider application of the concept of the moral duties of motherhood, and as a response to the evangelical impulse to action. Hence, they were particularly active in religious and moral movements. Temperance was one field in which they were very involved, and by the 1870s women had a separate organisation – the Scottish Women's Temperance Association. Within voluntary bodies, they tended to specialise in fund-raising activities such as bazaars and house-to-house collections. Visits to households were frequently assigned to women, mostly because it was believed that they would receive a more sympathetic hearing than men. In many charitable societies, the role of females rather replicated the domestic set-up, in that office-bearers were overwhelmingly men, while women constituted a large share of the rank-and-file workers. But there were some bodies which were run by women with a very limited role for men. Most towns had a Dorcas society, in which women made and provided clothes for the poor, and it is striking how often women's charities were devoted to overseas causes. Paisley, for example, had both a Ladies' Society Promoting Female Education in India and a Ladies' Society for Promoting the Christian Education of Jewish Women in Alexandria (Egypt) – presumably the addition in brackets was lest anyone imagined they were working in the Vale of Leven's Alexandria.

Even within the realm of the domestic sphere, the role of women was not totally subservient. Perhaps as much as a quarter of middle-class households in mid-century Glasgow were headed by women, and thirty years later, in 1881, this had risen to nearer one-third. A good proportion of these were, of course, widows, but a growing number were spinsters, and often there were adult males living in these households. Women also frequently took charge of their financial and property assets, effectively managing investment and property portfolios; in 1879–80, they formed almost 30 per cent of the shareholders in three large Dundee-based investment trusts. A number were widows, and some may simply have inherited their spouses' investments, but single women made up just under one-half of the female total.

Underpinning these processes was a rising assertiveness of women's rights which had a distinctive Scottish accent. A seminal moment was the publication in 1843 of Marion Reid's *A Plea for Woman*, which advocated equal civil and political rights for women. A prominent manifestation of such concepts was the campaign to persuade the Scottish universities to admit women as undergraduate students. In 1869, Sophia Jex-Blake unsuccessfully sued Edinburgh University's Senatus for thwarting her bid to enrol as a medical student. However, from the later 1860s, Edinburgh, Glasgow and St Andrews universities offered courses specially designed for women, successful completion of which led to the conferment of a diploma. These were often well-attended; in 1873, 141 women enrolled for a course on biblical criticism at Edinburgh University. A Glasgow association to promote the cause of women's right to a full university education, launched in 1877, was supported by many women across Scotland, and drew in many of the city's professional, academic and business men with progressive views. Success for the campaign came in 1889, when women were permitted to attend arts, science and medical courses alongside male students and to graduate on equal terms with men.

THE LOWER MIDDLE CLASSES: INCOME, GENDER AND LIFESTYLE

Below the comfortable middle-class band lay the lower middle class, which included office-workers and minor semi-professional occupations, but the substantial majority consisted of self-employed shopkeepers, tradespeople and master craftsmen. Their circumstances were markedly less affluent than the solid middle class. In the mid-1850s, the median income earned and the estate left by professionals and large businessmen was three to five times larger than lower-middle-class individuals. Whereas the comfortable middle class earned upwards of perhaps £300 per annum, most petit-bourgeois people existed on between £60 and £100 a year. This differential seems to have widened: between 1850 and 1890 the gap between the average annual income of Edinburgh professionals and that of small businessmen had doubled, up from five to ten times greater. Significantly, very few of the latter could afford to retire, instead working for as long as possible. The petit bourgeoisie generally lived in smaller homes, often adjacent to or above their business premises, rarely in suburbs, and had only one or two servants, normally not living in.

Women had a major role in sustaining small businesses; they frequently dealt with the retail and secretarial aspects, while the menfolk handled the production side. As part of the struggle to keep afloat financially, women often augmented household income by doing other paid work, either at home – dressmaking, for example, or taking in paying lodgers – or outside, running restaurants and small shops, such as grocers.

Survival for the self-employed was perilous: a third of these small businesses had a lifespan of about three to five years, and few survived to a second generation, as sons and nephews were instead more likely to move into ancillary trades. Their position was progressively eroded by two trends which formed a pincer movement on their profitability. On one side, the rapid spread of the co-operative movement from the mid-1850s substantially weakened the working-class customer base of small producers. From numbering around 134 in the early 1850s, retail co-operative societies had grown to 275 by 1873, and between 1872 and 1880, the total membership, sales and profits all doubled. Co-operative societies steadily extended their range of products from groceries to a broad spectrum of goods, including clothing, footwear and dry goods, whose prices frequently undercut those of individual shopkeepers and tradesmen.

From the other side, petit-bourgeois artisans and retailers were squeezed by the remorseless logic of large-scale capitalism. Sales to the solid middle-class market were heavily dented by the emergence of department shops and chain retailers, who benefited hugely from the reduction in costs brought by the spread of the railway system. The former, for instance, Jenner's in Edinburgh and Arnott's in Glasgow, which opened in, respectively, 1838 and 1848, offered mass-produced goods such as clothing and furniture at low prices which small businesses could not match, so that demand for bespoke products shrank drastically. The latter, epitomised by Thomas Lipton's grocery shops, which began in Glasgow in the 1870s and by 1894 had branches in 243 British towns, undercut individual shopkeepers by reaping considerable economies of scale.

Simultaneously, consolidation of wholesalers took place in most sectors, creating an oligopolistic market, so that the prices of raw and semi-processed goods rose steeply for small traders and craftsmen. By the 1850s, a mere two mills supplied flour to Edinburgh's bakers. It proved very hard to bring together small firms in a sector to act in unison, as many were tempted to break ranks and persevere independently, while a good number of trades were relatively easy to enter. There was a profound tension between the doctrines of laissez-faire, to which they subscribed piously, and the stringent realities of the market economy, and there was never a resolution of this dichotomy.

The precariousness of their position had several consequences. In social and economic terms, most lower-middle-class people were more akin to skilled working-class journeymen than to the echelon above them. Their incomes were near to those of artisans, and they mostly employed only a handful of workers; in Edinburgh in 1851, 98 per cent of baking firms had fewer than ten employees. Moreover, they themselves had often risen from journeyman status, and so shared many of the same values as their workers. Significantly, they and their children tended to marry more into the upper working class than into the solid middle class. Long hours and low incomes left these lesser bourgeois groups with limited opportunities for involvement in public life, unlike the higher middle classes. Few of them seem to have been very active in voluntary associations, and it was mostly only in less prestigious churches that they could aspire to become elders. As an instance of the latter, between 1824 and 1883, only 9 per cent of the elders of St Andrew's Church of Scotland Kirk Session in Edinburgh's New Town were lower middle class, but they comprised 64 per cent of the elders in the Canongate Congregational church.

Politically, there was a sharp contradiction between their stance in local and national politics. In municipal affairs, this squeezed middle class acted resolutely to minimise their outgoings. Rising rate burdens, or the threat thereof, were strongly resented by these people, and so they opposed local government proposals to improve town amenities. For example, in Dundee and Stirling, there were vigorous campaigns against municipal plans to provide water to all houses in the towns. As they frequently formed the largest social force in burgh electorates between 1832 and 1868, their political clout could be significant, as in Aberdeen and Edinburgh, where they were viewed as blocks to reform. Yet, the lower middle class were a major prop for the Liberals in parliamentary politics, where the key issues advocated by the party centred on questions close to petit-bourgeois beliefs, such as constitutional reform, free trade, laissez-faire social policy, financial retrenchment and the dismantling of monopoly power, especially in land and religion.

Over time, however, the predominant lower-middle-class stance shifted from radicalism, which prevailed until the end of the 1840s and was manifested in support for electoral reform before 1832, and then for Chartism, or its milder cousin, the Complete Suffrage Union. From 1850 or so, the petit-bourgeois voter tended to identify more with Palmerstonian Liberalism and then, and most enthusiastically, with Gladstone's giddy recalibration of the party's policies from 1865 – as is discussed in Chapters 9 and 10.

THE WORKING CLASSES: CHANGES IN SKILL AND STATUS

Between the 1780s and 1880 the working classes faced a complex, often interlocking set of challenges, which included technological change, management work practices, legal policy and economic fluctuations. Some of the major features of working-class experience across the period were: the changing status of occupations; shifting patterns in the control of workplace practices and the accompanying de-skilling of crafts; the gradual movement to replacing a family-generated household income with the concept of a sole male breadwinner earning enough to provide for the needs of the family; the tension between internal sectional differentiations and a wider spirit of class unity; and shifting from searching for an alternative economic system to compromising with the existing order.

The changes in industrial activity and organisation discussed in the preceding chapter swept away a number of existing labour hierarchies, so that a skill which hitherto had been the passport to regular well-paid work could fall into steep and irreversible decline. The classic instance is handloom weaving. In the 1790s, weavers had been the elite of the working class, with a high steady income and a comfortable lifestyle, often with cultural interests such as book clubs and debating societies. The impact of the introduction of power-loom machinery was devastating, especially in the case of cotton, the first textile to undergo such mechanisation. By the 1830s, the handloom weavers' condition was pitiful, especially as mechanisation had begun also to penetrate linen and wool weaving. Earnings had shrivelled from around £1.20 a week in 1791 to 40p in 1834, which included a fall of 34 per cent since 1821. By 1818, a teenage female power-loom weaver could earn more than experienced male handloom weavers, and destitution became widespread in weaving communities, with many so desperate that there were widespread appeals for assisted emigration. Despite the continuing crisis, the number of handloom weavers remained high: in 1803, there were 58,000; in 1820, 78,000; and by 1840, they had actually increased to 85,000. Part of the reason for this pattern was that many weavers migrated to Scotland from Ireland, where conditions were even more dire. But by 1850, a sharp downward trend had set in, with only 25,000 remaining at their looms, because machinery was now making deeper inroads into wool and linen, and in 1881, a mere 4,000 remained. Other trades and crafts underwent a similar process: for example, in paper-making, the skilled vatmen were effectively eliminated by mid-century; and male hecklers in the Dundee textile industry, who were replaced by women workers after an unsuccessful strike in 1827.

On the other side of the balance sheet, new well-paid skilled jobs were created: fitters, riveters and brassfounders in engineering and shipbuilding, and puddlers in iron manufacture all grew greatly. Certain trades threatened with decline converted to other skilled jobs: for example, wheelwrights moved to become planers in the expanding heavy engineering sector, while Clydeside shipwrights switched to working as riggers when wooden boat manufacture declined. Other crafts, however, survived virtually unscathed by technological innovation: for instance, several building trades, notably joiners and masons, persisted with modes of production which dated back to the eighteenth century, while limited mechanisation in coalmining meant that hewers still worked along the same lines in the 1860s as fifty years earlier.

In a surprising range of occupations, the practice of sub-contracting remained. It operated in well-established sectors, such as construction and, especially, mining, where the hewer employed his assistants and paid them out of his earnings. But in modern industries, too, the practice was applied: in shipbuilding, the black squad, a group of four or five men who carried out the riveting work in iron and steel ships, was recruited by the main riveter to do the subsidiary operations, such as heating the rivets and holding them in place for him to fit. In iron manufacturing, puddlers also hired and fired their assistants. The retention of sub-contracting meant that the organisation of working procedures was largely left to the craftsman, and for employers the main advantage of this arrangement was that problems of recruiting, paying and disciplining ancillary workers were not their responsibility.

This continuation of the customary control exercised by craftsmen did not, however, signify an undiluted general perpetuation of their independent status, because there were two broad ways in which their autonomy was clipped. One was that wide-ranging structural economic forces rendered them more vulnerable. In particular, self-employment became less viable for many as the size of units of production expanded sharply, especially in heavy industry and textiles. Another destabilising feature was unemployment, which became a frequent, but quite unpredictable, occurrence, as the behaviour of the Scottish economy was increasingly bound up with world trade and commerce. As an instance of this, the number of men employed at Denny's Dumbarton shipyard in 1858 was 1,122, yet the following year it had fallen to 408. This fluctuating pattern proved persistent, for in 1875 Denny's workforce was 1,321, but shrank to 558 in 1876.

A second challenge to these workers' autonomy was presented by the policies pursued by employers within the workplace, which were substantially driven by the decision that, as an alternative to applying high levels of capital investment, concentration on controlling labour costs would best improve profitability. There were three general facets to this strategy. Firstly, owners and managers decisively wrested control of workplace practices and decision-making from their employees; secondly, subdivision of the work process left skilled men in a weaker position in respect of their authority over the rest of the workforce; and thirdly, payment on a piecework basis was introduced, replacing a flat hourly or daily wage rate. Instances of the first process include the campaign waged in the 1820s and 1830s by Glasgow cottonmasters to end the various forms of control exercised by male spinners. These men had enjoyed the right to nominate their apprentices, who were frequently relations, and to determine who should serve as their factory overseers. A prolonged period of industrial warfare was conducted by both sides, characterised by the use of lockouts and black-listing of union activists by employers, and strikes and violence against blacklegs on the part of employees. In 1825, the masters won an early victory in a four-month-long dispute over the spinners' right to choose their apprentices, and a notorious trial in 1838 resulted in the breaking of the spinners' union, thereby ushering in a regime of full management control. Miners had also lost the power to select apprentices by 1830. Similarly, the custom of textile workers in Borders towns leaving their looms in warm weather or when conditions for fishing were good in the nearby rivers had well-nigh perished by 1850. As a consequence of this tilt in power, fines for lateness became prevalent across many sectors, and workplace customs in which heavy consumption of alcohol played a prominent part were sharply curtailed.

In the coal industry, the hewers historically had jealously guarded their right to work in their own way and at their own pace – to such an extent that visitors were not allowed to view miners operating at the coalface, and underground lighting was not accepted. In Scotland, 'stoop and room' was the normal method of winning coal, in which pillars of coal some four metres in depth were left intact, thus holding up the roof, while the hewers worked in the corridors behind these columns. Hence, it was virtually impossible for managers to monitor work practices, and so miners were paid on a standard hourly or daily basis. Gradually, the owners moved towards imposing longwall hewing, which involved teams of colliers working in a line along the coalface with no pillars to obscure visibility. The coalmasters also introduced payment by piecework, which meant that the pace of work was driven by the faster hewers, and slower men were exposed to discipline by managers. By the 1870s, longwall had usurped stoop and room in many Scottish mines. Greater discipline was further imposed on the workforce with the introduction of winding machinery, which sped up the delivery of coal to the surface. Additionally, the employers tightened their control by progressively reducing the contractual length of employment offered to miners. Across the various mining regions, in the twenty years from the 1840s, annual contracts were replaced by ones stipulating only a fortnight's notice of dismissal.

The second general approach deployed by managers to reduce the power of skilled workers was to exploit the prospects offered by the application of technology to subdivide the production process, primarily by intensifying simultaneously the differentiation and concentration of the workforce. For example, in textiles, the all-round skills used in manual spinning and weaving were broken down via machinery into simplified component tasks requiring much less expertise. A detailed survey shows that in one woollen mill in the Borders, the tasks previously carried out by a single handloom weaver were apportioned to seven different occupations, and the proportion of those in skilled trades fell from 34 to 14 per cent of all workers.[4] The gains for factory owners were twofold. The control (and therefore the independence) which the craftsmen had enjoyed was severely diminished, and accordingly, a much more docile labour force was created. Simultaneously, the wages bill was pruned, with semi-skilled hands paid much less than the previous craftsmen.

THE SEMI- AND UNSKILLED WORKFORCE

The advent of the factory system thus created many jobs in the semi-skilled category, which were often filled by younger people. The woollen mill referred to above increased its labour force after mechanisation from 82 to 274, but with only a handful of skilled workers. An important associated development was the emergence of the factory-floor supervisor, whose primary function was to

Figure 3.1 Furnacemen at Dalmellington Iron Works, c. 1850. This squad worked at one of eight furnaces. In the front row are twelve young boys, who made the sand beds which the molten metal was poured into, and they also carried pitchers of beer to the men working at the furnace. © Dalmellington and District Conservation Trust. Licensor: www.scran.ac.uk

oversee the rank-and-file workforce and improve production by a mixture of rewards and punishments. These foremen were invariably male, even if the bulk of operatives were women, as in textiles. They were mainly recruited from the ranks of highly skilled workers, as they had the practical know-how to deal with technical problems, and were customarily the highest-paid employees in the production process.

Below the skilled and semi-skilled lay the unskilled workers, whose position was highly insecure, for they were offered little other than manual labouring jobs, many of which were available only on a casual basis. A prime instance of this was dock-working, where hiring was done each morning and depended on how busy the dock was that day; other examples included building labourers, porters, messengers and carters. Much employment for the unskilled was seasonal, for instance gas production was high in winter, but fell away sharply in warmer weather, while breweries faced heavier demand in hot summer months, but consumption diminished in cooler conditions. Thus, unskilled workers faced a twin problem: their pay was set at a much lower level than others, but additionally they had no guarantee of enjoying a full working week – or indeed even one day's work in a week. The numbers in this category were substantial: by 1890 in Glasgow, it has been estimated that they formed between one-fifth and one-quarter of all adult male workers, and the figures before then are unlikely to be very different.[5] In small and medium-sized towns, however, the percentage might have been lower, as large cities seem to have acted as a magnet for urban immigrants with no special aptitudes.

THE FAMILY ECONOMIES OF THE WORKING CLASS

These gradations in skill and status in the working class were reflected in pay levels, and consequently in living standards, lifestyles, aspirations and family relationships. Broadly speaking, skilled male workers' wages were between two and three times those of semi- and unskilled men. Thus, data gathered in the early 1840s indicates that the average weekly earnings for a skilled man was 65p, and for a labourer, it was 30p. Across time, wage levels changed, but the broad ratio persisted. Between 1846 and 1880, the wage rates of a range of skilled crafts in both Clyde shipyards and Lanarkshire ironworks were almost continuously at least double those of the unskilled labourers.

The implications of these varying wage levels for living standards were considerable. A calculation made in 1843, based on the cheapest foodstuffs (primarily oatmeal, barley, potatoes and milk) and very limited per capita consumption levels, concluded that an annual income of £26.80 was required to feed a family of two adults and two children on this meagre fare. But only an artisan, with an annual income of £34.30, could support his family entirely from his wages. A semi-skilled factory worker's yearly earnings of £24.80 would fall just below the target line, while a labourer, bringing in £13.20 per annum, reached only one-half of the standard. If, however, the wife and family of the latter worked, the household income reached 95 per cent of the target. These figures are predicated on full employment throughout the year, which, as we have seen, was never guaranteed for any worker, regardless of skill.[6]

For unskilled workers, with a small and unpredictable weekly pay, household income had to be augmented by other members of the family going out to work. Wives and daughters sought jobs as cleaners or in catering, and, increasingly as the second half of the century unrolled, in sweated tailoring trades. Adult males chased casual jobs in town centres, and the younger ones often worked as shoe-blacks, street-crossing sweepers or delivery boys. The necessity of maximising total family income meant that the poorest of the working class rented houses in or very near town centres, where employment opportunities were greatest.

Over the nineteenth century, the use of child labour in industry in Scotland took a different trajectory from England. For some fifty years, until the 1830s, the use of young children in textile factories and in mining was quite commonplace; famously, Robert Owen employed large numbers at New Lanark. Until the mid-1840s, colliers were accustomed to having family members working beside them, clearing away the hewn coal and transporting it to the point where it was taken up to the surface. So, young girls, often aged only eight or nine, worked underground, while their brothers, of about the same age, began to learn the rudiments of hewing, so that by their early teens these boys were able to do much of the work of an adult. In spinning factories, too, the male workers expected to be able to recruit kin as assistants, a demand which precipitated the industrial unrest in the later 1820s and mid-1830s. Before the restrictions imposed in the 1830s, a twelve-hour working day was not unusual for children aged from eight years working in mills.

But the use of child labour changed sharply during the 1830s and 1840s. Whereas in Glasgow in 1833, child labour in textile factories was proportionately 50 per cent higher than in Manchester, partly because Scottish cotton-masters used less advanced technology, thereafter the figures for Scotland steadily shrank. In 1851, in England, the percentage of ten- to fourteen-year-olds at work and at school were virtually equal at 40 per cent each, but in Scotland, 54 per cent of the age group were in education and 33 per cent were in employment (the others – 20 per cent in England, 13 per cent in Scotland – were unemployed). The difference had several causes. For one thing, most Scottish factory owners, except in Dundee, had no interest in operating a half-time education system. More practically, as the average of looms per worker in Scottish cotton factories was almost half that in Manchester (respectively, 2.1 and 3.7), the former had less need for child workers. Additionally, the cotton industry in Scotland in the 1840s was stagnant, with no demand for more labour. The 1842 Mines Act struck at the employment of children aged ten years and under, but there was still a large pool of older children working in pits; in the east of Scotland as late as 1870, one-sixth of the labour force was under sixteen.

In Scotland, for much of the nineteenth century, about one-quarter of women were in paid employment and they formed one-third of the whole labour force, a larger share than in England. As discussed in Chapter 1, this applied in agriculture, but it was also the case in manufacturing and industry, for several reasons. The rigorous nature of the Scottish Poor Law denied benefit to able-bodied females, and the tendency for Scotswomen to marry a couple of years later than their English sisters added to the numbers. Moreover, as Scottish wage rates for men were generally lower than in England, the incentive for women to augment household income was considerable. The textile sector had a particularly pronounced bias towards female labour. In the 1830s, while the ratio of men and women workers in Lancashire cotton factories was equal, in Glasgow the ratio was 100 men to 160 women, and in linen mills in the east, the ratio was 280 women per 100 men. In the eighteenth century, women worked in coalmines only in the Forth Valley, but by the early 1840s they formed one-quarter of the mineworkers in the whole eastern area, where they were mostly employed as bearers, and not as hewers.

In 1851, one-quarter of all women in work were engaged in agriculture, domestic service or textiles, and one-sixth in clothing, thereby making up 90 per cent of all employed females. Thereafter there was a tendency for women to move from factory and agricultural labour to working as shop assistants and in food and drink preparation, which were less demanding and offered better working conditions. Dundee was quite exceptional for the high presence of women in employment. In 1881, 57 per cent were in paid work, forming 43 per cent of the city's labour force, and they dominated textile manufacturing, providing 75 per cent of jute workers. Women's pay rates in all jobs were almost invariably much lower than men's – usually one-half – and only unskilled male labourers might earn less than a skilled woman.

Between 1850 and 1880, there was very little effective trade unionisation of the many women employed in the textile industries. Partly, this was because few male trade unionists displayed much interest in organising women workers. An additional factor was that a great many female factory operatives were young – under twenty-one years old – and they expected to spend only a very few years in a factory before marrying and leaving the labour market. For these people, trade unions seemed irrelevant. Furthermore, it has been suggested that the culture and processes of trade unions reflected male values which women found alien. The formalised meetings and rule-bound procedures characteristic of unions was unpopular with women, and they were uncomfortable with the male unionists' favoured approach of protracted negotiations and discussions with employers. Instead, it is argued, women preferred spontaneous action, often involving noisy, colourful processions through city streets to attract public attention and support.[7] It is instructive to note that between 1851 and 1890, there were around 100 strikes by women textile workers, mostly in Glasgow or Dundee, and primarily triggered by wage disputes, victimisation allegations and working conditions. Normally the female strikers had rejected the advice of male trade unionists to find a compromise resolution of the dispute.

While unskilled men were compelled throughout the era to rely on other family members to boost household income, the trend in other segments of the working class moved steadily to the assumption that the male head of the family would be the sole breadwinner, with commensurate pay levels. In the first half of the century, it had been quite normal for the families of skilled male workers to be in paid employment. However, the rise in men's real wages after about 1850 revolutionised the role of women in the family economy of the skilled elite. Women, it was felt, contributed more to the general good of the household if they stayed at home, cooking, cleaning and raising the children instead of relying on child carers or, more likely, using older children to look after their siblings. In any event, the impact of the 1872 Education Act, with its requirement of compulsory education for all, effectively removed the latter option for mothers. Men tended to approve of the withdrawal of women from the labour market, which, they claimed, removed them from the moral dangers they were exposed to in factories. The end result of this new disposition was, of course, to rearrange the balance of power within the household decisively in favour of the male breadwinner, and so the emergence of the macho male culture of Scottish workingmen was taking shape.

THE SKILLED WORKINGMEN: LIFESTYLE AND ETHOS

Enjoying higher pay and greater regularity of employment, skilled workers were in a much more favourable position than other workers. Often they seemed closer to the lower middle class: for example, as noted above, in the post-1850 era in Edinburgh, intermarriage between these two sub-classes was more prevalent than marriage above or below. These bonds were strengthened by the very real possibility that many artisans could move from journeymen to small masters with relative ease. As we have seen, the size of the average building firm in Scotland was under ten employees, and as the normal life expectancy of a small business in Edinburgh was no more than five years, there were always spaces in the marketplace for new entrants.

With increased spare time created in the 1860s by the widespread reductions of working hours, along with rising real incomes, there were further signs of a change by skilled workers towards an apparent acceptance of middle-class values. Artisans used their leisure hours purposefully: rambling groups explored their rural hinterland, frequently combining this with scientific interests such as geology and natural history, while horticultural societies and competitive flower shows became very popular. Others took up literary pursuits; the rise in working-class interest in Robert Burns was a prominent feature of the era, with a concomitant surge in proto-McGonagalls cluttering the pages of local newspapers.[8] The growth of rational recreation among skilled workers was widespread, with all types of sporting activities from athletics to swimming taken up in large numbers. In mining villages, too, there were clear signs of changing cultural and social norms from mid-century. Friendly societies and co-operatives flourished vigorously, while reading rooms spread and brass and pipe bands both grew in popularity.

Sport in society

Developments in sport reflected in many ways wider evolving aspects of social organisation and behaviour. At the outset of the period, sporting events frequently took place on special festive occasions, such as New Year's Day and Fasten-e'en (Shrove Tuesday), and involved mass unrestricted participation, often attended by violence, drink and disorder. So, at New Year in 1836, a football match was held at Perth, with fifty players on each side, and uproar ensued when Lord Stormont (the heir to the earl of Mansfield) bit a man who was arguing with him.

But by mid-century, a transformation was occurring. These older rough-and-tumble games were either suppressed by the authorities, who were concerned about outbreaks of riot and disorder, or fell naturally into desuetude. Curling and golf persisted from the earlier age, but numerous newer games flourished, such as rowing, athletics, bowls, cricket, cycling, rugby and – of course – soccer. The expansion was remarkable: in 1872, there were 200 Scottish cricket clubs, and by 1880 around one-quarter of all males aged between fifteen and twenty-nine in Stirlingshire were members of sporting clubs. Sports were increasingly organised on a nationwide basis (thanks in great part to transport improvements), with agreed rules and universally accepted codes of conduct. In 1838, the Royal Caledonian Curling Club was formed, and under its aegis, the game's rules and equipment were standardised, while in 1847 the first national curling competition was held. International matches began in the 1870s, with the first Scotland–England football game held in 1872, while Dr W. G. Grace played at selected Scottish cricket grounds in the same year.

The rise of organised sport had several sources. By the 1860s, the reduction in the weekly hours of work meant that many men had Saturday afternoons free, and the gradual rise in living standards allowed money to be spent on sporting equipment and outfits. Thanks to improved dietary standards and medical advances, more young men were healthier and stronger than hitherto, and so able to undertake strenuous exercise. But there was also a moral imperative. 'Rational recreation', namely, organised sport, was preferable to dissolute pastimes which centred on drink or gambling and made no contribution to a better lifestyle. Instead, the new sports offered a heady blend of the qualities which middle-class reformers wished to inculcate in working-class men, such as the pursuit of physical fitness, team effort and co-operation, while the mandatory acceptance of the verdict of referees and umpires underlined the need to observe the orders of authority in a wider framework.

Most of those taking part in sports were drawn from specific social sectors. These included the professional and business middle classes, the

> lower-middle-class tradesmen and shopkeepers and the skilled echelons of the working class. Unskilled and semi-skilled men were mostly not much involved in sport, mainly because they did not have any spare time and were too poor to pay subscriptions to clubs or to buy clothing and equipment, while their physical condition was markedly lower. Indeed, most could not afford to attend sports matches as spectators. Class-based differentiation obtained in sport, as in most facets of social activity. The solid bourgeoisie predominated in tennis, curling and golf, while athletics, cricket and football drew support from the lower-middle-class and skilled workers. Where a game attracted a broad social spectrum, the better-off participants frequently established clubs with high subscription levels, often with strict dress codes to maintain exclusivity; this practice was prevalent in golf and bowling.
>
> Women's participation in many games was limited to little more than being spectators and presenting prizes, but in 1867, a women's golf club was formed in St Andrews, and it had 500 members in 1880. Additionally, mixed foursomes in golf and tennis became acceptable among the middle classes by the end of the era, as is depicted in John Lavery's 1885 painting of a tennis match in the Glasgow suburb of Cathcart.

There was, furthermore, a flourishing range of voluntary associations which seemed to underline the accommodation of workingmen to the wider economic and social framework, and their general desire to achieve moral and intellectual improvement as well as economic and social betterment. There was a sustained increase both in the number of individuals opening accounts and in the volume of money deposited with local savings banks, and, in 1867, Scotland boasted one-quarter of Britain's 874 Post Office Savings Bank branches. The number of friendly societies, to which working-class people contributed from a desire to have financial protection against sickness, unemployment and death, languished for some ten years before surging upwards between 1859 and 1866, and by 1890 there were some ninety in Glasgow alone. There was wide-ranging working-class interest in education, whether it was schooling for their children or provision for adults, through mechanics institutes and universities – Alexander MacDonald, the Scottish miners' leader, attended Glasgow University. Working-class involvement in Temperance displayed an aspiration for moral advancement. Thus, for a period, Edinburgh Trades Council meetings took place in a Temperance café, and as noted, from the mid-1850s there was a marked decline in traditional drinking practices, which had often been work-related. Additionally, working-class people made up the majority of congregations in all church sects, including the Church of Scotland, despite their pronounced elite lay leadership.

A key concept which emerged among skilled workers in the 1860s was that of property in labour, which was linked to the values of sobriety, independence and respectability. The leader of the Glasgow joiners' trade union expressed this approach very clearly when he told a parliamentary committee in 1867: 'I think that a man's remuneration for his labour ought to be sufficient to keep him in respectability', which he identified as including living in a two-roomed house with an annual rent of about £9 and the wife owning a silk dress.[9]

WORKING-CLASS UNITY AND DISUNITY

The segmented nature of work, pay and family circumstances impinged on working-class unity in cross-cutting directions. For most of the period, trade unions, essentially representing skilled men, displayed at best limited solidarity with the less skilled. The trades councils of Edinburgh and Glasgow, for example, showed little inclination to unionise non-artisan workers in the 1860s and 1870s. Moreover, harmony among the unionised occupations was from time to time badly frayed, with demarcation disputes in the engineering industries a growing feature of the last twenty years. Certain Scottish unions and occupations were viewed rather unsympathetically by the broad labour movement. Handloom weavers in the 1830s attracted hostility because some acted as strike-breakers in a period of tense industrial relations, particularly in the coalfields, and behind this lay a resentment at the aloof stance towards less fortunate workers which the weavers had adopted when in their pomp. A similar attitude lay in part behind the distancing shown by other trade unions in Glasgow during the cotton-spinners' strike and subsequent trials in 1837–8, because of the acts of extreme violence – including the fatal shooting of one strike-breaker and throwing acid into the faces of others – which occurred during the strikes they staged. This aggressive attitude was contrasted unfavourably with the peaceful conduct of the Tolpuddle Martyrs a few years earlier.[10]

Another field of working-class fissiparity began to merge in the final two or three decades of the era, and subsequently bulked very large in the political and social evolution of modern Scotland. On the whole, until perhaps 1850, relations between Irish Roman Catholic immigrants and the host community had been relatively amicable. The Irish were regularly involved in political movements from the reform campaigns of the 1790s to Chartism, and participated in industrial struggles, providing activist leaders in weavers', cotton-spinners' and miners' trade unions. But a changing environment became detectable after mid-century, with some native workers militantly hostile to Irish incomers. This trend was particularly evident in the western coalfields, where sectarian riots, usually associated with so-called 'marching days' – especially 12 July – became a feature from the early 1850s, and an explicitly anti-Catholic body, the

Free Colliers, grew exponentially. Orange versus Green tensions had spread by the early 1870s to working-class parts of Glasgow, such as Bridgeton, Govan and Partick, in all of which there was a sizeable presence of Ulster Protestant immigrants, often working in engineering shops and shipyards. But in other places, there was much less inter-community tension.[11]

Nevertheless, the period witnessed numerous episodes in which working-class solidarity and unity were the uppermost features. While there was at best only limited participation for the abortive radical rising in 1820, the simultaneous general strike in the west of Scotland was solidly observed, and lasted about as long as the 1926 general strike.[12] Another feature was the coming together of inhabitants of neighbourhoods to protect existing rights and privileges, such as opposing plans to close off public spaces for private use, or, as in Glasgow, massing to assert the right to walk on the grass in a newly opened public park in defiance of a city council veto. Trade unions frequently supported industrial action by other workers: for example, the Glasgow cotton-spinners' strike of 1824–5 was backed by workers in Renfrewshire and Lanarkshire, while the cotton-spinners themselves lent support regularly between 1816 and 1837 to other trades involved in industrial disputes, so belying their image of aloofness. For most of the 1840s, the Chartist movement generated a united mentality at its peak, pulling together workers in old and new crafts, those in semi- and unskilled occupations, along with a spread of shopkeepers and small businessmen.[13]

Trade unions suffered serious setbacks in the first quarter of the nineteenth century, as the previous reliance on the legal system to settle rates of pay – for instance, in 1803, the Court of Session raised the wage rates for compositors – was effectively terminated by 1813, when the courts severely restricted the right to strike. The revival of trade unions was assisted by the repeal in 1824 of the Combination Laws. But too many of these new unions were local, and had only a few links with either other unions in the locality or workers in the same job elsewhere. The history of trade unionism among miners illustrates both features. For much of the period, the most that could be built up was county-level organisation, but establishing a permanent national body remained a chimera until 1855, when Alexander MacDonald established the Scottish Coal & Iron Miners' Association. The county unions were easily broken, especially in periods of recession, because either strike-breakers were readily obtained in an era of abundant labour or adjacent coalfields simply increased output. Miners also played little part in attempts to forge an alliance of unions in an area, thus they were not members of Glasgow Trades Council in the 1860s.

The first half of the 1830s was marked by high levels of inter-union co-operation. A key institution was the United Trades of Glasgow, one of whose activities was to co-ordinate comradely assistance during labour disputes, such as when the engine-makers' union aided striking masons and carpenters. In this period, there were also inter-city linkages, as delegates from Dundee and

Edinburgh attended meetings of the Glasgow United Trades. This sense of a broader movement was sustained by the growth in newspapers aimed at a working-class readership. Most were part of the unstamped press, which tended to be rather ephemeral because the authorities strove to suppress them quickly, but Glasgow in particular had a range of such papers, with a radical edge and addressing the concerns of workers.[14] The United Trades foundered during a major economic recession in the mid-1830s.

From the middle of the 1850s there were clear signs of a resurgent spirit of collaboration and mutual sustenance among the organised sections of the working class. Trades councils emerged in larger towns, pulling together in one body affiliated unions to consider issues of common concern, either local or national. The first council in Britain was established in Edinburgh in 1853, followed by Glasgow, and later by Dundee and Aberdeen. The councils demonstrated the width of topics of interest to workingmen. Edinburgh opined not just on industrial disputes, but commented on city matters such as education reform and urban redevelopment projects. As considered later, Glasgow and Edinburgh both took leading roles in British-wide campaigns to amend laws deemed hostile to workers, notably the Master and Servant Act and the proposed trade union legislation in the early 1870s.[15] But they almost exclusively represented skilled artisan labour, the only level of workers with unions, and showed little interest in unionising the semi- and unskilled segments, so that in 1892, as a percentage of the total adult population, there were one-third more English unionised workers than in Scotland. It is perhaps revealing that whereas the British-wide Trades Union Congress was set up in 1868, it took almost another thirty years until its Scottish equivalent was established in 1897.

The trend among the skilled elite apparently both to accept laissez-faire economic and social doctrines and to evince a willingness to embrace ideas of moderation and respectability was not a full representation of working-class values and attitudes. For instance, societies promoting self-improvement and thrift were highly prized by workers, but frequently it was the mutualism of organisations that was admired by members. Friendly societies were attractive not just for the financial security they promised, but also for the friendship and sociability which was integral to their regular weekly or monthly meetings. Again, co-operative stores provided cheaper, better-quality food, while the dividend rewarded thrift, but they also highlighted the power of collective action. In many respects, too, both movements were close in values and structure to trade unions. Middle-class cultural and religious norms were treated with an element of detachment by workers. The respectable theatres which channelled bourgeois standards were never popular with working people, and there was a raffish component to working-class public entertainment. The 'free and easies' of the mid-century era were, from contemporary accounts, a form of talent nights and singalongs, accompanied by some serious drinking, while the music halls of the same period were described by a working-class radical as very low, with heavy drinking and crude stage acts.[16] While the Scottish working class had many churchgoers in their midst, there was a readiness to reject certain middle-class theological trappings, such as rigid Sabbatarianism. Edinburgh Trades Council vigorously pressed for the opening of the city's Botanical Gardens on Sunday – but only after the morning services were completed.

It is apparent that the tendency from the 1850s was for trade unions not to plunge headlong into withdrawals of labour when a dispute with employers arose; instead a negotiated compromise was sought. Nevertheless, strikes did occur if there was a breakdown in talks, and out of all the British coalfield regions, the west of Scotland miners had the highest rate of work stoppages, and their 50 per cent success rate was the best of all. In 1874, rank-and-file miners rejected Alexander MacDonald's strategy of conciliation, and struck for shorter hours and improved working conditions in lieu of the leader's preference for restricting output. The protracted agitation in the 1860s and 1870s to reduce working hours is further testimony to the readiness to reject the prevailing economic orthodoxy. The aim was to have nine hours a day as the maximum, and this was adjusted to demands for a fifty-hour week, which would give workers Saturday afternoons off. Strike action in the Clyde shipyards in 1866 won the workers a fifty-seven-hour week, and in 1872 this was reduced to fifty-one hours, which was the shortest working week in Britain until the 1890s.

These episodes powerfully suggest that the dictates of classic political economy were not viewed as sacrosanct, and indeed the minutes of the Edinburgh Trades Council reveal a regular stream of resolutions which challenged these tenets. In 1859, the council repudiated the claims made in a speech by the local MP that the laws of supply and demand as applied to wages were inviolable, instead asserting that these concepts were unsound in principle and contrary to the best interests of masters and men alike. Trade union legislative proposals were rejected outright in 1873, for similar reasons, and continuously from 1861 until 1873 (when the published minutes end), the council championed the demand for a fifty-hour working week. The council also resolved that the classic statement of mid-Victorian bourgeois values, Samuel Smiles's *Self Help*, was not worth buying, as it offered nothing of value to trade unionists.

Middle-class social policies were also sharply criticised when they were deemed to harm working-class interests. There were voluble objections to the urban slum-clearance programmes of the 1860s, because they would not increase the provision of decent housing for working-class families. Education changes provoked bitter resistance. In Edinburgh, the proposal in the early 1870s to convert the merchant schools such as George Heriot's from their original role of admitting able children of all backgrounds to becoming essentially middle-class kraals was vigorously denounced by the trades council. Another revealing instance was working-class opposition to plans by some city school boards to introduce domestic science as a compulsory subject for female pupils. The board members saw this as a means of disseminating better housewifely practice among working-class women. Working-class parents protested vociferously against this policy on two grounds. Firstly, mothers resented the implication that they had poor housekeeping standards, insisting they were quite capable of transmitting domestic skills to their daughters in their own homes. Secondly, parents complained that the introduction of domestic science to the school curriculum would mean their daughters having to forgo studying academic subjects, which was unfair and undesirable.

In the 1820s and early 1830s, working-class activists sought an alternative to the emergent economic and social system. The main lodestar which they were drawn to was Owenite co-operative principles, which aimed to transform society, especially with regard to poverty and education. A community based on these ideas was set up at Orbiston, in Lanarkshire, in 1825, but internal disputes resulted in its disintegration by 1828. After the decline of Owenite socialism in the late 1820s and the failure of Chartism twenty years afterwards (fully discussed in Chapter 9), there seemed to be no credible alternative to the capitalist system until the emergence of socialist ideas in the early 1880s. There was thus still a degree of faith in laissez-faire doctrines, even among radical working-class people. Until the 1880s, several leaders of the labour movement, including Keir Hardie, persisted in arguing that the main cause of many social problems was high levels of intemperance among the working classes.

NOTES

1. S. Nenadic, 'The Victorian Middle Classes', in W. H. Fraser and I. Maver (eds), *Glasgow, Volume II: 1830 to 1912* (1996), 267–71.
2. E. Gordon and G. Nair, *Public Lives: Women, Family and Society in Victorian Britain* (2003), 35–47.
3. For a full discussion of Chalmers's influence, see pp. 117–18, 126–8.
4. J. Holley, 'The Redivision of Labour: Two Firms in Nineteenth-Century South-East Scotland', Edinburgh University PhD Thesis (1978), ch. 4.
5. J. H. Treble, 'The Market for Unskilled Male Labour in Glasgow, 1891–1914', in I. MacDougall (ed.), *Essays in Scottish Labour History: A Tribute to W. H. Marwick* (1979), 115–42.
6. I. Levitt and T. C. Smout, *The State of the Scottish Working Class in 1843* (1979), 107–13, 274–5.
7. E. Gordon, *Women and the Labour Movement in Scotland, 1850–1914* (1991), chs 3 and 5.

8. William McGonagall (1825 [or 1830]–1902) was a Dundee weaver whose poetry was characterised by poor scansion, wobbly grammar and much bathos. He is widely regarded as one of the worst English-language poets.
9. *PP* 1867, XXXII (3873), *First Report of the Commission on the Organisation and Rules of Trade Unions*, q. 8042.
10. Six Dorset farm labourers were arrested in 1834 for forming a trade union. They were sentenced to seven years' transportation to Australia, but a large protest movement resulted in the quashing of the verdict.
11. See pp. 171–3 for a more extended analysis.
12. For a fuller account of this episode, see pp. 214–15.
13. See pp. 260–1 for an extended discussion.
14. In 1815, the government sharply raised the stamp duty on newspapers, putting their price well beyond the reach of working-class readers. In response, cheaper unstamped journals proliferated, but their lifespan was ephemeral because the authorities quickly suppressed them. The duty was reduced in 1836, and abolished entirely in 1855.
15. See pp. 270, 281, 293.
16. W. Freer, *My Life and Memories* (1929), 33–4; cf. A. B. Cook, *Aberdeen Amusements Sixty Years Ago* (1911), 9.

CHAPTER 4

Urban Social Conditions

THE RANGE AND EXTENT OF ISSUES

The impact on living conditions created by the economic and social changes outlined in the previous chapters, as evidenced in health, housing and environmental standards, was for many people negative, rather than beneficial. What is striking about these problems is both their depth and their longevity, as even by about 1880, the degree of improvement in many respects was barely perceptible.

One factor behind this challenge was demographic. Scotland's population grew steeply from 1,608,420 in 1801 to 3,735,573 in 1881, and the pace of growth in towns and cities was extremely rapid. In 1750, Scotland was the seventh most urbanised European country; by 1850, it was the second. The share of the Scottish population living in settlements inhabited by over 5,000 people grew from 21 per cent in 1801 to 48.9 per cent in 1881, but in the western Lowlands (i.e. Ayrshire, Dunbartonshire, Lanarkshire and Renfrewshire), the degree of concentration was far higher: in 1801, 39.7 per cent, and in 1881, 68.8 per cent. Several places developed at a hectic rate: Dundee's population doubled between 1801 (31,000) and 1851 (61,000), and in 1881 it had swollen to 140,000 – a total very close to its current figure. But this was exceeded by Glasgow, which increased from 147,000 in 1801 via 345,000 to 511,000 in 1881. Other towns sprang from small towns to sizeable ones: Motherwell leapt from 1,726 inhabitants in 1841 to 13,853 in 1881, and Airdrie's population doubled in twenty years, moving from 6,594 in 1831 to 12,922 in 1851.

Under the huge and sustained pressure of urban population growth, the infrastructure of towns and cities would struggle, even with the most active responses. House-building, for instance, had little prospect of coping with demand, as the population density per hectare in Glasgow surged from 38 in

Table 4.1 Death rates per 1,000 living, 1861 and 1881[a]

	Scotland	Four largest cities	Rural
1861	21.5	28.1	17.9
1881	19.7	23.3	17.3

Note:
[a] Derived from M. W. Flinn et al., *Scottish Population History* (1977), 382

1801 to 135.5 in 1841, and thence to 235 in 1871. Clearly health and sanitary provisions were adversely impacted by such circumstances. Yet unsatisfactory conditions were not restricted to burghs which experienced rapid expansion. Stirling, whose population grew at a statelier pace – up from 5,000 in 1801 to 15,000 in 1881– had grave problems. Other factors, then, beside the intensity of demographic change played a vital role in creating and perpetuating this dire situation. In consequence, the manifold nature and degree of nineteenth-century urban living conditions bequeathed a legacy of multiple deprivation which remained a feature of Scottish society for much of the succeeding century.

The urban–rural gulf can be seen in the death rates for 1861, which in the four largest cities was over 50 per cent higher than in rural areas, although the gap diminished somewhat over the next twenty years. Health statistics for Glasgow reveal the long-term trend. The city's annual death rate for the period 1820–4, namely, 24.8 per 1,000 living, was exceeded for the next seventy years, with a continuous increase until the 1870s, when a steady downturn set in, and one commentator has noted that life expectancy in the city's slums was worse than during the Black Death.[1]

Towns and cities were hit by waves of epidemics, such as a serious typhus epidemic in the late 1830s and scarlet fever in the 1870s. But occasionally cataclysms struck, notably cholera, which marched across the urban Lowlands in 1832, 1848, 1854 and 1866, killing at least 10,000 in the first outbreak and between 6,000 and 7,000 in the second. The specific killer illnesses changed across time. Smallpox had been a prime taker of lives at the turn of the century, but inoculation reduced its prevalence from the early 1810s. Typhus was another major disease in the first half of the century, pushing Dundee's death rate in 1847 up by 75 per cent. By the 1870s, however, deaths from zymotic illnesses were declining, but those from tuberculosis, bronchitis and other pulmonary illnesses remained very high.

Despite the shifting ratio of causes of death, some general features can be highlighted. Almost all of these illnesses were brought on by inadequate nutrition, poverty, an unhealthy environment and the wider economic context. There was frequently a close correlation between periods of high unemployment and outbreaks of typhus in the first half of the century, so that it was the poorer people who were most affected. Cholera was the main exception to this rule, as it was not primarily caused by social or economic factors, but was water-borne. A prominent feature of the health crises was that mortality was concentrated in the youngest age groups; around half of all deaths in Glasgow between 1855 and 1859 comprised children under five years of age. This was a clear indicator of poverty and malnutrition in large numbers of households, as was the city's static rate over the thirty years from 1855 for maternal deaths during pregnancy and parturition (1.9 deaths per 1,000 live births).

Another indicator of declining urban health standards can be seen in data for height, which is greatly influenced by nutrition and environmental factors. Evidence derived from military recruitment lists suggests that across the eighteenth and nineteenth centuries, the tallest recruits to the British army came from rural Scotland. But for urban-born male Scots, gaol statistics indicate that the height of those born between 1800 and 1840 fell appreciably, with a modest recovery thereafter. These urban Scots were on average just under 2.5 centimetres below the national norm of 170 centimetres – and Glaswegians were over a further 2.5 centimetres smaller.

Poor health was intimately linked to the urban housing provision for the Scottish working class, which differed radically from England in several ways, and was in most respects substantially inferior. The tenement was virtually the universal housing structure in Scottish towns, with the typical English back-to-back terraced houses extremely rare. The tenement had some positive qualities: it gave protection against weather extremes, it could foster close social relations, and it afforded security against burglary and anti-social behaviour in general. But as the century advanced, its negative features became the focus for concern, because of both conditions within the flats and also the external environment. The 1861 census showed that two-thirds of the Scottish population lived in one- or two-roomed houses, and in some towns it was substantially higher. The normal dimensions of a one-roomed house were around 4 metres by 3.350 metres and the additional room in a two-roomed property was usually 3 metres square. A one-roomed house was just that: there was no separate kitchen or bedroom; and in a two-roomed flat, the second room had only space for a bed, and little more. So whole families lived, slept and – given the mortality rates – died in these small houses. Notwithstanding these already congested conditions, in 1871, one-quarter of Glasgow households took in lodgers, including 20 per cent of two-roomed and 8 per cent of one-roomed houses. There were also houses which held two families simultaneously: in Glasgow in 1871 the number of families exceeded the city's housing stock by 5.6 per cent. These aspects may help explain why in 1861, 2,200 one-roomed dwellings in Glasgow contained a total of over 17,000 people – i.e. nearly eight per house.

98 INDUSTRY, REFORM AND EMPIRE

Figure 4.1 Close no. 80, High Street, Glasgow, 1868–71. Shortly after this photograph was taken, the property was demolished under the Glasgow Improvement scheme. Edinburgh, National Galleries of Scotland

Tables 4.2–4.4 indicate simultaneously the enormity of the crisis and the stasis in responding to it. While there was a fall between 1861 and 1901 in the percentage of the population living in these smallest houses, the actual number rose by 15 per cent – and the 1911 census revealed a further increase. It is remarkable that construction of these smaller houses continued unabated

Table 4.2 Scottish housing stock by room size, 1861–1901 (Source: *PP* 1913, LXXX, *Census of Scotland, 1911, Report*, 568)

	1 room %	1 room N (000s)	2 rooms %	2 rooms N (000s)	3–7 rooms %	3–7 rooms N (000s)
1861	34.0	227	37.9	247	27.5	185
1881	26.0	211	38.9	316	35.3	353
1901	17.6	170	39.9	385	42.5	414

Table 4.3 Population in house sizes, 1861–1901 (Source: *PP* 1913, LXXX, *Census of Scotland, 1911, Report*, 568)

	1 room %	1 room N (000s)	2 rooms %	2 rooms N (000s)	3–7 rooms %	3–7 rooms N (000s)
1861	26.2	863	37.7	1,155	35.2	1,078
1881	18.0	670	39.5	1,476	42.8	2,058
1901	11.0	493	39.5	1,882	48.9	2,211

Table 4.4 Overcrowding in Scottish houses, 1861–1901 (Source: *PP* 1913, LXXX, *Census of Scotland, 1911, Report*, 568)

	Persons per room					
	2+		3+		4+	
	%	N (000s)	%	N (000s)	%	N (000s)
1861	58.6	1,732	33.8	1,036	18.7	575
1881	50.8	1,896	27.7	1,034	13.2	493
1901	45.7	2,042	22.9	1,024	9.6	428

right up to the end of our period. Between 1867 and 1878, 80 per cent of new properties built in Dundee were one- and two-roomed flats, and in Glasgow from 1872 to 1877, the figure was 75 per cent. In England, by contrast, the standard working-class dwelling was a four-roomed terrace house. One- and two-roomed houses were rare, apart from a few north-eastern towns, and here progress in reducing their number was speedy: in 1866, 43 per cent of the population of Newcastle-upon-Tyne lived in these properties, but by 1884, this had fallen by nearly one-third, to 31 per cent. Hence, the levels of overcrowding (defined as more than two persons per room) prevalent in Scotland were seldom encountered anywhere else in Britain; in 1891, the figure for Glasgow was 59 per cent, for London, it was 19 per cent, while in Manchester, depicted by Engels half-a-century earlier as the epitome of appalling housing conditions, it was 8 per cent, and in several cities, the problem was virtually non-existent – in Nottingham, a mere 1 per cent of the inhabitants were affected by overcrowding.

The smallness of the houses and the number of people packed into them contributed greatly to the poor Scottish health standards. Contagious and infectious diseases such as scarlet fever spread rapidly within them, as it was virtually impossible to isolate those affected. The poor quality of air in the rooms led to high rates of lung and respiratory diseases. The deleterious impact of these houses was graphically illustrated by Glasgow's Medical Officer of Health in a comparison of the city's Blythswood and Bridgegate and Wynd districts for 1880–2. In Blythswood, the mean number of persons per room was 1.25, in Bridgegate, it was 2.95; in the former, 9 per cent of houses were one-roomed, in the latter, 49 per cent were. Blythswood's death-rate – 16.1 per 1,000 living – was under half Bridgegate's 37.1, while the respective infant mortality rates were 111 and 206.[2]

Public health and environmental conditions were exceptionally poor, with sanitation a particular concern. A systematic survey conducted in the early 1840s revealed that almost every town had inadequate drainage and sewage systems. Most houses were not connected to the main sewers, which in many cases were very limited in extent. The length of Glasgow's sewerage system in 1832 ran to seven miles in forty-five streets, and by 1850, it had extended to forty miles, still insufficient. Even better-class houses were rarely linked to the sewage system: a wealthy Aberdeen lawyer's house, built in the early 1860s at the top of Union Street, then a highly fashionable area, relied on cess-pits. Open sewers existed at mid-century in Stirling, Inverness and Glasgow. The provision of drains was also sporadic: they were not installed in Edinburgh until the 1850s, and then a mere two miles were initially provided.

This meant that the presence of human manure posed a major obstacle to sanitary improvement. For one thing, in working-class tenements, individual toilets were not provided: sometimes there might be a single privy for the occupants of an entire close. As late as 1876, in Paisley, the ratio of water-closets to population was 1:96; in Perth, it was 1:33. In these circumstances, closes became public conveniences, a feature compounded by the tardy introduction of public toilets in many places. This led to passers-by using stairways and entries to houses to relieve themselves.

The arrangements for the removal of this night soil occurred at two- or three-day intervals. In the interim, different strategies for accumulating the manure were adopted. In Edinburgh, it was kept in pails within the house, while elsewhere it was gathered in public middens, either in streets or in tenement backlands. In some places, the removal of human waste was left to private individuals, so in 1847, there were over 300 separate dung-heaps in the medium-sized town of Montrose. As noted in Chapter 1, town manure was used by nearby farmers to improve agricultural yields. But as well-rotted manure gave the best results, wherever possible large deposits were built up and allowed to break down. In Stirling, one farmer had the contract to clear away night soil, but he did so at six-monthly intervals, so for half-a-year a massive mound of mouldering excrement festered in the burgh. Where the local authority cleared the ordure, the attraction of selling town manure to farmers was irresistible to cash-strapped local authorities. The amount produced was considerable: in Glasgow in 1880, it came to 700,000 kilograms each day, and the annual removal cost to the city council at mid-century was £12,000, which was almost cancelled by sale proceeds of £10,000. Hence, there were vested interests in perpetuating this arrangement.

In addition to the challenges posed by human manure, sanitary problems were intensified by the needs of providing food for the urban populace. In Edinburgh in the 1840s, there were 78 slaughterhouses, as well as 171 byres containing 2,085 cattle, which supplied the dairy needs of the city. Seventy of these byres were deemed dirty, and 160 were situated below inhabited houses. Stirling had over 100 piggeries in 1874, and everywhere there were countless stables to accommodate the army of horses deployed in urban traffic and haulage. The vast amounts of animal manure generated by these commercial outlets, along with waste meat, bones and skins from the abattoirs, were added to the piles of putrefying human ordure. In Greenock, the result of this nauseating cocktail was defined in graphic detail by a local doctor:

> In one part of the street there is a dunghill – yet it is too large to be called a dunghill. I do not mistake its size when I say it contains a hundred cubic yards [c. 90 cubic metres] of impure filth . . . The proprietor has an extensive privy attached to the concern. The collection is fronting the public street; it is enclosed in front by a wall; the height of the wall is about 12 feet [3.6 metres], and the dung overtops it; the malarious moisture oozes through the wall and runs over the pavement . . . There is a land of houses adjoining, four stories in height, and in summer each house swarms with myriads of flies; every article of food and drink must be covered, otherwise, if left exposed for a minute, the flies immediately attack it, and it is rendered unfit for use, from the strong taste of the dunghill left by the flies.[3]

The limited availability of water added to poor levels of sanitary provision. Until the late 1840s, for the majority of the inhabitants in most towns there were three possible sources of water supply. One was to take water from nearby burns and rivers, but, as discussed shortly, many of these had become increasingly polluted and therefore unusable. A second option was to have recourse to public wells and standpipes: in Edinburgh in the 1840s, these were the sole providers for about 40 per cent of houses valued at less than £4 rent a year. But they had two deficiencies. The water contained in many wells was of very inferior quality: only fourteen of thirty-four wells in Glasgow in 1834 were deemed to be satisfactory for public consumption. On top of this, the numbers of people seeking to use the wells made accessibility very difficult. One standpipe in Queen Street in Stirling served over 800 individuals, with the result that there were regular queues of between 80 and 100 waiting to draw water. The third choice was to take supplies from a private water company. These had been established in Edinburgh and Glasgow in the decade after the end of the Napoleonic war, but the cost was high, so that customers were mostly in the more affluent households, who could afford to have it piped into the home. Before the 1840s, very few places had a public supply of water on an adequate basis, the major exception being Greenock, where from 1827 water was supplied from nearby Loch Thom.

The upshot of these factors was abysmally low water consumption levels: annual per capita use in the 1840s was 90 litres in Edinburgh, and half that in Aberdeen, and in 1876, the figure for Glasgow was 202 litres. Inadequate provision existed not just in larger towns, but also in medium-sized burghs such as Dumfries, Lanark, Arbroath and Ayr. After the publication in 1842 of Edwin Chadwick's detailed survey of working-class sanitary conditions, and more so following the establishment in the early 1850s of the link between poor water quality and cholera, many towns acted to introduce a public water supply. The flagship initiative was Glasgow City Council's decision to bring water from Loch Katrine, a project completed in 1859. But this process was slow, and some burghs were still rejecting such schemes a decade afterwards – for instance, Cupar in 1869. Even where a municipal supply was introduced, its availability was often selective. In several towns, water was not piped in to houses with a low valuation. Dundee only supplied water on a wide basis in 1870, and in Edinburgh the houses built under the Improvement scheme inaugurated in the mid-1860s had no cisterns to store water. The decisive breakthrough came in the 1870s, as medical knowledge of the benefits of a universal water supply percolated down to local authorities, and simultaneously the Poor Law Board of Supervision became more interventionist in pushing councils to act, as discussed below.

The wider environmental framework was also detrimental to living standards. Urban air quality was very poor, due to two scourges: smell and smoke.

Chemical and town gas plants emitted foul odours, as did glue factories, breweries, etc. There was also the ever-present stink created by the dung heaps, which permeated towns. In Edinburgh, the practice of spreading manure over the Meadows and farms near the city created an all-pervading stench, which Queen Victoria unavailingly complained about when in residence at Holyrood Palace. The chimneys of factories and workshops pumped out smoke on a massive scale: prints of Glasgow from the early nineteenth century depict the city wreathed in smoke emanating from industrial plants. Additionally, domestic consumption of coal grew exponentially, with 1,000 million kilograms used annually by Glasgow households in the 1830s. At mid-century, the city's atmosphere was stated to be more polluted than any other city in the United Kingdom. The omnipresent pall of smoke hanging over urban Scotland was alluded to in Alexander Smith's poem in praise of his native city, 'Glasgow', composed in 1854: 'A sacredness of love and death/Dwells in thy noise and smoky breath.'

The connection between bad air and pulmonary illnesses must have been evident to most contemporaries, and was confirmed by parliamentary enquiries, yet there were few concerted attempts to curb smoke pollution. Efforts to curtail the output of noxious vapours was stymied by wealthy influential business interests: J. B. Russell, Glasgow's stalwart Medical Officer of Health, could not stop Tennant's chemical works from discharging smoke from the famous St Rollox Lum, as the fines were too trivial to have a serious impact on such a massive industrial undertaking.

The contamination of watercourses added to urban environmental hazards. Here, too, both manufacturing and domestic polluters played a part. Factories regularly discharged waste from production processes into adjacent waterways, and among the worst offenders were chemical plants, paper and textile mills, dye manufacturers and breweries. The Almond, Esk and Kelso rivers were badly affected by industrial refuse, showing that the problem existed beyond large towns. Lochs Long and Goil were identified by the early 1880s as being smelly and polluted to an unacceptable degree. With inadequate sewerage systems, rivers, burns and lochs became receptacles for human waste. By the 1870s, 190 million litres of human and industrial refuse generated by Glasgow and the surrounding localities were deposited every day in the Clyde, so that from Glasgow to the Cart tributary, the river was 'very foul and turbid, in short a gigantic open sewer, noxious gases being continually evolved which, during the summer, are so overpowering as to force the bulk of passenger traffic from the river to the rail'.[4] The quality of water in the Clyde near the mouth of another tributary, the Kelvin, it was further reported, was so poor that it could not be used in the boilers of steamboats, as the deposits in the water caused engine pinking.

THE HOUSING CRISIS

The causes of the escalating housing crisis provide insights into the varied range of influences and attitudes at play in urban localities. The obduracy of poor housing conditions in Scotland, when compared with the less intractable situation in England, was partly the product of the differing intersection between supply and demand factors. Briefly put, building costs per unit of working-class housing in Scotland were higher than in England, and the levels of affordable rent in Scotland were lower. These elements were created by a mix of technical, legal, bureaucratic, social and economic issues which did not operate to anything like the same degree south of the border.

The retention of the feudal system in land law made Scotland significantly different from England, where it had been abolished in the seventeenth century. Under feudal law, there was a crucial distinction between the physical ownership of land and the superiority rights, which could be retained after the disposal of the asset. The rights of the holder of the superiority in property were acknowledged by the payment of an annual feu duty by the physical owner. The crucial aspect was that unlike leasehold in England, which ultimately returned the property to the original owner, feudal superiority rights conferred no claim to regain physical ownership of the property. In other words, it was a permanent alienation, and consequently it was in the interest of the feuar to delay relinquishing ownership for as long as possible, in order to maximise the feu duty charge. This carried immense implications for housing costs. When new land was released by the owner, the high cost of feu duty, plus the charge for ground annual, which could easily be double the comparative burden in England, compelled the developer who had purchased the land to cram more houses onto the area than in England. Builders were often short of capital, and an effective method of funding building projects was to divide up the feudal rights and sell them on at a profit to others, who then made an extra charge on the physical owners. These feu farmers became a regular feature of the urban financial landscape, in some cases raising an income up to fifteen times higher than the original charge. An extra burden which owners of feudal rights imposed was casualties, which were levied when a change of real ownership of a house occurred, whether through death or sale. The general upshot, according to the most authoritative study, was that feu duties, casualties and ground burdens constituted approximately 20 per cent of the total rental – a more substantial proportion than in England.[5]

The cost of house-building was adversely influenced by the structure of the industry in Scotland. As already noted in Chapters 2 and 3, most firms in Scotland were quite small outfits; about four-fifths employed fewer than ten men, and they had only a very brief existence, with the average concern surviving for only eight to ten years. These small businesses were perennially cash-strapped – between £150 and £200 seems to have been their normal working capital. Because of their precarious finances, providing homes for working-class tenants carried risks for these building firms, for reasons discussed below. Their first preference was to build to sell, which gave an immediate injection of capital to the firm. In effect, this meant providing for the solid middle-class market, which mostly sought villas, substantial terraced houses and spacious flats.

House-building in Scotland required more expensive materials and applications, partly because of tradition and partly because of the challenges posed by the elements. So, bricks were rarely used in house-building, apart from in some mining villages; instead stone was preferred, being better able to withstand the rain and harsh climatic conditions, and this was not only a more expensive material, but it required more skilled labour. Slates were almost universally preferred for roofing, at least in the western and central Lowland areas, although it was much more expensive than tiles, whose use in Scotland was mainly confined to some eastern areas. Underneath the slates, a layer of material, called sarking, was placed in order to resist water penetration. This protective sheeting was not normally used in England.

An extra ingredient of the higher building costs was the imposition after the middle of the nineteenth century of very strict regulations regarding building materials and construction methods. This development ensued from numerous scandals in the earlier period caused by jerry-building, scamping and corner-cutting procedures, which had resulted in many property collapses and fires. After 1860, Glasgow City Council revived the medieval Dean of Guild Court's power to regulate construction methods, while the 1862 Police Act gave all local authorities similar powers. This laudable bid to curtail rogue builders ironically added substantially to housing costs, so intensifying overcrowding. The new rulings meant that in Glasgow, walls had to be 25 per cent thicker and foundations at least one-quarter deeper than was required in London. The overall result of the influences discussed in this and the preceding paragraph was that by the mid-1860s, house-building costs in Scottish towns were about 75 per cent above those in London.

Rent levels were further increased by the difference between rating procedures in Scotland and England. In the latter, rates were charged on a net valuation, that is, after deductions for costs such as repairs and insurance. But in Scotland, the gross valuation determined payment. This of course meant a higher bill, which tenants were expected to cover in their payments to landlords. This issue became more salient from the 1850s as places such as Edinburgh shifted their municipal revenue sources from tolls and customs to taxes on business and private properties, with the consequence that rates rose by 30 per cent between 1855 and 1870. Additionally, increased expenditure by local authorities on public health and civic improvement schemes from the early 1860s contributed to the rising rates bill.

While these supply-side elements made the cost of providing housing higher than in England, there were two major influences bearing on the demand side which also contributed to the low quality of working-class accommodation. Firstly, Scottish wage rates for many occupations were lower than those obtaining in England. While there were variations from one trade to another, as a general rule, the disparity was between 20 and 25 per cent in the 1830s and 1840s, and there was only a mild reduction in the gap thereafter: in the 1860s, Scottish wage rates were around 16 to 19 per cent lower. But, secondly, the prevalence of lower wage levels in Scotland seems not to have been compensated for by a cheaper cost of living. Comparative data for the period before 1880 are not easy to find, but it is clear from a government study in 1905 that food and fuel costs in a selection of Scottish towns were about the same as in London, and a remarkable 11 per cent above the north-east of England. There is no obvious reason why the position thirty or more years earlier should have been radically different, and, if this is accepted, it indicates that real wages in Scotland were at the very least 10 per cent below non-metropolitan England. This difference went a good way to explaining the puzzlement among middle-class commentators, who could only interpret poor housing standards as an indication that Scots preferred inferior-quality accommodation in order to spend their income on other, implicitly dissolute, options.

The Scottish rental system applied extra downward pressure on housing choices. In England, most working-class housing was let on a weekly or, at most, a monthly term. This permitted tenants to adjust their housing options with great speed and flexibility in response to shifting economic and personal circumstances. In Scotland, however, year-long leases were the norm; 80 per cent of tenancies were held on that basis, with only some 20 per cent as monthly leases, and very few for less. From the property-owners' standpoint, this was a highly advantageous set-up. A full year's income was guaranteed, with no vacant letting periods; management costs were low, and there was less likelihood of heavy repair bills, as tenants who were staying for a full year would keep the house in a good state. As an added attraction, whereas landlords using a monthly lease system were responsible for collecting rates due on the property, they were absolved from this under an annual let.

The benefits of yearly lets for landlords were not balanced by offering positive features for tenants. The nature of much of the Scottish economy and its employment characteristics made this a highly risky venture. Firstly, around one-fifth to one-quarter of the adult labour force in larger towns worked on a casual or seasonal basis, mostly in unskilled jobs like dock work, portering, building labouring and transport.[6] For these people, there was no guarantee of employment from one day to another, still less for a full year ahead. Secondly, much industrial production, such as textiles, iron, coal and, above all, heavy engineering, was geared to international markets and so subject to fluctuations in world trade.[7] These movements were volatile and quite unpredictable – if businessmen could not foresee these cyclical patterns, workingmen were unlikely to do so. Hence there was, in this context of extreme uncertainty, a marked reluctance to commit to renting a superior house for so long a period. The penalties for failing to honour the rental obligations if there should be a trade recession were severe. Landlords had greater rights under Scottish law than their English counterparts. The law of hypothec, which was unique to Scotland, allowed the seizure of a defaulting tenant's possessions. Between 1867 and 1874, one-fifth of all Edinburgh Small Debt Court cases – 21,000 – were landlord hypothec claims. Evictions for non-payment of rent in periods of a trade slump reached very high rates: in Glasgow they soared from 4,261 in 1875 to 7,092 in 1880, in the wake of the economic crisis caused by the collapse of the City of Glasgow Bank. In comparison, such court-endorsed evictions in London between 1886 and 1890 averaged 2,327 annually. Furthermore, once evicted, it was very difficult to secure another tenancy in a reasonable property. It was the practice that prospective new tenants had to provide a letter from the factor of their current flat certifying that they were of good character and were not in arrears of rent. Without this evidence, they would have to move downmarket to very unsavoury property.

Caution on the part of intending tenants was reinforced by the consequences which the Scottish Poor Law imposed on those evicted as a result of unemployment. Unlike England, the Scottish system gave no relief to the able-bodied of either sex, whatever the circumstances. Hence, evicted able-bodied individuals were not entitled to any benefit whatsoever, and the result would be the break-up of the family, with the children placed in a poorhouse, while the parents were left to fend for themselves, which could mean having to move from their town or area in search of work. No self-respecting working-class parent would lightly contemplate such a traumatic consequence of failing to calculate the rent which could be met in the most trying conditions. It followed from all these features that the safest option for a careful working-class family was to rent a house which they stood a reasonable prospect of being able to afford, even in adverse conditions, which meant one at a relatively low cost.

It is no coincidence that overcrowding and general housing problems were markedly less severe in towns whose primary economic function was either to serve a regional hinterland, or to meet the local needs of a solid middle or upper class, whose demand for goods was not determined by world trade conditions. Aberdeen was an example of the regional centre, and Edinburgh of the high-end stable market. The housing statistics for these two cities were appreciably better than urban centres in the west of Scotland, and also Dundee.

PUBLIC HEALTH PROBLEMS

The persistence and apparent insolubility of public health problems had a variety of causes, which ranged across scientific uncertainty over the causes of and cures for major diseases, institutional confusion, political pressure and ideological determinism. A fierce debate on the spread of diseases raged in the middle of the century between the miasma theory, which stressed that disease was airborne, and those who contended that infection and contagion were the real causes. Eventually the latter won the argument, but until the issue was resolved, the general public had no way of knowing how best to proceed. Cholera was not accepted by experts as related to contaminated water supply until the early 1850s. Likewise, there was no clear differentiation by doctors between typhoid and typhus until the late 1830s, when it was agreed that the former was an enteric fever spread by contamination of food or water by excreta and urine discharges, while the latter was transmitted by lice.

In some cases, moreover, the medical profession itself proved resistant to new concepts and policies. In the late 1860s, Dr Littlejohn's suggestion that doctors should notify local cases of infectious diseases was vigorously resisted by many private practitioners. As late as 1872, Dr Andrew Fergus, a well-known Glasgow doctor and city councillor, contended that water-closets were dangerous to public health, because of the sewage gases they generated. Given this attitude among medical practitioners, it is not surprising that the general public was frequently sceptical of, and sometimes hostile to, public health measures.

Scots law also worked against an active co-ordinated approach to health and housing problems. The only valid grounds for objecting to a building development, however insalubrious its consequences, were if a private individual was adversely affected, whereas considerations of general public interest were not entertained. Again, objections to an existing nuisance could not be raised by a new claimant. In any case, the cost of undertaking a legal process on such matters could prove costly and lengthy: the average charge in mid-century came to about £3,500. Furthermore, legislation seemed at times poorly drafted, with the result that in some places, the powers of local authorities were circumscribed by limited powers. Stirling Council had no authority to enter private houses, while the Edinburgh Police Act of 1848 restricted action to individual nuisances, and did not permit proceedings in cases of general nuisance. The 1876 Pollution Act applied only to urban, but not to industrial, waste, which was arguably at least as serious a problem.

A crucial lacuna was that it was not until the end of the 1860s that a nationwide authority acted to manage and direct public health policy in Scotland. The Scottish New Poor Law of 1845 had established the Board of Supervision, the first large Scottish state agency for a century, to provide central administration.

As the title implies, this body had a rather limited role, which was a marked difference from its English equivalent, for while it exercised oversight of the local Poor Law units, it did not have not outright control. No right of initiating policy was conferred on the board, and it did not have the power to issue orders to parochial authorities; in England, these important levers were available and frequently used.

For the first quarter-century of the board's existence, its attention was focused on dealing with voluminous appeals by applicants for relief against parochial-level decisions, rather than elaborating a wider scheme of improving environmental surroundings. This meant its influence on overall policy was reactive, and not interventionist. It was not until 1859 that the board was explicitly given a broader role, when the Privy Council endorsed the need for intervention after an outbreak of cholera in Wick which the local powers had failed to deal with. Subsequently, the Scottish Public Health Acts of 1867 and 1875 definitively established its supervisory role over parochial boards by extending its scope to embrace public health and environmental issues.

But there were still barriers to an effective system being implemented. For one thing, towns and cities whose population exceeded 10,000 were exempt from the board's influence if they had a local Police Act, unless a government minister ordered compliance. The process by which the board became more directive in handling recalcitrant local bodies was a slow, gradualist evolution. The method adopted by the board was to issue policy regulations and circulars in the expectation that forward-looking places would adopt them. But these suggestions could be ignored by lazy or complacent parochial boards, so that it was often only a major medical emergency which afforded the board an opportunity to shift practice to a higher standard. Moreover, it had no powers over the appointment or dismissal of parochial board Medical Officers of Health, so trouble-makers and whistle-blowers could not be shielded from the wrath of local worthies. The Board of Supervision faced other obstacles: for instance, it was given no prior notification of private or local parliamentary bills introduced to address specific sanitary and environmental contexts, and so could not enshrine uniform practice across the country.

Additionally, the board's officials, understaffed and under-resourced, struggled to cope with onerous workloads. Initially, to handle 886 parochial boards, there were only two inspectors, and numbers rose marginally over the following forty years. Stretched so thinly, officials had little opportunity to acquire an intimate understanding of more than a handful of parishes. In contrast, the English Poor Law authority had 67 inspectors monitoring around 600 Poor Law unions, and they were paid much more generously than the Scottish officials. Even after the 1867 Sanitary Act, the Board of Supervision could rely only on the services of a solitary Medical Officer, Littlejohn, and he was part-time. It is illuminating that Littlejohn was paid £200 p.a., but his full-time English counterpart, Sir John Simon, drew an annual salary of £2,000.

The social profile of the board's members militated against a more active approach. They were mostly a blend of landowners, sheriffs and Edinburgh lawyers, with a couple of municipal dignitaries lobbed in to give the impression of a broad range of experience. The first chairman was Sir John MacNeill, a son of the laird of Colonsay. The officials acting under the board's guidance were also predominantly upper middle class; they included MacNeill's nephew, Malcolm, a product of Eton and Sandhurst, and William Smythe, the proprietor of a large Perthshire estate, who was the son of a judge and educated at Westminster and Oxford University. In contrast to the overall political colour of Scotland, many of the board's personnel were Conservatives – indeed, Sir John MacNeill's brother was Lord Advocate in Peel's 1841 government. The backgrounds of most of the board's top echelons suggest that they might well be unacquainted with, and not very sympathetic to, the realities of life for poor people in urban areas.

Thus, there was either no national body to co-ordinate and direct policy, or, if it did exist, it failed to give leadership. In the first case, a vexed dispute between Edinburgh and Leith burgh councils in the late 1830s over the abominable state of the Water of Leith could not be resolved by a verdict from a supervisory institution, as would have occurred in England. Again, the lack of a central organisation dealing with pollution resulted in uneven approaches from place to place, with no sharing of information. In the second case, the dilatory approach by the Board of Supervision in addressing social problems was significant. It was only in the 1890s that the board became actively engaged in tackling poor conditions in house interiors, one of the prime causes of low health and social standards. It is indicative of the time lag between England and Scotland in this area that while in 1871 the English Local Government Board was created, expanding the functions of the Poor Law Board to encompass health and destitution policy, it was not until 1894 that a similar process of consolidation occurred in Scotland.

These failings at a national level were compounded by profound weaknesses in administration in the localities, which ranged from structural incoherence to a retarded growth in professional competence. Conflict between authorities could delay improvements, and a major difficulty was that Scottish urban government did not repose exclusively with town councils. It has already been noted in Chapter 3 that from the end of the eighteenth century, the device of creating police commissions was deployed in order to fill gaps in the provision of burgh amenities. The continuation of police commissions after the burgh council reforms of 1833 posed difficulties. Co-ordination did not always occur, notably if there were tensions between the two bodies. There were disputed demarcation lines between council and commission, so that in some places, responsibility for street cleansing lay with one, whereas pavements and closes fell within the ambit of the other. Gradually these rivalries (which were frequently rooted in pre-reform conflicts) were removed: councillors increasingly sat *ex officio* on commissions, and the councils had the powers exercised by commissions transferred to them in an amicable arrangement, which happened in Dundee in 1850. The unitary authorities which emerged from mid-century made for greater efficiency and uniformity, and at last facilitated the growth of greater professionalism and specialisation in burgh management.

Constricting financial conditions also inhibited a forward improvement programme. In some places, such as Edinburgh, this was because the inherited burden of indebtedness long prevented any ambitious programmes. Elsewhere, the financial strength of councils was curbed because, as a sort of spill-over from policy on poor relief, many Scots were resolutely opposed to levying statutory rates in order to relieve social problems. So, in Stirling, voluntary contributions persisted until the later 1840s. This meant that, generally, the funding base for councils was very narrow, at least until the mid-1850s, and it was only in the mid-1860s that the situation became easier, with both a tax base now widened beyond traditional customs revenues, and cheap government loans on offer.

Local government structures were sometimes inarticulate and underdeveloped, and councils' administrative competence was uneven. In some places, the office of sanitary inspector was treated as a virtual sinecure, and it was not until the 1880s that professionalisation of the job became standard. Glasgow council appointed an Inspector of Cleansing in 1843, but until 1868 he headed a seriously understaffed department. The city's first Medical Officer of Health worked on a part-time basis, and moreover, he had a team of only five part-time police surgeons, one sanitary inspector and three policemen to deal with nearly 400,000 Glaswegians, so that the city's problems continued to escalate. Additionally, the lines of management authority were frequently blurred, as in Glasgow, where the medical officer and the sanitary inspector were in the same department and were of equal status. This led to regular disputes and malfunctions between the two sections. In England, however, the medical officers were placed above the sanitary inspectors in all matters, so ensuring clear policy formulation and implementation. Enforcement of laws and regulations was often slack, or even non-existent. Measures to control pollution were extremely ineffective: there were few inspections carried out in cases involving rivers and lochs under the 1876 act.

But besides these technical obstacles, there was also a range of ideological elements operating against reform. One was electoral: before the Second

Reform Act of 1868 and its concomitant extension of the municipal franchise to a substantial section of the working class, municipal voting power lay with the middle classes. Two factors motivated them to resist improvement. Many of this class had the facilities which working-class people were denied, such as a good water supply, adequate sanitation and satisfactory housing provision. They were therefore quite content with the existing provision of public services. Possibly more importantly, there was widespread rejection of measures which would raise the rates burden on the middle classes. The lower-middle-class shopkeepers and self-employed tradesmen formed a significant presence in the municipal electorate, and, as we have seen, the financial position of these groups was highly precarious. In Edinburgh, they comprised about 15 per cent of those in work, but paid 25 per cent of the total rates bill, and as they operated on very thin margins, any potential rise in local taxes would affect them adversely. After 1868, the balance of electoral power shifted from the petit-bourgeois class to an alliance of high-minded urban elites keen to enhance the image of the burgh and a mass working-class vote simply craving better provision of health and housing amenities. Thus, as noted earlier, it was only in 1870 that piped water was supplied to every house in Dundee.

Because of the slow march to electoral democracy, middle-class values and fears tended to prevail in determining responses to social problems, and these were intimately fused with the ideology of laissez-faire that was so dear to them. For instance, there were more deadly epidemics than outbreaks of cholera, but this disease was especially threatening to the comfortable classes because it tended not to be contained by social boundaries, so that solid respectable members of the community were as prone to succumb as the inhabitants of poorer housing districts. In Jedburgh, more people died in a smallpox epidemic in 1849 than from cholera in the previous year, but there was no public outcry, and in 1847 in Stirling, typhus swept through Irish navvies working in the town, killing many but evoking a limited reaction from the town council, unlike its vigorous response to cholera in 1832.

An additional political barrier to drastic action by local authorities was the composition of the councils. Manufacturers frequently sat on burgh councils – at least one-half of Glasgow's Lord Provosts between 1833 and 1880 were in this category, and in general they wielded influence on deliberations in municipal chambers, either by their direct presence or by means of pressure groups such as chambers of commerce. Attempts to curb pollution were stoutly resisted by these men: for example, Dundee factory owners opposed cleaning up rivers and burns in Lochee. Many were also inimical to serious housing reform, believing that higher rents would inevitably result in pressure to raise wages. A second lobby with a vested interest in preventing major changes in housing was well represented in many town councils. This consisted of those who were either landlords or whose livelihood was tied to the private rented sector, such as house-builders, conveyancing solicitors, surveyors and house factors; over two-thirds of Edinburgh councillors fell into this category.

URBAN IMPROVEMENT PROJECTS

The limitations of prevailing ideological tenets were clearly illustrated in the most ambitious approach adopted in the period to formulate a comprehensive attack on the worst housing conditions, namely city improvement schemes. Glasgow was the first place to embark on this project, in 1866, to be followed by Edinburgh (1867), Dundee (1871), Greenock and Leith (both 1877) and Aberdeen (1881). Glasgow's was, naturally, the largest in scope, and it laid the general template for the others.

The plan for Glasgow dealt with an area of approximately 35 hectares in the eastern part of the city centre, where 50,000 people were crammed into some of the city's worst housing blackspots. The property owners were bought out, the bulk of the buildings were razed to the ground and new streets were laid out. By 1884, half of the original inhabitants had been removed and the total cost had reached £1.5 million, funded by a rise in the rates. Edinburgh followed a similar trajectory, with the clearance of 2,700 houses in 20 hectares of one of the Old Town's most overcrowded and decayed districts scheduled, effectively removing 18,000 people – one-quarter of the Old Town's and one-tenth of the whole city's population. The projected cost of the venture was put at £300,000. The results of these schemes provided, superficially at least, a great deal of vindication to their initiators. Population density in these areas fell markedly: in Edinburgh, it was halved from 617 persons per hectare in 1861 to 367 per hectare in 1881, and the death rate dropped by a third, from 27 per 1,000 living in 1867 to 19 in 1884.

But some would contend that there are grounds for regarding this optimistic standpoint as jejune, rather than well-founded.[8] The improvement schemes, it is claimed, simply relocated the problems, instead of completely abolishing them, and in some instances may rather have intensified the housing crises. Also, the unquestioned advances in health and environmental standards in the cleared districts are not necessarily attributable to the improvement programmes by themselves. Many of the reasons for these shortcomings are seen as arising from a blinkered analysis both of the roots of the problem and of the best way to implement a long-term amelioration. Firstly, the improvers assumed that those removed from the slum quarters would migrate further afield and find higher-quality accommodation in the outlying parts of their city. In reality, however, the bulk of the ejected people moved no further than a mile at most from their flattened houses, because they were mostly unskilled workers whose day to day employment was uncertain, and so they needed to be near alternative sources of employment. If they lived outside the city centre, job availability was severely circumscribed. Furthermore, rents in more attractive outlying areas were beyond the resources of these people. So, overcrowding in the seven Old Town localities not participating in Edinburgh's slum-clearance initiative actually increased. While health levels did rise in the city's improvement area, the undeveloped parts of the Old Town shared in this progress, indicating that wider environmental factors, rather than slum clearance in itself, were responsible.

Equally crucially, a basic flaw in the overall framework underpinning the regeneration blueprints highlighted a fundamental problem which remained unresolved until after the First World War. There was no consideration by any of the cities' authorities that the free market might not provide decent housing for the working class, and hence the question of affordable rents for these people was never seriously debated. No provision was made for constructing better-quality homes in the cleared sites for the poorer working classes, as it was assumed that those removed would be re-housed through the free market. Councils envisaged that a major financial bonus of these schemes was that not only would unsightly and unhealthy hovels be removed, but their replacement by either middle-class housing or business premises would yield a large increase in municipal rate revenues. Simultaneously, it was anticipated that the former slum-dwellers would be morally reformed by settling into new, better accommodation, and so the overall bill for poor relief would shrink. In pursuit of this strategy, councils sold land to private developers at high prices, effectively precluding the viability of constructing working-class housing. Glasgow council received £2 per square metre for its cleared areas, while £1.25 to £1.50 was the upper limit for builders providing rented property for working people.

The success of the improvement schemes was inhibited by opposition from two sources. One was the opinion of moral reformers in the Thomas Chalmers tradition, who complained that the programme would merely encourage the pauper classes in their depraved condition, whereas temperance and other evangelical measures offered a better long-term solution to the housing difficulty. The second category of objectors were, as noted above, rate-payers of slender means, mostly the shop-keeping and self-employed tradesmen classes. They were especially incensed that those in houses with a low valuation were exempt from paying rates, yet they would be the beneficiaries of these schemes, while the lower middle class faced a rise in their rates. Acting together, these forces created political problems for the councillors' projects. Every Edinburgh ward committee voted against the 1867 proposals, and in Glasgow, Lord Provost Blackie, who drove through the Improvement scheme, lost his seat at the first election after its inception. He was defeated by a Temperance candidate, who also reached out to fretting rate-payers. In such circumstances, there was no continuous rolling programme of slum clearances.

POOR RELIEF: IDEOLOGY AND FINANCE

Laissez-faire ideology also played a central role in the formulation and implementation of the Scottish poor relief system, which, as already discussed, was pronouncedly harsher than that in England. Around 1840, those in receipt of relief made up 3 per cent of the population of Scotland, but in England, the proportion was 7.5 per cent – even after the English New Poor Law Act of 1834 had considerably tightened entitlement rights. At that point, per capita expenditure in England was 29p but only 7p in Scotland. As a result, the disparity in benefits was wide; in the mid-1840s, while a widow with a family in England would receive between £10 and £17 a year, in Scotland she would get at best only £5 per annum, but in many places much less, down to under £1 in the harshest regimes, such as in Glenelg. The severity of poor relief in Scotland as compared to England derived from both its treatment of applicants and its financial resourcing.

Entitlement to support in England was based on a residential qualification of forty days in the parish. In Scotland, however, before 1845, a three years' residency rule operated, which was extended under the new law to five years, and those who failed to meet this strict requirement were returned to their parish of origin. While a lengthy residential qualification might have made sense in an earlier age of a settled agricultural society (itself a highly idealised vision), it was utterly impractical by the nineteenth century, where agrarian reform in both the Highlands and Lowlands, as well as industrial growth and urbanisation, created very high levels of population mobility within Scotland. Moreover, there were simultaneously inflows from Ireland at a higher proportional rate than that experienced in England. The rule was especially harsh on widows with children, who had to make their way back to their appropriate parish, however far from where they had lived with their spouse. The consequence of these settlement rules was that there were constantly bands of itinerant poor moving across the country to their parishes of origin, or, in the case of the Irish, making for ports to sail back home.

A second uniquely Scottish provision was that no relief was supposed to be given under any circumstances to an able-bodied person, whether male or female, so that even in a severe depression, with mass unemployment, benefit should be denied. This policy was much more stringent than in England, where even under its much-reviled New Poor Law, some support could be forthcoming. In reality, the Scottish rule was not always enforced, particularly in bouts of acute economic dislocation, as when several Lanarkshire parishes provided a degree of temporary assistance during downturns in activity in the coalfields. Also, in some places – notably in the Moray-Banffshire and Galloway areas – it was not unusual for mothers with illegitimate children to be supported. But decisions by the Court of Session in 1849 and 1864 explicitly stated that only those who were both destitute and disabled were entitled to relief, thereby substantially restricting the freedom of parochial boards to deviate from the general principle. This precept reflected the values and realities of an earlier economic and social era, where work was seen to be available for all. But it failed to recognise that periods of unemployment were a constituent part of industrial capitalism, which was especially pronounced in the case of Scotland, whose economy was heavily dependent on world trade, rather than on domestic demand, so that joblessness was not a moral deficiency but an economic reality. The rigorous enforcement of this policy added to the volume of roving groups of people travelling from place to place in search of work.

The hardships experienced by poor people were greatly exacerbated by the distinctive Scottish mode of financing poor relief. The traditional source of funding was primarily the proceeds of collections taken at the local parish Church of Scotland services. This was augmented by other sources such as fines imposed by church courts, fees for burials and the use of the church mortcloth at funerals, together with bequests and endowments. The drawbacks of this approach were serious even in the most propitious circumstances, but were exceptionally severe in parishes containing a high proportion of poor people, since they were very likely to have the fewest funds to provide relief. This was the case, for example, in many Highland parishes in the north-west mainland and the islands. But this long-standing system came under increasing pressure for several reasons. The growth in Secession congregations from the 1790s meant that numbers of parishioners, frequently including the better-off, ceased to contribute. Yet simultaneously, those seeking relief grew steadily, most notably in industrial and urban centres, as downturns in economic cycles generated swelling numbers of applicants. But pressure also mounted elsewhere, because of the decline in work opportunities for women as domestic textile production was hit by the rise of factories, while legislation in the 1840s severely reduced the numbers of women working in mining.

The inadequacies of the traditional financing of poor relief were only very slowly acknowledged and acted upon, and there was widespread resistance to a shift to compulsory assessment and the levying of poor rates on the whole community. The reasons for this resistance were essentially twofold, and allied some of the most powerful influences in Scottish society. One objection was economic. Landowners were particularly opposed to a compulsory regime, arguing that they already bore enough financial burdens and that the valuation of their estates would be damaged by its introduction. Hence an attempt to bring in a measure to facilitate compulsory assessment in 1815 was vetoed by landowners. As discussed above, lower-middle-class town ratepayers were also hostile to any increase in the burden of local taxation.

The second stream of objection was ideological, and was most forcibly articulated by Church of Scotland clergy, with the main exponent being

Thomas Chalmers. In numerous publications, Chalmers argued that an obligatory assessment would wreak damage on the moral and social fabric of the nation. Voluntary contributions were immeasurably to be preferred, as they sustained a bond of affection and responsibility between the wealthy and the poor. Compulsory assessment removed the scope for discretion in appraising the moral worth of the applicant and determining the amount of relief to be given. It was also costlier to administer, and it removed the personal ties which voluntary giving required, so reducing social cohesion. Worst of all, Chalmers contended, compulsory assessment would inevitably create a culture of pauperism, with the poor regarding relief as an absolute right, to be given with no scrutiny of their moral worthiness to receive support, thereby encouraging idleness, profligacy and immorality in various forms, such as sexual misconduct, gambling, intemperance and criminality.

For some thirty years after the end of the Napoleonic wars, the Church of Scotland waged a vigorous agitation to retain the voluntary approach. Chalmers himself established the most ambitious scheme to rebut the case for compulsion when in 1819 he launched an experiment in his new Glasgow parish, St John's, to prove that a voluntary set-up would be both cheaper and more effective than the existing arrangement, which was a city-wide system funded by assessment. The project was not a success, despite Chalmers's voluble assertions to the contrary, as within a decade it was financially unviable and so by the mid-1830s it was wound up. Significantly, despite the enormous prestige Chalmers enjoyed, barely any parishes adopted his scheme, and most of these few foundered quite quickly. Chalmers made a second bid at West Port parish in Edinburgh from 1844 to confirm the superiority of voluntary poor relief, but this was also a failure.

Thomas Chalmers and the St John's Parish Poor Relief Scheme

In 1819, Chalmers became minister of St John's church, which had been created to cover the easterly area of his previous charge, Glasgow Tron. The population of the new parish was 10,513, accommodated in 2,237 houses. As part of his aim of winning the population to Christianity by evangelical ministry, Chalmers envisaged that St John's would serve as a laboratory for his ideological project to reform existing poor relief practice. As he saw it, the growing trend towards funding poor relief by compulsory assessment promoted pauperism by making relief a right, destroying both the incentive for claimants to look for work and also eroding the natural social bonds of sympathy which voluntary donations fostered. He believed that the re-creation of a rural parish set-up would eliminate pauperism, and to this end he appointed twenty-five deacons, who each would have responsibility for some sixty families. These deacons would critically appraise requests for relief, by applying strict criteria. The first layer of responsibility was the family and kin of the applicant, next came neighbours and acquaintances, followed by private charities. Only when all of these proved unable to offer adequate support would parochial assistance be available, always provided the individual was not able-bodied. The funding for this relief, as in all non-assessed parishes, came from the proceeds of the collection at the church service. St John's had two Sunday services: the morning one had high seat rents and was intended for the better-off, most of whom came from outwith the parish, while the evening was less expensive and was aimed at the local working-class population. Chalmers was confident that the evening collections would suffice to cover poor relief, while the larger morning sums were to be devoted to providing schooling for parish children. Education, he contended, was the best means of instilling morality and Christianity in future generations of the working-class. Chalmers left the parish in 1823, but his scheme was persevered with until 1837. He maintained in various publications that the experiment fully vindicated his stance, pointing to a significant reduction in poor relief expenditure and a marked fall in the number of recipients.

But critics argued that this was misleading. Firstly, they stressed, it was the economic recovery of the 1820s, and not Chalmers's scheme, which reduced the incidence of poverty, and moreover, by 1830, the number of paupers was greater than in 1819. Additionally, after a few early years in surplus, the scheme regularly fell into deficit, which by the mid-1830s was irretrievable, despite regular private donations. Moreover, the inhabitants of the parish were for the most part not in the poorest stratum; rather they were drawn from skilled and semi-skilled occupations, such as craftsmen and textile workers. So, on the eve of the inception of the scheme, only 3 per cent of Glasgow's paupers resided in the new parish. Lastly, there was no beneficial impact on church-going, for the church-going percentage of the population actually dropped from 28.7 per cent in 1819 to 22.6 per cent in 1834.

The trend towards introducing compulsory assessment had begun in larger towns towards the end of the eighteenth century – Glasgow, for instance, adopted it in 1774 – but in 1800 only ninety-six parishes (around 10 per cent) had abandoned the traditional system. But thereafter there was a steady march towards compulsion, especially in the 1840s, as a severe recession placed heavy burdens on poor relief resources in towns, with the result that by 1843 almost every burgh with a population in excess of 10,000 was using assessment. The New Poor Law facilitated the introduction of assessment, so that parishes using it jumped from 230 in 1844 to 420 in 1846. By 1890 virtually every parochial board applied compulsory assessment.

Poor people living under an unassessed regime were generally likely to receive appreciably less relief than those in assessed parishes. But, as we have seen, the move to assessment did not necessarily raise provision to the levels prevalent in England, and indeed for some people it may have been disadvantageous. Until the 1845 act, it had been customary for relief to be given on an outdoor basis, a much cheaper system than taking the poor into institutions. After 1845, however, there was a trend to offering relief in poorhouses in preference to the previous mode. This was particularly pronounced after 1870, as two factors induced the Board of Supervision to press for greater indoor provision. Firstly, expenditure on poor relief had risen from £295,000 in 1846 to £795,000 in 1868, and ratepayers, already facing rising council rates for expanded municipal services, were becoming restive. Secondly, alarmed at the apparent swelling in the numbers of vagrants around the country, middle-class opinion urged that these paupers be offered relief only in poorhouses. Those receiving outdoor relief fell from 128,000 in 1868 to 73,000 in 1890, while indoor recipients rose across the period from 9,000 to 91,000. As an example, in Dunfermline, 8 per cent of recipients were given indoor relief in 1846, but by 1875 the figure was 25 per cent.

Scottish poorhouses did not impose the harsh work regime which characterised those in England, simply because the able-bodied rule automatically applied the less eligibility test: hence in England, they were 'Work Houses', in Scotland, 'Poor Houses'. Nevertheless, conditions in the Scottish institutions were much inferior to outdoor relief. The quality of food provided was not just very poor, but purposely humiliating: in certain institutions, the meat used to make stock for soup was carefully removed from the finished product, and so was not given to the inmates. There were no opportunities for rehabilitation and medical care was often rudimentary, with other – untrained – residents acting as nurses; in 1882, 55 per cent of poorhouses had no qualified nursing staff. Psychologically, the poorhouse regime was, to put it mildly, not very positive. The segregation of sexes within some institutions meant that couples and families were split up, partly in a bid to stop further breeding by married paupers. Wards mixed inmates with no regard to age or medical or mental health condition. The moral and personal degradation implicit in this arrangement was rendered tangible by the practice of supplying a communal night-time urine tub in each ward, which was to be used by all those sleeping in the room. Children in particular were given a very poor level of support: multiple occupancy – in some cases as many as five or six children – of one bed was quite commonplace. Schooling provision was often of a low standard, while Monkland Poor House contained no toys for the first thirty years of its existence.

BOARDING-OUT

A distinctive feature of Poor Law policy in Scotland was the regular practice of boarding-out pauper and, particularly, orphan children from an urban background. These children were placed with carers in rural areas, who received payment from the parochial board to cover expenses. By the 1880s it has been estimated that in each year there were around 1,000 such cases. While many went to individual family households, Quarrier's Homes and the Aberlour Orphanage, established in, respectively, 1873 and 1875, provided accommodation for such children on a large scale. Boarding-out in England was extremely rare, with pauper children either entering workhouses or remaining with their parents.

There were two reasons why the Scots adopted this approach. One was economy: it was calculated that the cost of boarding-out was appreciably less than using the poorhouse – possibly as much as 70 or 80 per cent cheaper. In addition, by using almost exclusively rural placements, it was argued that children were being placed in a healthy setting, far from the overcrowded and disease-ridden environments in which most were accustomed to live. But there was also an ideological concept behind boarding-out, and one that carried echoes of some of the moral elements of Chalmers's doctrines of the first half of the century. It was believed that boarding-out would remove children from the temptations and vices of urban life, so that juvenile criminality and immorality – which were growing preoccupations of social reformers from mid-century – would diminish. Accordingly, there was a preference for sending children to households in the Highlands and islands, where religious beliefs were particularly strong, in preference to, say, mining villages or small textile centres. For the crofters and suchlike, the gains from involvement in boarding-out were substantial, namely, a welcome income boost and availability of free labour for farmwork. But there was a further bonus for social reformers in the scheme. It was highly unlikely that those parents who were seen as having poor parenting skills would be able to maintain contact with their offspring, once removed. The physical distances were too great for poor people to travel, and written communications could easily be intercepted by the host family. Hence many children who were not orphans, but viewed as real or potential social problems, were whisked away from their families, rarely to re-join them. Those despatched to Aberlour and Quarrier's were often then sent out to live on farms in Canada, never to return.

NOTES

1. S. Szreter and A. Hardy, 'Urban Fertility and Morality Patterns', in M. Daunton (ed.), *The Cambridge Urban History of Britain* (2000), Vol. III, 631ff.
2. A. K. Chalmers, *The Health of Glasgow, 1818–1925: An Outline* (1930), 82. Infant mortality rates are for deaths of children under one year of age per 1,000 live births.
3. *PP, HL*, XXVIII (1842), *Sanitary Inquiry: Scotland – Report on the Sanitary Condition of the Labouring Population of Scotland . . .*, 256–7: W. D. Laurie, M.D., *Report on the General and Sanitary Condition of the Town of Greenock*.
4. *PP* 1872, XXXIV (c603), *Fourth Report of the Commissioners on River Pollution*, Vol. II, *Evidence*, 22.
5. R. Rodger, 'The Law and Urban Change: Some Nineteenth Century Scottish Evidence', *Urban History Year Book* (1979), 78–80.
6. See pp. 82–3.
7. See pp. 61–2, 158–9.
8. P. J. Smith, 'Slum Clearance as an Instruments of Sanitary Reform: The Flawed Vision of Edinburgh's First Slum Clearance Scheme', *Planning Perspectives*, 9 (1994), 1–27.

CHAPTER 5

The Presbyterian Churches

THE ESTABLISHED CHURCH, 1780S TO 1830

At the start of the nineteenth century, the established church in Scotland looked in a healthier condition than its English counterpart. Scotland was preponderantly Presbyterian; other Protestant churches enjoyed only a very modest degree of support, in contrast to the rest of the United Kingdom, while the number of Roman Catholics was, until the 1840s, extremely small. The abuses found in the Church of England were virtually absent in the Scottish state church. Two-thirds of Anglican clergy were non-resident, which was barely known in the Church of Scotland, and while about one in ten Anglican parishes lacked a priest, all livings in Scotland were routinely filled. Pluralism (i.e. one clergyman simultaneously holding several charges), rife in England, was uncommon in Scotland. In England, tithes were a cause of anticlerical protests, but in Scotland, teinds were not contentious, since they were not perceived as a barrier to agricultural improvement. Teinds were a lesser charge than tithes, not having been revalued for many years, and in Scotland the payment was deducted from the rent due, and so was not an additional burden on tenants. The social background of Church of Scotland clergy was closer to their congregations, most being drawn from the middling urban and rural classes, with a smattering from the working classes. Hence, the Anglican 'squarson' (a priest with a gentry background and interests) had no real equivalent in Scotland.

Moreover, the Church of Scotland also reached more widely and deeply into the fabric of society than its English equivalent. Until 1845, the administration of poor relief lay in the domain of the Kirk Session, and the local church had oversight of the parish school; in England, meanwhile, responsibility for the former was undertaken by laymen, and the Church of England had no statutory involvement in schooling.

Yet the Church of Scotland was plunged into profound turmoil in the second quarter of the nineteenth century. Nearly two-fifths of both its clergy and

The major non-Presbyterian Protestant sects in Scotland

The Congregational Church grew dramatically in the first decade of the nineteenth century, due to the missionary efforts of John and Robert Haldane, who sold their estate near Stirling to fund their work. By 1807, there were eighty-five congregations, against a mere fourteen a decade earlier, but this progress fell back when in 1808 the Haldanes switched to the Baptists, taking with them many followers. The formation of the Free Church in 1843 led to another seepage of support. Moreover, unity proved difficult, and a major secession occurred in 1843, when the Evangelical Union was formed. Traditionally, Congregationalism adhered to conservative Calvinist doctrine, but from the 1870s liberal theological and liturgical currents emerged. In 1880, there were just under 10,000 adherents, whereas there were a quarter-of-a-million Congregationalists in England and Wales. Probably the most eminent Scottish Congregationalist was David Dale.

The Baptist Church was greatly boosted by the adherence of the Haldane brothers in 1808, but subsequently sustained growth was inhibited by doctrinal disputes and breakaways. Additionally, as with the Congregational Church, the Free Church attracted a good number of Baptists. Nevertheless, membership almost doubled from 1860 to 1880, by which time it was around 10,000 – but the figure for Wales, with only half of Scotland's population, was 80,000. Leading lay Baptists included Thomas Coats and William Quarrier.

Methodism made virtually no headway against the implacable Calvinism prevalent in Scotland, despite John Wesley's missionary efforts. The sole significant success came in Shetland, where, by 1860, a local convert, John Nicolson, had built up a membership of 2,000. The stunted growth in Scotland is shown by a very modest rise in worshippers from 4,000 in 1830 to 5,000 in 1880. Welsh membership, however, doubled over the same period to a total of 26,000 in 1880.

The Episcopalians fared better than the other three sects. In 1788, the church formally abandoned its identification with the Jacobite cause, and in 1792 it was granted toleration. Membership increased steadily from some 11,000 in 1801 to 44,000 by 1851, and reached 68,000 in 1881. The geographical and social distribution of support shifted appreciably. In the eighteenth century, many Episcopalians were based in the Highlands, but emigration and Presbyterian evangelism eroded this base, so that by the 1840s, only Appin and some places along the Great Glen, for example Fort William, retained healthy numbers. Aberdeenshire, particularly Buchan, was another traditional Episcopalian area, and here membership held steady between 1800 and 1860. A religious revival in 1859, however, drew many in the local fishing villages over to more evangelical sects, such as Baptists. The great bulk of the nineteenth-century expansion came in Lowland urban centres, most notably Edinburgh and Glasgow. While the adherents in Buchan were preponderantly working class, many of these cities' members seem to have been more middle class, to whose growing artistic sensibilities the ambience of Episcopalian worship appealed, which found the Presbyterian order of service too severe. Numbers were also swollen by the arrival of immigrants not just from England, but also from Ireland, as Ulster Protestants were fairly evenly split between Presbyterians and Episcopalians. Many of the Irish Episcopalians were likely to have been working class, so broadening the social composition of the church. Additionally, a good sprinkling of the landed elite were members of the church, but overall, the social profile of Episcopalianism in Scotland was not vitally different from the Church of Scotland.

its laity seceded in 1843, and over the succeeding thirty years, the church lost its formal control of education and poor relief. For a period in the middle of the century, the very survival of the Church of Scotland appeared acutely parlous, and although it recovered somewhat in the third quarter, in 1880 it still seemed vulnerable. There were several interlocking aspects to the church's crisis: namely, the challenges of urbanisation and social change, the rise of Presbyterian churches outside the state church, internal divisions in the church and the political ramifications of being an established church.

The intense rapidity of urban growth in the early nineteenth century presented serious problems for the state church. Existing church accommodation was utterly inadequate: Paisley Abbey, for instance, accommodated 6,000 worshippers, but by 1812 the parish's population exceeded 25,000. Building new churches was not easy: in formerly rural parishes whose population had expanded with the growth of manufacturing, heritors resisted meeting the costs, while town councils, responsible for burgh churches, had very limited resources.

The growth of an urban middle class posed another challenge. Growing in numbers, its members were also more confident and assertive than hitherto. Their increasing wealth gave them the wherewithal to act independently of the state church, which was manifested in the striking growth of Presbyterian dissenting congregations. Secessions from the Church of Scotland had begun in the middle of the eighteenth century but accelerated from the 1790s, so that by the 1820s, perhaps one-third of Scottish Presbyterians were Seceders. These churches were mostly established in Lowland urban communities and spearheaded by the middle classes: for instance, all the church officers in a dissenting congregation in Edinburgh's Cowgate in 1828 were at least lower middle class. The reasons for this trend were varied, but there were no profound theological disputes behind these rifts, as the Westminster Confession – the doctrinal creed of Scottish Presbyterianism – was subscribed to by all. Clashes of personality sometimes led to breakaways, and lack of accommodation in parish churches played an increasing part. But the most important factor was opposition to lay patronage, which had been restored by a parliamentary act of 1712, against the wishes of the majority of Scottish Presbyterians. By the early nineteenth century, rather more than half of parishes had a lay patron, and about another one-third were under Crown patronage. From the middle of the eighteenth century, resistance grew to the patron's right to choose the parish minister. Many patrons were not overly interested in choosing someone sympathetic to the inclinations of the congregation. They entertained a preference for a Moderate minister, who would be socially acceptable and more likely to deliver low-key sermons, and would emphasise a culture of gentility and civilising tendencies, rather than expounding the robust evangelicalism which was more in line with the leanings of many parishioners. Secession permitted the new church to choose a preacher who met the congregation's criteria.

Without state funding, Secession churches were entirely reliant on internally raised finance, which gave rise to their generic term, the Voluntaries. As a corollary of this and because of their social background, Voluntaries were very prone to apply the ideas of a market economy to religion. For them, a state church was in a quasi-protectionist position, and it was unjust that non-observants were compelled to contribute to its upkeep either by teinds or burgh taxes, as well as supporting their own church. If a church could not survive on the financial backing given by the congregation, it should not be artificially kept afloat, any more than a non-viable business should receive state support. But this approach highlighted the fact that it was often difficult to maintain Voluntary churches in poorer areas, where congregation-derived funding might be inadequate; hence by the 1820s Secession churches in towns tended to be located in more affluent districts.

STATE CHURCH MODERATES AND EVANGELICALS

The response of the Church of Scotland to these difficulties was hampered by internal divisions between the Moderates and Evangelicals. The latter held that mere exhortation and morality were inadequate for salvation; instead, they stressed the centrality of individual conversion, as faith was more important than good works for eternal life. Commitment to parochial engagement, especially visitations by ministers and elders, and, more widely, missionary work were core Evangelical principles. Moderates instead emphasised that a broader social context of civilised, rational discourse would best promote Christianity. Salvation would not come simply by doctrinal belief, and the Bible gave sensible advice for moral conduct, rather than providing good news of redemption. Preaching by Moderates tended to be restrained in tone, and there was no great involvement in pastoral work or in developing the role of elders. In 1830, no ministerial visit to a parishioner in Cullen had occurred in thirty-four years, while in Tarland there was only one elder. Evangelicals were perceived, not least by themselves, as pious, sober, non-worldly and morally strict. Moderates, in contrast, were portrayed as sociable, mixing freely with the middle and upper classes, and they often pursued non-religious interests, especially in science, history, literature and the arts in general.

The Moderates' control of the church between the 1760s and the 1820s was not as total as sometimes asserted – not least by their Evangelical opponents. The Moderates' dominance primarily operated at the level of the General Assembly, but in presbyteries and synods, Evangelicals frequently prevailed – notably in the west-central area. The Moderates' influence was enhanced because they accepted the need to work with the government, and so they benefited from the ecclesiastical patronage dispensed by politicians through some 300 Crown-controlled livings. The lines between the two camps were not fixed, and on some issues, fluidity in support occurred. Unity between Moderates and Evangelicals was, however, unquestioned on the indispensable need for a state church as the guarantor of social and political stability. As the national church, it had a duty to minister to everyone in society, the poor as much as the better-off, whereas Voluntaries had no such obligation, and were prone to attend only to the interests of their own adherents.

The balance of power within the Church of Scotland began to tilt decisively towards the Evangelicals after about 1815. The death of the veteran Moderate leader George Hill in 1820 left that party without an effective head for many years. Moderate management of the General Assembly thus became more fragile in the 1820s. More or less simultaneously, the Evangelical camp benefited from the emergence of the most charismatic Scottish clergyman of the nineteenth century. Thomas Chalmers began as a Moderate, but became a fervent Evangelical after a conversion experience in 1810–11. He was a brilliant preacher: people fainted with emotion during his sermons, assuredly a very rare occurrence with Moderate clergy, and he was also an outstanding organiser, as his work on church extension in the 1830s was to reveal. In 1817, Chalmers was appointed to Glasgow Tron Church and this proved almost as revelatory an experience as his earlier conversion to evangelicalism. His previous charge had been Kilmany, a rural Fife backwater, and the transition to a teeming city parish jolted him into advocating the urgent necessity of a radical response

Figure 5.1 Rev. Thomas Chalmers, photograph by D. O. Hill (1847). © Special Collections, University of Glasgow. Licensor: www.scran.ac.uk

to the urban challenges facing the state church. The Tron parish inhabitants were mostly artisans and textile workers, and not the poorest labouring classes, yet Chalmers was alarmed at the absence of religion among his parishioners, evinced in immorality, pauperism and ultra-radicalism. Glasgow thus gave practical reinforcement to his belief that only a state church, and assuredly not Voluntaryism, could address these problems. His views were summed up in *The Importance of a National Church* (1827), where he explained that national character was formed by the church and education, and that individuals, however well-intentioned, could not produce this universal provision; only state aid would.

This sense of social and political foreboding among Evangelicals intensified with events in the early 1830s. The 1832 Reform Act was regarded as posing a serious challenge to national and religious well-being, because it fuelled an expectation that legislation by a secular government would ameliorate the condition of the poor. Evangelicals instead contended that nothing but a reformation of character, induced by religious conversion, could achieve that goal, and that an endowed territorial national church alone offered a viable solution. Neither a secular state nor a Voluntary church framework could provide the required combination of complete national coverage and religious instruction.

Accordingly, a central prong in Chalmers's bid to reassert the primacy of his church was to lessen the attractions of Voluntaryism. Initially, since lack of accommodation was assumed to lie behind the rise of secessionism, a programme of church-building was agreed to by the General Assembly. Moderates supported an approach to the government for assistance in adding to church provision in scattered parishes, mostly in the Highlands, and in 1824 the state responded positively. £180,000 was made available, and by 1831, fifty-three churches had been erected across the Highlands.

The Voluntaries reacted vigorously to this challenge. Their disparate sects were mostly consolidated into two churches: namely, the United Secession Church, formed in 1820, and the Relief Church, dating from the 1760s, so that henceforth there was much greater unanimity among Voluntaries. Moreover, the United Secession Church, which was more hostile than the Relief Church to the state church and accordingly strongly in favour of disestablishment, grew more rapidly in the 1820s. The passage of Catholic Emancipation in 1829 sharpened the hostility of Voluntaries to the principle of Establishment. In that year, the Rev. Andrew Marshall of Kirkintilloch published a highly influential pamphlet, arguing that the measure led to the risk of Roman Catholicism becoming the state church in Ireland. The only safeguard against this was to have no state churches anywhere in Britain.

THE DEEPENING CRISIS: FROM THE VETO ACT TO SPIRITUAL INDEPENDENCE

Relations between Moderates and Evangelicals, generally amicable in the 1820s, deteriorated acutely in the following decade. In 1834, the Evangelicals won control of the General Assembly, ending seventy years of Moderate ascendancy. One factor in this sea-change was a sharp shift in the social and religious characteristics of the elders attending assemblies. Until the end of the 1820s, many parishes at a considerable distance from the capital nominated either an Edinburgh-based lawyer or a member of the gentry as a representative elder, rather than sending a local communicant of the congregation. Between 1820 and 1832, 80 per cent of elders at general assemblies were either landowners or lawyers, and were mostly associated with the Moderate side. But by the mid-1830s, many of these men were replaced by local elders, often middle-class businessmen, who now had both the money and confidence to participate in assembly proceedings. The great majority of these new men were Evangelicals.

A second factor was that recently ordained clergy were overwhelmingly Evangelicals, many having been taught or influenced by Chalmers. After a short stint as professor of moral philosophy at St Andrews University, in 1827 Chalmers moved to the chair of divinity at Edinburgh University. Here, in the largest theology department in Scotland, he trained and influenced a generation of clergymen who became his ardent supporters in the struggles of the 1830s and 1840s. So, in Aberdeenshire, in 1822 there were seventy-five Moderate ministers and only eight Evangelicals, but twenty years later, Evangelicals numbered thirty, with Moderates reduced to fifty-five.

The newly secured Evangelical majority in the 1834 General Assembly passed two measures designed to win back Voluntaries to the state church. In a continuation of their thinking in the 1820s, Evangelicals assumed that if sufficient established-church accommodation were available in burghs, many Voluntaries would opt to return, as the financial costs would be significantly lower. Accordingly, the Chapels Act launched a second Church Extension programme, this time focusing on Lowland urban under-provision.[1] Chalmers was put in charge of the scheme. When the Whig government refused to fund this project, Chalmers revealed his remarkable skills in administration and fund-raising. Aided by a group of lay supporters – mostly urban businessmen, such as the Glasgow publisher William Collins – Chalmers masterminded an astonishing achievement: £305,000 was raised in six years from 1834, and this sum funded the building of 222 new churches, about one-fifth of the existing number.

Chalmers devised a format by which sizeable donations from a nationwide elite were joined to weekly subscriptions of a penny from the poor and the working classes, with the objective of giving the scheme a secure grounding in social solidarity. These Extension Scheme churches were carved out of existing parishes and had no responsibilities for poor relief or parish schools, which remained with the original parish. The existing parishes were termed Quoad Civilia parishes, and the newcomers, Quoad Sacra. Hence Quoad Sacra churches had added popularity, as lower financial contributions were required from congregations. Further, these churches tended to have recently ordained men as ministers, and these, as we have seen, were strongly Evangelical, thus adding to that party's strength at general assemblies.

The second tactic deployed by the 1834 General Assembly was to restrict the untrammelled authority of the patron, which had been such a recruiting sergeant for Seceders. The Veto Act prescribed that while the patron retained the right to nominate a candidate for a vacant living, that appointment was subject to a veto exercised by a majority of the male heads of households in the congregation. The act ingeniously kept to the letter of Parliament's Patronage Act of 1712, while simultaneously acknowledging the gravamen of long-running Seceder grievances. The implicit assumption was that patrons and congregations would reach a satisfactory outcome by negotiation and consultation, rather than have a protracted dispute. At first, most Moderates were prepared to support the Veto Act scheme as an effective riposte to the Voluntary challenge. Chalmers was emphatically against the abolition of patronage as it was a legal right, and this appeased Moderates, especially as the extreme Evangelicals wanted an end to patronage and were dismayed by the compromise position endorsed by Chalmers.

Despite initial euphoria about the positive impact of the twin measures, after some five years the Church of Scotland found itself mired in a cat's cradle of judicial and political obstacles. The central issue in several legal disputes was the relative weight of church and parliamentary sovereignty. The attraction of Quoad Sacra churches was severely diminished in 1839 by Court of Session judgments in cases raised by Stewarton and Brechin Quoad Civilia churches. The court ruled that these complainant churches had the right to use funds raised by the local Quoad Sacra churches for Quoad Civilia responsibilities, such as poor relief and education. This left Quoad Sacra churches financially unviable, not having full access to the entire funds raised by their congregations. Additionally, the court also decreed in the Stewarton case that only Quoad Civilia church minsters and elders had a right to attend general assemblies. This was potentially a serious erosion of the Evangelicals' grip on the General Assembly.

More profoundly devastating consequences, however, arose from litigation over the Veto Act. In the first four to five years of the operation of the measure, conflict between patrons and congregations was averted in some 90 per cent of appointments to livings, and so the act was regarded as broadly successful. In 1838–9, however, this appraisal was challenged irreversibly, starting in Auchterarder. Here, in 1834, the choice of the patron, Lord Kinnoull, was rejected by the congregation, and a new presentee was accepted by parishioners and installed. The original nominee then went to law, claiming that the 1712 parliamentary act could not be superseded by an act of the General Assembly. The case went on appeal to the House of Lords, which in 1838 resoundingly found for the rejected minister and asserted the unequivocal supremacy of parliamentary statute over any subordinate agency. Other cases followed, all confirming in detail the general principle promulgated in the Auchterarder ruling. The Evangelicals responded to this challenge by articulating the concept of Non-Intrusionism, namely, the state should not insist that a minister be appointed against the settled will of the congregation. Non-Intrusionism was then expanded to the doctrine of Spiritual Independence, enunciated at the 1839 General Assembly. This asserted that the church acknowledged the state's role in financing the physical aspects of the Church of Scotland, such as minsters' stipends and building costs. But the Non-Intrusionists absolutely rejected any role for the state in spiritual questions, which included the method of choosing ministers:

> The government and discipline of Christ's Church cannot be carried on according to his laws and the constitution of his Church, subject to the exercise, by any secular tribunal, of such powers as have been assumed by the said Court of Session.[2]

Evangelicals thus argued that Spiritual Independence was necessary to protect the Church of Scotland from dangers implicit in changes to the nature of the British state, namely the rise in influence of Voluntaries and Roman Catholics in the political process.

Any solution to the escalating religious conflict was rendered less achievable because, by about 1840, it had become closely enmeshed with national political considerations. Hitherto, the Tory party appeared to be umbilically linked to the Moderate wing and Evangelicals were closer to the Whigs – even although Chalmers was a Tory. Hence, the Evangelicals confidently expected support from the Whig governments in the struggle for mastery of the Church of Scotland. But discomfort set in from 1834–5 as Lord Melbourne's ministry failed to meet the Evangelicals' demands, mostly because the Voluntaries appeared to be exercising more influence with the government. The Whigs were heavily dependent in several constituencies on the votes of Voluntaries, who in 1834 had set up the Scottish Central Board of Dissenters as a political pressure group whose top priority was disestablishment in Scotland. The Veto Act deeply disquieted Voluntaries, and their concerns were loudly conveyed to Whig politicians. When the government refused to give financial support to the Evangelicals' Church Extension Scheme, after 362 petitions objecting to the request were organised by the Board of Dissenters and were signed by 148,000 individuals, Chalmers not unreasonably ascribed this decision to Voluntary lobbying.

In this context, the Conservatives naturally became interested in garnering Non-Intrusionist support, but a delicate balancing act was called for, to avoid alienating the party's traditional Moderate supporters. However, the irresistible juggernaut of legal decisions quickly corroded this new alliance. Angered by further court rulings, Non-Intrusionists became ever more implacable, and in the Claim of Right, endorsed by the 1842 General Assembly, an extreme declaration of the relations between church and state was adumbrated. The Claim, which carried undertones of seventeenth-century absolutist affirmations of Presbyterian rights, contended that secular government should simply hand funds over to the established church in Scotland, to be disbursed as the church saw fit, with no restraints imposed by the state:

> The General Assembly . . . DO . . . Claim as of RIGHT, that she shall fully possess and enjoy her liberties, government, discipline, rights and privileges according to law, especially for the defence of the civil liberties

of her people, and that she shall be protected from the foresaid unconstitutional and illegal encroachments of the said Church Of Scotland, and her people secured in their Christian and constitutional rights and liberties.[3]

This had two significant consequences. Firstly, the unity of Evangelicals within the church was ruptured: a crucial group of about forty ministers, labelled the Middle Party (alternatively known as 'the Forty Thieves'), broke away because they felt the Evangelicals were too much in thrall to the aptly named 'Wild Men', who opposed any dilution of full-blooded Non-Intrusionism. Ironically, the departure of the Middle Party simply entrenched the power of the Wild Men, as Chalmers now had fewer moderate (or, less extreme) Evangelicals to work with. Secondly, the Tories recoiled in horror from what they interpreted as a serious erosion of the rights of patrons in an established church. By extension, this could also be applied in England, where the position of the Anglican Church seemed less secure. The Tories were adamant that the British constitution could not be breached by undermining the doctrine of parliamentary sovereignty or the destruction of one of its pillars, namely the established church. This confirmed the party leadership's determination that no concessions aimed at keeping the Church of Scotland should be offered to the intransigent Non-Intrusionists. Hence, when in office from 1841, they refused to act to avert the impending schism.

BREAKAWAY, 1843: COURSE AND CAUSES

Confronted by this legal and political impasse, the Non-Intrusionists took up their nuclear option, namely, to leave the church and form a new one. The secession was carefully prepared, and had little spontaneity. In November 1842, when it was clear that legal decisions had rendered the prospects of success within the existing framework extremely bleak, a convocation of clergymen was held in Edinburgh. Some 465 ministers attended (no laity were present), of whom three-quarters – 354 – agreed to a plan to secede. In February 1843, an Act of Separation was drawn up, outlining Non-Intrusionist grievances and justifying secession. The act was signed by 470 ministers, of whom all but 16 did eventually leave. At the meeting of the General Assembly in May 1843, a stage-managed walk-out took place. After solemnly signing the Deed of Separation, the Non-Intrusionist ministers and elders left the Assembly Hall, walked in procession down the Mound to Canonmills, by the Water of Leith, where the Free Church of Scotland was formally inaugurated.

There were two conflicts coinciding in the Disruption crisis, so making a compromise resolution highly unlikely. In the first instance, there were implacable forces outside the church's parties for whom constitutional practice and political calculation meant that very few concessions could be made to the Evangelical standpoint as it had evolved by 1841–3. The consistency with which the higher courts in both Edinburgh and London repudiated Non-Intrusionist claims indicated the clear line that the judiciary saw as flowing from the fundamental principles of British constitutional law, namely, that parliamentary sovereignty was supreme in all circumstances. It was fruitless to argue that Scottish constitutional practice suggested otherwise, and in any case, the position before 1707 – or indeed 1688 – was not one that many Scots wished to revert to. Moreover, the general acquiescence in the patronage system introduced in 1712, which was not effectively challenged by the Church of Scotland itself until around 1830, undermined the argument that this was a long-standing, widely held grievance.

At the less elevated level of political manoeuvring, the Evangelicals had become increasingly isolated and friendless. Their erstwhile supporters, the Whigs, grew steadily more estranged from 1836–7. The retiral of Lord Advocate Francis Jeffrey and Solicitor-General Henry Cockburn – who had both been supportive of the Veto Act – from frontline politics to the bench was a blow, because the next Lord Advocate, John Murray, was more hostile. Andrew Rutherfurd, who replaced Murray in 1838, was initially sympathetic, but he was soon alienated by the Non-Intrusionists' uncompromising stance. As discussed above, the Tories, superficially well-disposed towards earnest champions of the establishment principle, were, in the light of cold analysis, not prepared to endorse the Evangelicals' drift to an extreme standpoint.

These profound legal and political obstacles were compounded by tactical blunders committed by the Evangelicals, which revealed weaknesses in Chalmers's character. Melbourne quite rapidly came to distrust him, estimating him as devious and unyielding, and by 1840 his verdict on Chalmers was trenchant: 'Chalmers, I feel certain, knows no theology . . . I particularly dislike Chalmers. I think him a Madman and all Madmen are Rogues.'[4] Even without pressure from the Voluntaries, the Whigs became disenchanted with the Evangelicals' manipulative conduct, epitomised by the latter's activities during the 1840 Perthshire by-election.[5] Like the Whigs, Conservative leaders found the Non-Intrusionists very difficult to work with. Chalmers gained a reputation among the Tory hierarchy for duplicity after he was held to have reneged on a deal negotiated in early 1840 with Lord Aberdeen. By its terms, the peer would sponsor a bill providing a compromise solution to the patronage crisis which would accommodate a great deal of the Non-Intrusionists' demands. But as the measure was proceeding through parliament, Chalmers publicly pronounced its proposals to be insufficient. Aberdeen was outraged at Chalmers's repudiation of what the peer considered a firm agreement, and Chalmers's conduct at the 1840 General Assembly, where he seemed to encourage rejection of any measure short of full implementation of spiritual independence, reinforced his reputation as devious and unreliable.

The unwavering obduracy of the Evangelicals, rather than the stance of the Moderates, came to be regarded as the major obstacle to a settlement.

Chalmers's negotiations with politicians and with non-Evangelicals in the Church of Scotland were vitiated to a considerable degree by the problems of keeping his supporters united. A particular challenge was presented by the 'Wild Men', who constituted perhaps one-eighth of the General Assembly's membership in the pre-Disruption decade. They were not an organised bloc, for while they acted together in opposition to patronage, they were disunited on other issues, such as the mode of choosing elders to attend general assemblies. The Wild Men increased both their saliency and their militancy after the Auchterarder case, and pressed for the outright abolition of lay patronage, which the General Assembly carried in 1842. Chalmers was always concerned to accommodate these firebrands, as he feared they might otherwise leave the church. They were typical of Chalmers's base support – younger men, restless for reform – and they included future leaders of the Free Church, most notably Robert Candlish, Chalmers's immediate successor. But, as noted above, in yielding to the demands of these Young Turks, Chalmers lost the backing of less extreme Evangelicals, and also confirmed Moderates in their complete opposition. The tensions imposed on Chalmers's delicate equipoise by the slew of court cases in 1839 and after became impossible to contain. As well as the emergence of the Middle Party, previously supportive public figures distanced themselves from the Evangelicals' response to the Auchterarder verdict. The prominent Whig, Fox Maule, later Lord Dalhousie, was a significant instance of this process. Revealingly, the Scottish press moved solidly to a critical standpoint as the crisis intensified, so that by 1843 the papers founded specifically to advocate the Evangelicals' case, such as the *Witness*, were virtually alone in championing Non-Intrusionism.

Numerically, the Free Church's support was impressive: some 38 per cent of Church of Scotland clergymen quit, and at least as high a share of the laity joined them. Additionally, nearly 400 parish schoolmasters left. Even more encouraging for the new church was the breakdown of these global figures. The outgoing clergy tended to be younger: only one-quarter of ministers ordained before 1820 left, as against approaching one-half (45 per cent) of post-1820 men, and for those taking up livings in the 1830s, the figure rose to three-quarters (297 out of 397). Some 30 per cent (289 out of 970) of Quoad Civilia ministers left, but 70 per cent (163 from a total of 234) of Quoad Sacra ministers went out. This suggests that the Free Church clergy, being for the most part younger, had less to lose emotionally and socially in leaving a parish, and perhaps felt confident that they would in due course replace the ageing state church incumbents. But there were intriguing counter-currents at play. Just under two-thirds of ministers who identified with the Evangelical side before the Disruption actually opted to leave. These who stayed in the state church may have been older men, reluctant to break with congregations and unsure of future prospects, or they may have been disturbed by the mounting stridency of the Non-Intrusionists in the years just before the Disruption; in other words, the forty members of the Middle Party may have been the visible evidence of a large submerged body. Moreover, the sense that the Non-Intrusionists had overreached themselves is hinted at in the data for ministers ordained between 1840 and 1843. These newest members of the clergy ran against the pattern of the 1830s; whereas three-quarters of the latter left, the more recent ministers were fairly evenly split: forty-five chose to remain, thirty-nine to leave. This was perhaps a pointer to the unexpectedly buoyant recruitment trend after 1843 enjoyed by the established church.

The Free Church had a very distinctive geographical and social shape. The bulk of its support came from two areas. Firstly, in the larger Lowland burghs, the church often matched or exceeded the rump state church: in Aberdeen, all nine parish ministers and the great body of the congregations left; and in Glasgow, Edinburgh, Dundee, Paisley and Greenock, church attendance data gathered in 1851 showed that there were at least as many Free Church as Church of Scotland worshippers. But elsewhere in the Lowland areas, in small towns and in rural parishes, support was much lower: in the south-west, less than 25 per cent joined the breakaway. Secondly, in the Highlands, the movement out was immense: in many parishes, it was reported that only a handful remained with the Church of Scotland, and overall between two-thirds and three-quarters of members left.

The reasons for joining the Free Church varied by location and class. The mass defections in the Highlands probably included a degree of social protest against clearances, since landowners were usually patrons of local churches. Yet this is not convincing as a complete explanation. In some of the most notorious areas of forced depopulation, ministers who had been at least complicit in the policy of clearance seceded in 1843, and were accompanied by the bulk of their congregations. Thus, in Farr parish, which included Strathnaver, David MacKenzie, the minister who had read out the landlord's notice of removal in 1814, joined the Free Church, along with almost all of his flock. Furthermore, the Free Church was equally popular in areas where mass clearances had been less prevalent, as in south-east Inverness-shire. By contrast, it was relatively less successful in mainland Argyllshire, although there had been several evictions there. For at least a generation before 1843, a substantial evangelisation campaign had been carried out in the Highlands, so that joining the Free Church can be read as a spiritual decision rather than a social protest. This religious conversion movement spanned the whole region and drew high levels of support among the population. It had mostly been undertaken by committed evangelical laymen, often called 'The Men', who dressed in a long blue cloaks and wore a spotted cotton handkerchief round their heads. They were teachers, missionaries and, particularly, elders, who had the advantage of being native Gaelic speakers, whereas many ministers in these parishes spoke only English.

In Lowland towns and cities, lay support was largely drawn from several social groupings. The first category covered those whose wealth was relatively new, such as manufacturers and traders, who felt excluded from eldership in the established church by those of older wealth and higher status, such as bankers and lawyers. For these new men of substance, the Free Church offered access to eldership, which in burghs was normally the next highest status position to a town councillor. The evidence from places as disparate in socio-economic structure as Aberdeen, Edinburgh and Glasgow seems to confirm this disparity in origins and status between office-bearers in the post-Disruption Church of Scotland and those of the breakaway Free Church. For instance, in New Leith parish, 69 per cent of the elders in the pre-Disruption Church of Scotland can be classified as upper middle class, and 23 per cent lower middle class. In 1844, the breakaway New Leith Free Church's eldership virtually inverted the balance: 30 per cent were upper middle class, and 60 per cent lower middle.

In most Lowland Free Churches, the majority of the congregation seems to have been composed of working-class people; usually they made up between 55 and 65 per cent of the total membership. There is, of course, no way of determining the motives which induced working people to commit to the Free Church. Doubtless, most of them adhered to the new church from deeply held religious convictions, but some contemporaries claimed to detect a tendency in which the adhesion of an employer of a large works to the Free Church often led to many employees accompanying him. This may be viewed as a form of industrial paternalism, a feature characteristic of the Lancashire cotton factory system, akin to the rural deference so widespread in England. More cynical spirits have contended that by joining the boss's church, workers hoped to be preferred for promotion, or, at worst, to escape losing their jobs in a round of dismissals. Moreover, there was a prospect of their children being admitted to the Free Church school, which was likely to be of a high standard, given the presence of children of prosperous churchgoers. Also, at points of crisis and need, a reasonably affluent Free Church parish might augment the highly austere relief doled out by the Poor Law authorities to a faithful communicant.[6]

THE SURVIVAL OF THE CHURCH OF SCOTLAND, 1843–80

With large-scale support from the newer middle class and skilled workers in urban areas, along with crofting communities, combined with the commitment of a young and dynamic clergy, the Free Church felt assured that quite soon the surviving Church of Scotland would collapse from inanition and senescence, whereupon their church would assume the position of the state church, reborn and transformed. In this mood of optimism, the decade after the Disruption was characterised by an immense Free Church building and staffing programme, so that by as early as 1847, some 730 churches had been erected, 669 minsters had been ordained and 513 schools had been built, with 500 schoolteachers and 200 probationers to staff them. The Free Church's confident assumption about future trends seemed confirmed when the 1851 census of religious attendance appeared. Although acknowledged by historians to be riddled with imperfections,[7] the census revealed that the Church of Scotland and the Free Church were neck and neck, each with 32 per cent of all churchgoers, while the United Presbyterian Church (UPC) had 19 per cent;[8] but in the larger cities the established church was mostly in third place. The eclipse and terminal decay of the state church thus looked to be not far off, and its centrality in the life of the Scottish people seemed to be steadily diminishing. This was evidenced by the 1845 Poor Law Act which stripped the Church of Scotland of its direct responsibility for poor relief; the abolition in 1854 of the religious test for university professors (except for theology chairs); the introduction in 1855 of state central registration of births, marriages and deaths; and the rapidly growing trend for burials in privately run cemeteries, replacing the traditional venues of state church graveyards.

Yet, within a generation, the great expectations of the Free Church were irretrievably punctured. In the Lowlands, the Church of Scotland revived in the towns and retained its former redoubts in the countryside, so that by 1880 its membership exceeded the combined total of the UPC and the Free Church, and it was especially successful in attracting the younger generation. A telling statistic is that between 1855 and 1880, the number of marriages celebrated in the state church rose by 27 per cent, in the Free Church by 13 per cent and in the UPC by only 1 per cent. A Glasgow Free Church minister ruefully commented in 1893 on the surge in support for the established church that '[i]t is easily accounted for by the great influx of young people into the Church of Scotland in the last twenty-five years'.[9]

The recovery of the established church was due to three broad factors. Firstly, its adoption of new approaches to worship, along with its response to advances in scientific knowledge and theology, drew in a large part of the new aspiring middle classes. The Church of Scotland, despite the loss of high-calibre clergy at the Disruption, steadily built up a cadre of exceptionally able preachers and teachers. These included John Caird and John Tulloch, professors of divinity and then principals of, respectively, Glasgow and St Andrews universities; R. H. Story, Caird's successor at Glasgow University; Norman MacLeod of Glasgow Barony church; and Robert Lee of Edinburgh Greyfriars' church.

The church's attraction for the solid middle class took two lines. Robert Lee led a movement to supersede the dreary, dry and formalistic order of traditional Presbyterian worship with a more colourful and uplifting ceremony. Stained glass windows, floral arrangements and wall paintings replaced whitewashed walls and plain windows. The Church Service Society, headed by Lee, was set up in 1865 with a view to modernising the order of service in the Scottish churches. Church music moved from the singing of psalms with no instrumental accompaniment to the use of organs and the introduction of hymns, with choirs leading the singing instead of a precentor holding the line for the congregation to follow. Thus, by 1845, the Springburn Church of Scotland congregation had just such a choir. All of this reached out to a middle-class audience who were becoming more culturally sophisticated and cosmopolitan in their taste for music, art and theatre. This period, after all, marks the rise of Scottish businessmen as serious art collectors. In a further sign of the softening of hallowed Calvinist practices, in 1873 a state church in Dundee held a Christmas service for the first time. The UPC and the Free Church were usually much slower to embrace these innovations.

The advances in scientific knowledge and scriptural analysis also benefited the established church. The impact of Darwinism was probably less cataclysmic for orthodox belief than in England; the discoveries of Hutton, Lyell and Chambers – all Scots – had already introduced Scottish opinion to the implications of geology, and Robert Chambers had made a particularly significant impact with *The Vestiges of Creation*, which appeared in 1844. The theological concepts of the Higher Criticism were absorbed quickly and sympathetically by Church of Scotland scholars, beginning in the 1860s, with Caird and Tulloch fully espousing these ideas in their teaching. The Free Church was divided in responding to the new currents. Its new leader, Robert Rainy, quite explicitly embraced evolutionary theory in his inaugural address as principal of the Free Church College in October 1874, and many Lowland adherents and clergy were comfortable with his standpoint. But the Highland portion of the church was implacably hostile to these modernising trends, and little formal advance was made. Indeed, the removal in 1881 of William Robertson Smith from a teaching post at Aberdeen Free Church College because he had advocated in print some Higher Criticism ideas showed how tortuous progress would be. The UPC, somewhat surprisingly, was the first of the three churches to acknowledge formally that parts of the Bible were not compatible with modern research when, in 1879, it officially modified the Westminster Confession by means of its Declaratory Act. It was not until 1892 that the Free Church followed suit in diluting the tenets of the Westminster Confession, and this precipitated a secession in the Highlands, with the formation of the Free Presbyterian Church.

The second sphere in which the Church of Scotland gained a significant advantage over its rivals was in recruiting working-class adherents in towns

> **The Higher Criticism**
>
> Until the middle of the nineteenth century, virtually all Scottish Presbyterians accepted unquestioningly the complete veracity of both the Old and New Testaments of the Bible. However, this approach was challenged, primarily by several German scholars, whose approach was termed the Higher (or Historical) Criticism. They contended that the Bible should be subjected to the same tests as any other historical document, such as who wrote the text, the exact dates of composition of the books, and the intentions of the authors. Close study of different literary phrases and formulations within the texts often indicated that several hands were involved. Thus, these scholars argued that the psalms were not all written by David, but were composed by various writers over many generations. The Pentateuch (the first five Old Testament books) was not written solely by Moses, and included pre- and post-Mosaic interpolations. The four Gospels were composed one or two centuries after Christ died, rather than by the named disciples, and the discrepancies between them reflected differing theological emphases in the early church. Other biblical passages were held to be either mistaken or improbable – for example, the account of the creation in Genesis, or the ages of many Old Testament patriarchs – while certain of the miracles ascribed to Christ mirrored similar accounts in other cultures.

and cities. A scholarly survey of a selection of congregations in Glasgow drawn from the three main Presbyterian denominations covering the two decades after the Disruption revealed that the working class constituted 61 per cent of the overall membership.[10] But this average cloaks a major discrepancy: while in the two non-established Presbyterian denominations, the working classes made up 54 per cent of the total, in the Church of Scotland, the figure was 79 per cent. Moreover, the state church proved more appealing to the less skilled sectors: 31 per cent of its working-class adherents were unskilled labourers, and 69 per cent skilled artisans. The figures for the UPC and the Free Church were 20 per cent unskilled and 80 per cent skilled. Similarly, in the small burgh of Kirkintilloch, the skilled workers comprised 75 per cent of the Free Church members, and the unskilled a mere 10 per cent. The main reason for this disparity was ironically what Chalmers had emphasised, namely, it was much less costly to be in the Church of Scotland than in a Free (or Voluntary) church. The Free Church was de facto as much a Voluntary church as the UPC, so for the less affluent members the demand for contributions was a perennial drag on their income. Moreover, the Church of Scotland was markedly less interested in conducting inquisitions into the moral conduct of its adherents than the Free Church, which continued to be vigilant against intemperance, fornication and non-observance of the Sabbath.

THE ABORTIVE FREE CHURCH MERGER WITH THE UNITED PRESBYTERIAN CHURCH, 1863-73

Lastly, the survival and growth of the established church after the difficulties of the 1840s was considerably aided by the conduct of its two Presbyterian rivals. As shown in Chapter 9, between 1843 and around 1860, the UPC and the Free Church were locked in controversy over a range of issues which essentially derived from their polar opposition on church establishment, rather than co-operating against the state church. The 1860s, however, initially suggested that the two non-established churches were changing tack to jointly threaten the Church of Scotland. In 1863, negotiations began to unite the UPC and the Free Church. This extraordinary shift in the stances of both – something akin in nineteenth-century ecclesiastical history to the Nazi–Soviet pact of 1939 – had enormous transforming potential. The bigger jolt was felt in the Free Church, as effectively it would have to abandon its fundamental founding principle. Going in with the Voluntaries meant that it no longer saw itself as a successor established church, but this was accepted by many, especially in the urban Lowland congregations, as a realistic appraisal of the current situation, namely, that the Church of Scotland, far from withering away, was growing at a faster pace than the Free Church. But the projected union would render the position of the state church untenable, since between 60 and 70 per cent of Presbyterians would be in the new merged church, and hence disestablishment would be virtually irresistible. Furthermore, the practical viability of a merger had been established in Australia, when the associated churches of both sects entered into a full union in 1861.

The outlines of an agreement were quite quickly settled between both sides, with the Free Church's acceptance of Voluntaryism confirmed at an early stage. But there soon arose an agitation within the Free Church against the scheme. One major component of opposition came from the Highland Free Churches, who refused to budge from the establishment principle propounded by the church at its inception. Embracing Voluntaryism was anathema to these adherents, and they were joined by a group of Lowland church members, the most prominent being the Rev. James Begg, a veteran of the 1843 crisis. The Constitutionalists, as they were called, were always a minority within the Free Church, but they were well-organised, vocal and utterly immovable in their position. The bulk of the Free Church concluded that, although in favour of union, it could not permit the threatened secession of the Constitutionalist wing, as the loss of the mass of Highland-based adherents was not acceptable, and would impact adversely on their church's relative strength within the union body, putting it in a subordinate role to the Voluntaries, who were virtually unanimous in accepting a merger. The threat of legal action by the Constitutionalists, who suddenly, despite the Claim of Right, found the secular courts indispensable, hastened the abandonment of the merger talks. Although it was recognised by the later 1860s that the scheme was not achievable, it was not until 1873 that the Free Church formally signalled the collapse of the union project.

The failure of the union talks marked a decisive turning point in nineteenth-century Scottish church history, almost on a par with the Disruption itself. The demographic challenge to the Church of Scotland had now lapsed. The UPC and the Free Church promptly turned to seek a political end to the state church by deciding to lobby the Liberal party to legislate for disestablishment. But it was always likely that the success of this route would be difficult, as is explored fully below.[11] Further, while the UPC and the Free Church had been preoccupied for ten years with the negotiations, as we have seen, the Church of Scotland availed itself of this breathing space to consolidate its bases of support and expand its membership more successfully than its two challengers, and this process continued for the rest of the century. The Free Church can be regarded as having made a strategic blunder in appeasing the Constitutionalist faction. Rainy's biographer observed that

> From the date of this controversy, the Free Church was different from what it was before, and had 'parties' in it as it never had before, and the problem of its guidance, which was the problem of Professor Rainy's career, became one of peculiar difficulties and embarrassments.[12]

The gap between the urban Lowland majority, essentially quite liberal and open to change in doctrine and practice, and the Highlands, still rigid in rejecting any whiff of revisionism and modernisation, could never be bridged. But by letting this gulf continue for another quarter-of-a-century, the church undoubtedly lost momentum in the Lowlands. Eventually, in 1900 the bulk of the Free Church did join with the United Presbyterians to create the United Free Church (UFC), while the Highland Free Churches remained outside, to be known as the 'Wee Frees'. But the 1900 union was essentially defensive, forged in the face of a still rising Church of Scotland, whereas the aborted union of the 1860s would have been an offensive union. Soon after the UFC was formed, a merger with the Church of Scotland was widely acknowledged as inevitable, and in 1929 the UFC joined the established church – which both of the former's component parts originally had been formed to overcome.

THE CHALLENGE OF THE 'LAPSED MASSES'

The main Presbyterian churches devoted much effort to winning over the churchless – or, as they were sometimes described, 'the lapsed masses'. One reason was that a natural feature of evangelicalism was to convert individuals to

Christianity. This need for this function was heightened by the clear evidence by the 1820s that many, especially in towns, had no connection with organised religion; in Chalmers's newly created Glasgow parish of St John's, in 1823, 30 per cent of households had no attachment to any church, and another third were at best occasional churchgoers. The 1851 religious census, however imperfect, confirmed that across Scotland, non-attendance was rife, especially in urban settings. Scant comfort was derived from the disclosure that levels of attendance were higher than in England; instead the urgency of addressing the situation within Scotland was emphasised. Added impetus was derived from the struggle, greatly enhanced after 1843, between the sects to achieve the greatest numerical support.

The range of devices deployed to try to reach unbelievers was considerable and changed with time and experience. The earliest home mission efforts distributed bibles to the populace, but it soon became apparent that a lack of spare time, together with low literacy levels, meant that no serious breakthroughs were being made. In the 1820s and 1830s, there was a vogue for visits to homes by committed lay persons, such as elders and deacons, with the aim of offering detailed support and guidance. The model for this was Chalmers's St John's scheme, which sought to replicate the intimate personal relationships which were felt to exist in small rural parishes. This approach did not yield convincing rewards: households in St John's with no sittings in any Presbyterian church rose from 39 per cent in 1819 to 41 per cent in 1836.[13]

Many town churches instead opted to establish 'mission churches' in working-class parts of their parish. The main argument for this approach were that poorer people could not afford the system of pew-renting which fully blown churches, especially the non-established ones, operated. But by the final third of the century, mission churches were perceived to be struggling. One crucial factor was that the middle-class flight to the suburbs left churches in both the town centre and in working-class areas under-populated and under-funded. Most of the new churches built from the 1860s were erected in the outskirts of towns, with the result that links with those left behind by the bourgeois exodus were seriously attenuated.

A variety of focused missionary bodies were also set up to reach sectors of the irreligious, such as seamen, cabdrivers and even the police. Broader approaches were epitomised by the Glasgow City Mission, but these all achieved at best only fitful success. Part of the problem lay with organisational defects. The Glasgow City Mission used divinity students, who usually only served for one or two years, so there was no continuity of commitment, and most of these men were from middle-class backgrounds, with little knowledge of working-class attitudes. But also, as mission workers frequently commented, there was also a distinctly instrumental response evinced by the recipients of mission efforts, as material benefits – especially food and clothing – were accepted, but concrete religious conversions were less forthcoming.

In light of the evident deficiencies of these approaches based on individual conversion, a different strategy was elaborated from mid-century. This new departure instead sought to create a more favourable environment in which the Evangelical message would attract a more positive response. The barriers to conversion were now identified not so much as personal failings, and more as structural social factors. Poor standards of educational attainment, inadequate housing and high levels of intemperance were among the problems highlighted as demanding drastic action. For many in this camp, as examined in Chapter 10, involvement in political action was viewed as necessary in order to address these obstacles efficaciously.

While most avenues of domestic missionary endeavour had at best patchy success, the Sunday school movement succeeded in reaching many children. In 1819 the Sabbath School Union of Scotland was formed, with the twin aims of educating the many children who did not attend day schools, and of instilling religious values in the young which would promote their social assimilation. The movement grew steadily, but exceptionally rapid progress was made between 1851 and 1881, when the number of registered children rose from 240,000 to 430,000, and it has been estimated that by 1891 almost 50 per cent of all Protestant children were enrolled.[14] Individual Presbyterian churches, especially in cities, were involved to an intense degree in providing Sunday schools. In Dundee in 1845, the newly formed Free Churches had set up some 50 schools, with 2,051 pupils and 123 teachers.

While the scale of the operation is impressive, it is questionable how far the Sunday schools fulfilled their declared objective. Irregular attendance was common; the standard of instruction was highly variable, as many teachers were young adults who often lacked the requisite pedagogic skills, and found maintaining interest and discipline a perennial problem. Moreover, there was a high turnover of teachers, so that an essential continuity of contact was hard to sustain. In addition, some have suggested that increasingly from the 1860s, the social class of children at Sunday school shifted from being mainly working class to middle class.[15] The decline in child labour, as well as the impact of the 1872 Education Act, reduced the educational role of Sunday schools. In a wider framework, the direct benefits to the churches in terms of winning new members was often viewed as very limited. One commentator observed in the mid-1890s that few former Sunday school attendees actually became practising Christians in adulthood.[16]

Despite these strenuous efforts, by 1881, the landscape of religious attachment had not appreciably improved. An unofficial census showed that church attendance had, if anything, fallen. In a Glasgow east end parish, only 8.1 per cent of the 5,000 adult working-class inhabitants were members of the area's two Presbyterian churches. Elsewhere in the social scale, too, a dwindling of commitment could be detected. The most prestigious Free Church in Aberdeen encountered great difficulties in inducing members to act as elders in 1889. The congregation of the West Free Church elected ten of their members to serve as elders, but they all declined to take office, and it was only after personal appeals by the minister that five relented and were inducted.

Nevertheless, although the tangible dividends of home missionary efforts were disappointing, the broader long-term influence of Presbyterianism on Scottish society was important. For instance, the great majority of the pre-1914 pioneers of the Labour party in Scotland – not least Keir Hardie – saw socialism as applied Christianity, and they revered the seventeenth-century Covenanters as forerunners in the struggle for reform. The deliberations of church bodies in all three denominations were as fully reported in the local press as burgh council meetings. The persistence of virtually total Sabbatarianism in all spheres of public life testified to the churches' impact on the national mindset. Although the New Poor Law formally terminated church responsibility for poor relief, in practice Presbyterian clergymen and committed lay adherents continued to play a leading role in the new framework, especially in rural parishes. The school board election results from 1873 onwards provided another pointer to the pervasive acceptance of Presbyterian values extending beyond those formally attached to a church. In most constituencies, the 'Use and Wont' candidates – who advocated the retention of the Presbyterian practice of using the Bible and the Shorter Catechism as the means of instructing schoolchildren to read and write – emerged as the largest grouping. This occurred not just in rural areas and douce country towns, but also in large towns, such as Glasgow, where barely one-fifth of the population attended church. The school board electorate included very many who were excluded from the parliamentary and municipal franchises; that is, they were among the poorest. In this context, it is not surprising that so much of Scottish politics revolved around religious questions, as is fully examined in Chapters 9 and 10.

THE PRESBYTERIAN CHURCHES' STANCE ON SOCIAL QUESTIONS AND ON THE ROLE OF WOMEN

It is noteworthy how little overt social criticism emanated from the Presbyterian churches across this period. The conditions in textile factories rarely elicited critical comments from the clergy compiling the *New Statistical Account* reports – mostly written at the height of the factory reform campaign of the

1830s – and where remarks on the use of child labour in mills were given, they were as often as not positive. At the same time, Scottish coal mines employed appreciably more women and young children of both sexes than most parts of England, but few clergymen either knew this or else felt it worthy of comment. Apart from the erratic Patrick Brewster of Paisley Abbey, Chartism gained little support from mainstream Presbyterian ministers, although it had a heavy religious content, as indicated by the number of Chartist churches.[17] James Begg was pretty much a lone voice inveighing against housing conditions, although even he seemed more preoccupied with rural than urban squalor. In the debate on poverty and health, the Presbyterian churches effectively rejected the opinion of doctors like W. P. Alison, who argued that destitution was a main cause of epidemics, so poor relief levels should higher. Instead, churchmen ascribed such problems to personal inadequacy.

In great part, the impress of Thomas Chalmers must have shaped the views of his fellow ministers. A fervent exponent of laissez-faire, Chalmers's vigorous opposition to any support for able-bodied unemployed, and his insistence that voluntary contributions to aid the 'deserving poor' were preferable to compulsory assessment, coloured Scottish Poor Law policy for the entire century.[18] Nevertheless, it is striking that Scotland had no parallel to the doughty Anglican clerics who opposed the New Poor Law and lobbied for the restriction of hours of work in factories in the 1830s. It was not until the end of the 1880s – at the earliest – that some Presbyterian churchmen began to display any interest in domestic social problems, and even then, as critics suggested, it may have been stimulated as much by the rise in support for socialism among the working class as by a fresh appraisal of radical social messages contained in the New Testament.

A somewhat similar reluctance to move from traditional standpoints is revealed in the Presbyterian churches' attitude to women. Calvinism apparently decreed that women were spiritually equal to men, but practice suggested this principle was more honoured in the breach than the observance. In mid-nineteenth-century Glasgow, women formed two-thirds of the membership of the Free Church and three-fifths of the Church of Scotland, but their role and influence was not even in inverse proportion to their presence, and the universal assumption was that they would be subordinate to men. Their primary duty was to foster the religious transformation of society by concentrating on their domestic responsibility to instruct their children in moral conduct, and any involvement in the public sphere would be subordinate to this. And when churchgoing women did engage in public life, it was expected that their interest would be an extension of their domestic role; hence many became Sunday school teachers – in the 1870s, 63 of the 111 such teachers at Glasgow Cathedral (Church of Scotland) were female. They tended to be active in campaigns which were pre-eminently moral, rather than political or economic. Temperance was a major field, as excessive drinking was presented as a male problem which impacted severely on women and their children and undermined the mother's role as a home-maker and a moral guardian of the family. Many women were heavily committed to the charitable societies founded by the Presbyterian churches and mostly worked as fund-raisers, although from mid-century they acted as home mission visitors, as the feminine touch was judged likely to elicit a sympathetic response on the doorstep. A substantial share of the active rank-and-file members in charitable bodies was frequently women, but the key office-holders were invariably male. Women had an infinitesimal share in church governance. Until the Disruption, the United Secession Church was the only sect to allow women communicants a vote, but soon after 1843, this privilege was conceded by both the Established and Free Churches. However, even after this, there were very few admitted to church committees and boards – the presence in the later 1870s of two women on the building committee of an east end Glasgow UPC was highly unusual.

NOTES

1. Decisions passed at General Assemblies were termed 'acts'.
2. W. Hanna, *Memoirs of the Life and Writings of Thomas Chalmers* (1849–52), Vol. IV, App. C, 544.
3. Ibid., 548 (caps in original).
4. NRS, Dalhousie MSS, GD45/14/640, Melbourne to F. Maule, 28 October 1840.
5. See p. 246 for a detailed account of this episode.
6. A. A. MacLaren, *Religion and Social Class: The Disruption Years in Aberdeen* (1974), 145–51, 162.
7. Ibid., 30–46; D. J. Withrington, 'The 1851 Census of Religious Worship and Education', *RSCHS*, 18 (1972–4), 133–42.
8. The United Presbyterian Church was formed in 1847 by a merger of the Relief and the United Secession Churches, the two main Voluntary bodies.
9. R. Howie, *The Churches and the Churchless in Scotland* (1893), xvi.
10. P. Hillis, 'Presbyterianism and Social Class in Mid-Nineteenth Century Glasgow: A Study of Nine Churches', *Journal of Ecclesiastical History*, 32 (1981), 47–64; see also Hillis, 'Working-Class Membership of the Presbyterian Churches of Scotland, 1840–80', *SLHJ*, 33 (1998), 31–50.
11. See pp. 283–6.
12. P. C. Simpson, *The Life of Principal Rainy* (1909), Vol. I, 149 (inverted commas in original).
13. See pp. 117–18.
14. C. G. Brown, 'The Sunday School Movement in Scotland, 1780–1914', *RSCHS*, 21 (1981–3), 3–26.

15. Ibid.; P. Hillis, 'Education and Evangelisation: Presbyterian Missions in Mid-Nineteenth Century Glasgow', *SHR*, 66 (1987), 46–62.
16. Howie, *Churches and the Churchless*, xxvi.
17. See p. 263.
18. See pp. 116–18.

CHAPTER 6

Assimilation and Acculturation

NATIONAL IDENTITY: EDUCATION AND PRESBYTERIANISM

At the outset of the period, many Scots probably regarded their national identity as being shaped by two interlinked influences, which were markedly different from the other component countries in Britain. The first was Presbyterianism, which almost the whole population subscribed to, notwithstanding its division into numerous sects. The doctrine and practice of this severe form of Protestantism was held to have stamped its brand on the national character, with positive outcomes. The Scots saw themselves as hard-working, sober in dress and demeanour, socially disciplined and generally law-abiding, virtues which were highlighted in many of the parish reports contained in the original *Statistical Account*, written by parish ministers in the mid-1790s. To some degree, there was in this rose-tinted vision an implicit contrast with England, many of whose inhabitants were depicted – not least by other English people – as prone to riot, public disorder, debauchery and criminality.

The second was the educational system, which had several distinctive features. By an act of 1696, every parish had to have a school, whose costs – which included the teacher's salary and his schoolhouse – were met by the heritors and parishioners, while in burghs, the town council was responsible for providing and financially maintaining a school. England, until the 1820s, had two universities, which were socially highly exclusive, whereas Scotland had five – until 1860, when King's and Marischal colleges merged to form the University of Aberdeen. Moreover, the intake to all the Scottish universities was open to all (male) students of ability, almost all progressing from the parochial and burgh schools.

A major reason for the original provision of universal schooling derived from the belief among the early Scottish Presbyterians that a literate laity would hold their clergy to strict adherence to biblical texts, since what was deemed the errors of Catholicism supposedly arose because the congregation could not read. Under the influence of the Enlightenment, the virtues of the education system were broadened into wider social benefits. The mixing of children from different backgrounds promoted social harmony, and an educated populace would be more likely to resist the superficial lure of radical doctrines. The opportunities offered by the system for upward social mobility for any boy with suitable abilities tended to enhance social stability, as a feeling of grievance against a hidebound caste structure was not sustainable. In addition, access to higher education based not on status but on ability would broaden the intellectual capacity of the country, thereby greatly enhancing the prospects for economic transformation and the extension of civilised values.

Girls' schooling before 1872

The Scottish Enlightenment provided a core reason for teaching girls, namely that it would produce intelligent wives and mothers, who would train their offspring in sound moral principles, thereby contributing to social harmony and advancement. This high-minded argument, however, ran up against two countervailing influences: firstly, the stark economic circumstances of low wages and fluctuating income levels; and secondly, the growing utilitarian approach advocated by those — frequently evangelical moralists — concerned about working-class living standards. This complex blend of motives resulted in educational provisional for girls in Scotland being far in advance of England.

In 1834, the total number of girls attending school was 70 per cent of the figure for boys, and on the eve of the 1872 Education Act, it had risen to 95 per cent. Moreover, until the last decade or so, children were mostly not taught in segregated classes — or schools. As a result, a fair number of girls learned subjects widely regarded in England as suitable to be studied exclusively by boys. So, proportionally, in 1850, twenty times more Scottish than English girls were learning Latin, and ten times more studied modern languages. Between 1851 and 1875, the percentage of girls studying Latin grew from 5.3 to 14 per cent; for mathematics, the respective figures were 4.1 and 9.6 per cent; and for modern languages, 37.7 and 49.9 per cent. But by the 1840s, there was a growing emphasis on instructing working-class girls in housework, in the expectation that cleaner, better-run homes would raise health standards and encourage men to remain at home rather than go out to pubs. Female Industrial Schools spread from around 1850 in towns, with a heavy focus on domestic training, so that by 1872, two-thirds of girls were being taught sewing.

For many working-class girls, education was restricted by various factors, such as being withdrawn from schooling to look after younger siblings if both parents worked. Others were put to work to eke out the household income, often when they were eight or nine years old. Elsewhere, cultural influences – as, apparently, in the Highlands – decreed that girls should be removed from school once they had acquired the most basic literacy skills, i.e. reading, but not writing. Moreover, in remoter areas, the provision of schools was quite inadequate. In sum, for many girls, schooling was over by the age of eight or nine.

Middle-class girls had much better educational opportunities. Many went to parochial and burgh schools, but a feature of the Victorian era was the growth of private institutions, of which the Young Ladies' Institutes were arguably the most significant. The first of these was founded in Edinburgh in 1830, followed by Glasgow in 1840 and Aberdeen in 1860. These schools offered a full, well-organised academic curriculum, covering subjects like science, history and German, and employing specialist teachers to give instruction in each discipline. So, while schooling for working-class girls had shifted from high Enlightenment ends to more pragmatic, utilitarian objectives, for the middle-class students, training to contribute to the enrichment of civil society remained the over-riding goal. By the 1870s, the latter were participating in higher education classes provided by the four universities.

Figure 6.1 A Premonstratensian priest with schoolchildren, Whithorn, c. 1890. © Whithorn Photographic Group. Licensor: www.scran.ac.uk

The education system fostered a powerful Scottish stereotype, namely the lad o' pairts. This concept articulated that a student could advance through the various levels of instruction as far as his intelligence would carry him, without any restraints, such as financial costs. Most parish schoolmasters had attended university and were thus able to give some instruction to promising children in key university subjects. There was no formal university entrance test, and the costs of attending university were, certainly compared to England, very low. Course fees were not much higher than burgh school fees, and accommodation was not in expensive college halls of residence, but in lodgings. It was estimated that the annual cost of studying at Glasgow University in the middle of the nineteenth century could be as little as £20.[1] Moreover, financial assistance at all universities was available through bursaries which had mostly been bequeathed by grateful former students; at Aberdeen there were enough to cover about one-third of the student population. The upshot was that, in 1880, the proportion of men attending university in Scotland was six times greater than in England.

Several careful studies of the social origins of Scottish students at various points across the time span covered here indicate that the majority came from middle-class or working-class families.[2] This, of course, is radically at variance with the composition of Oxford and Cambridge undergraduates, who were predominantly upper class: in 1839, 67 per cent of Cambridge students came from the landowning and kindred classes, while 61 per cent of Glasgow students were drawn from the business and tenant-farming classes. Instances of men from lowly origins abound. David Livingstone, a weaver's son, went to Glasgow University. Among those achieving academic excellence was Alexander Murray, a former shepherd boy, who became professor of Hebrew at Edinburgh.

From these two forging factors, an interpretation emerged that the Reformation and the rise of Presbyterianism bestowed religious liberty on the Scots by replacing the authoritarian Catholic regime with one in which power was largely devolved to local parishes. Hence, John Knox and other Scottish Reformers were often invoked as fighters for freedom from state tyranny, because of their conflicts with Stuart monarchs over the structure and governance of the national church. This perspective was vividly illustrated at the first mass political meeting of working people after the Napoleonic Wars, which took place at Thrushgrove, just outside Glasgow, in 1816. One of the leading speakers at this great reform rally hailed Knox and George Buchanan, as key figures in the struggle for liberty in Scotland. At the same time, the national education framework served to mould the Scots into a knowledgeable, literate people, ensuring both national and individual progress in economic and social affairs. But increasingly, the confidence reposed in this depiction of national identity became less assured.

THE ENLIGHTENMENT'S REVISIONIST CRITIQUE OF NATIONAL IDENTITY

Prominent figures in the Scottish Enlightenment offered a distinctly divergent analysis of the evolution of Scotland towards modernity. In this interpretation, the crucial turning point for the establishment of freedom and economic development was not the Reformation and its heroic figures. Rather, it was the wide-ranging impact of the Union of 1707 which provided the catalyst, because pre-Union Scotland was backward in terms of both its economic situation and its intellectual standing. Some Enlightenment writers, particularly William Robertson – himself the most prominent Moderate minister of his generation – and John Millar, opted to stress the negative influence of Presbyterianism on Scotland, rather than to praise its positive contribution. Instead, the importance of 1707 was, firstly, that it swept away the archaic power of the feudal nobility, which had long inhibited cultural and social growth in Scotland. Secondly, it provided long-term stable government for Scotland and ensured that the threat of a Stuart seizure of the throne would not come to fruition. Thirdly, Scots were able to study at close quarters the example of England as an advanced economic and social nation, and then to apply back home the lessons learned. The Union thus opened the door for Scottish landowners to reform their estates' agricultural practices, and later allowed manufacturers to benefit from English expertise, as at Carron and in cotton manufacture.

The contribution of the Union to Scottish liberty was given added resonance by the guarantee which was enshrined in it that the principles of the Revolution settlement of 1688–9 would be permanent and would enhance personal freedom in Scotland. The diffusion of these concepts was also witnessed elsewhere in religious affairs. Many Presbyterian Seceders were so grateful for the toleration and religious freedoms that they enjoyed under the Revolution-Union settlement that they were vehemently hostile to the Jacobite rising of 1745–6, fearing the return of the Stuarts. For the same reasons, in 1788, members of the Secession churches publicly celebrated the centenary of the Revolution. It is also noteworthy that the grounds most frequently used by nineteenth-century Evangelicals to attack patronage in the Church of Scotland were not derived from seventeenth-century theology. Instead, they deployed arguments heavily influenced by the Enlightenment, namely, that patronage was a gross infringement of the freedom and natural rights of citizens.

The Enlightenment critique, however, ramified more widely and deeply than approval of the Union. The high regard in which the literati held England led to an analysis which emphasised that Scotland was divided into two peoples, with those in the Lowlands much closer in culture and character to the English than to Highlanders. This interpretation contended that both Lowlanders and English people were Teutonic in origin, not Celtic, for the ancestors of the

Lowland Scots were the Picts. This shared Teutonic identity had been crucial in making the Union work smoothly and successfully, and heroic individuals from the past and present were wheeled out as evidence of the pedigree of Teutonism in Scotland. Wallace and Bruce, Knox and Buchanan all met the criteria, and among more recent figures, Burns was particularly singled out for membership of the pantheon.

THE ASSIMILATION OF GAELIC SOCIETY INTO SCOTLAND: MIGRATION AND MILITARISATION

The Teutonist theory served as a springboard for drawing further distinctions between Highlanders and Lowlanders which were widely held until the middle years of the nineteenth century. Its impact was reinforced by developments in both science, such as evolution, and pseudo-science, for example, phrenology, and hardened into an almost racist doctrine. Enlightenment thinking was preoccupied with the concept of stages of social and economic development, and in this schema, England was evidently at the highest level, to which Lowland Scotland was steadily advancing because of its agricultural reforms and the initiation of commercial and manufacturing activity. The Highlands, however, remained languishing at a lower, essentially undeveloped, phase, which of course tended to confirm the Teutonist categorisations. Many Lowlanders considered Highlanders to be little more than savages; for instance, Patrick Sellar dismissed the Sutherland peasantry as akin to native Americans, and the Highlanders' role in the Jacobite risings left the impression that they were innately opposed to the Scottish modernisation project. A large preponderance of travellers from the south remarked critically on the abject poverty and squalid living conditions which seemed to prevail across the Highland region.[3] If the Gaels were to be raised from their backward condition, they would have to abandon their cultural distinctiveness and embrace the values of their southern neighbours. In essence, the Gaelic language should be suppressed, and the inhabitants should receive education in order to learn English, which would open the world of improvement to them, permitting them to evolve to a higher plane of development. In consequence, up until the 1840s, the reaction of many 'Teutonic' Scots to the processes of eviction and removal in the Highlands was not particularly hostile. Clearances were not widely covered in the press, the churches were generally reticent about evictions and many heirs of the Enlightenment were in the van of Highland estate improvers: for instance, Patrick Sellar and James Loch, who subsequently wrote the earliest and most extensive apologia for the Sutherland Clearances.[4]

This negative image of Highlanders went into steep decline from the 1840s, and the somewhat racist critique was largely abandoned, with a great deal of empathy replacing previous derogatory opinions. There were several reasons for this. The depiction of the Highlanders as uncivilised and dangerous was largely undermined by their role in the Disruption of 1843. The area in Scotland which gave the most solid support to the Free Church was the Highlands and the difficulties encountered by these seceding congregations in trying to find buildings for worship had a profound impact on their Lowland co-religionists. This reappraisal was strengthened by the concurrent Highland Famine, when Free Churches in the Lowlands organised very successful fundraising efforts. The fortitude and dignity shown during these crises by ordinary Highlanders did much to disperse previous perceptions of barbarism.

These shifts in perspective were deepened by the greater interest taken by sectors of the press in local clearances, which developed from the 1840s. The *Witness* and the *North British Daily Mail*, published in, respectively, Edinburgh and Glasgow, carried many articles criticising evictions, while in the 1850s, the *Inverness Advertiser* and the Wick-based *Northern Ensign* repeatedly printed polemics denouncing the removals of Highlanders. A highly significant indicator of shifting opinion occurred towards the end of the 1840s, when J. Hill Burton, one of the pillars of the second generation of Whig Edinburgh Reviewers, wrote a piece for the *Edinburgh Review* which roundly denounced a recent wave of evictions.[5] Wider public opinion adjusted its standpoint under the influence of Queen Victoria's enthusiastic encomia about the region. She waxed lyrical about the landscape, which was not especially novel, but her admiration for the Highland people and their customs profoundly recalibrated attitudes. Her acquisition of the Balmoral estate, and the subsequent outbreak of rampant tartanry throughout the castle, created a wholly positive picture to the outside world.

The movement of displaced Highlanders to Lowland urban centres made a major contribution to the homogenisation of Scottish society. There had been migration from the Gaeltacht to towns from at least the middle of the eighteenth century, but the numbers grew markedly after 1820. However, the impact of Highland immigrants on the overall demography of Lowland towns was not substantial, certainly compared to that created by Irish settlers. In 1851, 11 per cent of Greenock's population was Highland-born, easily the highest share of any town, followed by Perth, with just over 5 per cent. In no other Lowland burgh did the presence of Highlanders reach 5 per cent. In the main, these immigrants merged relatively easily into the host community; in almost all places, there were no areas with a heavy concentration of Highlanders. Unlike the Irish arrivals in towns, they were not primarily confined to poorly paid, unskilled occupations, and while a fair number did indeed conform to stereotype and serve as policemen, most worked in skilled craft occupations. There was also a solid core of middle-class Highlanders, frequently merchants and shopkeepers, as well as a smattering of professionals, particularly clergymen.

As ever, a useful indicator of integration is marriage patterns, and it is evident that in places like Greenock, there was a high volume of marriages outwith the Highland community, certainly compared to Irish Catholic immigrants.

Integration was promoted by three salient factors. Firstly, many of the immigrants came from Highland areas quite near to the Lowland towns which they settled in. Glasgow and Greenock attracted primarily people from Argyllshire, while Perth recruited from the Highland parts of that county and also from south-east Inverness-shire. Movement from further north and west was less prevalent until the final years of the period. Thus, the transition experienced in coming to the Lowlands was less of a total culture shock than for those from far-flung parts. Secondly, as discussed earlier, many had experienced a degree of acculturation to Lowland society because of temporary migration by large numbers of Highlanders to towns and cities in the nineteenth century.[6] These people acquired an awareness of the practicalities of city living before deciding to settle permanently in such places. Thirdly, following on from these previous points, they had at least a smattering of English before moving. In the Lowlands, the general pattern was for Gaelic-speakers to follow the precepts of the Teutonists and abandon the language in favour of English in order to advance in Lowland society, as Gaelic was regarded by ambitious Highlanders as the language of the poorer working class. The numbers attending Gaelic chapels were a small proportion of the Highlanders resident in a town: for example, no more than 20 per cent in Perth in the 1850s and 1860s. Services were held in Gaelic for the less well-off, but were in English for the middle class, and the purpose of these churches was not to preserve Celtic culture, but rather to promote moral improvement and to introduce civilising practices. Indeed, over two generations, the language was largely lost, as most children of urban Gaelic-speaking parents spoke only English, which of course was the language used in the schools.

The most important means, however, by which the image of Highlanders was transformed positively was their role in the British army. Although there were Highland regiments from the middle years of the eighteenth century, the wars with France from 1793 to 1815 greatly enhanced their visibility among their fellow countrymen. We have already seen that recruitment from the region to the armed forces was at a much higher level than in any other part of Britain, and regiments were raised by Highland landowners, such as Lord Breadalbane and the duke of Atholl.[7] Their valorous conduct during these wars confirmed that Highlanders were completely loyal to the Hanoverian dynasty and all lingering suspicion of covert Jacobite sympathies were discarded. The prestige of the Highland regiments continued to rise during the nineteenth century, especially after their central roles at the Battle of Balaclava in 1854 and in the Siege of Lucknow in 1857. The use of Highland dress uniform for army units became very popular, and from a mere two kilted regiments in the middle of the eighteenth century, there were twelve in 1856. Thus, the garb which had been proscribed for much of the eighteenth century had become honoured as the national costume of Scotland by the high Victorian age.

The Highland army units contributed in another way to the appreciation and acceptance of Highlanders by the rest of Scotland. From the very start of the nineteenth century, these regiments encountered severe and persistent problems in recruiting Highlanders in sufficient numbers, partly of course because of the loss of population in the region resulting from clearances. The gap in manpower was met by men from the Lowlands, England and Ireland. In 1798, only 51 per cent of the 42nd Battalion were Highlanders, but by 1824, it had fallen to 32 per cent. In 1851, three-quarters of Scots enlisting in the army came from Lowland towns and cities. This intermingling of men from varied regions did much to create a sense of national unity among Scots.

This heightened appreciation of the positive qualities of Highlanders led to a pronounced shift away from the earlier opinion that Gaelic culture and lifestyle were barbaric and should be suppressed. The drive to build up the Highland military presence did much to preserve and promote traditional practices, beginning with the withdrawal of the ban on wearing the kilt in 1782 and the restoration of the Forfeited Estates in 1784 to a number of their original Jacobite owners. Highland Games were also reintroduced in 1782, and spread very widely after 1815, starting with St Fillans in 1819. Another reinvigorated tradition was piping, which received a huge boost from its central role in the Highland regiments. A notable feature of the growth of both Highland games and pipe bands was that they were taken up enthusiastically across the Lowlands. As early as 1845, the small Hillfoots textile town of Alva inaugurated its Highland games, and in many mining villages pipe bands became as popular as brass bands.

Beyond the level of popular interest in these Highland cultural features, a major factor in the rehabilitation of Celtic Scotland came from learned academics. Three of the most eminent English historians of the era, namely, Sir Henry Maine, F. W. Maitland and Sir Frederick Pollock, lauded the medieval Celtic social system for its many virtues, which they identified as loyalty, industriousness and the absence of any concept of private property. Equally influential were the studies by German scholars of folklore, anthropology and linguistics, which stressed the major contribution made by Celtic to the development of the Indo-European languages. Thus, by the 1870s there was a greater sense of self-confidence about Gaelic language and culture. The Gaelic Society of Inverness, set up in 1871, provided a forum for celebrating the literary and cultural achievements of Gaels and also acted as a lobby for the advancement of the language, a trend reinforced by the *Celtic Magazine*, founded in 1876 to promote the study of Gaelic civilisation. An Islay man, John Murdoch, founded the *Highlander* in 1873, which immediately became the vehicle for championing all aspects of the Highland way of life. In the urban Lowlands, Highland immigrants organised associations to advocate the Gaelic cause. The Glasgow Celtic Society was launched in 1857, and bodies like the Glasgow Skye Association (1865) celebrated the songs and customs of their locality. The formation of the Federation of Celtic Societies in 1878 represented a further step forward in the mobilisation of the pro-Gaelic lobby. The ultimate acknowledgement of the restoration of Gaelic as a central thread in the tapestry of Scottish culture was the establishment in 1882 of a chair of Celtic at Edinburgh University. This was the culmination of a protracted campaign spearheaded by J. S. Blackie, the university's professor of Greek, and it meant that Gaelic was now to be treated on an academic par with all other non-English languages, ancient and modern.

SCOTLAND AND BRITISH IDENTITY

The integration of the Highlands into the broader Lowland Scottish society was matched by the assimilation of both into a wider sense of a British identity. In part, of course, this followed from the appreciation which most Scots felt for the perceived benefits flowing from the Treaty of Union, yet various episodes contributed to a generalised anti-Scottish animus entertained by many English people for much of the eighteenth century. The causes of these hostile sentiments included the two main Jacobite irruptions, and climaxed in the early 1760s, when opposition to the appointment of Lord Bute as prime minister by the young George III was whipped up by John Wilkes into public disorder and extreme Scotophobia. It appears that only the French were more despised than Scots. However, a permanent readjustment in the English appraisal of the loyalty of Scots began with the American Revolution. Most of the colonists with Scottish origins declared their continuing attachment to Britain during the war, and many migrated north to Canada. The stance taken by the Scots colonists was widely contrasted with that of the Irish, who predominantly sided with the rebels from the outset.

In Scotland itself, there was general disapproval of the American revolt, resulting in a determination to manifest an explicit endorsement of British Whiggish and Protestant values. In 1776, David Hume and Adam Fergusson switched their position away from their previous criticism of the British government's handling of the colonists' demands. They now declared that it was vital to retain the integrity of Britain and its empire, hence it was the duty of citizens to support the government, since the British constitution was the finest system. This line of argument was also pursued by the Moderates in the Church of Scotland, and the General Assembly sent a loyal address every year throughout the war. More concretely, Scots enlisted in very high numbers compared to elsewhere; in Ross-shire alone, 4,000 men enrolled in the army and a further 1,000 joined the navy, while Glasgow citizens subscribed heavily to fund the raising of regiments. This contrasted with what was deemed a lack of vigorous participation in England, so the Scots presented themselves as the protectors of British rights. This display of support for the Hanoverian state was more than matched by the reaction to the French wars and the threat of invasion in the succeeding decade. As is discussed more fully below, loyalism in Scotland was exceptionally strong among all ranks of society.[8]

The expression of this commitment to Britishness was most clearly seen in two interwoven strands, namely, military participation and imperial involvement. During the two decades of war with France, Scots contributed considerably more of the armed forces' manpower than their share of the British population. Thus, 17 per cent of army personnel in the Napoleonic Wars were Scots, who also made up 36 per cent of those enrolling in the Volunteers in 1797. Overall, between 1773 and 1830, the presence of Scots in the army grew from 8.5 to 13.5 per cent of all serving soldiers. The impact of this increase in numbers of Scots in the armed forces was deepened by the leading role occupied by several Scottish-born commanders in key engagements in the wars. Admiral Duncan crowned his career in charge of the North Sea squadron with a masterly victory over the Dutch fleet in 1797 at the Battle of Camperdown, while the death of Sir John Moore at the Siege of Corunna in 1809 was commemorated in perhaps the most celebrated poem about these wars, namely, Charles Wolfe's 'The Burial of Sir John Moore'.

EMPIRE AND SCOTTISH IDENTITY

Much of the prowess of the armed forces in the nineteenth century was devoted to protecting and expanding the British Empire, and so inevitably Scots were deeply involved in many imperial operations, notably on the Indian subcontinent. In the later eighteenth century, fully one-third of the officer corps in the East India Company's army were Scots. But the part taken by Scots in fostering the development of the empire percolated into much wider spheres than the military, and indeed at times it appeared as if the imperial project was spearheaded by them. As noted earlier,[9] the burgeoning Scottish economy was disproportionately dependent on foreign markets, and while Europe and the United States were important outlets, the links with colonies were crucial. In terms of supply of raw materials, India was vital for cotton, jute and tea, while Canada supplied timber and potash. Exports, for instance, textiles, railway engines, bridges, coal and iron, were dispatched to almost every part of the empire. Furthermore, shipbuilding and heavy engineering were intimately tied in with the fortunes of shipping lines, and many Scottish ship-owners specialised in trade with British dominions and colonies. Scottish overseas investment was substantially directed towards the empire, and the United States was the only other country which received a significant inflow of capital. The North British Australian Company, formed in 1839 and funded by Aberdeen-based investors, was one of the first British financial enterprises in that country.

Missionary work was a major focus for Scottish endeavour in the empire, both formal and informal. Such activity grew markedly from the 1810s onwards, for several reasons. Firstly, in 1813, the East India Company permitted Christian missionaries to work without hindrance in the subcontinent, whereas until then it had rather frowned on such activity. Secondly, evangelicalism expanded greatly from the middle of the decade, and Thomas Chalmers strongly approved of overseas missions, seeing them as a logical extension of the campaign to spread Christianity at home. A phalanx of his outstanding students committed themselves to spreading the gospel message overseas, six of whom served in India. The foremost of this group was Alexander Duff, who in 1829 founded a pioneering settlement in Kolkata, where he established an educational system closely resembling the Scottish model in curriculum and pedagogy.

While the Indian subcontinent was a prime area of missionary activity, the abolition of slavery in British colonies led to an increasing commitment from the 1830s to the West Indies and Africa, with the latter a particular object of attention by Scots. Other Scots ventured much further afield, notably in the Pacific Islands, where the most well-known missionary was John Paton, who worked in the New Hebrides from 1858. Through his efforts in central east Africa, David Livingstone became arguably the most iconic national figure in the third quarter of the century, stimulating a widespread presence of Scottish missionaries in the region, thereby creating an influence which persisted into the second half of the twentieth century. In Scotland, national pride in these achievements was illustrated by the large domestic market for autobiographies and biographies of missionaries. While Livingstone was obviously the most lionised, readers also keenly devoured accounts of the lives of several others, including Duff, Paton and Mary Slessor, as well as Robert Moffat (Livingstone's father-in-law).

One feature of this work abroad was that women were frequently involved, so that by 1880, they made up fully 40 per cent of those engaged in overseas missionary work under the auspices of the Free Church. Most were wives or daughters of male missionaries, and they took a particular interest in fields such as the education and health of the indigenous people. But there were some who served as missionaries in their own right, of whom the outstanding example was Mary Slessor, a Dundee mill-girl who went to Calabar in Nigeria in 1876 at the age of twenty-eight, and remained there for almost forty years.

Scots were also prominent in a range of professional roles throughout the empire. There were numerous doctors, trained in the Scottish universities, who were distributed across colonies and dominions. In the fields of science and technology, Scots proliferated. Botany and forestry experts included William Roxburgh in India and George Lawson in Canada, while A. G. Bain became the foremost student of the geology of South Africa. Naturally, Scots were to the front in civil engineering, particularly railway and bridge construction. Administration in colonial territories also attracted many, and the wider provision in Scotland of university education ensured a higher than proportionate presence. The Scottish peerage gave a public face to their countrymen's imperial work, as several became governors of dominions and colonies. The eighth earl of Elgin served as governor of Jamaica, then as governor-general of both Canada and India, while the tenth earl of Dalhousie was Viceroy of India.

The links between Scotland and those parts of the empire which had large settler populations were particularly strong because Scots were well-represented in almost all of them. In certain regions of Canada, Australia and New Zealand, there were proportionately more immigrants from Scotland than from any other country in Britain. In 1881, they formed about one-fifth of foreign-born residents in Canada and New Zealand, and in the latter they were concentrated in Otago, where 55 per cent of all Scots-born settlers resided. The prominence of Scots in many walks of life in these new countries was often remarked on. This was especially true of Canada, where two-thirds of the country's bankers were Scottish. In the dominions, numerous leading politicians had a Scottish background: for the first quarter-century of the Canadian confederation after its inception in 1867, two Scots – Sir John A. MacDonald and Alexander MacKenzie – had a monopoly of the premiership; while in Australia, James MacCulloch served four times as premier between 1863 and 1877, to be followed by James Service (twice between 1880 and 1886) and James Munro (once, 1890–2).

But the importance of the imperial identity should be handled carefully, as it did not reach its full flowering until after our period. Anti-imperialism was a strong current running through Scottish economic and political ideology throughout this period. Free-market opinion was highly critical of the case for exercising formal sovereignty over colonial possessions, and there were many devoted followers in Scotland of the Manchester School's championing of this laissez-faire doctrine. Its chief exponents, Richard Cobden and John Bright, were highly influential voices among mid-Victorian Scottish Radicals, including Duncan MacLaren, who was Bright's brother-in-law. Hence, at the end of the 1840s, the overwhelming share of the Scottish press, including the *Scotsman*, looked forward expectantly to the dissolution of constitutional ties with British colonies. This reluctance to embrace full-throated imperialism persisted to the end of our period. The Disraeli-inspired jingoism which swept through most of England in 1878–80 was much more muted in

Scotland, where public demonstrations of approval were infrequent and drew little mass support. Instead, Gladstone's Midlothian campaign in late 1879, awash with scorching philippics against imperialist adventures, attracted unparalleled mass audiences in many parts of Lowland Scotland, and the resounding Liberal triumph in the 1880 general election was widely attributed to the impact of his oratory.[10]

Thanks to their enhanced presence in military and imperial endeavours, Scots felt enabled to regard their country as no longer an inferior partner, still less a client state, in Britain. The empire afforded a further indicator of parity between the two home countries, for it was portrayed as not an English, but a British, construct, thereby acknowledging the key contribution made by Scotland.

THE UNION OF 1707, SCOTLAND AND BRITISHNESS

Across the nineteenth century, the concept of the 1707 Union being a fusion of equals was developed by Scots, and an important approach was to yoke venerated figures from pre-Union Scottish history to a contemporary Britishness. The two most heroic fighters for Scotland's national independence, William Wallace and Robert Bruce, were adroitly invoked as part of this process. Of the two, Wallace easily held the prime position in the nation's estimation, as is indicated by the considerable number of memorials in Scotland dedicated to him, with the Wallace Monument at Stirling the most impressive. The monument, completed in 1869, immediately became immensely popular, attracting between 10,000 and 15,000 visitors a year in the 1870s. In contrast, there were fewer memorials raised to Bruce in this period, and the reasons for this discrepancy are revealing. Blind Harry's narrative of Wallace's life and struggles, written 200 years after his death, was widely read in the nineteenth century, and went through numerous reissues. Wallace was revered as an idealistic fighter for Scottish freedom, and his supposed plebeian background appealed to working- and middle-class readers, especially since he was allegedly let down by most of the Scottish nobility at crucial episodes. This chimed with the self-image of Scotland having a democratic social ethos, and also fed into the rising levels of antipathy to aristocratic landowners occurring in the Victorian age.

But Bruce, although subordinate in this pantheon, nevertheless was admired because he succeeded in securing the survival of Scotland as an independent nation, and so offered a model of patriotic aristocracy in lieu of the despised Stuart dynasty. Wallace and Bruce were constantly bracketed together as the founders of freedom for Scotland, and at several of the mass reform meetings held between 1815 and 1820, such as Thrushgrove, they were referred to as the forebears of modern democratic aspirations. Another facet of the Wallace cult was that he was treated as the precursor of nineteenth-century mainland European champions of suppressed nationalities. Within the Abbey Craig monument at Stirling, there are portraits of, and congratulatory messages from, Garibaldi, Kossuth and Karl Blind, thus neatly stressing the relevance of the thirteenth-century patriot to contemporary continental struggles for freedom and national independence.

But the highly potent twist to this quasi-veneration of Wallace and Bruce which was elaborated in the second half of this period was that their achievements were emphasised neither as being anti-English nor as undermining the Union of 1707. On the contrary, from around 1840, the argument was posited that they had made a concrete contribution to the creation of Britishness and eased the progression to the unified country. This was because their ultimately successful challenge to England meant that Scotland entered the new constitutional arrangement on an equal footing, rather than as a failed state. The implication was that Scotland enjoyed a higher standing than Wales or Ireland, both of which had been conquered and were subservient to full-blooded English sovereignty. This stream of thought may help to explain the vehemence in 1886 of the Scottish reaction to Gladstone's decision to grant Home Rule to Ireland, giving that country greater self-government ahead of Scotland.

Britishness thus became the dominant theme of much political and cultural discourse in this period. This trend was clearly delineated among working-class reform movements. Scottish radicals felt there was no incongruity in invoking England's Magna Carta as an essential bulwark of liberty, as was done by those who masterminded the abortive 1820 radical rising. At the very same time, at some radical meetings in the north of England, 'Scots Wha' Hae' was sung to acclaim.[11]

The most striking instance of this mid-Victorian pro-Union cast of mind came with the grandiosely named National Association for the Vindication of Scottish Rights (NAVSR). The association, which began in 1853, was, prima facie, a bizarre alliance of diametrically opposed tendencies. On the right, there were crypto-Jacobites, out-of-office Conservatives and followers of Sir Walter Scott's ultra-romantic Toryism. This element embraced James Grant, a historical novelist, his brother John and the earl of Eglinton, who organised a famous medieval tournament in 1839, and subsequently served in two Conservative administrations as lord-lieutenant of Ireland. The radical component of this movement was equally disjointed. The Rev. James Begg, an ardent Free Churchman, was particularly exercised by the need to improve the housing of agricultural workers in the Lowlands. The radical Edinburgh politicians, Duncan MacLaren and Charles Cowan MP, also threw their weight behind the campaign. Less easily pigeonholed were people like William Burns, a Glasgow lawyer preoccupied to the point of obsession with striving to end the careless use of the terms 'English' and 'England', instead of 'British' and 'Britain'.

The platform which the NAVSR advocated was, perhaps unsurprisingly, an ostensibly ill-coordinated ragbag of demands, some of which appeared marginal and almost frivolous. For instance, one of the twenty-four grievances listed in the association's manifesto concerned allegations of abuses of heraldic devices. But there were several clear themes preoccupying the association, on which even these superficially trivial complaints had a bearing. One ground of concern was indifference on the part of England to acknowledging Scottish sensitivities about inequality of treatment. Another was divergent priorities in important areas of national concern, such as the lack of adequate preparatory defences in Scotland against a foreign invasion, whereas appropriate measures had been put in place in England. Then there were complaints about the increasing tendency for the administration of Scottish government business to be centralised in England, such as the abolition of the separate Scottish agencies for the collection of income tax and of customs. The NAVSR, in line with mid-Victorian thinking, emphasised that local devolution was to be preferred, and went on to argue that the lack of Scottish control might lead to political and social instability on a par with the upheavals which had occurred in many European states in 1848, and which fed the swelling national independence movements in Poland, Hungary and Italy.

THE GOVERNMENT OF SCOTLAND BEFORE THE SCOTTISH OFFICE

Probably the most momentous topic raised by the association was the need for Scotland to be given a proper, explicit presence in the structure of the British governmental system. This demand essentially encapsulated the spectrum of complaints aired in the twenty-four points, and foreshadowed the main direction of the evolution of Scottish self-government during the remainder of the century. The NAVSR argued that the neglect of the interests of Scotland in both Westminster and Whitehall owed a great deal to the absence of a minister with a defined and specific function to deal with Scottish business, and therefore a Scottish secretary should be appointed. Since the abolition in 1746 of that office, the government's main Scottish law agent, the Lord Advocate, had been in practice responsible for dealing with the full gamut of business relating to Scotland. This included drafting and introducing all Scottish legislative proposals in the Commons, and steering bills through parliament, as well as responding to debates and questions on Scottish topics in the lower chamber. Frequently, the Lord Advocate also handled electoral arrangements. All these responsibilities were in addition to his official job, which covered all aspects of the Scottish legal system, such as appointing judges and sheriffs, and representing the Crown in major criminal and civil cases.

There were three core problems with this set-up. Firstly, the Lord Advocate was not a member of the Cabinet, only attending by invitation. Frequently, therefore, what in Scotland was considered to be a matter calling for prompt action made little impact on English ministers. Thus, repeated attempts by Lord Advocate James Moncrieff in the 1850s and 1860s to reform Scottish education were not supported in cabinet, to his great distress. The Scottish Education Act eventually came in 1872, but only after ministers had accepted the case for an English measure, which was enacted in 1870. More profoundly, sometimes the Scottish law officers were left outside the decision-making circle on Scottish matters. Lord Advocate Francis Jeffrey and the Solicitor General, Henry Cockburn, complained repeatedly that they were being kept in the dark about the details of the First Reform Acts, both for England and Scotland, so that deficiencies and anomalies were difficult to address. The second difficulty was, at bottom, logistic. The Lord Advocate spent a great deal of time shuttling between London and Edinburgh, trying to combine representing Scottish interests in the former and prosecuting in leading trials in the latter. Until the arrival of the rail link between the two countries at the end of the 1840s, this involved a forty-five-hour journey by stagecoach, and even after about 1850, the train still took thirteen hours. The physical strain on men often in later middle age must have been considerable, especially as some, most notably Jeffrey and, in the 1806–7 Ministry of All the Talents, Henry Erskine, were already in poor health.

The third aspect of dependence on the Lord Advocate for effective government of Scotland was that virtually none of the holders of the office were career politicians, and instead they used the office as a means of securing a judicial appointment, usually at the first available vacancy. Between 1801 and 1880, nineteen men were appointed Lord Advocate, and all but two (Henry Erskine and Sir William Rae) advanced to the bench. Only three men held the post for any duration: namely, Archibald Campbell Colquhoun (1807–16), Rae (1819–30, 1834–5 and 1841–2) and James Moncrieff (1851–2, 1852–8, 1859–66 and 1868–9). The average term for the other sixteen was about two-and-a-half years. These men had little time and no profound commitment to develop political skills or to establish any influence among the political class. Some indeed were barely ensconced in office before they joined the judiciary. For instance, Adam Anderson became Lord Advocate in February 1852, and acceded to the bench in May of that year. The same pattern of impermanence applies to the Solicitors General, the Lord Advocate's second-in-command, for only two of the thirty-three between 1800 and 1880 did not ascend to a judgeship, and the average spell as law officer was two-and-a-half years.

This vacuum was filled rather inadequately by having someone with a Scottish connection acting as adviser to the government: for instance, Disraeli normally consulted Sir James Fergusson of Kilkerran, while Fox Maule, a junior Home Office minister in the Melbourne administration, kept an eye on issues north of the border. There were intermittent calls for a designated Scottish ministerial post to be instituted. In 1828, the *Edinburgh Observer* denounced the neglect of Scottish business by Westminster: 'Scotland, poor Scotland! . . . Bills exclusively affecting her are either thrown out, or passed in silence as unworthy of discussion.'[12] The question was debated among Scottish Whigs at the time of the First Reform Act, but influential individuals, especially James Abercromby, felt that there was not enough work to justify such an appointment.

The thrust of the NAVSR's manifesto was not for separatism, but for a full and fair application of the Union of 1707, so that Scotland would be treated on a completely equal basis with England in all respects, however trifling these might appear. The association contributed greatly to significant long-term shifts in Scottish attitudes, as the earlier approach of striving to emulate England had been replaced by a search for equity, with a willingness to be vociferous in objecting to slights and asserting rights, real or imaginary. Hence, the impetus to lobby for a Scottish minister in Whitehall became more pressing in the quarter-century following the association's demise.

CULTURE AND SCOTTISHNESS

Throughout the period, Scottish literature was completely dominated by Robert Burns and Walter Scott, and they influenced other Scottish cultural forms. Burns's popularity was widespread among all social classes, for his poetry appealed on a variety of grounds. His depiction in *The Cottar's Saturday Night* of traditional rural society as embodying the core values of the Scottish character was heartily approved of, especially by conservative opinion generally. As a poet of nature, he was popular with a broad range of readers, including skilled artisans, many of whom were keen students of natural history. His exposition of Enlightenment principles in *A Man's a Man*, chimed with the instincts of many in a country which saw itself as socially democratic and egalitarian. His use of Scots had a profound impact, for he showed that the language had both a vibrant vitality and was also fully capable of expressing contemporary political and social concepts. For many who felt that Scots was a language held in low esteem, Burns gave them the self-confidence to use it.

Scott's achievements were multiple and wide-ranging. By reinterpreting the country's history in a positive light, he offered his country's people an alternative vision of their past to the negative account purveyed by Enlightenment historians and commentators. Thus, Rob Roy MacGregor was not a thuggish bandit, but rather a resolute defender of Highland values, pre-eminently courage and loyalty. In *Old Mortality*, the Covenanters are seen to have displayed, in some respects, admirable qualities, such as adherence to principles and resistance to overweening state power, while their religious extremism was, thankfully, a thing of the past. Likewise, the theme of *Waverley* was that Jacobitism expired as a political force soon after Culloden. Hence, Scottishness became more inclusive, embracing previously ostracised social forces. At the same time, Scott – a strongly committed champion of the Union of 1707 – stressed the continuing distinctiveness of Scotland's character and institutions. Equally importantly, his atmospheric deployment of place and landscape as almost characters in a story's plot transformed Scots' appreciation of the scenery of their native land. This was, of course, outstandingly the case with the Highlands, which were reconfigured from a rain-swept, desolate terrain to a majestic region filled with a brooding awe and mystery.

A further achievement of Scott's oeuvre was to raise Scotland's standing in the context of European culture from being a neglected backwater to constituting a central icon in the broad Romantic movement, which dominated the period. His work was warmly admired by men as disparate as Goethe and Marx. Novelists elsewhere heavily influenced by Scott included the Brontë sisters, Dickens, Dumas, Balzac, Hugo, Tolstoy and Turgenev. Bizet, Donizetti and Rossini based operas on Scott's novels; Mendelssohn's *Third Symphony* owed much to his writings; and Berlioz's *Opus No. 1* is the overture 'Waverley'. This adulation, and the consequent visits to Scotland of figures like Mendelssohn and Stendhal, gave Scots a sense of pride at the enhanced international reputation of their country.

Scott and, to a lesser degree, Burns profoundly affected the development of Scottish painting. Until the early nineteenth century, most artists in Scotland were working within a formal classical framework. Many, notably Gavin Hamilton, imitated the Italian masters and others were shaped by Graeco-Roman influences. From the 1820s, however, new directions were opened. For one, landscape pictures shifted from Lowland scenes celebrating the order and progress which mankind had imposed by taming wild nature. Instead, artists turned to presenting dramatic views of Highland hills and glens, almost invariably with lowering skies and devoid of any human presence, although frequently adorned with stags. The prime purveyor of this trend was Horatio MacCulloch, as instanced by his painting of *Glencoe* (1864).

Another evolving approach was illustrations of scenes from the works of both Scott and Burns. David Wilkie's *The Cottars' Saturday Night* is the classic example of the latter's inspiration. Scott's novels were raided for dramatic historical episodes, ranging from his medieval-based novels to his eighteenth-century stories; R. S. Lauder's *The Trial of Effie Deans* (1842) depicted a key episode in *The Heart of Midlothian*. Partly derived from Scott, artists increasingly turned to episodes in the sixteenth and seventeenth centuries in order to point up a particularly Scottish context, and also to link contemporary issues with past struggles. Thus, several paintings made in the 1830s and 1840s dealing with incidents in Covenanting history (e.g. Thomas Duncan, *The Death of John Brown of Priesthill, 1688* [1844]) drew clear parallels with contemporary religious conflicts.

Another sphere where Scott assumed a pathbreaking role lay in the revolution in Scottish architectural design. Until around 1820, strict classical formalism was the prevailing norm applied, both for urban landscapes (Edinburgh New Town, begun in 1769) and for country mansions (Robert Adam's Culzean Castle, 1777). But when, in 1817, Scott embarked on drawing up plans for his new residence of Abbotsford, he boosted the appeal of an emerging architectural style – the Scottish Baronial – which became the dominant mode until the end of the nineteenth century. Abbotsford rejected the dictates of existing architectural principles, such as discipline, order and proportionality. Doric columns and Trajan pillars were no longer de rigueur; now crenellations, castellations and crow-step gables were indispensable. The house's external structure evoked the castles and grand houses of medieval and Renaissance Scotland. In most Scottish towns, wealthy individuals commissioned mansions designed in the baronial style, and country houses were also part of this new trend, whose apotheosis was Balmoral Castle (1853).

This fashion reflected a prevailing feature of nineteenth-century Scotland, which is that the new bourgeoisie upheld individual choice and liberty above the constraints of the pre-existing order, whether in economic and social policy, politics, religion or cultural standards. Accordingly, the baronial influence steadily permeated the design of public and commercial buildings, such as law courts, hospitals, banks and municipal premises. The wider significance of the Scots baronial style was that it provided a distinctively national design format: generally, neither neo-Gothic nor neo-Classical edifices were much seen in Scotland, in marked contrast to, say, England. The climax of the triumph of the baronial style as embodying national identity came with the construction of the Wallace Monument, near Stirling. In this tribute to the country's greatest patriot, the prevalence of a specifically Scottish genre was an unmistakeable signal.

The literary and painterly outputs in the Victorian era display an almost total absence of engagement with the issues posed by industrialisation and urbanisation. The novel in England was preoccupied for about twenty years from the mid-1830s with the 'Condition of England' question, which addressed the impact of the new laissez-faire economic and social order on workers and the poorer segments of society. Among those who grappled with the wide-ranging implications were Dickens, Disraeli, Mrs Gaskell, Charles Kingsley and George Eliot. But very little Scottish fiction of any serious import in this era engaged with similar changes occurring here, although in their rapidity and depth they were arguably more profoundly challenging to existing values and norms. John Galt is the main exception to this neglect, most notably in *Annals of the Parish* (1821), which charts economic, social and political change between 1760 and 1810 in a Lowland village. But Scott and Burns had set the dominant stereotype, namely a rural-centred and essentially time-frozen backward vision of Scotland, and subsequent writers tended to plough the same furrow, which over time decayed into the flummery of the Kailyard. Among poets, only Alexander Smith wrote seriously about urban life; his ode to his birthplace, Glasgow, begins: 'City! I am true son of thine', but he had virtually no siblings.

Scottish painting followed a rather similar pattern. English artists in the Victorian era illuminated the new economy and society, while most French Impressionists delighted in depicting urban landscapes and the lifestyles of all classes of town-dwellers. Very few Scottish painters dabbled in city life and manners: in the early years of the century, Alexander Nasmyth's two panoramic treatments of Edinburgh in 1825 are a major exception. The best treatment of a Scottish industrial scene, significantly, comes from the English artist, Caleb Stanley, whose *Gartsherrie by Night* (1853) is a dramatic and vivid picture. It is illuminating that the group of painters styled 'the Glasgow Boys' were more preoccupied with rural scenery and the families of agricultural workers than any aspect of their own city.

Equally revealing was the response of the panjandrums of the Scottish art establishment to a movement in the 1860s which conveyed frankly the harsh conditions of contemporary Lowland agricultural labour, rather than dwelling on Highland scenes and ruined castles. The leader of this school, George Reid, was influenced by European painters such as J. F. Millet and G. A. Mollinger, who had produced realistic descriptions of peasant labour, using colour in a subtler, more restrained manner than the Scottish landscape artists. When Reid submitted pictures in this new style at the Royal Scottish Academy's 1867 exhibition, the reaction was virtually uniformly hostile, particularly as hitherto Reid had been a devout disciple of MacCulloch. Sir George Harvey, the president of the Academy, called Reid to a meeting, at which he conveyed his displeasure at the new departure, adding that the most eminent members of the Academy shared his views. Sections of the press and prominent art patrons joined in the chorus of disapproval. Reid subsequently concentrated on portraiture, painting very few studies of rural life.

IRISH IMMIGRATION AND EMPLOYMENT

While a Scottish identity was growing and becoming more inclusive, the increasing presence of Irish immigrants presented challenges. Irish people had been moving to Scotland from the late eighteenth century in search of work, but until the 1840s, this had not generally been viewed as problematic. There were two main reasons for this: firstly, many were temporary residents, either working seasonally as harvesters in the modernised Lowland agricultural sector, or spending longer, being employed in large-scale construction works, but moving away on completion of the project. Secondly, the numbers settling on a permanent basis in Scotland before, say, 1815 were relatively small. After the end of the French wars, the flow of incomers from Ireland grew, as the lure of working in a developing economy was very attractive. In 1841, there were 126,000 Irish-born enumerated in the census, which was just under 5 per cent of the total population, and in 1881, they made up 9.5 per cent. Moreover, as the century advanced, the Irish community naturally included Scottish-born offspring of first-generation immigrants.

There are three key aspects of this process. Firstly, the Irish-born were a much larger presence in Scotland than in England: in 1851, the Irish-born constituted 2.9 per cent of the English population, as against 7.2 per cent of the Scottish, and this disparity widened thereafter. Secondly, the distribution of the Irish immigrants was highly concentrated, rather than evenly spread across the whole country. By 1870, two-thirds were living in the four west Lowland counties of Ayr, Dunbarton, Lanark and Renfrew. Dundee, which in 1851 was the Scottish town with the highest percentage of Irish-born, was virtually the sole place elsewhere which contained a substantial number of Irish. By contrast, both Aberdeen and Edinburgh had more English than Irish residents. The consequence of these two factors meant that several Scottish towns had markedly higher levels of Irish residents than was found in England. For instance, the Irish formed 18 per cent of Glasgow's population in 1851, whereas the figure for London was 4.6 per cent, and Liverpool was the only English town with a higher percentage than Glasgow. Perhaps the largest share in Scotland was Coatbridge in 1861, which recorded 40 per cent of the population as Irish-born. An additional aspect of this demographic movement was that the increased presence of Irish people in many places occurred at a rapid speed. In Dundee, they doubled from around 9 per cent of the city's population in 1841 to 19 per cent a decade later, as between 9,000 and 10,000 new arrivals reached the city.

The start of this surge was caused by the catastrophe of the Irish Famine, but there were significant nuances to the stereotypical portrayal of the immigrants as overwhelmingly drawn from the lowest segments of the agrarian proletariat.[13] The great preponderance of those moving to Scotland – at times almost 80 per cent – came from the nine counties which made up the historical province of Ulster. Ulster had been less severely affected by the famine than the other three provinces, and it possessed a more advanced manufacturing and commercial sector than elsewhere on the island. This meant that there was a lower component of impoverished small peasantry and landless agricultural labourers among those crossing to Scotland. These poorest people were mainly found in the west and south of Ireland, and they tended to travel to either England or America, which were more accessible than Scotland. Hence, a considerable number of immigrants to Scotland were not unskilled workers; for instance, the bulk of Irish textile workers in Dundee's mills had been engaged in Ulster's important linen industry. In mid-century Paisley, 22 per cent of male Irishmen were classified as being in artisan occupations, only a little below the 29 per cent of Scottish immigrants to the city, and virtually identical with the 23 per cent of native Paisleyites. But in other towns, the Irish tended to be disproportionately concentrated in labouring and kindred low-paid work, as in Greenock, where they dominated the labour force in the town's sugar refineries – a particularly onerous and unpleasant form of employment – while in the western coal- and iron-fields, they took up the less high-status positions. Access to better-paid and less arduous occupations, such as the police force – the classic American escape route for the Irish – was almost completely closed off, as Highlanders had entrenched themselves in this niche. It would appear that for many Irish, the opportunity to ascend the ladder from unskilled work did not occur too often. In Greenock, the sons of first-generation immigrant dockworkers overwhelmingly followed in their fathers' occupation, a situation that carried on at least into the 1890s. The reasons for this limited avenue of advancement include religion, sectarian tensions carried over from Ireland and educational attainments.

IRISH IMMIGRATION: THE RELIGIOUS ELEMENT AND SECTARIANISM

The considerable bulk of Irish incomers were Roman Catholic, and their arrival vastly expanded the number of Catholics in Scotland, yet simultaneously created tensions with the indigenous co-religionists and fuelled apprehensions among Protestant Scots. In 1755, the number of Catholics in Scotland was estimated at just under 16,500, a little over 1 per cent of the total population, with four counties – Aberdeen, Argyll, Banff and Inverness – containing well over four-fifths of the total. In 1841, Catholics were thought to number 140,000 and in 1878, 320,000, i.e. 5 per cent and 7 per cent, respectively, of the total population. The real significance, in psychological terms, for the host population was that almost all of the increase was located in the industrial Lowlands, instead of the remote Highlands.

Given the time-honoured highly critical view of Roman Catholicism held by Scottish Presbyterians, it is not surprising that some displayed hostility to any increase both in the numbers and influence of Catholics. This feeling was explicitly manifested when a campaign of resistance was mounted in 1779–80 against a bill proposing to grant relief in selected fields to British Catholics. While in England and Wales the measure was accepted, albeit reluctantly, the agitation in Scotland was so widespread and intense that the sections of the bill relating to the country were dropped by ministers. The strength of opposition was most pronounced in the western Lowland presbyteries, the very region into which Irish Catholics subsequently moved in large numbers. Fifty years later, the Catholic Emancipation bill was likewise stoutly opposed by the majority of Scottish Presbyterian clergy and laity, the most vehement protests emanating again from the western Lowlands.

However, hostility to Catholics was not omnipresent, as Moderates in the late eighteenth century were quite sympathetic to several Catholic clergy who shared important Enlightenment values. Bishop John Geddes, for instance, composed the entry on the abolition of slavery for the *Encyclopaedia Britannica*, the great collaborative opus of the Scottish Enlightenment. Moreover, Geddes was a close associate of Robert Burns, who gave the bishop first sight of several of his poems. A cooler atmosphere intruded in the years after 1798, when the uprising in Ireland led many Moderates to adopt a more distant relationship with Scottish Catholics. In addition, the Catholic Church retreated somewhat from its Enlightenment stance in the years after 1800, and began to accentuate trends of greater religiosity, with more elaborate liturgies and a stress on pilgrimages. But prominent Presbyterians, ministers and laity, continued to champion Catholic Emancipation in the quarter-century preceding the act of 1829. For the most part these were Whiggish Moderates, but a major proponent of the measure was Thomas Chalmers, the acknowledged leader of the Church of Scotland Evangelicals.

Subsequently, virulent anti-Popery remained a strand in Scottish Presbyterianism, usually, however, restricted to its more extreme wings. In the 1850s, a Free Church minister, Dugald MacColl, was a sort of missionary in the Glasgow Wynds district, an area of heavy Catholic settlement. MacColl specialised in delivering open-air anti-Catholic sermons on Saturday nights as the pubs were closing, often provoking violent reactions. But it is significant that while the restoration of the English hierarchy in 1850 met with a huge outbreak of vociferous indignation against so-called 'Papal Aggression' across the spectrum of Protestant opinion, the equivalent Scottish restoration in 1878 drew only a very limited critical response beyond the usual ultra-Protestant elements.

From the middle of the nineteenth century, the Orange Order emerged as the most organised militant opposition to Catholics in Scotland. Although the movement was proscribed in 1836, when there were forty-four lodges in Scotland, the Scottish Grand Lodge appears to have continued in existence. It remained, however, fairly dormant for twenty years, apart from sporadic incidents in Lanarkshire and Ayrshire in the 1840s. The order expanded significantly from the 1850s, and in Dundee, the number of lodges doubled from six in 1859 to thirteen in 1873. But the central core of Orangeism was in the industrial west. The Lanarkshire coalfields were a particularly strong area, and there was a large presence in Glasgow, along with Greenock, Paisley and mining areas in Ayrshire, Lanarkshire and Stirlingshire. By the 1870s, public rallies attracted large numbers, so that 15,000 to 20,000 demonstrators were regularly reported attending Glasgow processions in that decade.

Two predominant motives for the growth in the Order can be posited. One was that in the mining districts, the Irish Catholics had seemed from the 1840s to pose a threat to the levels of wages and employment enjoyed by Scottish colliers. This threat was less present in the engineering and shipbuilding areas, as the highly skilled labour force was not economically threatened by newcomers from Ireland. Moreover, the rise of Orangeism in these places only started in the 1860s, by which time the movement of Irish into Scotland had settled at appreciably lower rates than in the Famine era. The influence of Protestant immigrants from Ulster may well have been significant. Data from the very end of the period indicate that incomers from the four counties of Ulster which were predominantly Protestant in religious affiliation (Antrim, Armagh, Derry and Down) contributed 59 per cent of the Scottish total, but they made up only 25 per cent in England. Many of these Protestant immigrants to Scotland had worked in the Belfast shipyards, where sectarian practices were universal, and they would probably have imported these attitudes, since parts of Glasgow and Greenock where Orangeism had a significant base were at once shipbuilding centres and areas of Irish Protestant settlement.

Sectarian rioting and strife had been an intermittent feature of the coalfields from the 1840s onwards, but the 1870s witnessed an escalation in disorder in places like Glasgow, where the Orange marches around the twelfth of July and the nationalist equivalents in mid-August were frequently attended by breakdowns of law and order. An especially serious episode took place in 1875, when a protracted outbreak of violence erupted in Partick and the authorities lost control of the situation for three days, and there were significant disturbances in Springburn in the following year. Unsavoury as these episodes were, a sense of proportion suggest that Orangeism was, in essence, a marginal influence at this time. Membership figures are not easy to determine, but it seems likely that the Order was rather less successful in Scotland than in other places outside Ireland. Around 1880, there were probably no more than 30,000 members in Scotland, whereas Liverpool alone had in the region of 17,000 in 1880, and Canada by 1870 boasted 100,000 adherents, when its population was about the same as Scotland. Unlike Ulster, where an upper echelon of landowners, businessmen and professionals provided a leadership cadre which conferred a veneer of respectable legitimacy, very few middle-class Scots joined the order. The outbreaks of violence and disorder associated with Orangeism repulsed Scottish opinion, for Scotland, in contrast to Ireland and, indeed, England, did not have a strong tradition of unruly mob action, while the scenes of drunkenness which accompanied Orange marches offended the influential Temperance interest. The bulk of Scots thus regarded Orangeism as a rather regrettable import from Ireland, and as its anti-Catholicism was a different strain from the Scottish strain, there were no significant links forged between the two. Hence the Orange Order never occupied the place in the Scottish political and social environment which it enjoyed in Liverpool and Ulster.

INTERNAL CATHOLIC TENSIONS

The more prevalent attitude of native Scots to the immigrants seems to have been one of benign yet wary tolerance, but certainly not a welcoming inclusive embrace. A Glaswegian brought up in a deprived quarter of the city's east end, which had a large Irish element, reflected late in life on inter-communal relations around 1880. He observed that the Scots did not mix much with the Irish, who were regarded as inferior since they mostly had unskilled jobs. Although there were decent people among the Irish, this social distance existed, he explained, because of the disorderly behaviour of some of their fellow countrymen, which it was feared might otherwise afflict the Scots.[14]

Animus towards Irish Catholics was, however, not restricted to Protestant Scots, as their co-religionists from elsewhere were also often antipathetic. There were two branches of the latter category. Firstly, there were non-Scottish clergy and nuns who were brought in to minister to the burgeoning Catholic congregations. Most, such as the Jesuits based in the north of England, were very critical of what they viewed as crude and ill-educated Irish priests and a superstitious laity. These groups, particularly the women religious, who mostly came from the continent or were middle-class recusants, were assiduous in promoting the ethos of the absorption of British (i.e. not Irish) values and culture. Secondly, there were broad divisions among the indigenous Scottish Catholics. There was a smattering of aristocratic and gentry recusant families, such as Lords Lothian and Lovat, and this elite social stratum was bolstered by the accretion of upper-class converts, who became a pronounced feature of the Victorian era. Among these newcomers were the third marquess of Bute, the duchesses of Buccleuch and Hamilton, along with Robert Monteith of Carstairs, whose family had been early cottonmasters. These people had little contact with the Irish Catholics, partly for reasons of social distinction and because few of them lived in the areas where the Irish had settled. It is instructive that only Monteith, with his estate in the west-central region, became involved in supporting the immigrant Catholics, and he made generous donations to various Glasgow-based religious charities. But otherwise, the impoverished Irish Catholics were pretty well left to their own financial resources.

The less socially exalted Scottish Catholics were little friendlier, and this was especially true of the indigenous clergy. The hierarchy of the Scottish church was recruited from their ranks, even in centres of Irish settlement, such as the Western District, where until 1869 the bishops were all Scotsmen, and then the Englishman Charles Eyre was appointed. There were two facets which fuelled a sense of grievance among the incomers. Firstly, very few clergy with an Irish background were brought in to serve Scottish parishes, so that in 1867, there was a sole Irish-born incumbent of a Glasgow church. It was widely believed by Irish Catholics that the Scottish clergy kept the best posts for themselves and that they also monopolised cushier administrative positions, while nepotism was rife in the allocation of plum jobs. Perhaps more significantly, the Scottish-born priests were almost openly dismayed by the influx from Ireland which they felt was an irritating diversion from their long-term goal of winning Scottish Protestants back to Rome. Likewise, Irish nuns were blocked from promotion in the religious orders until long after this period. The segregation between the two components of the church in Scotland was starkly illuminated with the formation in 1876 of the Glasgow Caledonian Catholic Association, whose membership was, as its name suggests, exclusively restricted to native Scots.

The tensions between the mass of communicants and the Scots-born clerics impeded the adjustment of immigrants to the host society, and the friction between the two camps underlines that there was a mood of independence among many Irish Catholics, which ran counter to the depiction so prevalent at the time – and long thereafter – of the total unquestioned hegemony exercised by the priesthood over their parishioners on a wide range of issues. It was, however, generally the case that where the menace of Protestant proselytism was feared, there was solidarity among Catholics to defend their religious values. This was very evident in the field of education, as is examined below.

But in other spheres, the clergy's pronouncements were often open to challenge. Although both bishops and parish priests were almost uniformly opposed to radical political campaigns, especially those related to Irish questions, the evidence suggests that many adherents simply ignored these denunciations. For instance, Chartism was strongly condemned from almost every pulpit, yet it attracted widespread support among the laity. Later on, there were serious misgivings among the clergy about the Irish land agitation of the later 1870s; nevertheless there were numerous mass demonstrations across Scotland in support of the campaign, and Charles Parnell and Michael Davitt were given heroes' welcomes on their Scottish speaking tours. Again, the politicisation of St Patrick's Day celebrations in Glasgow and Dundee was carried through successfully in the early 1870s, despite the almost universal desire among the clergy to retain it in its original format as a purely religious occasion.

THE CATHOLIC CHURCH AND THE SOCIAL
DEVELOPMENT OF IRISH IMMIGRANTS

For Catholics in an urban Lowland setting, the parish rapidly became the focal point not just for religious observance, but also for a broad range of cultural and social institutions, so that it conferred identity and stability in times of economic fluctuation for the adherents, and also shaped their values. The physical expansion of the church during the half-century after Emancipation was remarkable. In 1838, there were 83 priests, and in 1870, 190. The improvement was most evident in the west, where in 1840 only five chapels existed in the western area, but by 1884, there were 54. There was a two-way relationship at play in the wide-ranging role of the parish, for while Catholic values were disseminated through various mediums, these associations sustained the piety of many when churches were undermanned. Thus, it was estimated in 1851 that only about one-third of Irish Catholics attended church services, whether because of distance, work patterns or high mobility levels, and the networks of parochial-based organisations kept the absentees in contact.

The most impressive organisation was the St Vincent de Paul Society, whose primary role was to deliver welfare services to the needy. This remit covered a very wide range of problems, and there were many applicants; in Glasgow in the 1850s, the society handled some 750 cases each week. The care of children was a prime focus of attention, as instanced by the society opening an orphanage at Smyllum in North Lanarkshire in 1866. The society also gave solid financial and material assistance to schools and their pupils by donating clothes and shoes, providing free meals, paying class fees – by 1870, 700 children in Glasgow benefited – and even finding jobs for school leavers. Additionally, it met the costs of medical care and burials for the poor, and dealt with housing difficulties. While, of course, the over-riding motivating factor for those active in St Vincent de Paul was the compelling Christian obligation to look after the less fortunate in society, two other factors undoubtedly operated. Firstly, the rigid severity of the Scottish Poor Law bore down particularly harshly on Irish immigrants because of its residential requirement of five years to receive relief. Secondly, there was a justified fear that engagement with a Scottish welfare agency might expose the recipients to proselytising pressure, as Presbyterian clerical and lay influence were normally very high in these bodies, particularly where children were involved.

Cultural and social interests were also well covered. Most parishes had a library, containing mainly religious literature, but also in some instances catering for more secular tastes. The Catholic Young Men's Society served the needs of those often deemed most at risk of going astray. For more mature adults, the Guilds of St Joseph (for men) and of St Mary (for women) grew steadily from the 1840s. Both blended sociability with self-improvement, as for instance the prize awarded by the former to the member with the cleanest house. While many contemporary outside observers habitually depicted the Irish as heavy drinkers, there was a strong strand of teetotalism in parochial organisations.[15] The Catholic Total Abstinence Society was started as early as 1839, the Catholic Young Men's Society also advocated temperance, and the Irish National Association in Glasgow imposed a no drinks policy at its annual St Patrick's Day celebrations in the 1860s.

This parish-based system thus created a distinctive Irish Catholic community in Scotland. The wide spectrum of organisations which sprang up – one Dundee church had nine societies – encouraged people with differing interests to cohere. Group support and solidarity was promoted by communal events, such as bazaars and other fund-raising activities, including concerts and parish soirees. The emergence of voluntary associations – from none in 1838, there were eighty in Glasgow by 1851 – developed the self-confidence of the immigrants and fostered pride in their new identity. One important step in building the willingness of Catholics to appear in the civic sphere outside the safe confines of the parish was the rise of public processions on important ceremonial days in the church's calendar. Marches through town centres, with bands playing, emblems and flags flying, and religious effigies and icons borne aloft, all gave physical embodiment of their pride in their faith.

Equally significantly, the mushrooming of voluntary associations yielded a corps of secular leaders who acquired influence both within the parish and in the wider urban context. These people were perforce obliged to assume the responsibility of running parish societies, especially in the period between 1830 and the 1860s, when, as we have seen, priests were very sparsely spread over the western Lowlands. The majority of this lay cadre was drawn from a distinct middle-class segment, which, for the most part, was petit bourgeois. They were shopkeepers, traders and small businessmen, with a smattering of professionals such as doctors, lawyers, teachers and journalists. Thus, the leading figures who founded the Glasgow St Vincent de Paul society in 1848 included a coal merchant, a commission agent, a schoolteacher and several shopkeepers. Patrick Rogan, a Glasgow shopkeeper, was one of these people; he had been active in church affairs for a quarter of a century since 1840, over which period he had donated £1,800 to churches in and around the city.

As an indication of the formation of this social cohort, a newspaper – the *Glasgow Free Press* – was launched in 1851, initially to counter the anti-Catholic 'Papal Aggression' propaganda triggered by the restoration of the English hierarchy, and, more generally, it promoted the interest of the Irish in Scotland. The circulation of the paper, which was owned and edited locally, fluctuated between 1,200 and a peak of 5,000 during its lifetime of eighteen years. These figures compare quite favourably with the contemporary press: in 1855, the *Glasgow Herald* sold 5,200 copies, and all the Edinburgh papers, apart from the

Scotsman, were below 1,500. Like most other newspapers of its time, the readership of the *Free Press* would very probably have been mainly middle class.

IRISH CATHOLICS AND BRITISHNESS

The accommodation of the immigrants to the host society was strongly propelled by the clergy, who were predominantly cosmopolitan and not Irish in this period. The education of Catholic children was rarely undertaken by Christian Brothers, who were the major teaching force in Ireland and almost totally Irish in personnel. Instead, the less intensely Irish Marist Brothers had a larger Scottish role, while French and English nuns had a vital part in providing schooling from mid-century. All these organisations, but especially the women religious, stressed the central need for the Irish immigrants to dilute their cultural traditions and instead to embrace British and Scottish values in order to become respectable and successful. At the apogee of this lobby was Archbishop Eyre, who repeatedly insisted on following British, not Irish, practices and customs.

In line with much of the indoctrination purveyed by the church and parish associations about loyalty to Britain, the general stance taken by the immigrants to most political developments in Ireland was not one of passionate engagement, and there was little support for historical myth-making and memorialising. Violent uprisings in Ireland drew only vestigial support from Irish people in Scotland. This was largely true of 1798, and Young Ireland's abortive revolution in 1848 produced no major sympathetic demonstrations in Scotland, in contrast to England, where unrest broke out in London, Liverpool and Manchester. Fenianism likewise broadly fell flat in Scotland, as few participated in the 1867 rising, and after the Second Reform Act of 1868, interest turned to parliamentary politics.

Part of the failure of the Fenians to make headway in Scotland was because of opposition from the intensely pro-British church hierarchy, and the desire of post-Famine immigrants to focus on advancement in their new country. But another factor was the rise in the 1870s of moderate nationalism in Scotland, firstly in the form of the Irish Home Government Association, then as Parnellite Home Rulers. This movement was led by John Ferguson, an Ulster Protestant who ran a profitable printing concern in Glasgow. He was the first prominent Irish nationalist in mainland Britain to endorse both the leadership of Parnell and his strategy, and he rapidly became one of Parnell's closest colleagues. Ferguson skilfully directed the Scottish wing of the movement away from a narrow focus on exclusively Irish questions, and he strove to allay native Scottish concerns about Irish nationalism by adhering to a strictly constitutionalist approach and ensuring that neither Fenians nor Catholic clergy wielded any great influence within his party.

An appreciable portion of Ferguson's success derived from a significant shift which occurred in the 1860s, and was brought about by two organisations, namely the National Brotherhood of Saint Patrick, formed in 1861, and the Irish National Association of Scotland, which began in 1864. These both encouraged a shift among revolutionaries to embracing constitutional politics, which in great part was achieved by emphasising citizenship and nationalism as core objectives. The Brotherhood was essentially cultural in its focus; it provided reading rooms, containing, among other matter, publications on Irish history, but it also sought to demonstrate that Irish national consciousness was not totally identical with Roman Catholicism. The Irish National Association directed its attention to those born in Scotland of Irish descent, and it strove to link an awareness of Irish heritage with goals of self-improvement and respectability. Hence, as noted, it was teetotal, and it had a hall available for use by, for example, dancing classes and drama groups, while books and papers were provided for self-education. Additionally, the association reinforced its credentials as a socially aspirational institution by organising boat trips down the Clyde. In such ways, these two bodies opened up a vista of a democratic, sophisticated nationalism which was independent of an overweening Roman Catholic influence.

Ferguson constantly sought to establish connections between Irish problems and domestic Scottish social issues. This was especially evident as the land crisis escalated in Ireland after 1877, which obviously had parallels with the emerging tensions in the crofting regions, and links between the two movements were established. Michael Davitt, a driving force in the Irish Land League, toured the western Highlands, speechifying and dispensing advice on tactics. Edward McHugh, who came from Ulster Catholic stock, was active in the Glasgow Irish Land league branch, and then became Scottish organiser for the Land League of Great Britain. McHugh had a very influential impact on crofters when he visited several Highland localities in 1882, urging the case for a common front against landowners. But the land issue also stimulated a political reappraisal among sections of the Lowland urban working class, for it raised questions about the links between property rights and poor social conditions in towns. The outcome was the development of socialist groups in the early 1880s, culminating in the formation of the Scottish Labour Party in 1888, five years before its English equivalent, the Independent Labour Party. Ferguson was highly sympathetic to this new direction, and served on the first executive board of the Scottish Labour Party. Additionally, like several early socialists, he was an enthusiastic supporter of Scottish Home Rule.

Ferguson's approach chimed in with the prevailing feeling among Irish Catholic immigrants of loyalty to Britain; for instance, the 1845 Dundee Irish Repeal meeting concluded with three cheers for Queen Victoria. The highly influential upper-class converts were, not unexpectedly, unswervingly in favour, but so were the office-bearers of the St Vincent de Paul Society, while the Glasgow Guild of St Joseph toasted Queen Victoria at soirees and dinners.

Indeed, as has been touched upon in Chapter 3, Irish people participated alongside Scots in most of the major political movements of the period. They were very active in the Radical years between 1815 and 1830, and they took part in the agitation for the First Reform Act. The consequences of Catholic Emancipation and then the 1832 Reform Act gave the Irish in Scotland greater confidence about their political role, so that they were prominent in subsequent British reform campaigns. They had a visible profile in Chartism, where they were mostly identified with the moderate moral force wing, although two of the fiercest champions of physical force in Britain were Irishmen, namely, Bronterre O'Brien and Fergus O'Connor. When in 1865 the Radical Robert Dalglish was elected to parliament for Glasgow, there were Irishmen acting on his committee, and the Scottish National Reform League, which organised the campaign for the Second Reform, had many Irish delegates on the various trade societies. As discussed in Chapter 3, many trade unions had dedicated support from Irish workers, notably in mining and textiles. Naturally, most labour questions, especially where legislation was involved, necessitated a British perspective.

CATHOLIC SCHOOLING

A critical dilemma for the Catholic community was posed by educational provision, as good schooling was seen as the most effective means of achieving social mobility. But a range of factors combined to make this goal well-nigh unattainable in this period. The more prominent obstacles were very limited financial resources, a lack of trained teachers, economic pressure on parents to put children to work from an early age, and an unwavering resolve to have children taught in a Catholic religious environment.

One of the first attempts to establish schooling in the Lowlands for Irish immigrants' children was the Catholic School Society, founded in Glasgow in 1817. The initiative for this came from both Protestants and Catholics, and Kirkman Finlay, the city's MP, was the first chairman, but all the teachers were Roman Catholic. By the later 1820s, the society catered for 1,400 pupils in day and evening classes, but with perhaps 30,000 Irish Catholics in the city, this was only a very partial coverage, and these inadequacies were deepened under the impact of heavy immigration in the Famine period. Two developments alleviated the crisis. Firstly, government funding was made available with the creation in 1847 of the Catholic Poor Schools Committee, which assisted expansion, especially by awarding grants to cover the cost of using pupil-teachers, so that in 1851 Glasgow had 12 schools, containing 2,500 children. The second influence was, as noted, the advent of teaching religious orders. In the 1850s, two female orders set up schools for girls, and the Marists and the Jesuits provided education for boys.

Yet, shortly before the 1872 Education Act, the extent of the challenge facing the Lowland Catholic community was apparent. In all of Scotland, in 1870 there were sixty-one Roman Catholic schools, but there were seventy-four Episcopalian schools, although adherents to the latter church were no more than a quarter of the former. In Glasgow, limited growth had taken place since 1850, as there were now sixteen church schools, but less than one-third of eligible children were in regular attendance, the schools were badly overcrowded and the education offered to most was very basic. One city parish had no school, and there were only two institutions in the city teaching students above the elementary level. Grim as these Glasgow data were, the situation in the adjacent counties was bleaker; thus, in Lanarkshire, Hamilton and Airdrie alone had a school each, with a combined tally of 150 on the rolls.

The 1872 act stipulated the context within which Catholic schooling could continue to function, but it also rendered the delivery of good-quality education more problematic than ever. While the act permitted voluntary schools to exist outside the state system, it prescribed that they would receive no building grants or financial support from funds raised by school rates, although everyone was obliged to pay this tax.

The Catholic hierarchy opted to remain outside the state framework, primarily because they suspected – correctly, as was soon apparent – that, while Protestant control had formally been ceded, the new schools would retain a substantial element of Presbyterian indoctrination in various modes of instruction. A determined effort was made to meet the requirements of the new regime, with some impressive results. In 1872, there were 12,000 pupils in 65 grant-aided schools, and 10 years later, this had grown to 33,000 children and 138 schools. Even so, in 1879 at least one-quarter of the eligible children in the Glasgow archdiocese were not at school. Even among those enrolled, irregular attendance was a persistent problem, which reflected the precarious financial position of many Irish Catholics, as did the pattern of most children leaving education at an early age; pupils aged 10–11 years comprised 11.3 per cent of the total number of scholars, but the 12–13-year-olds made up only 4.8 per cent.

These figures were all significantly worse than in the state system, and they were reinforced by the paucity of post-elementary schooling on offer for Catholic children, which was arguably the most profound long-term barrier to achieving the objective of social advancement by means of education. In 1872 there were only three Glasgow Catholic secondary schools, and the two boys' colleges were in a threadbare state; St Aloysius's had 40 students, and St Mungo's, 150. Elsewhere in the western Lowland heartlands, the situation was just as bad: for example, Ayrshire had to wait until 1909 – almost forty years after the Education Act – for its first post-primary school.

The consequence was that the Catholic school sector found itself in a vicious circle. It could only improve the quality and number of trained teachers if there were more secondary school pupils, who could then proceed to be trained as qualified teachers, which in turn would generate more income from the government grant system. But there were two drawbacks. Firstly, employing more trained staff, although highly desirable from a pedagogic standpoint, carried a considerable financial burden, whereas pupil-teachers and unqualified teachers were much less well paid. Secondly, with so few post-primary students, the impetus to create a teacher training institute was not pressing, and it was not until 1894 that one was built. Before then, teachers had to go to English training colleges. The consequence was that in 1886, unqualified teachers in the state sector comprised 24 per cent of men and 29 per cent of women, but in Catholic schools, they made up 39 per cent of men and 59 per cent of women.

At the core of this stark situation was the acute financial burden which was laid upon the Catholic population. They were compelled by law to pay the education rates levied by the local school board, which went entirely to defraying the expenses of the state education system. Additionally, however, they were exhorted by their church to contribute generously on a voluntary basis to meet the costs of maintaining their own Catholic schools. But many of these parishioners were among the least well-off and most financially vulnerable people in Scottish society, so their donations were not able to match the resources which the state schools received from the rates. In consequence, in 1886, income per pupil in state schools (£2.12) was one-third higher than in the Catholic sector (£1.60). The outcomes of this disparity in resources intensified the qualitative and quantitative disparities between the two educational spheres. Class sizes in Catholic schools were much larger than school board institutions, and in 1877 there were 150 pupils per teacher in the former, a ratio which had not altered appreciably since about 1850. With most staff untrained, teaching amounted to little more than instruction in literacy and numeracy to fairly rudimentary levels.

NOTES

1. W. M. Mathew, 'The Origins and Occupations of Glasgow Students, 1740–1839', *Past & Present*, 33 (1966), 82–4.
2. Ibid., 78–84; R. D. Anderson, *Education and Opportunity in Victorian Scotland* (1983), ch. 4.
3. K. Fenyo, *Contempt, Sympathy and Romance: Lowland Perceptions of the Highlands and the Clearances during the Famine Years, 1845–55* (2000), 46–65, gives several instances.

4. J. Loch, *An Account of the Improvements in the Estates of the Marquess of Stafford in the Counties of Stafford and Salop, and on the Estate of Sutherland, with Remarks* (1820).
5. J. H. Burton, 'Celtic Clearings – Free Sites – Highland Passes', *Edinburgh Review*, 86 (1847), 499–511.
6. See pp. 23, 31.
7. See pp. 29–30.
8. See pp. 195–201.
9. This is discussed at pp. 61–2.
10. See pp. 285–6.
11. See pp. 214–15.
12. *Edinburgh Observer*, 24 June 1828.
13. E.g. A. D. Gibb, *Scotland in Eclipse* (1930), 55–7. Gibb was Regius professor of Scots law at Glasgow University, and a prominent Scottish nationalist in the inter-war era.
14. J. Devon, 'The Calton Fifty Years Ago', *Transactions of the Old Glasgow Club*, 6 (1930–1), 3.
15. J. E. Handley, *The Irish in Modern Scotland* (1947), 157–62, gives numerous critical case studies.

CHAPTER 7

Politics in the Era of Revolutions, c. 1780–1815

CURRENTS OF REFORM ON THE EVE OF THE FRENCH REVOLUTION

The outbreak in 1789 of the French Revolution galvanised opinion in Scotland across most levels of society. The prominent Whig memoirist, Henry Cockburn, famously recalled that '[e]verything rung, and was connected with the Revolution in France; which, for above 20 years, was, or was made, the all in all. Everything, not this thing or that thing, but literally everything, was soaked in this one event'.[1] As with most of his *obiter dicta*, this description mainly embraced the confined world of Edinburgh lawyers and literati, but the reverberations of 14 July ramified more generally.

There was initially widespread approval of the revolution, although the reasons for this broad spectrum of support were not uniform, rather ranging from high-minded principles to baser calculations. The last apostles of the Scottish Enlightenment, John Millar and Dugald Stewart, professors at, respectively, Glasgow and Edinburgh universities, hailed the revolution as welcome evidence of the movement of society in a progressive direction. Whigs acclaimed the Paris events as the French equivalent of Britain's 'Glorious Revolution', whose centenary had just been enthusiastically commemorated, and immediately the news reached Scotland, the Whig Club of Dundee sent a congratulatory message to the French National Assembly. Many, such as the independent MP George Dempster, warmly anticipated a wave of constitutional advances across the whole of Europe.[2] Presbyterian clergymen in both established and secession churches were in general well-disposed to the new regime: Thomas Somerville, the Moderate Church of Scotland minister in Jedburgh, was but one example. Given the influence in the state church of Moderate men, who were resistant to democratic tendencies in church government, the positive response seems surprising. It may be that some of the enthusiasm arose from a sense of *Schadenfreude* at the blow dealt by the revolution to the strength of the Roman Catholic Church, as France had been its main champion in Europe. For Tories, too, there were reasons to be cheerful: the long historical threat posed by Bourbon France to the security of Britain and its empire seemed removed, as the new rulers stressed peace and the international brotherhood of man. Businessmen saw the prospects for closer economic ties and a reduction in French protectionist tariffs as a distinct possibility. This consensus of opinion was reflected in the Scottish press, which, broadly speaking, looked on the early stages of the revolution with favour.

This widespread outburst of celebration had several deeper causes. Partly it chimed with political developments within Scotland during the 1780s, a good deal of which emanated from the consequences of the American War of Independence. The war had a double-faceted impact on Scotland. As outlined in Chapter 6, much of Scottish opinion initially supported the British government enthusiastically. This new status of reliability and integration may have given the Scots confidence to assert demands for fuller political and civil rights.

But the American revolt also fitted into the case for political reform. For a growing body of opinion, the incompetence of the British government in handling both the run-up to and the conduct of the war became a source of concern. The Whiggish MP for Roxburghshire, Gilbert Elliot, gradually progressed from supporting the war at its outset to becoming by 1782 a stern critic of British policy. Many agreed with him: in Aberdeen, where sentiment at the start of the war was behind the government, there was a clear shift to bewailing the deficiencies of the British political and military elites. This analysis reinforced the Whig critique that the constitutional balance between executive and legislature was being corrupted by the growing influence of the Crown, with patronage and placemen eroding the independent power of parliament.

More specifically Scottish issues were raised by the colonists' war. The link between taxation and representation was highly relevant, given Scotland's distinctly narrow electoral base, and the bromide offered by the theory of virtual representation was also effectively challenged. Both burgh and county political reform movements emerged in the early 1780s as a natural outcome of these factors. The campaign for burgh reform had two origins. One was discontent in several places at the refusal of the constituency MP to listen to the views of the citizenry, which led to demands to make MPs more responsive to their constituents – an emergent principle resoundingly established in the United States. The most significant instance of this occurred in Glasgow, where grievances about the impact of the American war on the city's trade and prosperity – it was claimed that income of about £1,500,000 had been lost – were ignored by the local MP. Glasgow's disapproval of government policy was highlighted when Edmund Burke, the most eloquent critic of the administration's handling of the American crisis both before and during the war, was elected rector of Glasgow

University in November 1783. The election of the rector lay in the hands of the students, who were overwhelmingly drawn from mercantile and commercial families in the city and its environs.

The second impetus for burgh reform arose from the inadequacies of Scottish municipal government, which were glaringly exposed in the aftermath of the American war. The grievances aired in the 1780s were manifold, and while the specific complaints naturally differed across burghs, depending on which abuses were locally more pronounced, the general tenor was clear: the principle of no taxation without representation had an irresistible appeal. A further grievance related to parliamentary representation. All the fifteen burgh MPs were chosen only by the self-elected councillors of the component burghs, with no regard to the wishes of the generality of the inhabitants. This explained why, as in the case of Glasgow over the loss of the American colonies, the views of the populace had no weight with members of parliament; all that counted for the MP was to have the councillors on board.

> **Unreformed municipal government abuses**
>
> Apart from the highly restricted electoral systems, whereby councillors were not approved by any form, however frail, of a popular vote, the focus of complaints about the operational aspects of unreformed burgh councils can be grouped into three categories.
>
> **Finance:** Accounting records had at least four problems. Firstly, they were often difficult to understand, as in Aberdeen, where there were six separate accounts. Secondly, several were incomplete or destroyed. The Fortrose accounts had been handled for twenty years by one man, who had variously been provost, burgh treasurer, dean of guild and a councillor, and there were no substantiating cash books or vouchers. Thirdly, other financial reports were, intentionally or not, inaccurate. Fraserburgh kept two sets of accounts, one to show to creditors, while in 1809, Aberdeen Council claimed its indebtedness came to £6,874, whereas in reality it owed between £130,000 and £140,000. The valuation of property was sometimes overstated, in order to secure advances to help service spiralling indebtedness. So, the council's valuation of Dumbarton burgh assets rose from £10,658 in 1810 to £17,911 in 1833, while total debts grew from some £10,000 in 1819 to around £19,000 in 1833. Fourthly, some councils kept the accounts hidden from public scrutiny: Dunfermline permitted only a select group of councillors to see them.
>
> **Property:** Council-owned assets were often given to councillors, their relatives and associates at bargain prices and with no public transparency. Between 1774 and 1816, all the property owned by Tain Council was sold off to councillors, while in Lochmaben, the provost's father-in-law acquired

a council-owned farm, with no mention of the transaction recorded in the burgh minutes. Between 1812 and 1817, Edinburgh Council sold several properties it owned in Midlothian to councillors and their friends, with no public advertisements.

Patronage: Contracts for council works were regularly allocated to those in or connected to the inner circle on highly favourable terms. In Anstruther East, one councillor repaired harbours and streets every year, without submitting estimates and with no assessment made of the need for the works to be carried out. Over-runs on Edinburgh Council building works in which councillors were involved came to £20,000 on St George's Church and £23,000 on the Royal High School. Appointments to jobs under a council's purview was another fruitful source of abuse. In 1803, the new town clerk of Forfar was the young son of a councillor, and in 1822 an application was made to the courts that he be removed on the grounds that he was 'retarded', but this failed as the appointment was for life. In Fraserburgh, the town clerk and harbour master was a twelve-year-old apprentice serving in a councillor's legal firm. Expenditure on entertainment was a third form of patronage. Between 1819 and 1822, Edinburgh Council spent some £2,600 under this heading, while the small and impecunious burgh of Inverurie paid £600 in tavern bills between 1805 and 1817 to a local innkeeper, who was the long-term burgh provost.

It was emphatically not the case that every burgh council was riddled with corruption. Several places, such as Perth, Paisley and Glasgow, were regarded as pretty well pure in most major aspects.

The case for burgh reform gained saliency in 1781, when Stirling Council had its original constitution replaced by a new, more open system: there were now no non-resident councillors, and burgesses with property worth over £5 were enfranchised. A pamphlet published pseudonymously in 1783 by an Edinburgh merchant argued the general need for reform, and the movement quickly gathered pace.[3] By 1788, fifty of the sixty-six royal burghs were involved in the campaign to improve municipal administration, although the strength of the movement was somewhat vitiated by Glasgow's refusal to participate. But wider political sentiments than local complaints were raised, as in 1787, when burgh reformers contended that the Treaty of Union offered more than narrowly economic benefits, namely the prospect that

> the liberties of England, which had rendered that nation illustrious, happy and powerful, might in time be communicated to Scotland. Until this event shall happen, it cannot with justice be said that the Scottish nation has experienced in their full extent the fortunate and brilliant consequences which were expected from the Union.[4]

In an interesting foreshadowing of subsequent radical Scottish movements, by 1788 reformers in fifty-two burghs, including Aberdeen, Edinburgh and Stirling, had formed links with the Yorkshire Association, led by Christopher Wyvill, which sought to amend the English county franchise system.

Simultaneously, a campaign to eliminate defects in the county franchise system gathered momentum in the 1780s, also partly inspired by Wyvill's organisation. There were two interconnected problems in Scotland: the exceptionally small size of the electorate compared to England, and the basis on which the franchise was given. Between 1780 and 1832, the total Scottish county electorate ranged from around 2,500 to 3,000 or so. In 1790, there were in all 2,625 voters, which meant that only five of the 40 English counties had fewer voters than all of Scotland, and the largest, Yorkshire, alone had over 20,000. The biggest in Scotland, Ayrshire, had 220 voters; a mere eight Scottish counties boasted over 100 voters, but 12 had fewer than 50, and Cromarty, with six, was the smallest.

The reason for the minuscule electorate was the peculiar Scottish county franchise system. The right to vote, which was in most cases based on possession of land valued at £400 Scots (about £35 sterling), was conferred not through the actual ownership of land (*dominium utile*), but by ownership of the feudal superiority of the property (*dominium directum*). These two forms of ownership were separate legal entities in Scotland, whereas in England feudal superiorities had been abolished in the seventeenth century. When alienating real property, owners took care to retain the feudal rights, partly because feu-duty was a source of regular income, but also to wield power at elections. Hence, in all counties there were many lairds with good-sized estates who were voteless, but in England they would have been electors. In Stirlingshire in 1775, 205 landowners possessed property worth over £100 sterling, but only 51 of these were on the electoral roll; while in Kirkcudbrightshire, under one-sixth of owners of property worth more than £100 sterling were voters.

Further discontent was fomented by the practical operation of the franchise system. With the assistance of a competent lawyer, it was relatively straightforward for a feudal superior with property above the minimum qualification to carve up the feudal rights into packages of £400 Scots, thereby creating additional votes. These voters could be non-residents in the constituency, and frequently were Edinburgh lawyers or London-based individuals with political or personal affiliations to the feudal owner. Egregious as ever, Henry Brougham stated the implications in 1810: 'all the Scottish county members may be elected by a few Jews living in Amsterdam, provided they visit Scotland at the election'.[5] Clauses inserted in the transfer of the superiority provided for the qualification to be taken back in a change of circumstances, such as death or political differences. In 1793, it was claimed that around 1,200 voters out of the total county electorate of 2,650 were fictitious. In many counties, the fictitious outnumbered the real voters; in Banffshire in 1795 there were about forty real and seventy paper voters, most of the latter created by the earl of Fife, the largest feudal proprietor in the county. In 1790, General James Grant won in Sutherland without receiving a single vote from an elector with a real property qualification.

There were therefore two disgruntled sets of lairds: those who did not hold the superiority to the land they owned, and those who did have the vote, but felt swamped by an army of fictitious voters who followed the instructions of their benefactor. This latter group of critics frequently termed themselves the independent county voters, and had a better chance of effecting some improvement in their position than the voteless men, who would require an act of parliament to meet their demand. It was quite improbable that the government would embark on a measure of reform which could easily precipitate demands from Wyvill's Yorkshire Association for change in England. Accordingly, an agitation to address the creation of so-called parchment voters quickly spread across Scotland in the early 1780s. Where the disgruntled real voters managed to organise opposition to the great landowners, it often proved possible to severely reduce, if not entirely eliminate, fictitious voters. The Ayrshire electorate fell by half in the space of a year, from 220 in 1790 to 110 in 1791, while between 1790 and 1794, Inverness-shire shed four-fifths of its voters, dropping from 103 to 21. Dramatic though this process was, it had three aspects which rather blunted its long-term impact. Firstly, it relied on constituency-level activism: thus, Norman MacLeod of MacLeod led the Inverness-shire insurgents, and in Banffshire, a fall from 108 voters in 1790 to 39 in 1794 was brought about by an alliance of lesser lairds determined to curb Lord Fife's control of the seat. But elsewhere, lack of leadership or internal divisions inhibited action. The absence of an effective nationwide organisation prevented a sustained, broad-based assault on the abuse of fictitious votes. Secondly, dependency on energetic individuals carried the risk of a decline in activity over time. MacLeod lost interest in politics in the mid-1790s as he advanced in his military career: from 1794 to 1801 he served as a major-general. Meanwhile, the Banffshire reformers' alliance splintered in disagreement over subsequent electoral strategy. Thirdly, the offending vote manufacturers rarely accepted the curtailment of their power base because of a Damascene conversion. Many appreciated that clinging to fictitious voters risked alienating independent real voters, which could prove counterproductive; this was the stance taken by the duke of Montrose in Stirlingshire. But once the agitation faded, many resumed vote creation, sometimes on an industrial scale: by 1811, Ayrshire voters had swollen to 151 from 110 in 1791.

THE OPTIMISM OF THE WHIGS

These currents of dissent encouraged the Scottish Whigs in the later 1780s. In all parts of Britain, the Whig party had suffered a serious rebuff in the general election of 1784, when they were swept away by supporters of the prime minister, William Pitt the Younger, who enjoyed the unstinted support of George III. But the Scottish results, although disappointing, had not been as bad as in England, and this, combined with the growth of these reform-minded burgh and county movements, emboldened the Scottish Whigs. As an instance of this process, the party latched on to the campaign for burgh reform, and the Irish playwright and Whig MP Richard Sheridan became the parliamentary spokesman for the cause. Between 1788 and 1793, he raised the question on four occasions in the Commons, but made virtually no headway. Another avenue linked with the wave of reform mentality was opened in 1785, when Henry Erskine, who had briefly served as Lord Advocate in 1783, orchestrated the formation of the Independent Friends. This was a thinly disguised Whiggish organisation which sought to draw in those disenchanted with the Scottish political system and generally opposed to the imposition by George III of Pitt as prime minister. At its peak, the Independent Friends numbered between 100 and 150, including 16 peers and 12 MPs.

In the approach to 1790 general election, the Whigs entertained high hopes of dislodging Pitt's administration, some of whose policies had been unpopular in Scotland. In 1784, a proposed coal tax had to be dropped, and a revised duty on linen was widely criticised. In the following year, landowners objected to a government plan to import cheap Irish grain, and an attempt to reform the Court of Session was resisted as a breach of the Treaty of Union. The Whigs' optimism was heightened by a marked growth in organisational competence, as Erskine claimed in 1789, 'we have now for five years back maintained or rather created an opposition in Scotland without example in times past'.[6] William Adam of Blair Adam acted as the British party's co-ordinator in the run-up to the general election of 1790. Adam, backed by financial support from Whig grandees, pre-eminently the duke of Portland, carried out methodical preparations to ensure that candidates were in place in winnable constituencies, that voters had been canvassed and that arrangements were made to get supporters to the poll on election day. Adam's duties covered all of Britain, but, not surprisingly, he was very active in Scottish seats: of the eighty-three constituencies in which he was involved, around fifteen were Scottish. As a result, the increase in Scottish contests (33 per cent) was proportionately far higher than in England and Wales (2 per cent), and this number was not exceeded in the remainder of the unreformed era. But the results in Scotland were disastrous for the Whigs: whereas even in the dark days of the 1784 contest, they had held fifteen seats, in 1790 only six definite supporters got in – plus one 'independent', who was rather optimistically identified as a possible adherent. The party had been comprehensively outmanoeuvred by Henry Dundas. In this context, the widespread positive reaction to developments in France offered a promising escape from the electoral impasse confronting the Whigs.

Table 7.1 General Election results, England and Scotland, 1784–1812[a]

	Tory		Whig		Other[b]	
	England	Scotland	England	Scotland	England	Scotland
1784	282	24	188	15	21	6
1790	289	36	168	6	28	3
1796	361	43	93	0	31	2
1802	337	39	123	1	25	5
1806	65	14	234	28	186	3
1807	289	27	152	13	47	5
1812	293	29	147	9	45	7

Notes:
[a] Based on L. B. Namier and J. Brooke (eds), *The House of Commons, 1754–1790*, Vol. I, *Introductory Survey* (1964), 126–41; R. G. Thorne (ed.), *The House of Commons, 1790–1820*, Vol. I, *Introductory Survey* (1986), 110–277
[b] 'Other' includes Independents, Neutrals and Doubtfuls

SCOTTISH REFORM POLITICS DURING THE FRENCH REVOLUTION, 1789–96

As noted, the popular response to events in France between 1789 and late 1792 was strikingly positive. Trees of liberty were planted in various places, including Aberdeen and Perth, while red caps were widely worn, as a symbolic gesture of solidarity with the revolutionaries. There were mass displays of hostility to the representatives of the existing order, as at Perth in 1792: 'This is our Race Week and a great show of company. The Reformers have been burning Mr Dundas in effigy and making great disturbance – <u>Liberty</u> and Equality pasted up in every quarter.'[7] These responses occurred not just in larger towns, but also in smaller burghs and semi-rural villages across the Lowlands. In Ayrshire, the revolution was excitedly discussed by the Monkland Friendly Society, a gathering of tenant-farmers and tradesmen, one of whose members was Robert Burns. Lord Bute complained that 'even in this sequestered spot . . . liberty and the rights of man are inscribed upon every door of the cotton mill in Rothesay'.[8] In Perthshire and Angus, weaving centres were hotbeds of radical admiration for the French, while the existence of a group of radicals in Portsoy created alarm among Banffshire lairds.

Against this background, the response in Scotland to the publication in March 1791 of the first part of Tom Paine's *The Rights of Man*, the most celebrated paean to the ideology of the French Revolution, was impressive. It appeared to elicit great enthusiasm among the less exalted classes. Some 10,000 copies were sold in Scotland, and 123 groups were formed in 66 different locations to study the book. A Gaelic translation was available for Highlanders – a good decade before the official Gaelic Bible appeared. Part II of *The Rights of Man* appeared in 1792 and was just as enthusiastically received. Nevertheless, the full Paineite programme was taken up by very few Scots; J. T. Callander was virtually unique in so doing, and he fled the country in early 1793. Almost all the demands and rhetoric of the reformers were couched more in the traditional Whig terms of corruption and executive tyranny, plus the need to restore lost rights, with few allusions to Paine's core themes of social welfare and natural rights.

The emergence of considerable non-elite support for reform and the interest in Paine's writings prompted a concerted bid by upper-class Whigs to constrain and channel these new forces. In England, aristocratic Whigs had founded the Friends of the People in April 1792 as an exclusive body for the political elite, leaving more plebeian individuals to set up separate organisations, the most influential of which was the London Corresponding Society, mainly comprising artisans and tradesmen. Whigs played a key role in establishing the Scottish Friends of the People in July 1792; Henry Erskine, Norman MacLeod of MacLeod and Professor John Millar attended the inaugural meeting. In sharp contrast to England, however, the Scottish Friends aimed to embrace merchants, tradesmen and artisans by setting subscriptions at a low rate: in the Glasgow branch, it was 5p a year, compared to £2.62 in England. The objective of the Scottish Whigs was to lead and guide the broad reform movement, with the view both of gaining political support and of simultaneously restraining more radical tendencies among the middle and working classes. This strategy became their enduring principle down to the Reform Bill crises of 1832, and indeed it persisted long thereafter. These calculations were exemplified in the draft programme set out by the movement, which denounced the Corn Laws and the Test Acts, and called for equal representation and shorter parliaments, but studiously avoided any specific scheme of franchise reform and did not mention annual parliaments or the ballot. There was virtually no interest in the problems of the poor or in the redistribution of wealth, so the overall approach was closer to the Foxite than the Paineite agenda.

At the outset, the Scottish Friends attracted wide support, with branches springing up not just in the central Lowlands, but also in the Highlands, the Borders and the south-west. Membership in local associations was sometimes high; Glasgow claimed 400 members, in Perth four societies were formed, each with around 25 members, but it was Edinburgh which had the greatest number of supporters. The Scottish Friends also drew in support from both the burgh and county reformers, who hoped that greater weight would thereby be given by parliament to their demands.

The first national convention organised by the Friends met in Edinburgh on 11–13 December 1792, and was attended by some 170 representatives from 79 branches, based in 35 towns and villages. The majority came from the central Lowlands, with around one-half drawn from the Edinburgh area. In contrast, the north-east sent one delegate, and none came from the Highlands and Islands. Resolutions were passed which, for the most part, did not stray far from the Whigs' demands: annual parliaments and universal male suffrage were not approved. The case for reform was couched in terms of the restoration of the constitutional settlement of 1688–9, rather than referring to more radical arguments, such as those of the seventeenth-century English Levellers or Paine's natural rights theory. More militant voices were raised, notably Thomas Muir, a Glasgow advocate, who pressed for close links with Irish radicals and used Paineite rhetoric, but these were decisively rejected. The convention did, however, agree to co-operate with the English Friends and with the London Corresponding Society. The convention therefore seemed to have been successful and to have laid the foundations for future development, and it was decided to hold a second meeting in the first half of the following year.

But before the second convention could meet, the political environment changed drastically, with the result that significant groups and individuals involved with the Scottish Friends withdrew. There were four core influences at work. Firstly, the reaction of many erstwhile sympathisers to the French Terror, which was launched in autumn 1792, was one of shock and disgust. George Dempster moved far from his initial enthusiasm, now expressing dismay at events and disillusion with the fundamental principles of the revolution.[9] For many, such as the Rev. Thomas Somerville and Gilbert Elliot, it was these events, rather than reading Burke's jeremiad, *Reflections on the Revolution in France* (1790), which influenced moderate opinion adversely. Secondly, many upper- and middle-class people were unsettled by the behaviour of the urban working class in late 1792. There were riots against the authorities in several towns, with disturbances in Dundee lasting over nine days. In Langholm, some workingmen toasted 'George the Third – and Last'. The jubilant reaction of many working-class people to the victory of the French over Austria at the battle of Jemappe (6 November 1792) added to concerns among the better-off. Thirdly, the conviction in January 1793 of several reformers charged with sedition alarmed a substantial body of reformers who shrank from any taint of association with extreme radicalism. Fourthly, the outbreak of hostilities with France in February 1793 further tested many to breaking point, as patriotism was placed above support for reform.

As a result of these factors, three moderate groups detached themselves from the Scottish Friends in the early months of 1793. The bulk of upper- and middle-class Whigs, with Erskine in the van, announced they could not continue as members, on the grounds that the convention demanded ultra-radical measures of parliamentary reform, such as franchise extension. The reduction of the influence of the Crown was the Whigs' prime target, which would be more effectively achieved by eliminating electoral corruption and reducing the influence wielded by aristocrats on behalf of the executive. Thus, the position of Erskine – and John Millar – was that while changes to the burgh council franchise were acceptable, their extension to the parliamentary vote was not. Additionally, the Whigs steadfastly refused to endorse outright opposition on principle to the war with France.

Resistance to widening the franchise also caused the departure of those associated with the county and burgh reform agitations. The county reformers had never called for extending the right to vote, but rather targeted the abolition of fictitious votes as the essential – and more immediately achievable – improvement. Burgh reformers were more concerned at the unaccountability of town councils, which allowed corruption and malversation of funds to occur with impunity. They had frequently stressed that any amendments to the council franchise did not imply broadening the parliamentary vote qualification, as a leader of the campaign had stated in 1788: 'This you will be pleased to remark, has no connection with a parliamentary reform.'[10]

The second convention, which met in Edinburgh on 30 April 1793, was thus a changed and shrunken assembly from the first one. Only 28 branches were represented, compared to 79 at the first convention, and 117 delegates attended – a third fewer – with a higher proportion coming from Edinburgh and vicinity, while only three delegates came from Glasgow, against 12 before. As well as the changed geographical distribution, the social composition was appreciably altered, with those attending predominantly drawn from the lower middle classes; Lord Daer was virtually the only elite Whig present. With this diminished moderate presence, more radical motions were put forward and frequently carried, but while a resolution opposing the war with France was approved, the proposal to promulgate a Declaration of Rights on the French model was not passed. The government, alarmed at the tendency to extremist speeches at the convention, put Thomas Muir and T. F. Palmer, a Dundee Methodist minister, on trial for sedition in August and September 1793. The sentences handed down were ferociously severe – Muir was given fourteen years' transportation, and Palmer seven – especially compared to similar trials in England.

A third convention, sitting in Edinburgh for four days from 29 October 1793, suffered a further fall in support. Partly this was because it was called at short notice, in order not to alert government spies, and so it was poorly planned. But, more profoundly, attendance dropped because the repression after the previous convention resulted in a steep decline in both branches and membership. Some 163 delegates took part, but although this suggests a return to the level of the first convention, closer scrutiny indicates underlying problems. Fully two-thirds of those present hailed from Edinburgh, leaving only fifty-four from elsewhere, whereas at the first convention, ninety came from the 'country'. A distinctly more radical tone pervaded this convention. Styles and conventions used in the French National Assembly were adopted by the delegates; for instance, all were addressed as 'citizen'. A message from Irish radicals expressing views of a semi-revolutionary nature was read out, and resolutions calling for universal male suffrage and annual parliaments were easily carried, all of which had been firmly rejected in the two previous assemblies. Yet the prevailing tone remained constitutional, and connections with English radicals were maintained.

Shortly after the third convention closed, delegates from English reform societies arrived in Edinburgh and the Scottish delegates were recalled to attend the British Convention, which opened on 19 November. The English contingent injected a more radical content into debates, with firebrands like Maurice Margarot and Joseph Gerrald taking leading roles in the proceedings. The authorities quickly closed the convention, and four key figures, including Gerrald, Margarot and William Skirving (the secretary of the Edinburgh Friends), were tried for sedition. They were convicted by a hand-picked jury and, as with Muir and Palmer, condign sentences – transportation for fourteen years – were handed down. This was in part because the accused opted to defend themselves in order to use their speeches from the dock to publicise their political principles, which did little to soften the jury's attitude.

In anticipation of state action to suppress the reform movement, the third convention set up a secret committee (the Committee of Ways and Means – a nice nod to Westminster) to act as a co-ordinating agency for an underground existence. But the reformers had great difficulty in regrouping, as from late 1793 until 1797 the movement was in a state of near-hibernation, with activity quite dissipated. Moreover, in May 1794 a plot was uncovered in Edinburgh which sought to overthrow the agencies of the state and instal a people's government by means of an armed uprising. The ringleader, Robert Watt, was convicted of treason and executed, then he was decapitated, and this episode compounded the vulnerability of the reformers. This period of inertia contrasts strikingly with the situation in England, where radical reformers retained a significant presence, much to the concern of the authorities. In 1797, the London Corresponding Society was aware of seventy-two provincial radical societies, only eight of which were in Scotland. The London society was in correspondence with sixty-two of these bodies, but a mere five were Scottish. This discrepancy indicates the greater impact in Scotland of a harsher regime of general repression and of sentencing policy in particular.

In 1797, a hardcore element formed the United Scotsmen, which – like its Irish namesake – was an underground outfit with secret oaths and talk of armed action. But their numbers were not large, with no more than perhaps thirty branches, mainly in smaller towns in Perthshire, Fife and Ayrshire. But some places which had been hotbeds of radicalism until 1793 seem not to have been involved: Paisley is one instance of this. Until 1797, the Scottish underground radicals had closer, though intermittent, connections with English revolutionaries than with their Irish counterparts. In 1796, a deputation from the United Irishmen came across to rally the Scots, but the response was disappointing, and the Irish complained that the Scots lacked energy. The recourse to violence in Ireland in late 1797 and early 1798 led to divisions among Scottish revolutionaries, and there was little support even among committed United Scotsmen for the Irish rising in 1798. Talk of insurgency in Scotland in concert with French assistance came to nothing, and the United Scotsmen thereafter subsided from view, although there are hints that there was still a shadowy organisation bearing that name in 1816–17.

LOYALISM IN SCOTLAND

The failure of the democratic movement can be ascribed to several causes. On one hand, the authorities closely monitored the activities of reformers: Dundas instructed the Edinburgh postmaster to open the mail of suspected individuals, and he urged sheriffs to give information concerning local developments. Spies and informers, the latter often unpaid concerned members of the public, reported both to local magistrates and to central government, usually providing crucial details. But the reformers made self-inflicted errors. After the first convention, the Friends of the People alienated moderate opinion, especially by their support of France when war broke out, which placed them in a distinct minority, as Scotland responded enthusiastically to patriotic appeals. The reformers had no coherent strategy, beyond petitioning parliament or the monarch, and when this approach yielded no results, many became disheartened. The Friends did not manage to make connections with the range of protests and discontents which took place in the mid-1790s. There was widespread resistance to the Militia Act in 1797: in many places across the Lowlands non-cooperation by local people meant lists of eligible men could not be compiled, and numerous protest meetings were held. The most serious episode occurred at Tranent on 29 August, when troops killed eleven and wounded twelve demonstrators. But the opponents of the Militia Act evidently had no close links with the radicals. Moreover, while in England rising unemployment and food shortages led to unrest, in Scotland handloom weavers were thriving, and harvests were adequate. The Scottish reformers adopted Paine's political prescriptions, but ignored his social welfare proposals, which left them struggling to link a wider democratic system with reducing hardship among the working class.

A major inhibiting factor confronted by the reformers was the extent of loyalism in Scotland. The government assiduously cultivated this by a shrewd blend of subtlety and bludgeoning, both arts in which Henry Dundas, the dominant figure in the Scottish political landscape, was highly skilled. Firstly, propaganda was astutely shaped to marginalise the democratic movement through a wide range of instruments. Secondly, reformers were subjected to repressive measures which rendered them isolated, divided and disheartened. Thirdly, loyalists were encouraged to organise and display support for the constitution, and nowhere more so than in enrolling in military volunteer units.

By late 1792, the rising incidence of violence in France pushed most clergy to a highly critical position. The main outcome of clergymen rallying to the side of the government was that, given the high levels of church attendance – notably on fast days – the pulpit was probably the most effective medium for reaching the general populace, particularly the less literate. Sermons were delivered exhorting congregations to obey the monarch and the government as their Christian duty, stressing the benefits of law, stability, prosperity and the protection of property which the British people uniquely enjoyed, thanks to an almost perfect constitutional framework settled in 1688–9. Paine's views were singled out for denunciation, since the writings of an atheist were self-evidently false. Although a few ministers in Protestant churches outside the Church of Scotland espoused the democratic cause, the overwhelming preponderance in all sects endorsed the broad loyalist stance. In 1795, a large number of Presbyterian Dissenters subscribed to a loyal address, and Dundas was so impressed with the stance of the Scottish Roman Catholics that he gave them a subsidy in 1796. The limited level of Dissenter sympathy for reformers may be due to the lack in Scotland of a significant presence of radical sects like Quakers and Unitarians, who enjoyed a much larger following in England. The Irish insurgency in 1798 further cemented the attachment of Protestant churchmen to the government, as the threat of a Catholic uprising fed their worst nightmares.

Scottish newspapers, which had increased from eight in 1782 to twenty-seven in 1790, were with few exceptions – the most significant being the *Edinburgh Gazetteer* – solidly behind the government. This bias towards the administration was far more pronounced than in England, where the Whigs managed to sustain several papers. The instinct of much of the press to endorse the government's approach was reinforced by the judicious allocation of state funding to a number of them. At the same time, some papers associated with the opposition were weakened by trials in 1793: for example, the editor of the *Bee* was jailed for three months. As an added disincentive to anti-loyalist prints, most coffee houses were induced to ban their publications. In addition, the loyalist press printed lengthy reports of patriotic rallies, speeches, parliamentary proceedings, but allotted virtually no space to the reform side. The violent incidents in France were given prominence in their columns, while the proceedings of the Scottish Friends of the People were either ignored or attacked. The government also subsidised the printing and distribution of a veritable deluge of pamphlets which denounced Paine and his Scottish adherents and praised the beauties of the British constitution. One of the most influential of these was *The Present Happiness of Great Britain*, a printed version of a sermon delivered in 1792 by George Hill, the principal of St Andrews University, which sold over 10,000 copies.

The creation of Scottish loyalist associations did not occur spontaneously, for in late November 1792 Pitt urged Dundas to establish these on the broadest possible basis, following the success of the movement in England. Guided by Dundas, the formal organisation of loyalists differed somewhat from England, where Reevesite Loyalist Associations were a thuggish street-level movement enjoying significant popular support, having some 2,000 branches, whereas in Scotland only three branches have been identified. Instead, loyalist activists in Scotland tended to be middle class and elitist, as corporations and institutions like burgh councils, guilds and churches expressed faithful allegiance in addresses: the first of these was the Edinburgh Goldsmiths' Hall Association, established in December 1792. Indeed, by early 1793, there were more individuals in loyalist societies than in the Scottish Friends of the People. In Scotland, the violence that characterised organised loyalism in England was rare, and the common English practice of effigy-burning – mostly of Paine – was quite unusual. The staple of English loyalist street disorder, Church and King riots, were rendered nugatory by the extremely small number in Scotland of the main targets, namely Quakers and Unitarians. Moreover, many lower-class Scots were hostile towards the ruling Moderate party in the Church of Scotland. Barely any loyalist demonstrations were held to protest against the reform conventions of 1792 and 1793, and the Irish uprising of 1798 did not provoke mass meetings. Public gatherings were used infrequently, and were often associated with war victories – but to a much lesser extent than in England. The preference in Scotland was instead to submit petitions to the monarch and parliament as evidence of support.

Reformers and those identified as their supporters frequently endured harassment and intimidation. Tradesmen, publicans, booksellers and printers suspected of pro-reform tendencies were boycotted by patriotic customers. Discrimination against professional men in law, academia and religion who were seen as sympathetic to the French Revolution was systematically applied.

The revered Dugald Stewart, Edinburgh University's most eminent professor, was effectively silenced because in one of his publications he had referred approvingly to the Marquis de Condorcet, an eminent mathematician and a champion of Enlightenment values, who embraced enthusiastically the cause of the French Revolution. Stewart withdrew the book and soon after retired from his chair. Elsewhere in academia, appointments were based on political leanings, not merit. In 1795–6, the best applicant for the chair of medicine at Glasgow University was rejected because of his reformist connections. In law, the most notorious episode came with the deposition in 1796 of Henry Erskine, universally acknowledged as the finest advocate in Scotland, from the post of dean of the Faculty of Advocates, an office he had held since 1785. An aspirant judge was informed by Lord Bute in 1795 that he would not be appointed because he had attended a great dinner in honour of Charles Fox, where reforming sentiments had been voiced.

At a lower level, men in a range of professions could find their advancement blocked or, in extreme cases, lost their positions because of their political views. Professor Millar's son, a rising lawyer, opted to emigrate to America in order to escape the hostile environment he encountered in Scotland. He was but one of many of the political refugees who migrated to the United States from the British Isles in the 1790s, who left for similar reasons. It appears that to a greater extent than in England and Ireland, the Scots' occupational backgrounds were middle- and lower-middle-class professions, such as medicine, law and teaching. Dundas skilfully changed his policy in church appointments, and whereas before Moderates had a virtual monopoly of Crown patronage, he now promoted several Evangelicals – for instance, two were made royal chaplains.

The impact on the reformers of the trials for sedition was profound, and created a psychology of resignation and despair. The wider public, repelled by the evidence brought forward in these cases, was spurred to ostracise radicals, and to join volunteer movements to stamp out internal revolutionary threats. But, some show trials apart, the authorities were noticeably reluctant to make blanket use of the courts to silence the democrats, fearing a public reaction against what might appear to be overzealous hounding, and it was noted that juries frequently showed a marked unwillingness to convict in certain cases. Dundas was unhappy at Lord Braxfield's outrageously one-sided handling of Muir's prosecution in 1793, which was perceived to have been counterproductive, since it stimulated an upsurge in support for the Scottish Friends in the later part of the year. As intended, the outcome of these trials was the shattering of the reform movement. In 1794, an embattled Whig wrote to William Adam, who was soliciting funds to restore Charles James Fox's precarious finances, that

[t]he trials at Edinburgh have struck all his [Fox's] friends with terror. We dare not meet together in safety and no person will venture even privately to collect a subscription from his neighbour. Our conversations now turn reserved and guarded, and the most innocent actions are liable to misconstruction.[11]

But while in the short and medium term the government had won the support of much of Scottish national opinion, there was another side to the legacy of the 1790s. For those convicted became the earliest entrants to the pantheon of Scottish radical martyrs, a genealogy that was traced thence through the 1815–20 phase to the Chartists, the early Labour party and 'Red Clydeside'. The memory of these men and the treatment they received at the hands of the authorities enthused and mobilised subsequent generations of reformers.

Probably the clearest evidence for the strength of Scottish loyalist sentiment is participation in the armed forces, both in the regular divisions and in the reserve sectors. The contribution of Scots to the regular army was well ahead of the population ratio. Of the sixty fencible and forty-six horse regiments raised during the wars, thirty-seven of the former and fourteen of the latter were recruited in Scotland. One-sixth of officers in the British army were Highlanders, who constituted a very small percentage of the total population. Recruitment to the British Volunteer movement and, after 1797, to the Scottish Militia, ran at exceptionally high rates, much above the levels achieved in England. Enlistment in the volunteers came in two phases: the first in 1794–5, when the danger was seen as a domestic insurgency, and the second in 1797–8, when there was alarm about a potential French invasion which yielded enrolments on an even larger scale, and both served to confirm the marginalisation of reformers and the preponderance of unstinting loyalism in Scotland. By 1795–6, almost 48 per cent of British Volunteers were Scottish-based, and in 1797–8, the figure was around 35–40 per cent. In addition, many others were sworn in as Special Constables to reinforce the burgh police, mostly in larger cities like Edinburgh and Glasgow.

The social composition of the volunteers reveals that in the first surge, most were drawn from middle- and upper-class men, but in the second wave of 1797–8, the intake had a strong working-class component. By 1800, 32,000 Scottish Volunteers were artisans and labourers; between 50 and 60 per cent of the Musselburgh Volunteers in 1797 were artisans and no other socio-economic grouping contributed above 7 per cent. Virtually no English unit could match that level of workingmen recruits. Possibly workers were less disposed to join in the first phase because they were not too concerned by the supposed threat of an internal revolution, and may even have been mildly sympathetic to the Friends of the People. Several Scottish Volunteer units were reluctant to act against food rioters and Militia Act protesters. For instance, in 1800, the Peterhead Volunteers refused to protect a ship exporting grain from efforts by locals to stop the vessel sailing. But when the question was one of an existential national crisis, they were willing to participate, possibly indicating the percolation of a profound sense of a British identity.

Enrolment in the reserve forces was geographically widespread. Besides the cities and towns, which contributed significantly to the overall numbers, rural areas were also heavily involved; Perthshire alone supplied almost 2,500 men between 1794 and 1801. But the outstanding feature was the disproportionate involvement by the four Highland counties (Argyll, Inverness, Ross and Sutherland): 20 per cent of all Scottish Volunteers came from there, although they contained 16 per cent of the nation's population. In addition to enlisting in the regular British army, Highlanders swarmed to join the volunteers, and even the militia.

But some caveats may be logged up, as other calculations than pure patriotism could operate. For Highland landowners, as noted in Chapter 1, the financial benefits of raising a corps were highly attractive to a caste perpetually teetering on the verge of bankruptcy. For recruits everywhere, being a volunteer offered the security of being deployed solely within the locality unless there was an invasion, whereas in the regular army, soldiers could be sent anywhere within Britain or abroad. Thus, it was possible to continue in work and draw pay as a volunteer, which in Stirlingshire was 5p per day, with a pension payable if injured. Moreover, volunteers could resign at any time – which one workingman stated would happen on a grand scale if an invasion was imminent.[12] Commitment to the principles of the Glorious Revolution or devotion to the Protestant Constitution and reverence for George III may not, in other words, have been a priority in many nooks and crannies of Scotland.

Another field where Scottish loyalism had a different timbre to that in England was in ideology. To be sure, there was a great deal of common ground in the arguments wielded on both sides of the border. Since, however, Burke's polemic had perhaps not enjoyed the same éclat in Scotland as in England, other arguments had a useful role to play in promoting the loyalist case. A good deal of this Scottish discourse had a distinctly Whiggish tint, whereas in England, High Toryism was the most important ingredient. In Scotland, the importance of the Revolution settlement of 1688–9 was stressed, linking, along classic Whig lines, a balanced constitution with the rights of property. This, rather than the central role of the monarch, was the focus of resolutions carried by bodies as diverse as Edinburgh Town Council, St Andrews University and a meeting of the Roxburghshire gentry. Hence, Scottish loyalism was not coterminous with royalism. Elsewhere, the stress was on the vital connection between British liberty and Scottish economic growth. Unlike England, where the survival of the Anglican Church constituted a central pillar of loyalism, in Scotland there was very little stress placed on the need to preserve the state church. Thus, the English Tories' attachment to King and Church, which was a core ingredient of the party's appeal in that country well into the nineteenth century, had no close replica in Scotland. In the long run, the absence of such a visceral Tory slogan may well have left the Scottish party seriously deficient in appealing to a broad constituency, as became apparent in the middle third of the next century. Moreover, as discussed above, Burke's arguments, although highly influential in shaping the language and context of English conservatism for whole of the nineteenth century, had only a very limited and oblique appeal in Scotland, and finding an alternative rhetoric to mobilise Scottish Toryism proved very difficult for most of the nineteenth century.

HENRY DUNDAS AND POLITICAL MANAGEMENT

The upsurge in loyalism had a profound political impact, for it reinforced the adherence of the majority of Scots, and more especially the electorate, to the side of the government. Just as the strength of loyalism owed much to the efforts of Henry Dundas, so he adroitly exploited the benefits to consolidate the position of the Tories in the country. It was thus a part of the Whigs' problem that for a quarter of a century from 1784 they were confronted by the most skilful operator in Scottish politics during the unreformed era. Dundas was born in 1742 into a prominent legal family: his father, grandfather and great-grandfather had all been judges, and he duly became an advocate in his early twenties. He entered parliament in 1774, and was made Lord Advocate in 1775 in Lord North's administration, then in 1782 he was appointed Treasurer of the Navy, but fell from office in 1783, when the Fox–North government came in. He briskly shifted his allegiance to Pitt, who was made premier that year, and was restored to the navy post. Dundas soon became one of Pitt's most trusted lieutenants, and was a central pillar of government from 1783 until 1801, serving continuously in core offices of state, first as Treasurer of the Navy (1783–91), next as Home Secretary (1791–4), and then as Secretary for War (1794–1801). For Pitt, Dundas's value was that, firstly, he was a highly effective administrator in all the posts he held. Secondly, and of almost equal importance, through his mastery of Scottish politics, he was able to deliver a substantial block of votes in both the Lords and the Commons, which boosted the government's control of parliament in a very fraught period. Dundas's character was a vital component of his success as a political manager. Shrewd and adept in exploiting situations advantageously, he could still be genial and generous both in private and political relationships. But he was also quite single-minded in pursuit of his goals, and wielded a sharp tongue or pen against those he believed

Figure 7.1 Henry Dundas, 1st Viscount Melville, by Sir Thomas Lawrence, 1810. London, National Portrait Gallery

had crossed or double-crossed him. Above all, he never lost sight of his main objectives, which he stated at the end of his life to be: 'to support the great aristocracy of the country as the best bulwark against the attempts of Jacobins and Democrats, and those who, if of different principles, are so infatuated as to countenance them.'[13]

Dundas pursued two broad strategies in order to achieve political domination. The first was to use patronage and influence to win over voters, and the second was to forge alliances with powerful regional and local magnate interests to prevent opposition forces from gaining the ascendancy. Because of the more straitened economic circumstances in Scotland, the dispensing of patronage of any kind among almost all social categories had a greater impact than in England. Furthermore, the total Scottish electorate was so very small that the dividends were proportionately far higher than in England. By virtue of his continuous involvement in government at a very high level, a wide battery of patronage was accessible to Dundas, which he worked systematically.

India had long been a prized object of desire for eighteenth-century Scots; in the period from 1700 to 1774 they filled about one-quarter of all positions in the East India Company. Dundas had considerable input into the government of India because between 1788 and 1801 he sat on the Board of Control of the East India Company, which had responsibility for all matters there. Moreover, he had close associations with several individuals who had access to the innermost corridors of power in the company, the most fruitful of these being with David Scott, who acted as the conduit between Dundas's political needs and the availability of positions in India. One calculation suggests that in Dundas's era, between 30 and 40 per cent of posts in the subcontinent were allocated to Scots.[14]

The armed forces constituted another popular focus for Scots seeking state employment, and the army was a more fruitful orchard than the navy. This was because would-be naval officers faced the disadvantage of needing to possess some evidence of competence and ability as a prerequisite, while these were merely optional add-ons for the army. Between 1794 and 1801, Dundas was at the head of the ministry of war, and thus had enormous power in determining appointments. The outbreak of war with France in 1793 led to a steep increase in army officer numbers, around one-quarter of whom were Scots. Medical appointments to the army and navy attracted a disproportionately high number of Scottish applicants. Additionally, wartime contracts for a wide range of products offered scope for Dundas to favour Scottish businessmen: the Falkirk-based Carron Company, for example, enjoyed a sharp rise in income and profits from 1793, when it switched from domestic goods production to armaments manufacture.

Civilian life also yielded areas for Dundas to exercise patronage. One aftermath of the two Jacobite risings was that the patronage of about 300 state church livings was taken away from private individuals and vested in the Crown. This gave a far greater share of patronage to the government than in the rest of Britain, and Dundas exploited this highly effectively: relatives of voters were accommodated in livings which were well-paid or required little pastoral superintendence. University positions in the five Scottish universities also fell under Dundas's purview. As chancellor of St Andrews University from 1788 to 1811, all appointments there were carefully monitored by him to ensure the political orthodoxy of successful applicants. In the other universities, great noblemen held the equivalent office, and being in alliance with Dundas, they acted to carry out his wishes. At Glasgow, the duke of Montrose always consulted him over filling chairs, while in Aberdeen, Dundas had gained control of Marischal College promotions by the 1790s, and from 1792 King's College was also under his sway. At Edinburgh University, where the town council was the ruling authority, Dundas carried substantial weight as the city's MP; when the chair of logic fell vacant in 1808, the grounds for choosing a replacement were stated by a correspondent – clearly following Dundas's doctrine – thus: 'two things are to be guarded against: the appointment of a man not qualified in point of science and the appointment of one not well disposed in point of politics.'[15] Less exalted jobs also lay within the ambit of his influence, particularly Customs and Excise positions, which offered lifelines for individuals just about managing to get by, and many ordinary voters, including burgh councillors, sought these posts for needy kith and kin. In 1811, such patronage in Greenock and Port Glasgow embraced 41 posts, worth a total of £6,655 in annual salaries, ranging from £45 to £500. The most famous beneficiary of this lower-level patronage was Robert Burns, who became an exciseman in 1789.

While the provision of such *douceurs* helped win over individual voters, Dundas's other keystone policy was to work with the great landowners who had a substantial say in determining the outcome of elections. Frequently these arrangements were designed to deliver a single county for Dundas's party: a union between the duke of Montrose and Lord Elphinstone in Stirlingshire helped produce victory in 1796 in a seat long retained by the Whigs. Likewise, in Perthshire, where the Whiggish Lord Breadalbane posed a challenge, Dundas bolstered the position of the duke of Atholl by enlisting lesser lairds on the latter's side. In a more expansive approach, Dundas elsewhere encouraged the formation of alliances of magnates to establish regional power blocs, thereby conveying several constituencies to the government's side. In the north-east, Dundas forged a compact between the duke of Gordon, the dominant landowner in the district, and lesser, but still powerful, figures, such as Brodie of Brodie, Lord Findlater and Grant of Grant. This pact was sealed in 1787, and it became even more potent in 1789–90, when the earl of Fife signed up. The result was that four counties (Aberdeen, Banff, Moray and Nairn) and the Elgin Burghs were virtually guaranteed to return MPs favourable to Dundas. Similar nexuses yielded Dundasite hegemony in the south-east and the southwest, clustered around, respectively, the duke of Buccleuch and the earl of Eglinton. In return for the commitment of these grandees to his side, Dundas could offer attractive rewards. High-level military promotions were a recompense for some; for others, the conferment of a British peerage was inducement enough; and after 1794, appointment as county lord-lieutenant appealed to the vanity of many. Additionally, ministerial help with legislation relating to local issues, or shaping government policy to meet the interests of the county, were important levers of persuasion.

But these weapons at Dundas's disposal were not infallible, and so did not automatically deliver the desired outcome. The benefits of patronage were circumscribed in several ways. For one thing, in many areas, the volume was limited. The total number of posts in the East India Company, for example, was a mere eight to sixteen annually, and essentially these were restricted to younger men. Much of the low-grade patronage, for example, Customs and Excise positions, was placed at the disposal of the local MP, rather than handled directly by Dundas; moreover, the Treasury retained the authority to overturn such appointments in the general interests of efficiency. State patronage in church appointments was always susceptible to the need to accommodate the opinions of the congregation, as an unpopular nomination could lead to secession. Above all, electors were not automata, voting as instructed by their social superiors or dispensers of patronage. If they were not consulted on political questions, or if they felt their representative was not actively meeting them and working on behalf of the needs of the constituency, they were prepared to act, whatever Dundas or his local aides wanted. There was, indeed, a wider political culture which concentration on vote manufacture, patronage and corruption too easily overlooks. Voters expected their MP to pursue the general good of the county and the more specific interests of individual constituents, and were ready to hold him accountable for his voting record and the promotion of county interests. These factors of themselves tended to pull the MP towards the government side. David Scott, although crucial to Dundas's deployment of Indian patronage, lost his Angus seat in 1796 because he was perceived by local gentry to rely on a small inner circle of associates, while the broad body of lairds and independent voters felt ignored and by-passed. Hence, although personally well-liked and offering huge volumes of patronage, not to mention enjoying the vital endorsement of Dundas, he was turned out.

Burgh seats presented a different challenge for Dundas. Since, apart from Edinburgh, these seats had four or five constituent burghs, councillors in the individual places had considerable freedom to play candidates and patrons off against each other. Additionally, in burgh seats, the mood of the wider public opinion beyond the narrow electorate frequently had to be taken into account by all parties.

On the other side of the equation, alliances with county magnates could be problematic. These men were haughty, flighty, self-important and, in a number of cases, not over-endowed with intelligence. Hence disputes and ruptures could flare up at any moment, often concerned with trivial matters of protocol and convention, and frequently it proved difficult for Dundas to restore the status quo. Lord Fife, pulled into the north-east confederation, was never entirely settled and in 1793 withdrew in pique. The duke of Atholl broke spectacularly with Dundas in 1797, and a bitter exchange of letters left the fissure a long-term feature of Perthshire politics. While in Stirlingshire the Montrose–Elphinstone political marriage promised much for Dundas, the two peers soon fell out over electoral manoeuvrings in neighbouring Dunbartonshire. Again, if a great landowner felt Dundas had failed to reward him adequately, relations quickly cooled, especially if expectations of places or honours were not met.

Nevertheless, the strengths of Dundas's management were apparent in the general elections, as shown in Table 7.1. In 1784, he could claim twenty-four MPs on his side and fifteen against, which was a weaker performance than in England. But at the following contest in 1790, he had thirty-six solid followers, reducing the Whigs to only six MPs, with three non-aligned, and this time the Scottish results exceeded England. The 1796 election marked the apogee of Dundas's achievements: aided by the Portlandite defectors (discussed below), the administration had forty-three supporters. As well as his army of MPs holding Scottish seats, Dundas also had a loyal group of Scots, numbering perhaps twenty, sitting for English seats. The greater success in the 1790s of the Tories in Scotland compared to England increased Dundas's value to the government and accordingly made patronage more readily available for him to consolidate and expand his power.

Equally invaluable to the government was his role in delivering a body of backers in the House of Lords, which in the eighteenth century had parity of power with the Commons. The Treaty of Union laid down that all peers of Scottish creation would not automatically sit in the Lords: only peers of English creation, together with post-1707 ennoblements – i.e. British peers – had that right. At general elections, the Scottish nobles elected sixteen of their number to sit in the upper house for the duration of that parliament. As the peers in the Lords numbered between 180 and 200 in the later eighteenth century, of whom a good number were traditional aristocratic Whigs (and there were also several non-attenders), the sixteen Scots could tilt the balance of the house. Moreover, as the representative Scots tended to be more regular attenders than the others, the partisan inclinations of the Scottish representative peers had great significance.

At each election Dundas circulated a list of peers whom the government wished its supporters to endorse, but getting the Scottish noblemen to conform to these requests was not at all straightforward. Several felt compelled to deviate from voting for the whole bloc, either because of ties of blood, marriage or friendship with unendorsed candidates, or to maintain good relations with neighbours. As Lord Mansfield explained in 1812:

> in the choice of our representatives, I have ever supported those peers to whom I am connected in friendship and others mainly because I thought that they would do honour to our country, without regard to conformity in political opinions.[16]

On the other hand, a good portion of the Scottish noblemen were in straitened circumstances and could be persuaded to vote for the party ticket in return for pledges of aid, sometimes surprisingly modest. 'I understand', Dundas wrote in 1790, 'Lord Bellenden is in London. Somebody should be desired to convey to him a bottle of brandy and 20 pounds and I should think they might get his proxy."17 Others were influenced by the inducement of the prospect of a British title, which was bestowed between 1784 and 1800 on nine peers. Thus, Lord Galloway had his request for an upgrade rejected in 1789, but was given a British title in 1796, as he then controlled three Commons seats. Dundas's tight grip on this area increased to the extent that, whereas in 1784, his slate won twelve of the sixteen places, by 1796 he had a complete return of his sixteen recommendations.

WHIG DISARRAY AND DISMEMBERMENT, C. 1794–1811

Dundas's hegemonic position persisted through the 1790s. To a considerable extent, this was because the patriotic loyalist reaction served to reinforce his all-pervasive influence, but the disintegration of the Whig party in Scotland further boosted Dundas's dominance. As we have seen, the Whigs began to fall apart as events in Paris created alarm among moderate supporters at the end of 1792, but the turning point came when the duke of Portland's faction seceded to join the government in July 1794. Portland was accompanied by thirty-eight MPs, four of them holding Scottish seats, of whom the most influential was Sir Thomas Dundas (a distant kinsman of Henry Dundas), who was rewarded for his defection with a peerage, becoming the 1st Baron Dundas. A very wealthy landowner with estates ranging across Shetland, Stirlingshire and Clackmannanshire, as well as North Yorkshire, Dundas had spent a considerable amount of money in subsidising Whig candidates, working in close cooperation with Henry Erskine and William Adam to build up the party prior to the 1790 general election. Hence, his departure undermined a wider swathe of Whiggery than even his territorial interests would suggest. Some Scottish peers also joined Portland, including Lords Seaforth and Tweeddale. Not long after Portland's departure, a further major blow to the credibility and intellectual standing of the Scottish Whigs was sustained when Sir Gilbert Elliot went over to the government side. Elliot belonged to the Minto family, whose Whiggery went back to 1688–9 and had formed the bedrock of the party's influence in the Borders. The Whigs were thus reduced to a very small rump for the next dozen or so years, and not all were easy political bedfellows, being united only in veneration of Charles Fox.

In the early 1800s, however, Dundas's position became less secure. When the Irish Act of Union was passed in 1801, George III refused to countenance the introduction of legislation to emancipate Roman Catholics because it went against his coronation oath. Pitt, having promised the Irish that Catholic relief would be an integral part of the union settlement, resigned the premiership, and Dundas followed his leader out of office. Both declined to serve under the new prime minister, Henry Addington, who tried to wrest control of Scottish politics from Dundas in order to reinforce his somewhat precarious position. But Dundas remained resolute that he would not surrender his influence and sharply warned Addington not to intrude on his patch. Proof that Dundas largely retained his power was confirmed at the 1802 general election. MPs firmly tied to Dundas numbered twenty-six, with another nine more loosely associated, and only four supporters of Addington were elected. Nevertheless, many observers took Dundas's absence from office as a sign of his vulnerability. In December 1802, he was ennobled, becoming Lord Melville, and this further threatened to reduce his power to influence Scottish political affairs, since he was now removed from day-to-day management in the Commons.

Addington's premiership proved short-lived, and in April 1804 Pitt replaced him, whereupon he rewarded Melville for his loyalty by ensconcing him at the Admiralty. But the resumption of his dominant role in Scottish politics was derailed by his trial for impeachment, on a charge of financial mismanagement while Treasurer of the Royal Navy. The proceedings against him began in 1805 and lasted until the following year, when he was acquitted by a slender majority in the Lords. The hiatus in Tory fortunes in Scotland caused by Melville's preoccupation with his trial presented an opportunity for the Scottish Whigs to revive. This opening was enhanced by the disarray in the Tory party following the death of Pitt in January 1806, which led to the formation in February of the so-called Ministry of All the Talents, a coalition of Foxite Whigs and the followers of the more centrist politician, Lord Grenville. The general election in November 1806 attested to the eclipse of Melville's dominance: only fourteen Scottish MPs backed him, and the government supporters rose to twenty-eight, with three classified as independents. This appeared a tidal change in Scottish politics, and offered the Whigs the prospect of making the shift permanent by proving in office to be efficient and capable of passing reform measures. However, the ministry was an uneasy alliance, since Grenville had been in Pitt's government until 1801, and in the new administration he had some sharp policy disagreements with the Foxites. In any case, the ministry was short-lived, for in March 1807 it collapsed – partly because Fox had died in September 1806 – and the Tories were reinstalled in office under the duke of Portland.

The tensions which ran through almost all aspects of the 'Talents' government were fully present in its Scottish dimension. There were three central problems: the distribution of decision-making responsibility; the quality of ministers; and the actual policies adopted. Power over Scottish affairs was largely retained by Grenville and Earl Spencer, with the former taking the lead position in overall control of government business and appointments. The leaders of the Scottish Whiggery were marginalised, and Lord Lauderdale, one of the most experienced of the Scottish party's *prominenti*, played virtually no part in the governing process. Responsibility for Scottish political micromanagement was allocated to Lord Moira, whose promotion created dismay among Whigs, as he was firmly in the Grenvillite camp, and moreover was regarded as rather lightweight. Henry Erskine became Lord Advocate, but he proved pretty ineffective, in part because was out of action for a spell with an attack of gout, which rather left Scottish affairs becalmed. One MP wailed: 'As the Lord Advocate is unwell at Buxton, the people of Scotland are quite at a loss to whom to apply to regarding political matters.'[18]

The Scottish Whigs argued vociferously that a wholesale purge of Tory placemen and sinecurists was essential in order to send a clear signal that Melville's influence had been reduced and was not likely to be restored. Only on this basis, they asserted, would the Whigs establish a level playing field in Scotland. But the Grenvillites were not particularly interested in assisting the Whigs to capture political power in Scotland; they wished instead to protect their own position, which was somewhere between Tory and Whig. Moreover, as the coalition had a secure majority in England, Grenville and Spencer felt no urgent need to place any priority on the demands of Scottish Whigs. With the full approval of his leader, Moira removed very few Tories from public positions in Scotland, to the utter despair of the Whigs. Thus, the Whigs were infuriated when the Tory duke of Gordon was left as the holder of the Great Seal, the most important Scottish official position.

Another serious difficulty was that no significant piece of legislation relating to Scotland was passed by the ministry. It was intended that the main measure would be a bill reforming the Scottish judicial system in order to simplify procedure and reduce the pressure on the Westminster law lords created by the large volume of appeals emanating from Scottish court decisions. In 1807 Grenville brought forward a bill to effect this, but it was rejected by parliament. One problem was that, contrary to normal practice, the draft measure was not shown to the Scottish MPs, the Faculty of Advocates and the Writers of the Signet for consultation and comment before publication. When it did appear, the bill received a very critical response at county meetings, on the ground that it was a breach of the Treaty of Union and a threat to Scottish national identity. Further, a body of younger Whig advocates, mostly connected with what was to become the *Edinburgh Review* circle, vigorously attacked the proposals as 'unsound in principle, and unsuited to the condition and wants of Scotland'.[19] In these circumstances, it was not surprising that in the general election of June 1807, the Melvillite pre-eminence was restored, if not quite at the same level as before: there were twenty-seven Tory MPs.

For the Whigs, the years from the downfall of the Talents Ministry to the end of the Napoleonic War had very few encouraging moments, even although the 1807 election gave them thirteen MPs, the second best result since 1784.

Several of the long-serving stalwarts left the political scene: in 1811 Henry Erskine withdrew from public life, and William Adam resigned from parliament because of his difficult financial circumstances, and soon after took a judicial office. They were accompanied in retirement in 1811 by Sir John Sinclair, while Sir John Anstruther and Peter Baillie also died in that year. Other Whigs were tending to move to a less partisan stance; by 1807 Lord Selkirk had disavowed his radical views of the 1790s, and was rewarded with the post of lord-lieutenant of Kirkcudbrightshire.

In contrast, between 1807 and 1815, the Tories were relatively secure. Melville died in 1811, but his son, Robert, quite smoothly slipped into the role of managing Scottish politics in the Tory interest, which effectively he had been doing in the last years of his father's life, including masterminding the victory in the 1807 election. The 1812 general election produced another decisive majority for the government, which gained two more followers, making twenty-nine in all, while their opponents slipped from thirteen to nine adherents. The Whigs' espousal of Irish Roman Catholic emancipation was profoundly unpopular, as the 1826 election subsequently confirmed. The only difficulties for the government side were caused more by internal disputes than any serious Whig challenge. For instance, in Perthshire a dispute within the Murray clan between the duke of Atholl and Patrick Murray of Ochtertyre over the selection of a candidate resulted in the latter's camp supporting the Whigs in an unsuccessful bid to defeat the Atholl interest. Thus, in the closing phase of the wars with France, the dire position of the Whigs appeared virtually beyond retrieval.

NOTES

1. H. Cockburn, *Memorials of His Time* (1856), 80.
2. J. Fergusson (ed.), *Letters of George Dempster to Sir Adam Fergusson, 1756–1813* (1934), 197; Dempster to Fergusson, 3 August 1789.
3. [T. Macgrugar], *The Letters of Zeno to the Citizens of Edinburgh on the Present Mode of Electing a Member of Parliament for the City* (1783).
4. Northallerton, North Yorkshire Record Office [NYRO], Wyvill MSS, ZFW 7/2/57/10, *Memorandum by the Committee of the General Convention of Delegates for Burgh Reform in Scotland to Members of Parliament* (10 March 1787), unpaginated.
5. British Library [BL], Dropmore MSS, Add. MS 58965, ff. 2–9, Brougham to Lord Grenville, 18 April 1810.
6. NYRO, Zetland MSS, ZNK/X/2/1/744, H. Erskine to Sir T. Dundas, 5 January 1789 (stress in original).
7. Perth, Perth & Kinross Council Archives, Richardson of Pitfour MSS, MS79/42, J. Richardson to R. Richardson, 10 November 1792 (stress in original).
8. Blair Adam, Adam MSS, Box '1792', Lord Bute to W. Adam, 2 November 1792.

9. Fergusson, *Letters of Dempster*, 222; Dempster to Fergusson, 9 September 1792.
10. R. Graham, *A Letter to the Rt Hon. William Pitt, Chancellor of the Exchequer, on the Reform of the Internal Government of the Royal Boroughs [sic] of Scotland* (1788), 17.
11. Blair Adam MSS, Box '1794, M-Z', R. Small to W. Adam, 8 April 1794.
12. Glasgow City Archives, MacKinnon MSS, TD 743/2, ff. 6–12, Memoir by J. Mackinnon, 1859.
13. NRS, Melville Castle MSS, GD 51/1/198/61, Melville to J. Hamilton (copy), 11 May [1811].
14. M. Fry, *The Dundas Despotism* (1992), 111–12.
15. NLS, Melville MSS, MS 9, f. 11, Lord Advocate A. Colquhoun to Melville, 29 January 1808.
16. Scone, Mansfield MSS, 1413, Mansfield to the duke of Buccleuch, 15 October 1812 [rough draft].
17. BL, Dropmore MSS, Add. MS 59258, ff. 7–14, H. Dundas to Lord Lansdowne, 25 June 1790.
18. BL, Dropmore MSS, Add. MS 58996, ff. 166–7, Sir J. Sinclair to Lord Lansdowne, 18 October 1806.
19. H. Cockburn, *The Life of Lord Jeffrey, with a Selection from His Correspondence* (1852), Vol. I, 176.

CHAPTER 8

Politics in the Last Years of the Unreformed System, 1815–32

At the end of the wars with France in 1815, the Whigs seemed to have few hopes of making advances, given the weak position they found themselves in after the collapse of the 1806–7 ministry and the electoral rebuff in 1812. But several factors operated to give them a sense of forward movement. The first was the failure of militant working-class action in the period from 1815 to 1820; the second was the reorientation of the party's strategy and the advent of a new leadership cadre; the third was the wide-ranging impact of social and political change.

THE CHALLENGE OF WORKING-CLASS RADICALISM, 1815–20

Working-class unrest was primarily fuelled by pressing economic and social difficulties. The abandonment after 1812 of the practice by which local Justice of the Peace courts determined wage rates introduced a free market approach, which was blamed by many workers, especially handloom weavers, for a sharp reduction in income levels. The abolition of income tax at the end of the war resulted in a rise in indirect taxes, such as on sugar, malt and beer, which bore heavily on the lower-paid. The patchy data on real wages suggest a clear downward trend for a number of occupations in the later 1810s, and meal riots, for instance in Dundee in 1816, testify to the intensity of hardship. The rapid growth of manufacturing centres, with its concomitant impact on housing, health and communal well-being, added to a sense of a declining quality of working-class life. These trends were reinforced by post-war dislocation, as demobilisation offloaded many servicemen onto the labour market, adding to the pressure on jobs, wages and living conditions. Simultaneously, the position of those in or near poverty was rendered more precarious by the mounting concerns among the middle classes and evangelical clergy about the extent and expense of poor relief, as discussed in Chapter 4.

Working-class radicalism, although severely repressed in the 1790s, never totally disappeared, although only a few traces remain of its existence over the following ten to fifteen years. One glimmer is afforded by the short-lived *Glasgow Sentinel*, which appeared in 1809–10. In September 1809, it printed a letter which denounced the British state as 'a miserable and imbecile junta . . . rowing us down the stream of corruption and sacrificing our best and bravest troops to the manes [sic] of tyranny, superstition and priestcraft'. The writer added that the celebration of George III's golden jubilee as king was an affront to the widows and orphans of soldiers killed in the war. By contrast, the success of France was due to its political system and the resultant enthusiasm of the people, while other European powers, 'decayed at the heart', needed the sword to mobilise its population.[1] It is surely no coincidence that the sole press voice in Glasgow representative of working-class radicalism in the 1850s and early 1860s bore the same title, testifying to the sense of historical continuity so characteristic of this political strand.

But as economic conditions deteriorated after the peace, industrial action to defend living standards became less effective, and so there was a swing towards political action. These diffuse streams of discontent acquired a coherent ideological overview thanks to radical agitators, who re-emerged around 1812. Maurice Margarot, having served his sentence in Australia, returned to Scotland in that year, visiting old radicals in Paisley and Edinburgh in a bid to revive the spirit of the early 1790s. More weightily, Major John Cartwright, a veteran English radical, made contact with a number of long-standing Scottish reformers in 1813, and then undertook a three-month tour through the Lowlands in the summer of 1815, where he attracted large audiences, especially in distressed areas. Cartwright's reform message differed significantly from Paineite assertions of natural rights. He expounded a historicist argument that constitutional liberties, running from the Magna Carta to the Revolution of 1688–9, had been eroded by an all-powerful executive. Only a sweeping measure of parliamentary reform would produce a drastic retrenchment of state spending on the armed forces, pensions and sinecures, thereby instantly improving the lot of ordinary people. A pamphlet published in Glasgow at the end of Cartwright's tour conveyed his message: the war had, among other problems, resulted in 'a heart-sickening, a terrific TAXATION' because Britain was 'in all practical effect enslaved to a factious OLIGARCHY who have arbitrarily assumed a hateful power of Taxing her without her consent'.[2] These ideas were not greatly dissimilar to the views of middle-class radicals, so that co-operation in the 1830–2 phase of parliamentary reform was not too difficult.

The response in Scotland to Cartwright's campaign was, at one level, strictly constitutional; mass meetings were organised all across the Lowlands to endorse his programme. A rally held at Thrushgrove, near Glasgow, on 29 October 1816 was claimed to be the biggest ever public meeting in Scotland, with an estimated attendance of 40,000, and gatherings took place elsewhere, for example in Dundee, Paisley and some middle-sized Angus burghs. Cartwright's strategy of submitting mass petitions to parliament in favour of reform was enthusiastically taken up, and by March 1817, some 600 petitions signed by about 100,000 people had been submitted from Scotland to Westminster. All these petitions, however, were routinely rejected.

These repeated rebuffs played into the hands of more militant elements, who organised an underground conspiracy, plotting to use violence to bring down the state apparatus. Those involved in the project were mostly located in west-central Scotland, with outposts in Perth and Dundee. They were drawn from a range of occupations, which included not just those in declining economic circumstances, such as handloom weavers, but also workers in expanding sectors and some lower-middle-class occupations like teachers, publicans, shopkeepers and tradesmen. Their structure continued some aspects of the United Scotsmen, including secret solemn oaths, hidden signs and a weekly subscription. However, the cells into which they were organised proved quite porous: police spies and informers infiltrated the movement with little difficulty, and were able to keep the authorities fully briefed on the activities of the plotters. In February 1817, twenty-six suspected conspirators were arrested in a sweep of houses in the Glasgow area, but the trial of the leaders on charges of sedition collapsed when a key witness testified that one of the prosecuting counsel had promised him employment in return for his evidence. All the accused were discharged, with no convictions.

In 1819, economic conditions worsened, with new consumption taxes imposed in the summer, while wages did not rise. In July, between 20,000 and 30,000 met in Paisley to protest at the deleterious impact of taxation. Moreover, political discontent added to the sense of distress as the state crushed working-class protest with almost unparalleled severity. On 16 August 1819, at a peaceful reform meeting in Manchester, the local yeomanry shot 11 people dead and wounded some 500 others, provoking widespread protests across Britain. In Scotland, many towns witnessed large gatherings which deplored the Peterloo Massacre, and in Paisley there was rioting over seven successive days. These protests moved working-class discontent from the level of local grievances to a national movement. The reaction of the government was to pass the Six Acts, which prohibited the exercise of basic civil liberties, including holding mass meetings, thereby intensifying the depth of working-class alienation from the political system.

By late 1819, the authorities were receiving regular reports of a new underground movement in the west of Scotland. There were accounts of arms being manufactured, military-style training, and plans to capture army barracks and seize their weaponry. These activities were intended to be the prelude to a general uprising which would also involve radicals in northern England, with whom the Scottish plotters were in close communication. Placards and posters appeared across Lanarkshire, Renfrewshire and Ayrshire calling for a general strike to begin on 3 April 1820, as the first stage in the insurrection. While the means were extreme, the ideology of the radicals derived from Cartwright, rather than Paine, and still less the London-based semi-socialist Spencean movement. The proclamation of the rising stated, 'Equality of Rights (not of Property) is the object for which we contend', and explained that their objective was: 'to replace to BRITONS, those rights consecrated to them, by Magna Charta, and the BILL OF RIGHTS, and sweep from our shores, that Corruption which has degraded us below the dignity of Man.'[3] The response was a clear portent of the power of working-class unity. The west of Scotland economy was paralysed, as 60,000 workers struck, closing down workplaces of all sizes. Smaller towns well outwith the normal ambit of radical action were involved, such as Mauchline and Girvan. This unprecedented display of unity rattled the urban middle classes, many of whom rushed to enrol in the local Volunteers – including Francis Jeffrey.

When it became apparent that the planned simultaneous English rising had not taken place, most of those in the Scottish underground organisation took no further action, and there was a gradual return to work by the strikers. But a small group – no more than forty – marched from Glasgow with the object of raiding the armaments factory at Carron, near Falkirk, in the hope of triggering an armed uprising. Intercepted by troops at Bonnybridge, a few miles from their objective, the radicals were easily subdued and arrested. A smaller rising in Strathaven was equally unsuccessful, and the leaders there were also detained. Of eighty-eight men arrested, thirty went on trial for sedition. This time the government's law officers were thoroughly prepared, and several convictions were secured. Andrew Hardie and John Baird, the leaders of the Bonnybridge posse, were both executed, as was John Wilson of Strathaven, even though the jury strongly recommended clemency for him. Twenty other men were given long terms of transportation. As in the 1790s, the sentences handed down in Scotland were markedly harsher than those in England for similar offences, where the longest was seven years hard labour.

The consequences of the 1820 episode were, firstly, that working-class activities were diverted away from politics to industrial organisation. The economic recovery which took place through much of the 1820s promoted the new direction, and the repeal of the Combination Acts in 1824–5 was a further incentive. Secondly, the Scottish working class was in the long term highly averse to participating in violent or revolutionary political action, a stance clearly delineated in the Chartist era. Thirdly, there were no further instances of Scottish radicals liaising with underground conspirators in England or Ireland; henceforth, connections, as in the age of the Chartists, were overt. Fourthly, many radicals felt that some sort of co-operation with other reform-minded classes and groups offered the best prospects of advance, and this contributed to the co-operation between middle- and working-class campaigners during the 1830–2 reform crises – and for many years thereafter.

THE WHIG RECOVERY: THE *EDINBURGH REVIEW* AND THE MIDDLE CLASSES

The draconian sentences handed down in 1820 quelled the immediate crisis, but in the longer-term perspective, the Whigs felt it imperative to find ways of containing and channelling working-class discontent, in order not just to demonstrate that the reformers were peaceable and constitutional, but also to highlight the depth of disenchantment and the consequent risk of a social explosion. This challenge coincided with a decisive shift within the Scottish party, as from around 1810, a group of younger Edinburgh lawyers steadily assumed its leadership. The main figures included Francis Jeffrey, Henry Cockburn, John A. Murray, Francis Horner and Henry Brougham, and the vehicle by which they ascended to influence was the *Edinburgh Review*. Founded by them in 1802 and appearing quarterly, it was initially apolitical, concentrating more on scientific, cultural, social and economic themes. It acted as a megaphone for the ideas of the Scottish Enlightenment, which had been purged in the previous decade from both public discourse and the learned professions during Dundas's *Kulturkampf*. By 1810 its circulation was around 12,000 copies per issue, with about half of the sales in Scotland; but the actual readership was at least three times higher and, it has been claimed, it attracted a broader social audience in Scotland than in England.[4] A switch in focus was signalled in 1808, when an article jointly written by Jeffrey and Brougham denounced British policy towards Spain, and called for democratic reform in that country. This blistering attack on Spanish aristocratic government was also transparently applicable to the British political situation, and from this starting point the magazine became ever more firmly associated with a Whiggish reform programme. The dominance of these men, which had no parallel in the English party, had two causes: there was a gap in the leadership of the Scottish Whig party, and they offered a realistic strategy for recovery by broadening the party's appeal.

In England, the Whig party was solidly aristocratic, and the advent of a younger generation of noblemen, such as Lord Althorp and Lord John Russell, gave renewed leadership and direction. But in Scotland, the social elite had long been solidly in the Tory camp, thanks mainly to Dundas's management in the preceding era. In 1811, Melville observed that '[t]here are very few of the great families of Scotland of jacobinical principles', and he cited only Hamilton and Maule as 'genuinely attached to the real Foxite party'.[5] The duke of Hamilton's brother, Lord Archibald Hamilton, sat in the

Figure 8.1 Francis Jeffrey, by Colvin Smith, c. 1825. Edinburgh, National Galleries of Scotland

Commons from 1802, where he stoutly championed burgh reform, but when he died in 1827 there was no immediate aristocratic replacement. Other Whig peers, like Lauderdale, Rosslyn and Selkirk, grew increasingly detached to varying degrees from around 1807. This crucial leadership lacuna in Scotland was filled by the Edinburgh lawyers, the sole group to offer direction. These men tended to come from less exalted social backgrounds, mostly hailing from either minor gentry, such as Cockburn and T. F. Kennedy, or the professions, like Jeffrey, whose father was a middle-rank lawyer.

More significantly, however, the *Review* group carried Whig principles into a new phase. Profoundly influenced by the teaching of Dugald Stewart and John Millar, they wholeheartedly embraced Smithian economics and the idea of progress, two key elements of the Scottish Enlightenment. Their thorough exposition of the principles of free trade and laissez-faire social policy simultaneously shifted party thinking and reached out to the expanding middle classes, while their assessment of developments between 1815 and 1820 sharpened their strategies. They redirected the party's critique of existing institutions away from the Foxite credo, which stressed the primacy of curbing the growth of executive power and the Influence of the Crown, because they threatened the principles of liberty enshrined in the 1689 Declaration of Rights. Instead, they embraced the arguments of Smith and other literati that commercial society was the true guarantor of liberty and progress. Hence, the crucial need was for a broader reconfiguration of economic and social structures, accompanied by a specific political reform agenda. As to the last, they emphasised the pressing need for a comprehensive revamping of the governmental and political structures of Scotland, which lagged well behind England. The 1817 and 1820 state trials underlined the intolerable confusion caused by the Lord Advocate having dual legal and political functions, while these roles were carefully demarcated in England. The lack of jury trials in many cases and the antiquated procedures of Scottish courts compared unfavourably with England. English elections suffered from abuses which were eradicable, but Scotland endured systemic failings, namely a very small electorate and the prevalence of vote manufacture.

For Jeffrey and his circle, the middle classes had a crucial role in their grand modernisation project. The Reviewers appreciated business and professional people as wealthy, intelligent and, like themselves, completely opposed to monopoly, protectionism and all other breaches of laissez-faire. Hence, by admitting these individuals into the political process, they would act as a barrier to aristocratic tyranny and political corruption. James Abercromby observed in 1830: 'I must confess that the only particles of public spirit and feeling which can be found in this country [Scotland] exist among the middling classes.' The following year he added, 'I have long been a zealous friend of the middle classes as the real strength and support of the country.'[6] The spectacle of merchants and manufacturers joining the Volunteers in large numbers during the crises of 1819–20 confirmed the civic virtues of the urban middle classes. But the Edinburgh Whigs were emphatic that they did not advocate the total enfranchisement of the middle classes on grounds of natural rights or citizenship. They were to be given the vote on a pragmatic basis, namely, to restore the desired balance of mixed and virtual representation which alone would enable the Commons to fulfil its constitutional role.

The *Review* Whigs emphasised that it was essential to keep the entrepreneurial classes politically detached from the working classes, whom they regarded as posing a profound threat to the stability of the constitution. The latter's demands were too radical, and the violence of 1815–20 highlighted the menace which they presented to order and progress. Jeffrey railed in 1820 against 'so much madness in Scotland', elsewhere labelling the radicals as 'mostly ignorant and unthinking persons', while Abercromby gave a trenchant opinion on Peterloo and the 'abominable reformers':

> Vigour, however, I am persuaded, is the only way to put down these people, and there is no time to be lost. Delay gives them strength and increases the chances of the bad spirit ascending to the classes above the mere mechanic.[7]

Indeed, at almost every point in the half-century after 1815, Whigs were much exercised by fears of working-class violence breaking out during political crises, hence Abercromby declared that 'the proper sphere' of his party was 'to protect the constitution both against the Radicals and against the encroachments of Ministers and of the Crown'.[8] So concerned were the *Review* Whigs about working-class recalcitrance over the doctrines of political economy, particularly as regards trade unions, that they promoted educational classes to instruct workingmen in the concepts of Smithian economics, and thereby acquire the values of self-discipline, thrift and sobriety, which the middle classes already possessed in abundance.

These new Whig principles chimed plangently with evolving trends in middle-class attitudes. Although they had shown themselves patriotic during the earlier critical phases of the wars with France, from around 1810 there were two clear indicators that businessmen were becoming rather discontented with aspects of the political system. Firstly, the government's economic policies were increasingly viewed as featherbedding the agricultural and landowning sectors, and inimical to the interests of business, a bias which bore particularly adversely on Scotland. An early flashpoint was the issuing in 1807 of the Orders in Council, which stringently restricted commercial trade between Britain and those parts of Europe under French control. These had a severe impact on the Scottish cotton industry, which exported a far greater share of its products to Europe than England did. Meetings objecting to the orders were convened in manufacturing centres, with local chambers of commerce joining in the protests, and the orders were withdrawn in 1812. The government's decision at the end of the war to continue with income tax, which had been introduced as a temporary wartime levy, infuriated middle-class professionals and entrepreneurs, who claimed that it diminished profitability, reduced business investment and dampened domestic demand levels, while leaving landowners and state parasites relatively untouched.

This sense of class grievance was at once compounded and encapsulated by the policy of agricultural protection. The passage in 1815 of a Corn Law giving greater protection to domestic producers crystallised the reasons for middle-class hostility to the ministry, since, in pushing up the price of bread, the act portended both to increase wage levels and weaken domestic demand for manufactures. The measure protected landlords, whose rental income was sustained unnaturally, as tenant-farmers benefited from artificially high corn prices. Moreover, the Corn Laws preserved the monopoly in landownership, because high rents pushed up land values. Hence, the tariffs on corn contravened the sacred principles of free trade at numerous points, and became the focus for economic and social reform in the minds of the business community.

The second target of middle-class discontent was the unreformed burgh councils. As we have seen, this had been a major issue in the 1780s, before being effectively snuffed out in the reaction to the radicalisation of the reform movements in 1792–3.[9] The unimpeded continuation of the abuses complained of thirty years earlier rankled still more after 1815, especially as several councils had fallen into serious financial difficulties because of extravagance and corruption. The campaign revived in 1816, when, after the exposure of gross abuses by councillors, Montrose received a new, quite democratic constitution, and this reform emboldened critics elsewhere, as a local versifier observed: 'Through Scotland we're envied by ithers/ Wha fain would be as we are, I trow.'[10] Within six months, almost half of the sixty-six royal burghs had joined the movement. Aberdeen (which became bankrupt in 1818), Dundee and Inverness were prime targets for burgh reformers, and the demand was stated simply and clearly by an Inverness newspaper: 'All that is asked by the burgesses is merely the election of their representatives in the Town Council.'[11] Archibald Fletcher, a leader of the earlier campaign, returned to champion the cause by producing in 1819 a history of the previous phase, which showed the persistence of abuses.[12] The movement received added impetus in that year when Glasgow joined it, since in the 1780s the burgh had stayed aloof from that agitation. The clamour climaxed in debates in the House of Commons on the topic between 1819 and 1822, and although the government side was strong enough to defeat demands for reform, the Whigs benefited inordinately in urban Scotland.

Behind these various episodes lay a longer-term development of profound significance, namely the emergence of a coherent middle-class identity and world-view, aspects of which have been explored in Chapter 3. A major unifying ingredient was the rise of local Whig-supporting newspapers in the fifteen years after 1815. Hitherto, the Scottish press had been small in number, mainly sympathetic to the Tory governments and struggling to compete with London journals for the readership of the elite. The most emblematic example of the new phase was the *Scotsman*. Established in 1817 by a group of Edinburgh professionals and businessmen, it was from the outset vigorously on the side of free trade economics and reform politics. By the mid-1820s, similar broadly pro-reform titles had appeared elsewhere, for example, in Glasgow, Cupar, Aberdeen, Kelso and Paisley, and, like the *Scotsman*, they were usually the highest-circulation paper in the locality. The spread of business associations, notably chambers of commerce, added to this sense of communal solidarity; the first was formed in Glasgow in 1784, and other places steadily followed, while local bodies representing specialist commercial and manufacturing interests, like the Glasgow West India Association, were widespread. The formation in larger towns of Police Commissions as alternatives to the reviled burgh councils contributed to the attack on the *ancien régime* and reinforced the elan and confidence of the new urban commercial classes, as discussed earlier.[13] Not for the first or last time, Glasgow University rectorial elections suggested the shifting currents of opinion among west of Scotland businessmen. In 1820, Jeffrey won, followed in 1823 by another Whig, Sir James Mackintosh, famous as the foremost defender of the French Revolution against Burke's critique.

These primarily economic links were deepened as the Reviewers tied the Whigs to the rising force within Scottish Presbyterianism, namely, the Evangelicals – a tendency reinforced by a mutual distaste for the Moderate wing of the Church of Scotland. In the eyes of the Edinburgh Whigs, the Moderates formed a vital component of the Dundasite Tory regime which had repressed dissent and independent thought. The prominent Evangelical minister, Henry Wellwood Moncrieff, was very close to the Reviewers, and his son James rose to pre-eminence in the next generation of legal Whigs, serving as Lord Advocate for most of the years between 1852 and 1869. Cockburn and Jeffrey encouraged Thomas Chalmers to write articles for the *Review* advocating the reform of the Scottish Poor Law in strict accordance with laissez-faire principles, while the Whig MP Thomas Kennedy tried in parliament to amend the Scottish Poor Law along similar lines.

An additional cement between the Edinburgh Whigs and the liberal and evangelical middle class was support for moral causes. Foremost among these was the abolition of slavery, which revived as a vigorous campaign from 1814, after several years in abeyance. In that year, 141 petitions came from 67 Scottish locations, and the movement grew in the mid-1820s; a Glasgow petition in 1826 attracted the support of a quarter of the population. This phase of the agitation was less church-based than before; rather it involved many civic bodies, and Whigs like Cockburn and James Moncrieff took a prominent role. The Reviewers were deeply interested in penal reform, a cause shared with many individuals who approached the topic from a religious standpoint.

But relations between the Edinburgh legal Whigs and the middle classes were not just a meeting of minds: they actively co-operated in several campaigns. The agitation against the Orders in Council was initiated by an *Edinburgh Review* article written by Brougham, who then participated wholeheartedly in the movement and was thanked by Glasgow Chamber of Commerce for his leading role in the campaign. The highlight of a great Edinburgh rally held in 1816 against the continuation of income tax was a speech by Jeffrey, his first public appearance as a political orator, and the *Review* had once again been in the forefront of the agitation to abolish it. The earliest overtly political orchestration of this broad alliance came in 1820, when a large gathering met in Edinburgh's Pantheon building on 16 December. Masterminded by the Whigs, the meeting carried resolutions calling for parliamentary reform as part of the movement protesting against George IV's treatment of his estranged wife, Queen Caroline, whom the king proposed to divorce. The agitation drew together Whigs and middle-class and working-class radicals in a foretaste of the united front of reformers forged in 1830–2.

Queen Caroline

Caroline was the daughter of the duke of Brunswick, and her mother was George III's favourite daughter. In 1795, she married her first cousin, the prince of Wales, the future King George IV. Quite quickly, however, they separated, partly because of her erratic behaviour, but more because of his openly adulterous relationships. Caroline left Britain in 1814 and moved to Italy, but she returned in 1820, just before George III died, hoping to become queen and to attend her husband's coronation service. George IV tried to divorce Caroline, but he could not induce parliament to enact the necessary legislation, so instead a bill of pains and penalties (effectively, a trial of Caroline for adultery) was introduced in parliament. There was a considerable degree of public support for Caroline, mostly because her husband's unpleasant conduct and character had made him deeply unpopular, and also suggested that he would be an unsatisfactory monarch. Radicals and a section of the Whig party, most prominently Henry Brougham, championed her cause, and hundreds of petitions supporting her were submitted to parliament. Even Walter Scott, a staunch Tory, felt that Caroline had been badly treated. She received strong backing from a broad spectrum of Scottish society: there were addresses from a range of organisations, such as the Incorporated Trades of Perth, while public meetings championing her cause were held in Dundee, Edinburgh and Glasgow in 1820. Some 35,000 Glaswegians supported a pro-Caroline petition, as did 16,000 Edinburgh citizens, while only 2,000 supported one backing George IV. When the bill of pains and penalties was abandoned, over eighty localities across Scotland held public celebrations. Riots broke out in Ayr, Edinburgh, Glasgow and Paisley against local elites who did not participate in the general rejoicing.

Caroline was, nevertheless, barred from attending George's coronation, and she died shortly afterwards. But the episode was significant for two reasons. Firstly, it stimulated interest among the wider public in constitutional questions, which fed into a broader reform agenda. Secondly, it sharply illuminated the treatment of women in every social echelon, an aspect highlighted by the involvement of women in public demonstrations in favour of Caroline, especially those held after the parliamentary bill fell.

The unity and vigour of Whiggery in Scotland after 1815 were accorded public affirmation through the annual Fox memorial dinners, which were held in Edinburgh, Dundee, Glasgow and some smaller towns in Angus. These occasions fulfilled several vital functions. They emphasised the common ground between different social and political strands in the party, thereby stiffening their shared resolve to continue to support the cause. The 1820 dinner was acclaimed as being 'on a more splendid scale than before ... a kind of general meeting of the Whigs of Scotland', so that the committee wanted the stewards to be a mix of 'nobles, the landed interest, lawyers, writers and tradesmen'.[14] Three years later, some 430 attended, of whom fully 300 were middle class, and speeches by both Cockburn and Jeffrey stressed the central role of commercial society in the party. The wider significance was that a public display of commitment to the Whig cause was declared, since, as Cockburn noted, in Scotland, 'we have no other regular convocations', and the dinners 'prodigiously awakened the public spirit'.[15] The proceedings – speeches, toasts and a list of those present – were fully reported in Whig newspapers and thus broadcast the party's values and policies to a wider public, who might feel comforted that liberal opinions were not restricted to small isolated groups.

Nevertheless, the reformist momentum of the early post-war years went into neutral soon after 1820, and remained inert for virtually the whole decade; for instance, the volume of petitions submitted to parliament calling for political reform fell sharply between 1824 and 1829. Partly this was because of the improving economic landscape, but two other factors were at play. Firstly, the growing liberalisation of the Tory government's approach to a range of policies mollified middle-class hostility, as did its application of heavy cuts to public expenditure. Secondly, the Edinburgh Whigs themselves shifted their focus. Attention was directed less to parliamentary reform than to administrative improvements, such as devising schemes to reform the Poor Laws, and implementing effective judicial reorganisation. Symptomatic of this trend was the decision by several of the Whig lawyers to accept office in George Canning's Liberal Tory administration, formed in 1827. This apparent volte-face was justified on pragmatic reasons: it was hoped that some of the Whigs' pet projects would be enacted by a premier seen as sympathetic to a moderate reform agenda. The future Lord Stair claimed that 'my anxiety is to strengthen the new [Canning] government ... which all liberal men are so desirous of upholding'.[16] The following year, James Abercromby, a prominent Whig who had joined Canning's administration, described William Huskisson, a pioneering Tory free trade minister, in glowing terms as 'a powerful, liberal and strong ally'.[17] This was consistent with the stance of the Whigs, namely that parliamentary reform was not an end in itself, and that other avenues which would modernise Scottish institutions were equally valid. Bereft of the leadership of the *Review* Whigs in these years, the broad political reform movement rather fell away, at least while open-minded Toryism was in the ascendant.

But it is misleading to think that, on a broader perspective, the movement for change perished totally. For one, moral reform campaigns such as the anti-slavery movement maintained an active presence throughout the period. Moreover, in parliamentary elections, there is a body of evidence indicating popular protest against the unreformed system. In the general elections of 1820 and 1826 in the Aberdeen Burghs, the return of the radical Joseph Hume was greeted with joy, with calls for wider enfranchisement aired at mass victory celebrations in several of the constituent burghs; similar displays greeted the return of R. C. Fergusson for Kirkcudbrightshire in 1826. In 1820, Sir John Maxwell was carried on the shoulders of non-electors through Renfrew burgh upon his return as MP for the eponymous county. This legacy of protest helps to explain the remarkable effusion of extensive pro-reform activity which was exhibited between 1830 and 1832.

THE TORY HEGEMONY IMPERILLED

The Tories' dominance of Scottish electoral politics remained assured between 1815 and 1831 – more so, indeed, than in England. Robert Dundas, the second Lord Melville, who continued to manage the government's Scottish business for almost the whole period, achieved this in the face of considerable challenges. Firstly, there was a changing climate in Scotland. The Whigs were increasingly confident that the march of their ideas would triumph, especially as the Tories had little to offer beyond a blind, undiluted defence of the status quo. Secondly, cuts in government expenditure sharply diminished the scale of patronage; by 1819, only around one-half of the posts available to Melville's father remained, and the abolition of the Scottish Board of Customs in 1823 removed another major milch cow.

Nevertheless, Melville's control was apparent throughout: at the four elections between 1818 and 1830, an appreciably higher share of seats in Scotland was held by the government: in 1818, 75 per cent of Scottish MPs were Tories, against only 55 per cent of the whole Commons. Much of the Scottish Tories' support in the 1818 and 1820 contests partly derived from carefully targeted loyalist messages which concentrated almost exclusively on the solid middle-class elements of society, who felt alarmed at the signs of revolution and disorder among the working classes. County meetings everywhere passed pro-government resolutions, and, as noted, the urban business classes readily joined the Volunteer forces. Moreover, despite the widespread unease at the treatment of Queen Caroline, the Scottish reaction to the coronation of George IV in 1821 was highly positive in most places (but not Arbroath), and, as is well known, the king's visit to Edinburgh in 1822, a carefully contrived rehabilitation exercise to sanitise his image, was generally an unqualified triumph. The 1826 contest was fought primarily on Roman Catholic emancipation, which opinion in Scotland was overwhelmingly opposed to. In 1830, as noted in Chapter 1, Scotland was less affected than England by agrarian distress, so the government side fared better.

The Liverpool ministry's position in Scotland was greatly enhanced when William Rae became Lord Advocate in 1819, serving continuously until 1830. Rae's studiously moderate approach to issues, avoiding the adoption of hardline stances, neutralised much of the enmity between parties which had long been a characteristic of Scottish politics, especially in legal appointments. His less partisan style slotted neatly into the government's gradual change in policies which took place across the 1820s, often termed Liberal Toryism. Many of these more progressive measures proved very popular in Scotland, especially among the hitherto antipathetic business and commercial classes, because they covered a range of economic, moral and religious topics. In the economic sphere, the simplification of tax and customs regulations and the repeal of the Combination Acts were well received, while trade with South America and the colonies was boosted by steep reductions in import duties. The cuts in state expenditure achieved by cutting placemen and sinecures in the Scottish patronage system were universally popular, as was the depoliticisation of civil service appointments. Greater state support for moral and religious ventures attracted the enthusiastic encomia of middle-class evangelicals and philanthropists. The award in 1824 of a grant to fund a state church building programme in the Highlands and Islands was perhaps the most eye-catching of these initiatives.

Broader liberal policies were also adopted: under Canning's influence, foreign policy moved from instinctive support for repressive regimes to embracing nationalist causes. Reforms in Scottish judicial procedure were popular with middle-class opinion, as decisions became cheaper and quicker. Concerns at the harsh penal code and at appalling prison conditions were met by a reduction in the number of custodial offences contained in the criminal law and by measures to improve gaols. The move to a policy of making legal appointments on a strictly non-partisan footing had a significant impact. In 1823, Peel signalled the new departure in typically guarded terms:

> I am sure it is both just and politic to open general judicial situations to men of eminence, whatever their political principles, or rather, I should say, not necessarily to exclude political adversaries from the bench, because I can conceive political principles that ought to constitute a disqualification.[18]

In addition, the repeal of the Test Acts in 1828 benefited Church of Scotland adherents, who hitherto had been debarred from a range of public positions.

Nevertheless, the winds of Liberal Toryism which gusted through the English party made little headway north of Hadrian's Wall; rather Scottish Tories seemed somewhat out of kilter with the new currents, for disciples of Canning and Huskisson were rare in their ranks. They did include two ministers, Sir George Clerk and Charles Grant. But by 1832, Grant had decamped to the Whigs and subsequently served as a Whig minister. In the approach to the 1830 election, Melville and his close kinsman, Robert Dundas of Arniston, were not prepared to support Clerk in Midlothian, and a league of Tory grandees in Inverness-shire caballed against Grant because of his unwavering adherence to Huskissonian principles. Additionally, sections of the Scottish Tory press were hostile to Canning's administration: in Glasgow, the *Herald* and the *Courier* both felt he was too liberal. The staunchly Tory *Blackwood's Magazine* became increasingly antagonistic to laissez-faire policies in the early 1820s, so that by 1825 it roundly denounced the liberalising economic policy adopted by the Liverpool government.

Melville, rather out of touch with the new direction, left office in 1827 when the ultimate liberal Tory, George Canning, became prime minister. The new home secretary, Lord Lansdowne, assumed responsibility for managing Scottish affairs, working closely, as discussed earlier, with two Whig MPs, James Abercromby and T. F. Kennedy, a relationship which caused deep unease among traditional Tories. These worries, however, seemed fully dispelled when the duke of Wellington became premier in January 1828: the Whigs were dropped, and oversight of Scottish affairs was entrusted to the earl of Tweeddale's son, Lord Binning, a man firmly identified with the Toryism of the pre-Canning era. While Cockburn lamented what he saw as the clock being turned back, most Scottish Tories rejoiced at the restoration of true party principles. These hopes were quite quickly comprehensively dashed, as Wellington and Peel soon opted to legislate for Roman Catholic Emancipation. As examined above, the reaction in Scotland was far more hostile than in England. Some 900 petitions opposing the bill were sent to parliament, around 250 of which came from Scotland, outnumbering Scottish resolutions in favour by a factor of ten.

For most Tories, Catholic Emancipation was unthinkable, and the party notables lined up in implacable hostility: Melville and Buccleuch came out against the bill, with only Rae and Clerk among prominent parliamentarians prepared to champion it. Walter Scott did support the measure, but he had few Tory adherents. Emancipation was vehemently opposed by the Tory press, especially *Blackwood's*. In angry articles it denounced the bill as a breach of the Treaty of Union, and a threat to the principles of 1688–9. A major consequence of the passage of the bill was that many Scottish Tories, spearheaded by the magazine, came to the paradoxical conclusion that parliamentary reform was necessary in order to protect the constitution from the display of excessive power wielded by the executive in forcing through a measure stoutly opposed by the clear majority of public opinion. Contributors to *Blackwood's* argued that reform should concentrate on abolishing small rotten boroughs as the most efficacious remedy, rather than introducing the ballot or a wider suffrage, which would have incalculable democratic consequences.

The tensions posed for the Tories by issues like Catholic relief and economic liberalisation compounded more structural problems which were peculiar to Scotland. While the minuscule electorates in Scottish constituencies, burgh and county alike, made control and manipulation of seats relatively straightforward, in the long run this narrow electoral base proved counterproductive, and these defects grew ever clearer in the 1820s. The exclusion of the overwhelming majority of the population put the party in a different position from England, where the substantial numbers of voters in many county and borough seats meant that the Tories were compelled to develop some forms of social and economic appeal to constituents; in Scotland, however, patronage, corruption and influence seemed the sole requisites. Thus, unlike England, the grievances felt by the Scottish solid middle class who did not have the vote poisoned the Tories' appeal in the post-1832 era.

A further result of the small unreformed electorate was that, in contrast to England, the Scottish Tories had no need to develop any constituency party organisation, however rudimentary. After the Reform Act, the party in Scotland found it much harder to establish a grassroots structure, as there was no pre-history, and socio-economic bases were virtually non-existent. It was essentially a party of feudal landowners, with few other interests attached to it, whereas in England, prominent Tories such as Peel, Canning and Huskisson had risen from business backgrounds. The only national party institution in the pre-reform era was the Pitt Club, which held an annual dinner on the anniversary of Pitt's birthday. The main celebration took place in Edinburgh, but other places, such as Kilmarnock, also held commemorative meetings. As with the Fox dinners, toasts were drunk, songs sung and speeches delivered, all in the cause of party harmony and uplift. But after the passage of the 1828 Emancipation Act, the Pitt clubs declined in support.

The Tory party did try to establish a vigorous press to challenge the growth in Whiggish newspapers after 1815, but they encountered problems. It seems clear that the circulations of provincial Tory journals were mostly smaller than their Whig rivals, and several struggled to survive: in 1832, the party organ in Dumfries was bought up by the local Whig newspaper. The main exponent of Tory ideas was *Blackwood's Magazine*. Launched in 1817, its major focus was not political, but cultural, most notably in its development of an outstanding stable of literary authors, including James Hogg and Scott's son-in-law, J. G. Lockhart. It did, however, carry a growing amount of political matter in the 1820s, with most of the contributors non-Scots. But *Blackwood's* had a smaller circulation than the *Edinburgh Review* and a lower proportion of its readership was based in Scotland, so its impact was substantially less than its Whig rival.

Moreover, Tory policies were less attractive in Scotland: while the manufacturing interest was resolutely hostile to the Corn Laws, protectionism – even in certain agricultural seats – had much less appeal than in England, as wheat production formed a lower share of total farm output. In England, the Tories could appeal to the Anglican community as its protector, defending its establishment status against the challenge from the growing strength of Nonconformity, but the position in Scotland was less straightforward. As considered earlier,[19] the various versions of English Dissent were not a significant presence in Scotland, where the Presbyterian Voluntaries were the only sizeable body outside the state church. But within the Church of Scotland there was a further barrier to adopting the English Tories' stance, namely the rising volume of support after 1815 for the Evangelical wing of the church and its conflict with the Moderates. As discussed earlier, the latter were closely identified with the Tory party, so Evangelicals tended to see the Whigs as a more sympathetic party. Thus, in the fracturing Church of Scotland, there was little scope for political gain. A further reason why the national church was not an effective rallying point for Scottish Toryism was that, as Walter Scott noted, there was only limited opposition to Catholic Emancipation, as many in the party had a historic Jacobite connection. Accordingly, in 1821, as distinct from all Pitt dinners in England, Edinburgh ostentatiously did not toast 'The Protestant Ascendancy'.

THE REFORM MOVEMENT REVIVED

The Whigs were dismayed at the decision of the liberal Tories to stay loyal to their party after Canning's death in 1827 by joining the governments led firstly by Viscount Goderich (later the earl of Ripon), who was quickly followed in 1828 by the duke of Wellington; both high reactionaries. The Whigs evidently expected the followers of Canning, Huskisson and Lansdowne to leave the Tories and continue the alliance with themselves. Kennedy exploded to Lord Minto that their action was 'disgusting and reprehensible'.[20] Hereafter the Whigs returned to looking to co-operate with the extra-parliamentary reform elements, who were themselves stirring at around this point.

By the end of the 1820s, the urban middle classes had once again grown disaffected with the government. In several towns, for example, Paisley, deceleration in economic growth convinced businessmen that a more vigorous application of laissez-faire economic principles was necessary. The retention of the Corn Laws resurfaced as a focus for complaint, and fed into a wider critique that the government represented a landed elite innately hostile to the interests of business. A prominent Glasgow merchant exclaimed in 1830: 'Was there ever a period when we should be more careful to return active, practical and independent members to represent our great commercial and manufacturing interests?'[21] Significantly, this individual – James Ewing – became an MP for the city in the first post-Reform Act parliament. This frustration fused with escalating anger at the malpractices of the unreformed burgh councils, especially when contrasted with the effective performance of local police commissions, managed by the very middle class who were excluded from burgh councils. The particular objects of this indignation at this point were Dundee and Edinburgh. In 1830, Dundee lost the right to take part in parliamentary elections, and Edinburgh was on the verge of bankruptcy as a result of heavy spending on non-essential items. With two of the four largest cities manifestly misgoverned, the case for reform seemed overwhelming, as Ewing argued in 1830:

> As for the middling and manufacturing part of the population, among whom is to be found so much that is pure and honourable in patriotic feeling, they may be said to be without any organ of communication at all among the representatives of the nation.[22]

As noted earlier, working-class support for political reform had dwindled in the 1820s, in part because of the severe state repression of radicals, but also, as noted, because economic growth meant that employment rose and real wages probably picked up. However, when the economy drooped at the end of the 1820s, the search for improving living standards shifted from the workplace to politics. Trade unions, liberated from legal constraints in 1824–5, had initially made headway against employers, but, as explored in Chapter 3, they were now facing a counter-offensive which led to male workers in textiles and mining losing control of workplace practices, such as appointing foremen and choosing apprentices.

Working people and the middle classes had arrived, from different starting points, at a common analysis of the causes of economic and social problems, and they also established a consensus about how to improve their lots, as outlined above. The analysis was that the unreformed electoral system benefited landed and agricultural interests at the expense of both business and industrial labour, with high taxation and excessive state spending on placemen and pensioners reducing domestic demand levels, so that enterprise was stunted and workers' living standards were jeopardised. Instead, an electorate which reflected faithfully the interests of those in commerce and manufacturing would sweep away these abuses, so promoting economic growth and a concomitant rise in living standards. There seems to have been an acceptance that the vote would be conferred primarily on the middle class, but working people assumed that their interests would be promoted by their allies in the reform agitation.

For those of a more Whiggish disposition, reform was conceived as addressing historical inequalities while simultaneously acknowledging Scottish traditions of freedom. Sweeping away the feudal foundations of the Scottish county franchise would place the electoral system on the footing which England had achieved in the seventeenth century. In this way, Scotland would attain equality with English liberties, and a reform act would definitively address the deficiencies in the Treaty of Union, permitting Scotland to become a modern political state on a par with England. But these objectives did not necessarily require a major democratisation of the electorate, and early franchise schemes produced by Kennedy and other Whigs proposed a property qualification for burgh voters which at £20 per annum was double the actual figure of £10.

This swelling surge of discontent with the British political system was fortified by the French revolution of 1830, which deposed King Charles X and installed a democratic constitution. Thirteen places in Britain, including Edinburgh and Glasgow, held meetings to express approval of the new French regime. As an early instance of the social solidarity which characterised the campaign for parliamentary reform, a dinner attended by middle- and working-class reformers was held in Glasgow on 3 January 1831 to celebrate the events in Paris, and to express the hope that reform would quickly spread across the channel. Once again, support for European nationalist-democratic movements was linked to reform in Britain.

At the 1831 general election, the Whigs made a net gain of eight MPs in Scotland, a significant advance on past performances. The campaign embraced a broader debate than parliamentary reform *tout court*: slavery, agricultural protectionism and monopoly trading rights in India and China all featured prominently in constituency battles. This indicated that parliamentary reform was expected to open the way for wider social and economic changes which people had long campaigned for. Certainly, the intensity with which Scots joined in the reform movement suggests something deeper than a transitory spasm of enthusiasm. Thus, at a huge Glasgow meeting in September 1831, placards were carried depicting Daniel O'Connell and the Radical MP Joseph Hume, and there were calls for free trade and the protection of labour rights alongside franchise extension.

A prominent feature of the popular campaign for reform was the concordance of the urban reformers across class lines, a feature which had major implications for the development of politics in the post-1832 era. Although the specific details varied from place to place, the general characteristics were apparent in places like Dundee, Paisley and Glasgow. In these cities, there were separate organisations for middle-class and working-class activists. In Glasgow, the Reform Association was mainly middle class and the Political Union working class; whereas in Paisley, the Renfrewshire Political Union recruited mostly businessmen and professionals, and workingmen predominated in the

Paisley Reform Society. But in both cities, the associations normally collaborated closely: there was overlapping representation on the respective executive committees – one-third of the executive committee of the middle-class Glasgow Reform Association were members of the more proletarian Political Union. It was reported of the Glasgow Reform Association that

> its main use, if not its main object, has been to facilitate intercourse between them and the leaders of the working-classes. They find the [working-class] leaders quite disposed to be reasonable, so long as they have confidence in the ministers.[23]

Meetings and rallies were carefully co-ordinated, so that visiting orators were able to address both societies, either jointly or separately.

The conduct of the general body of reformers was exceptionally disciplined and observant of legal constraints, in frequent contrast to England. There, the rejection of the First Reform Bill in 1831 instigated scenes of violent disorder in several larger towns, particularly Bristol, Derby and Nottingham. But protests in Scotland, even though attracting huge crowds – for instance, 20,000 in Paisley and 100,000 in Glasgow – were mostly peaceable and well-disciplined. There was, however, rioting in Dundee at a demonstration attended by 20,000 people, and the severe sentences of seven and fourteen years' transportation imposed on those convicted may well have doused the ardour of protestors elsewhere. An attempt in October 1831 by English reformers to destabilise the economy by orchestrating a run on provincial banks was not replicated in Scotland. Adherence to constitutional procedures was scrupulously observed: at the Glasgow reform dinner held in January 1831 under the auspices of the trade union movement, the English agricultural outrages – the Captain Swing protests – were comprehensively rejected and full support for property rights was explicitly affirmed.

While the arguments of the reform camp received a massive enthusiastic response, the opponents of reform argued doggedly in favour of preserving the status quo. A major mouthpiece for these views was, of course, *Blackwood's Magazine*, although others, especially MPs, voiced the case for resisting reform. Several strands were developed by these critics. Firstly, it was stressed that the remarkable economic and social transformation of Scotland since 1707 suggested that the political arrangements were not relevant, and therefore parliamentary reform was unnecessary and undesirable. Secondly, the historicist arguments deployed by reformers were turned on their head; unlike England, Scotland had no historical rights and liberties which had been lost. Thirdly, any scheme of reform threatened to breach the Treaty of Union, which had laid down the distribution of seats for Scotland. Fourthly, Burke's case for gradual evolution, not violent change based on theoretical precepts, was applied.

The revolution of 1830 in France revealed the risk of radical political shifts, with uncertain long-term consequences. Fifthly, the agitation for reform was artificially got up by Whigs: there had been little evidence between 1820 and 1830 of an appetite among the populace for reform. Sixthly, the disturbances at elections (primarily, however, in England, not Scotland) showed the perils of enfranchising working people. Seventhly, the existing system allowed every interest to be represented: after all, Kirkman Finlay, the leading cotton manufacturer in Scotland, sat for Marlborough between 1818 and 1820, and many other Scots entered parliament via small English borough seats.

However, many of these points had rather lost credibility by 1831, when the demand for reform was clearly irresistible. Sheriff Archibald Alison led the Tory rethink in the columns of *Blackwood's*, stressing that while concessions were inevitable, it was vital to protect the British constitution against full democracy by admitting a portion of the middle class, although the impact of this change should be minimised. The most effective way to achieve this was to shift the focus of attention to the redistributive aspects of reform, so that the influence of the landed interest could be preserved by excluding the new class of voters from county seats.

WOMEN AND POLITICS IN THE UNREFORMED ERA

The role of women in politics before the First Reform Act, although oblique, was nevertheless, in certain circumstances, significant – and mostly occurred in county seats. Some women, usually widows or daughters who inherited an estate with feudal superiorities attached, could control votes, and hence had an active part in the political life of the constituency. The countess of Sutherland wielded the greatest power in this respect, for the majority of electors in the eponymous county was under her sway from 1786, when she succeeded to the title. Mrs Mackenzie Stewart, who inherited the Seaforth estates in 1815, had a considerable, but not dominant, interest in Ross-shire. Also, thanks to their control of some of the constituent town councils, both women had significant stakes in the Northern (Wick) Burghs seat, and Mackenzie Stewart also had some weight in the Inverness burghs. They both engaged at a close level in the political management of their interest. In 1806, Fox reported hearing that the countess 'is now a determined and a very eager politician', and in 1810 she negotiated directly with Lord Seaforth over the candidature for the Northern Burghs.[24] Her influence extended far beyond her native shire: in 1806, Lord Grenville refused to pledge ministerial support to the Whig candidate in Fife, as the countess supported the opposition candidate. Mackenzie Stewart communicated regularly with other Ross-shire landowners on county politics, and made it clear that she, and not her husband, was in command.[25]

There were other ways of exercising a political presence, most of which could be categorised as 'soft' power. A major source of this occurred where class and a strong personality blended, so that upper-class women frequently took a prominent role in politics. For example, the fourth duchess of Gordon was very active in several seats. In 1788, she opposed Dundas's project to bring Lord Fife into the alliance of north-eastern landowners, and in 1790, she was also reported to be intending to campaign in that year's peerage election. In addition, the duchess took a leading role in London and Edinburgh as a Tory party hostess.

Elite women made an additional contribution as intermediaries with influence either on political magnates or on voters. In 1801, Lady Elphinstone solicited the duke of Montrose for the support of his interest in Stirlingshire, while in the same year a candidate for Cromarty sought the blessing of Lady Elibank for his campaign. Furthermore, upper-class females passed on political information, both local and national, to men. Gilbert Elliot's sister explained the intricacies of vote creation to the Minto estate's lawyer in 1811, and in 1805 the wife of an aspirant candidate in Kincardineshire sent Lord Melville a full account of the political situation in the county, as well as a detailed survey of the voters.

An area where the presence of women was felt to be very potent was in the personal canvassing of voters, which broadly covered both family members and social acquaintances. Wives were frequently targeted as the most likely way to persuade voters to support a candidate, and daughters, sisters and mothers were also a prominent influence. Beyond family connections, women were also highly important in persuading male friends and associates in making voting decisions.

The role of sub-elite women in the 1790–1815 era seems to have been more restricted: the workingmen champions of French Revolution principles in Scotland tended to emphasise the virtues of fraternity and a male artisan culture rather than Paine's concept of an egalitarian citizenship which included women. Nevertheless, women took part in many of the food and militia riots of the 1790s. Between 1815 and 1832, a shift occurred, however, with women becoming more prominent in the public sphere, in good part because of the rise of processions and demonstration as vehicles for political protest. At a Glasgow demonstration in 1819, women in the weaving district of Anderston not only made red caps of liberty for marchers to wear, but also two rows of them – with caps on – participated in the march to the east end of the city. In the 1820s, there are reports of women involved in demonstrations at burgh elections; after Joseph Hume was re-elected for the Aberdeen Burghs in 1820, a female society with a standard and ribbons took part in the Brechin celebration, and women attended post-election celebrations in Aberdeen. A turning point in working-class men's attitude to women participating in political action seems to have come with the agitation supporting Queen Caroline. Sympathy with the suffering endured by Caroline at the hands of her male persecutors induced radical Scotsmen to reappraise the position of their own womenfolk.

For middle-class women with a professional or business background, there appears not to have been much scope for political involvement, especially given the restricted electoral character of burgh constituencies. Nevertheless, their entry into public affairs was initiated by the movement to abolish slavery, which grew in size in the 1820s. Women occupied a prominent place in the Scottish campaign, and an early sign of the more overt engagement which arose in the post-1832 era came with the formation in 1830 in Edinburgh of a separate women's anti-slavery association. There was, then, a growing body of intelligent women who had a sound grasp of political issues. Partly this reflected the provision of a fair amount of schooling for women which the impact of the Scottish Enlightenment promoted. Additionally, the impact of quarterlies, particularly *Blackwood's Magazine* and the *Edinburgh Review*, in encouraging women to take an active interest in politics was considerable, if unquantifiable. As a result, women at dinner parties in Edinburgh were wont to discourse animatedly on questions of the day, rather than passively listening to the opinions of the males. Jeffrey, for one, was greatly discomforted by this forwardness.

Appearances by women at public political meetings developed in the postwar period. The Edinburgh Fox dinners of 1821 and 1822 were attended by one or two women, but such intrusions were subsequently vetoed. A sign of a newfound confidence was that by the mid-1820s, women sometimes attended election polls, usually sitting in the front row, or in a restricted area. There were 'several high-born and elegantly dressed ladies' at the front of the gallery during voting in the 1826 Inverness-shire contest; and at the 1829 Ayrshire by-election, a somewhat perplexed man reported: 'I saw a number of ladies seated to the right, which I never before remember to have seen honouring a county election.'[26] During the 1831 general election, Lady Maxwell delivered a public speech to the Pollokshaws Masons in which she praised the consistent political principles adopted by her husband (the MP for Renfrewshire) and her son (the Whig candidate for Lanarkshire).[27] This was possibly the first occasion on which a woman delivered a full-length political speech in Scotland.

NOTES

1. *Glasgow Sentinel*, 23 September 1809.

2. *Affairs, being now settled ABROAD, 'tis high time to look at HOME* (5 September 1815), 1 (capitals in original).
3. London, National Archives, HO/102/32/296, *Address to the Inhabitants of Great Britain & Ireland* [1820] (capitals in original).
4. A. Benchimol, *Intellectual Politics and Cultural Conflict in the Romantic Period: Scottish Whigs, English Radicals and the Making of the British Public Sphere* (2010), 209–22; F. Stafford, 'The *Edinburgh Review* and the Representation of Scotland', in M. Demata and D. Wu (eds), *British Romanticism and the Edinburgh Review: Bicentenary Essays* (2002), 40–2.
5. NLS, Melville MSS, MS 1, f. 232, Melville to Lord Douglas, 30 November [1811].
6. BL, Holland House MSS, Add. MS 51575, ff. 14–17, Abercromby to Lord Holland, 13 July 1830; Blackford [by Yeovil], Kennedy of Dunure MSS, Abercromby to T. F. Kennedy, 13 January 1831 [typescript copy].
7. London, University College London Archives, Brougham MSS, MS 22135, Jeffrey to H. Brougham, 8 April 1820; *Substance of the Debate in the County Hall, Edinburgh, . . . December 22, 1820*, 34; Blackford, Kennedy of Dunure MSS, J. Abercromby to T. F. Kennedy, 20 August 1819 [typescript copy].
8. Blackford, Kennedy of Dunure MSS, J. Abercromby to T. F. Kennedy, 20 August 1819 [typescript copy].
9. See pp. 184–7, 193.
10. *Montrose Review*, 11 October 1816.
11. *Inverness Journal*, 27 February 1818.
12. A. Fletcher, *Memoir Concerning the Origin and Progress of the Reform Proposed in the Internal Government of the Royal Burghs of Scotland . . .* (1819).
13. See pp. 73–4.
14. NLS, Minto MSS, MS 12134, ff. 15–17, L. Horner to Minto, 3 December 1820.
15. [H. Cockburn and T. F. Kennedy], *Letters Chiefly Connected with the Affairs of Scotland . . .* (1874), 69 [21 December 1822].
16. NRS, Clerk of Penicuik MSS, GD 18/3313, Sir J. Dalrymple to Sir G. Clerk, 11 May 1827.
17. Blackford, Kennedy of Dunure MSS, J. Abercromby to T. F. Kennedy, 29 September (1828) [typescript copy].
18. BL, Peel MSS, Add. MS 40339, ff. 84–5, R. Peel to W. Rae, 20 October 1823 [copy].
19. See pp. 122–4.
20. NLS, Minto MSS, MS 12136, ff. 22–3, Kennedy to Minto, 21 January 1828.
21. *Authentic Account of the Proceedings Arising from the Election of Kirkman Finlay, Esq., of Castle Toward, to Be a Member of Parliament for Glasgow and the Clyde District of Burghs . . .* (1830), 20.
22. Ibid., 27.
23. BL, Bowood MSS, B 104, ff. 57–60, J. Abercromby to Lord Lansdowne, n.d. [c. November 1830].
24. BL, Fox MSS, Add. MS 47564, ff. 254–5, Fox to Lord Lauderdale, 2 January 1806.

25. E.g. NRS, Seaforth MSS, GD 46/120/3, Mrs Mackenzie Stewart to Sir A. Mackenzie, 14 October 1817 [copy].
26. *Inverness Courier*, 12 July 1826; Ayr, Ayr Council Archives, Hamilton of Rozelle MSS, AA/DC17/113/14, J. Hamilton to A. Hamilton, 14 May 1829.
27. Glasgow City Archives, Maxwell of Pollok MSS, T-PM 116/490, *Speech by Lady Maxwell to Pollokshaws Royal Arch Lodge* (12 May 1831), n.p.

CHAPTER 9

Politics in the Age of the First Reform Act, 1832–c. 1865

THE FIRST REFORM ACT: VOTERS AND CONSTITUENCIES

The Scottish Reform Act was passed on 11 July 1832, five weeks after the English act, and was greeted with widespread acclaim across most of Scottish society. A celebratory National Jubilee day, held on 10 August, was widely observed, and not just in bigger towns: in the north-east, quite small places such as Ballater, Mintlaw, New Pitsligo and Portsoy held demonstrations. The act was viewed on all sides as ending the Scottish *ancien régime* even more decisively than in England. The existing franchise systems were completely replaced, and recognition was given to new demographic and social factors by a major revision of constituencies. The upshot of these provisions was that the Scottish electorate rose by some 1,400 per cent from 4,571 in 1831 to 63,369, whereas in England it increased by 41 per cent, from 434,530 to 614,654.

The impact of the Scottish and English acts differed in two significant respects. Firstly, in England, broadly speaking, the franchise changes did not materially alter the social composition of the electorate, but rather simply increased the overall number. In Scotland, however, the control wielded by feudal superiors and self-perpetuating council cliques dissolved, and new social elements acquired the vote. In most counties, such as Perthshire, tenant-farmers made up just over half of the total electorate, with around one-third in the professional, business and artisan classes, and the remainder being proprietors and miscellaneous categories. However, in at least one-third of counties – almost all in the Lowlands – farmers were in a minority, usually because of sizeable numbers of town voters: in Roxburghshire, it was noted by Tories that the qualified electors in Kelso alone comfortably exceeded the county's agricultural voters. In burghs, tradesmen and shopkeepers tended to be predominant, as in Aberdeen, Edinburgh, Glasgow and Inverness.

> **The franchise provisions of the First Reform Act in Scotland**
>
> In county constituencies, the act removed henceforth the right to vote based on feudal superiorities, although existing electors – termed 'freeholders' – were left on the register. The franchise was now based on two main qualifications: firstly, real ownership of property with an annual rating valuation of £10 or more; and secondly, tenants who either paid an annual rent of £10 and held a lease of 57 years' duration or paid £50 rent and had a 19-year lease. Owners must have possessed the property for six months, although not necessarily residing in it; husbands could qualify on their wife's property and co-owners could vote if the property was worth multiples of £10. Likewise, joint tenants could claim the franchise if the value of the property permitted. These qualifications also applied to residents in towns and villages which were not part of a burgh constituency, thereby allowing them to vote in the county seat.
>
> In burgh constituencies, town councillors lost their role as the burgh electorate. Now, male owners and occupiers of property rated at £10 formed the new electorate, provided they had paid the rates and had not received poor relief in the previous twelve months. These voters had to reside within seven miles of the burgh that they were qualified to vote in. Occupiers additionally had to have resided in the property for twelve months, but this was not required of proprietors. Joint owners and occupiers could vote if the property was worth multiples of £10, and husbands could vote on their wife's property.
>
> The act was poorly drafted, mainly because it employed English legal terms (particularly 'occupation', 'ownership' and 'possession') which were not strictly applicable in Scots law.

Secondly, the English redistribution of constituencies created a more profound alteration than in Scotland. Around one-quarter of English seats, all in smaller boroughs, were swept away, and in the re-allocation, county MPs were increased by one-third and an equivalent number of new borough MPs were created, primarily in previously un- or under-represented manufacturing centres. In Scotland, no burghs were disfranchised, and eight extra MPs were allocated to burghs, so that there were now 23 burgh and 30 county MPs. England, in contrast, had 322 borough and 142 county MPs.

There were, however, aspects of the Scottish measure which were less positive. While vote-creation in county seats along the old lines was, naturally, eliminated, new forms were quickly devised to exploit faulty draughtsmanship

> **The redistribution of Scottish constituencies under the First Reform Act**
>
> The act had two key redistributive features. Firstly, the old practice of six counties being paired and represented in alternate parliaments (three in, three out) ended. Two (Bute and Caithness) became independent seats; two (Clackmannan and Kinross) formed a single seat; and the other two (Cromarty and Nairn) were joined to two adjacent constituencies (respectively, Ross and Moray). Secondly, Scotland received eight additional seats, so total representation rose from forty-five to fifty-three, and these were all allocated to burghs. Aberdeen, Dundee and Perth were disjoined from their groupings and given a separate MP, while Greenock and Paisley, both hitherto unrepresented, also became constituencies on their own. Edinburgh received a second member, and Glasgow became a stand-alone constituency, with two members. The act also reshaped the composition of nine of the fourteen burgh groupings, with eleven additional burghs admitted, three of which – Leith, Musselburgh and Portobello – became a separate seat, while the other eight were added to existing constituencies. Most of the newcomers were manufacturing centres, such as Falkirk and Port Glasgow, but Oban and Peterhead were also admitted. Three burghs (Peebles, Rothesay and Selkirk) were removed from their groupings and merged into their county seats in order to boost the size of their shires' electorate. But otherwise, no small burgh constituency had its right to return an MP removed, not even Wick (366 voters) or Wigtown (316). There were now seventy-six burghs represented in parliament, against sixty-six before.

in the legislation. The most common method was to create voters by establishing fictitious joint tenancies on properties worth more than twice the minimum qualifying value. This loophole was utilised by both sides, but the bulk of fictitious voters were created by the Tories, especially in the south-eastern counties. Although not carried out on a large scale – one survey estimates under 6 per cent of all county voters were so enrolled by 1844 – in a handful of seats they bulked much larger, and could possibly tilt the outcome in tight contests.[1] In Midlothian, life-renters soared from 3 per cent of voters in 1832 to about 25 per cent by 1842. While the level of vote-creation fell away after 1840, the practice was still being deployed in 1880, when Liberals and Conservatives engaged in the titanic struggle for control of Midlothian both indulged shamelessly in it.

Despite the enormous increase in the Scottish electorate, overall enfranchisement still lagged behind England. The ratio of voters to adult males in Scotland (1:8) was appreciably lower than in England (1:5); indeed, Scotland had merely caught up with the pre-reform English proportion. The prime reason for the discrepancy was that in Scotland, being the poorer country, property values and rental levels were significantly lower, so fewer individuals qualified. Also, registration was expensive and many in Scotland seem to have decided to forgo the right to vote rather than pay the fee. Furthermore, the twelve months' residency requirement in burghs probably had a greater impact in Scotland, where, so Jeffrey claimed, a third of families, including many middle-class ones, moved house annually.[2]

The franchise aspects of the act attracted the most attention, but the concomitant revision of constituency boundaries also had profound implications. Two cardinal features influenced the scheme. Firstly, seats were not allocated in accordance with numbers of voters, so that huge disparities occurred. Sutherland had eighty-four voters, while Glasgow, with two MPs, had 6,989, i.e. almost forty-two times as many voters per member. Secondly, the central Lowlands were under-represented, and the Highland and southern Lowland regions were heavily over-represented. The major manufacturing centres had 30 per cent of all the voters, but only 12 per cent of seats, while the northern and south-eastern areas together had 20 per cent of the electors, but 40 per cent of the seats. This geographically skewed disposition served to cramp the full electoral power of urban-industrial Scotland, and to protect landed and less radical interests. This is partly confirmed by the treatment of burgh constituencies. The consequence of introducing new burghs into groupings depleted by the creation of single-member constituencies was the removal from county electorates of many urban voters, thereby protecting the agricultural integrity of shire seats. Also, the retention of small county and burgh seats permitted the perpetuation of landowners' influence: Lord Bute firmly controlled the eponymous county, and the Wigtown Burghs continued to be a fiefdom of the earls of Galloway.

THE TORIES' DIFFICULTIES

Scottish election results under the new system diverged profoundly from England. In both countries, the 1832 general election resulted in a headlong rout of the Tories. In England, they won a quarter of the contests, and in Scotland, just under one-fifth. However, the Tories in England recovered quickly from the drubbing meted out that year, and in the 1837 election they emerged as the larger party. Of the seven elections from 1835 to 1859, in England the Tories won four consecutive contests from 1837 to 1852, and their share of seats never fell below 40 per cent. In Scotland, the party did not win a majority in any of these elections; only once (1841) did it manage to hold 40 per cent of seats, and on three occasions it dropped below 30 per cent.

Table 9.1 Conservative MPs, Scotland and England, 1832–59

Election	Scotland		England	
	Seats	%	Seats	%
1832	10	19.0	117	25.2
1835	15	28.3	200	43.1
1837	20	37.7	238	51.3
1841	22	41.5	277	59.7
1847	20	37.7	238	51.5
1852	20	37.7	244	50.3
1857	14	26.4	185	40.2
1859	13	24.5	208	45.2

One problem facing the Scottish Tories was the legacy of the unreformed system, which they had benefited from and had robustly defended, with the result that the newly enfranchised electors decisively rejected them. The intensity of this animus was deeper than in England, where, as discussed in Chapter 7, a large number of constituencies under the pre-reform set-up had sizeable electorates. Because of the magnitude of the change in Scotland, the Whigs attracted more numerous and more socially widespread support than in England. In the run-up to the 1835 election, a paper-mill owner in Midlothian stoutly rebuffed the Tory candidate:

> Those who advocated [Reform] are entitled to the approbation and gratitude of all classes of society. Had you, Sir George, been amongst its supporters, you should have commanded not my vote only but that of many others who with pride and pleasure would have hailed you as their Honourable Representative. You declared however in Parliament that I ought not to possess the Elective Franchise, and yet request me to exercise it on your behalf, to the prejudice of those who aided me in obtaining it. Figure yourself in my position – How would you have acted?[3]

This antagonism proved very long-lasting; in 1868, the Tory record of resistance to parliamentary reform was still being flagged up by Liberals. This image was perpetuated by the Tories' vote manufacturing activities in the 1830s, which were held up by their opponents as clear witness to the party's recidivist genes.

Some factors which aided the English Tories were less prevalent in Scotland. Like England, deference was a factor in counties, as tenant farmers and estate workers frequently followed the political lead given by their lairds out of respect to the leaders of the agricultural interest. But there were limitations. Most crucially, the prevalence in Scotland of long leases – nineteen years being the normal duration – considerably diminished the threat of loss of tenure which English landlords could hold over politically recalcitrant tenants, who were mostly on much shorter leases. In any event, on some issues – particularly religious ones – tenants might not comply with their landlord's wishes, as happened in Wigtownshire, where Lord Galloway's influence was diluted because a number of his tenantry who were dissenters voted Whig. Also, it was hard in Scotland to replicate key components of the English political culture of deference, with its paternalist ideology of landowners who were directly responsible as JPs for the welfare of all in the rural community, so eliciting loyalty from social inferiors. Scottish JPs did not wield anything like the same socio-legal influence, and landowners had at best a low-level presence in administering the Poor Law. The leisure symbols of a shared identity so lambent in England were largely absent in Scotland: fox-hunting was limited to a few areas, partly because of terrain, while village cricket was equally rare.

The Tory advance in England came to a considerable degree from gains in boroughs, which constituted over two-thirds of the total seats; in 1841, their best result, they captured almost exactly one-half – 157 out of 332. While some of these victories were sleepy backwaters and stately cathedral towns, over the period the party frequently won in many industrial towns, including Leeds, Liverpool, Newcastle-upon-Tyne, Southampton and Stoke. The Scottish Tories did nearly as well as their English counterparts in counties, but their performance in burghs was comparatively woeful. Almost all burgh seats remained permanently deaf to the enchantments of Conservatism. Over the eight general elections between 1832 and 1859, they won in only four of the twenty-three burgh seats, and these on rare occasions: two (Haddington and Kilmarnock) only once, one (Inverness) twice and one (Falkirk) three times – and there was more than a whiff of corruption at play in the last. They were virtually invisible in many burghs: in fifteen of the twenty-one constituencies, the party fought in less than half of these general elections, including Aberdeen, Dundee, Greenock, and Paisley, and in no seat did it stand every time.

The development of formal constituency party organisation played an important role in fuelling the Tory surge in English boroughs after 1832. In 1835, the old corrupt town councils were abolished, and the new municipal franchise differed appreciably from the parliamentary one. This reform had two interacting facets. Firstly, the Tories participated fully in local elections, not just for borough councils but also for the New Poor Law authorities, established in 1835, and for parish councils. Secondly, the party strove to maximise voting power by assiduous attention to registering supporters for these sub-parliamentary authorities. The near-annual electoral cycle and the yearly registration process kept activity at a high level between parliamentary contests. To reinforce their strength, additional organisational strategies were applied. Local newspapers were established to promulgate the Tory viewpoint, and reading rooms and clubs, for both the middle classes and workingmen, were founded – all in order to foster a local culture of Conservatism. Hence, the social basis of the party was broadened, while success in local government elections attracted able and ambitious urban middle-class men to the party.

In Scotland, however, there was only limited parallel urban organisation. The reform of municipal government in 1833 made the municipal franchise virtually identical to the parliamentary one, so there was less call for registration work. Until 1845, the Poor Law was administered by unelected individuals, and there was no direct equivalent to parish councils. Additionally, Scottish sub-parliamentary elections were customarily not fought on partisan lines; for instance, Glasgow and Edinburgh, staunchly Liberal in parliamentary elections, had several Conservative lord provosts in the half-century after municipal reform. Nevertheless, some elements of organisation were adopted in Scottish burghs during the 1830s. Tory papers were set up in selected towns. The *Glasgow Constitutional*, launched in 1835, aimed to supplement the city's two declining Tory titles, and new papers were also started in Cupar, Dumfries, Kilmarnock, Montrose and Perth. Significantly, the *Glasgow Constitutional* was set up by city businessmen, the very group Peel sought to recruit in his bid to reconfigure his party. Additionally, the major intellectual forum for Toryism in Scotland, *Blackwood's Magazine*, abandoned its ultra-Toryism of the closing years of the unreformed system, and was transmogrified into a loyal advocate of Peelite principles. The quarterly's most frequent Scottish contributor in this period was Sheriff Archibald Alison, who repeatedly emphasised that it was vital to reach out to the business community in order to overturn Whiggery. Another venture which echoed English tactics was to mobilise workingmen. Edinburgh and Glasgow each formed a Conservative Operatives' Association; the latter was launched in 1836, and some 270 members attended its first Annual General Meeting.

Tory Radicalism won support in English manufacturing centres from workers affected by the new industrial order, and it laid down a strand of social reformism which was revived – at least rhetorically – by Disraeli and others after the Second Reform Act. These radical Tories of the 1830s attacked the imposition of laissez-faire policies on the working class, particularly the introduction of the New Poor Law and the rejection of factory reform legislation. Its leading proponents were lesser gentry and Anglican clergymen. Scotland, as noted earlier, had no Poor Law reform until 1845, and the Factory Question was never as salient as in England; Scottish male textile workers were instead more concerned to defend their control of the work process and labour recruitment than to restrict hours of work.[4] Indeed, some working-class radical newspapers – for instance, the *Glasgow Evening Post* – were hostile to Factory Reform in the 1830s, and almost all the Conservative-inclined press in Scotland advocated a laissez-faire stance. Few lairds took up Tory Radicalism – Alexander Thomson of Banchory being the main exception – possibly because many landowners had interests in manufacturing and mining ventures. The leading Scottish advocate of legislation to protect working people was Sir John Maxwell, the Whig MP for Lanarkshire, who championed the cause of handloom weavers in parliament, abetted by W. D. Gillon, the Whig MP for Falkirk. Among the Tory intelligentsia writing for *Blackwood's*, Sheriff Alison was a lonely voice championing the Ten Hours Act and opposing a harsher Poor Law regime.

There were nonetheless distinctly positive features for the party in the middle to late 1830s. There were quite substantial shifts by voters away from Whiggery. By 1837, in some constituencies up to a quarter of those who had voted Whig in 1832 had either gone directly across to the Tories or had abstained, itself often a prelude to further movement away. For some, the feeling was that the Whigs were too radical in their policies, and so backing the Tories was necessary to stem the tide. For others, the apprehension loomed large that the Whig government's policies were inimical to the interests of the Church of Scotland and too partial to Voluntary Presbyterianism. It was for this reason that Sir Andrew Agnew, elected as a Whig in 1832 for Wigtownshire, in 1837 endorsed the ultimately victorious Tory candidate for the seat.

This unease among moderate opinion was exploited by Peel in a bid to win over the urban middle class in Scotland, as he was already doing in England. In the commercial towns in the west, he was informed in 1836, positive pro-Conservative stirrings were to be found:

> I am assured that many most respectable persons, who were friendly to the Reform Bill, will be found in Glasgow ready to meet you and bury all past differences in the earnest desire of making common ground against a republic.[5]

In that year, Peel was elected rector of Glasgow University, which seemed to herald a breakthrough for Conservatism in urban Scotland. The arrangements for a celebratory banquet held in Glasgow in January 1837 confirmed that Peel was focused on consolidating his appeal to business and professional men in burghs. The old High Tories in the landed classes and the Edinburgh legal establishment were excluded from the event, but a prominent role in the proceedings was accorded to the local Conservative Operatives' Association, which had initiated the idea of the banquet by getting up a petition signed by 2,000 workingmen.

Highly promising developments followed this start. In the 1837 general election, serious assaults were launched on five larger burgh seats. Only one of these, Kilmarnock, was won, but this limited advance was blamed on the suddenness of the dissolution, and there were confident predictions of more gains, including Glasgow, at the next contest. There were further propitious auguries: Sir James Graham, a former Whig turned close confidant of the Tories' leader, succeeded Peel as Glasgow University rector; in 1840 Glasgow and Edinburgh both had Tory lord provosts. So serious was the challenge that in Greenock, Whigs fretted lest the seat slip away: 'unless we stir, some influential mercantile Tory will be invited to stand and probably would sit.'[6] But these great expectations were wholly deflated in the 1841 election, as – quite unlike England – no advances of note were made in burghs. Greenock was emphatically not captured, Kilmarnock was reclaimed by the Whigs, and counties with a heavy input from urban voters, such as Renfrewshire, slipped away. Falkirk and Haddington were the only Tory burgh victories. As Graham lamented to the party's election manager, 'In Scotland we have been least successful'.[7]

THE CONSERVATIVES AND THE CRISIS IN THE CHURCH OF SCOTLAND

The prime reason for the Tories' failure lay in the Church of Scotland conflict. At first sight, this appears paradoxical, as a fundamental ingredient of English Conservatism throughout the period was the party's steadfast support of the Church of England, and, as a corollary, of the establishment principle everywhere else in the British Isles. In return, the Anglican Church gave highly effective political assistance, especially in organising electoral registrations and disseminating pro-Tory propaganda in parishes. While the Church of England remained largely united internally until the middle 1840s, the Scottish state church was fatally riven between Moderates and Evangelicals, a conflict which reached its climacteric in the decade after the Reform Act.[8]

As the Tories were historically close to the Moderates, the Evangelicals, who had long had close links to the Whig party, confidently expected support from the Whig governments in the struggle for mastery of the church. But in the mid-1830s, the Whig government frequently rebuffed their demands, instead responding positively to pressure from the Voluntaries, who were opposed to the Evangelicals' agenda.[9] As a result, disenchantment with the Whigs set in among Evangelicals, so that Peel was informed in late 1837 that: 'They [the Church of Scotland] consider that [the Whigs] are on all occasions ready to sacrifice the interests of the Established Church in order to conciliate the Dissenters.'[10] This unmooring had a crucial attraction for Peel and his political strategy of refocusing the Tories as a centrist, modernising party.

The Evangelicals had solid support among urban Lowland business and professional men, for instance, William Collins, a Glasgow publisher, and Charles Cowan, a Midlothian paper manufacturer. Peel wished to attract such politically moderate men, whose firm adherence to the establishment principle was unquestioned. In several Scottish by-elections from 1835 onwards, the Tories made headway thanks to the cry of 'the Church in danger', which in England had proved an inordinately powerful magnet. In his address at a Glasgow banquet in January 1837, Peel adroitly stressed the rights of the state church, and this seemed to elicit a greater response among his audience than his exposition of the case for modest political reform. The polling in the 1837 general election strongly suggested many Church of Scotland members had voted Tory.

But this symbiotic relationship grew more strained after the giddy heights of 1836–7, largely because the Evangelicals embraced the concepts, firstly, of Non-Intrusionsim and, secondly, of Spiritual Independence. These developments seemed to imply that the church stood above the law, which was anathema to a party fully committed to constitutionalism. English Tories began to view the threat to lay patronage as a dangerous precedent for an assault on the Church of England. Another implication of spiritual independence was equally unacceptable: property rights, in the form of secular patronage, could be abolished without compensation. In addition, like the Whigs, Conservative leaders found the Non-Intrusionists very difficult to work with.[11]

But the electoral benefits of Non-Intrusionist support, illuminated by a by-election for the marginal Perthshire seat in March 1840, seemed incontrovertible. Here, Non-Intrusionist pressure compelled the Tory candidate at the last moment to match the Whig by endorsing the full Evangelical standpoint. The Tory win, which quadrupled the party's majority from 116 to 458, was regarded by many in all political camps as decisively assisted by the Non-Intrusionists, who now insisted that the party owed them special consideration. Hence, at the start of 1841, relations seemed reasonably positive, especially as Melbourne's ministry remained deaf to the Evangelicals' demands.

However, one month before the 1841 election, Peel informed a deputation of Evangelicals that the Non-Intrusionists should submit to the courts' rulings. He also repudiated a bill sponsored by the duke of Argyll aimed at resolving the patronage difficulty, declaring it yielded too much to popular control of ministerial appointments. It was therefore clear that if his party formed the next government, it would not comply with Non-Intrusionist expectations. Scottish Conservatives instantly felt despondent when reports of the meeting emerged; the party's chief Glasgow agent wailed: 'It is with a heavy heart that I see the labours of years thrown away.'[12] The widespread predictions of defeat at the polls were vindicated, and the consensus across parties was that Non-Intrusionists overwhelmingly voted Whig in most seats, especially burghs, so depriving the Tories of victory in all but two urban seats. The party's losing candidate in Glasgow summed up the situation in a succinct understatement: 'I am sorry to say that this untoward Church question has damaged us not a little.'[13] Even in normally safe Tory seats, the party faced stiff competition: in Roxburghshire, the Whigs had initially withdrawn from the contest, but the vehemence of Non-Intrusionists' reaction to Peel's interview induced them to re-enter, and they won. In other constituencies, Tories declined to contest the seat, as in St Andrews, viewing the fight as pointless. The outcome would have been even worse for the Conservatives but for weaknesses in their opponents, as Whigs did not stand in some county seats previously held by them, such as Ayr, Dunbarton and Perth.

The formation of the Free Church in 1843 created a voting bloc of considerable weight, especially in the larger Lowland burghs and almost all Highland seats. This vote was virtually universally delivered against the Conservatives, who, being in office at the time of the Disruption, were held guilty of permitting the secession by their intransigence towards the Non-Intrusionists. One consequence was the wholesale loss of the solid urban middle class, as erstwhile Tories like James Forrest, a former lord provost of Edinburgh, were henceforth firmly in the Liberal camp. William Collins Jr, the son of one of Chalmers's most ardent lay supporters, had been a member of the Glasgow Conservative Operatives' Association, but by the 1860s he was a prominent influence in Glasgow Liberalism. Significantly, the city's Operatives' Association was dissolved after a heavy loss of members who resigned in protest at the government's responsibility for the Disruption. The Tories' setback in the 1847 general election was explained by some candidates as the inevitable outcome of the hostility of Free Churchmen.

Moreover, great resentment was aroused by the refusal of many landowners to release land for the new church to build places of worship. Many of the worst offenders tended to be prominent Tories, notably the dukes of Buccleuch and Atholl, while among the few sympathetic landowners were Whigs such as Lord Breadalbane and Fox Maule. In Ross-shire, the Liberal gain in 1847 was put down to the incumbent Tory, Mackenzie of Applecross, allegedly having refused sites in his estate, even though the Free Church had the vast majority of churchgoers in Wester Ross. The new Liberal MP, James Matheson, had the reputation of being fully amenable to releasing land for the Free Church.

THE IMPACT OF THE REPEAL OF THE CORN LAWS ON THE CONSERVATIVES

In the immediate aftermath of the Disruption, Tory hopes were dealt a second heavy blow. The repeal of the Corn Laws arguably had a more serious impact on the party's fortunes than in England, so that, taken in conjunction with the loss of support generated by the Disruption, the result was that for perhaps a decade after the split, the Tories were preoccupied with recouping their fortunes rather than expanding into Whig zones. As discussed earlier, the appeal of agricultural protectionism was less alluring in Scotland, even among the farming community, and several progressive tenant-farmers were in fact ardent repealers. In 1842, George Hope of Fenton Barns, probably the country's outstanding modernising farmer, was given a prize by the Anti-Corn Law League for an essay denouncing the policy of agricultural tariffs. Interestingly, the general election contests in 1847 in Fife and East Lothian, two prime

Figure 9.1 Kirriemuir weavers' banner celebrating the repeal of the Corn Laws, 1846. This indicates the broad cross-class support in Scotland for Peel's abolition of agricultural protectionism. © Angus Council. Licensor: www.scran.ac.uk

wheat-growing constituencies, revolved more around tenant-farmers' complaints about the operation of the Game Laws than the ending of protection. While protection yielded few dividends in counties, it was politically bankrupt in burghs, where free trade was overwhelmingly popular, even with sound Conservatives. The great ironmaster William Baird, the Tory MP for Falkirk, had campaigned in 1841 as a free trader. His brother James, who became the MP for the constituency in 1851, also opposed protectionism.

As outlined in Chapter 8, the case against protection was well developed before 1832, and persisted down to 1846, but with greater depth and intensity, and with some new angles. The theoretical underpinnings stemmed from Smithian economics, but the practical arguments for free trade were also well rehearsed. Scottish industry and trade relied heavily on international, not domestic, markets; lower corn prices would cut the cost of bread and so permit reduced wage levels, increasing competitiveness and boosting profitability. The Scottish middle classes were also keenly appreciative of the political potential of repeal, as it was expected to reduce aristocratic incomes and prestige, thereby forcing landowners to retreat from dominating parliament. Notwithstanding this broad appeal to employers and the middle classes, workingmen were also advocates of the abolition of the Corn Laws, primarily because the prospect of reducing food prices in a low-wage economy was powerful. So, in 1834, the Dundee working class organised ahead of the middle class to attack the Corn Laws. In Dundee and Glasgow, operatives' associations of the Anti-Corn Law League were set up in the early 1840s, and the members of the league's Kirkcaldy branch were almost wholly working class.

The critique of Corn Laws was widened after 1832 to include religious aspects. Non-Intrusionists believed that a major obstacle to patronage reform was that it struck at the property interests of landowners, so they harboured no wish to support the lairds on this issue. After 1843, the Free Church's grievance against landowners grew exponentially with the refusal of sites for churches. These matters exercised Voluntaries much less, but the Corn Laws presented them with a different grievance. They were obliged to pay teinds, which went to support the state church, as well as having to fund their own churches. As the level of teinds was determined by grain prices, the attractions of reducing these had obvious financial benefits, and moreover it was believed that the reduction in income for the Church of Scotland would render its survival more precarious, and this assumption was given credence by the almost universal opposition to repeal among state church clergymen. The most explicit expression of this strand of anti-Corn Law mentality came in December 1842, when an assembly of some 800 Dissenting clergy and a similar number of lay adherents (including George Hope, who was a Unitarian) met in Edinburgh and solemnly pronounced the imposition of tariffs on wheat to have no scriptural basis.

Hence, large numbers of Scots – proportionately more than the rest of Britain – signed petitions opposing the Corn Laws: in 1834, over 60,000 subscribed to a Glasgow protest, while in 1840, 11,286 Dundonians signed what was then the city's largest petition. Branches of the Anti-Corn Law League, which was formed in 1839, spread across the whole of Scotland, reaching as far as Shetland and Caithness, and Scotland could boast a higher proportion of branches, with 35 against 227 in England. This trend was reflected at Westminster: in 1845, while 41 per cent of Scottish MPs supported a motion for repeal, only 24 per cent of the rest of the Commons did so.

Further problems were posed by the split in the Conservative party over the repeal of the Corn Laws in 1846. Because of a degree of fluidity in voting patterns, absolute precision is difficult to establish, but it would appear that between 1846 and 1852, the ratio of Peelite to Protectionist MPs was higher in Scotland than in England. At the general elections of 1847 and 1852 a sort of informal non-aggression pact operated in a bid to avoid damaging clashes and thus hopefully facilitating a future reunion of the two camps, but events undermined this expectation. The two most prominent Scottish aristocratic frontline Tory politicians, Lord Aberdeen and the duke of Argyll, moved across from the Peelites to the Whigs in the early 1850s. In 1852, Aberdeen led an administration dominated by Whigs, while Argyll served in cabinets under Palmerston and Gladstone. Some of the largest owners of estates in wheat-growing districts supported Peel in 1846 – notably the duke of Buccleuch, the marquess of Queensberry, and Lords Dalhousie and Wemyss. These four peers between them had significant influence in at least seven county and three burgh constituencies – almost one-fifth of all seats. Buccleuch's adherence to Peel was highly damaging for the Protectionist Conservatives, not simply because he was widely regarded as one of the leading Scottish Tories. He also carried enormous political clout in the south-east, as evidenced by reports that in the 1847 elections he vetoed a Protectionist candidate standing in Roxburghshire, while the Peelite A. E. Lockhart retained Selkirkshire thanks to his support. Because there were so few Scottish Conservative MPs, the influence of peers was much greater than in England, hence the disarray created by these men was considerable.

For Protectionist Tories, relations with Peelites after 1846 took three forms. Firstly, a protracted internal process gradually ousted some Free Trade Tories. The best instance was in Ayrshire in 1852; after the mobilisation of local activists with encouragement from Lord Eglinton, the sitting Peelite MP, A. H. Oswald, withdrew to fight Weymouth and was replaced by a Protectionist. Secondly, in other places, less committed Peelites returned to the Tory party and were accepted as repentant prodigals: for example, Alexander Smollett in Dunbartonshire. More significantly, Buccleuch's heir, Lord Dalkeith, who in 1845–6 had lobbied junior ministers to stay loyal to Peel, entered parliament in 1853 as a Conservative. Thirdly, the formation of Lord Aberdeen's administration in 1852 triggered a realignment which left the Tories permanently bereft by the 1857 election of quondam Peelites, now wearing Whig colours; the duke of Argyll and Lord Aberdeen had used their considerable influence in their eponymous counties to replace Tory MPs with Liberals.

This transition was significantly reinforced by the advent of Lord Palmerston, another Peelite, as the dominant politician of the later 1850s, but now sailing under the Liberal flag. His reluctance to endorse sweeping internal reform measures, combined with a vigorous defence of British interests in the wider world, was exceptionally appealing to many moderate Scottish Tories. It was claimed that in 1857 at least two constituencies – Ayrshire and Lanarkshire – were lost by the Tories because middle-of-the-road party supporters, finding the Conservative candidates too hardline, opted to vote for Palmerstonians. In the latter seat, the Tories had not been challenged for twenty years.

Recovery from these two debilitating setbacks was inhibited by another difference between English and Scottish political cultures. Anti-Catholic feeling was stirred up by the introduction in 1845 of a government grant to Maynooth College (an Irish training seminary for Roman Catholic priests). In England, this mood was compounded by the restoration of the Catholic hierarchy in 1850, demonised as 'Papal Aggression'. The Tories, as the traditional defenders of popular Protestantism, exploited these events to great effect, making electoral inroads into Liberal strongholds in industrial areas. But in Scotland, the party could make little headway along these lines. Opposition to Maynooth, as discussed below, was the political prerogative of the alliance of the Free and United Presbyterian (UP) churches, who used it as an electoral battering-ram within the Whig-Liberal party. 'Papal Aggression' was at that point in time less contentious in Scotland (always excepting the lunatic fringe of Presbyterianism, which in some places was a very considerable hem), where the restoration of its Catholic hierarchy did not occur until 1878.

Furthermore, organisational defects were a persistent problem for the party. One pointer to the organisational inertia afflicting the Tories was the demise of many pro-Conservative newspapers. By the 1850s, the party had few popular journals backing it: in Edinburgh, the Whiggish *Scotsman* ruled supreme, while in Glasgow the Tory organs were in terminal decline – the *Glasgow Constitutional*, founded in the surge of Conservative enthusiasm generated by Peel's reformulation of the party's ideology, folded in 1855, leaving the heartland of industrial and commercial Scotland without a weighty Tory paper for nearly twenty years.

THE WHIGS: SUCCESS AND CONFLICT

For the Whigs, the disarray of their rivals was at once a boon and a challenge. The benefit was their unquestioned supremacy in many constituencies, particularly burghs. But the broad sections of Scottish society and politics encompassed by the party created tensions and divisions as differing groups sought to achieve ascendancy over policy. The upshot was that the dominance of the Whigs was largely overthrown in burghs for a decade or so from 1847, but then they recovered much of the lost ground in the 1857 and 1859 elections, although in many instances this arose as much because of rifts within their internal opponents as any surge in positive support for themselves.

One factor which contributed to the frailty of the Whigs was that whereas in England, there was something of an efflorescence of Whiggery in the two decades after the Reform Act, as a generation of young aristocrats imbued with Christian beliefs, for example, Lords Milton and Tavistock, strove to improve British society, this development was less present in Scotland. Few aristocratic Whigs were prominent after 1832, apart from Fox Maule, later the eleventh Lord Dalhousie, whose standpoint was close to his English counterparts. As a junior Home Office minister, he announced in 1837 that he 'would always advocate the interests of the poorer classes and do his best to reduce their grievances'; by 1842, he urged the repeal of the Corn Laws:

> It is impossible to see the starving thousands in this country, whose miserable pittance is counted by one-fifth of a penny and not feel that every penny by which the price of meal is kept up by a corn law is cruel and abhorrent to all reason.[14]

This humane response contrasts powerfully with the attitude of both the Edinburgh legal and the urban business Whigs, but Maule never became a beacon for Scottish aristocratic Whiggery. Other historic Whig families, such as the Mintos, provided lacklustre MPs in the period, while several were politically inactive, for example, the tenth duke of Hamilton.

Moreover, the other two strands of Whiggism faced problems. The influence of the Edinburgh lawyers became less pervasive, although they still wielded influence by providing lord advocates for Liberal governments throughout the half-century after 1832. But they were increasingly subject to vigorous criticism by the emerging middle-class radical groupings, who accused them of timidity and conservatism, and their hold on parliamentary seats was increasingly at peril from urban Radicals. Their in-house journal, the *Edinburgh Review*, rather lost influence within Scotland after the 1830s. Its editorship passed out of Scottish hands, and in 1847 the journal physically moved to London, while there was a concomitant diminution of articles addressing Scottish concerns. Rival Liberal periodicals sprang up, such as the *North British Review*, founded in 1844, which advanced a Free Church position. In 1846, its circulation – about 3,000 – probably rivalled that of the *Edinburgh Review* in Scotland. The great expansion from the 1830s of newspapers in Scotland advancing progressive political and social agendas arguably further dented the influence of the *Edinburgh Review*. In at least thirteen burghs, spread between Wick and Dumfries, such papers were started.

The third ingredient of Scottish Whiggery, the urban wealthy business-professional element, was steadily eclipsed for around a decade between the mid-1840s and the end of the 1850s by new, vigorous expressions of Radicalism. In Glasgow, the so-called Whig Junta had successfully managed electoral politics from 1832 until 1847, whereupon it went into eclipse for a decade, and this trend was repeated elsewhere: for example, Edinburgh and Aberdeen, although the causes and the timing could vary. This shift in Whig-Liberal politics reflected several trends in the structure and values of the new middle-class electorate, which produced deep disaffection towards Whig administrations and policies. The 1832 general election resulted in sweeping victories in most seats for the Whigs, including larger burghs like Aberdeen, Edinburgh, Glasgow and Leith, whereas Radicals were elected in only a few places, pre-eminently Dundee, Falkirk and Greenock. The overwhelming Whig triumph in 1832 raised expectations of further sweeping institutional changes, but, apart from the Municipal Corporations and the Police Acts, both passed in 1833, very little Scottish reforming legislation was placed on the statute book in the remainder of the decade.

Radicals quickly grew restive at Whig inertia, and by 1834, their discontent was being publicly aired, with calls to cut public spending, reduce the number of placemen, introduce the ballot and widen the suffrage in order to counter landlords' intimidation and nullify the impact of fictitious votes. One key component of middle-class radical discontent was the reluctance of Whigs to support the full repeal of the Corn Laws. This, as noted earlier, became a touchstone for Scottish Radicalism in the 1832–46 era, and several Whiggish electoral casualties in 1841 and 1847 fell in part because of their moderate stance on repeal. The political Radicals were reinforced by the creation of the Scottish Central Board of Dissenters in 1834, whose espousal of disestablishment was easily assimilated to the broad theme of sweeping change.

Between 1834 and 1837 the united political and religious Radicals challenged Whigs in several burghs. In the 1835 elections, they succeeded in Kilmarnock, replacing a tepid Whig with Sir John Bowring, a prominent English social reformer, and in a by-election at Paisley the following year, a radical won the seat previously held by a very moderate Whig. Moreover, 1835 was the first stage in the Tory revival, which removed one-third of Whig county MPs, so making the Radical element among Scottish Liberal MPs greater. Radicals made further inroads on the Whigs in the 1837 elections, gaining control of the candidacy in Renfrewshire, and pressing elsewhere in the west-central area.

THE IMPACT OF RELIGION ON THE WHIG PARTY

But the more profound shift against the Whigs arose from the intensifying religious controversy which preoccupied middle-class opinion for a decade or so after 1832. While initially they found common cause with political Radicals, as the conflict in the Church of Scotland became more potent in the mid-1830s, the Voluntaries switched to focus primarily on ecclesiastical issues. The initial consequence of the rift within the Radicals was to give the Whigs an electoral respite. By-elections in 1837 and 1839 in, respectively, Glasgow and Edinburgh were easily won by uncompromising Whigs; in the latter, T. B. MacAulay, the archetypal Whig intellectual, was returned unopposed. Both these constituencies had very recently been top Radical targets. As we have seen in Chapter 5, the Whigs' relations with their former allies, the State Church Evangelicals, became ever more fraught in the years before the Disruption, but the party retained the adherence of the vast bulk of Voluntaries in the 1841 election. For, despite the disappointment felt by the latter at perceived slights and neglect by the Whig ministries, it remained quite impossible for the Voluntaries to jump to the Tories. But this uneasy alliance was soon to be tested to destruction.

The Disruption resulted in the creation of a Free Church block vote, whose allegiance to the existing parties was fluid. A prospective Whig candidate who was sniffing out prospects in the Haddington Burghs seat in 1847 was cautioned that

> since the Free Church party has gained a firm footing and a high standing, and as much will depend upon this party being satisfied as to the views of candidates [on a range of issues] . . . a less correct idea can be formed as to the probable success of any candidate whatever.[15]

But the electoral weight of the Free Church vote was in most seats outside the Highland region not the crucial factor in determining the outcome. In by-elections held in the first two years after the Disruption, Voluntaries declined to collaborate with the Free Church, since there was a deep gulf between the two over the establishment principle. But a seismic shift took place in 1845–6, bringing adherents of the two churches into a political alliance. The decision by Peel's administration to give state funding to Maynooth College, a training seminary in Ireland for Catholic priests, provoked outrage among Voluntaries and the Free Church, albeit for different reasons. The latter opposed subsidising 'erroneous religious beliefs', whereas the former objected in principle to state finance being made available to any church. Both camps agreed to modify their rigid doctrinal stances, as the Scottish Board of Dissenters outlined it:

At a crisis like the present all friends of religious liberty should study to the utmost harmonious co-operation ... surely there may be an amicable co-agency in a parliamentary conflict. Where the same measures are approved of, there may be a mutual forbearance as to abstract opinion, and parties may unite on supporting this or that man, as the qualification of the individual and the circumstances of the locality render desirable. To be more specific, unless Dissenters can vote for Free Churchmen and Free Churchmen for Dissenters, union is impossible and defeat certain.[16]

This holy alliance deeply disturbed Whig party managers, and their concerns were vindicated at the 1847 general election, when in several burghs candidates backed by the militant anti-Maynooth movement were returned. This process operated, among other seats, in Glasgow, where two well-established urban Whigs were defeated, and in Aberdeen, Edinburgh, Stirling, Perth, Paisley and Dundee. Of course, other factors also applied in these contests, but Maynooth was a central topic of contention. The college was still being awarded government grants at the time of the 1852 general election, and the Free–Voluntary combination mostly held the seats gained in 1847, and notched up some additional wins, such as Greenock. The outcome was that while in one or two places the adhesion of Tory voters could materially assist a Whig candidate, in general Whigs were being expelled from many urban constituencies.

The political collaboration between the Free and the UP churches over Maynooth was based on successfully glossing over conflicting principles, but in the mid-1850s the need for educational reform provided a testing-ground for this alliance. By 1850, there was widespread discontent at the condition of the once-vaunted Scottish school system. Parochial schools could not cope with the demographic pressures of industrialisation and urbanisation. The rise of other types of schools to fill the gap only exacerbated the situation, as many of these were inadequate in quality and were not subject to any inspection. While there was a clear case for a sweeping reform to introduce a truly national system, the control of the parochial school system by the Church of Scotland created three major difficulties. Firstly, parish schoolmasters had to be members of the state church; secondly, religious teaching was a core element of the curriculum; and thirdly, religious instruction imparted the doctrines of the Church of Scotland. Hence, many of those outwith the established church – and some within it – wanted a non-sectarian system, with no religious teaching in the classroom.

In 1850, the National Educational Association of Scotland was formed to press for the introduction of a national secular non-sectarian schooling system. Its founders included Whigs, such as Lord Melgund; prominent academics, like Sir David Brewster, the Principal of Edinburgh University; and socially concerned public figures, for example, the publisher William Chambers. This essentially secularist group was joined by leading Voluntaries, notably Duncan MacLaren and Adam Black, because the United Presbyterians were opposed to all state finance of religion, including schools.

Rather unexpectedly, the Free Church also participated in the association. In pursuit of its founding principles, the church had set up schools as part of its claim to be a national church, and there were 712 by 1851. But its educational project was not succeeding. Only about two-thirds of congregations were served by a church school, with Lowland parishes particularly under-supplied, thus many children of Free Church families attended parochial schools, where religious teaching expounded only the doctrines of the established church. Financially, the expense borne by the Free Church in maintaining its schools imposed a heavy burden, and by 1850 the Educational Scheme teetered on the verge of bankruptcy. By campaigning for a truly national school system to replace the existing parochial schools, the Free Church would achieve two goals. Firstly, it would be liberated from the upkeep costs of its own schools. Secondly, the proposed scheme would deliver a possibly fatal blow to the Church of Scotland, as its control over parochial schools gave substance to its pretensions to be a truly national church. Having already lost responsibility for poor relief, if schools were taken out of its hands, the established church would lose credibility and be reduced to virtually the same status as the Free and Voluntary churches.

Thus, reform of schooling served as a strategy for both non-established Presbyterian denominations to assail the Church of Scotland's status, and this unity boosted their electoral alliance in the 1852 election. Supporters of the State Church were prompt to identify the underlying motive behind the religious advocates of a non-sectarian national scheme. A former Tory cabinet minister at the time of the Disruption crisis warned that 'I am quite sure that if an attempt be persevered in to uphold the Parochial Schools on their present footing, a struggle will ensue in which the Church [of Scotland] will be worsted and its existence endangered.'[17] But the Free Church's determination to retain religious instruction in a national non-sectarian system led to conflict within the reform camp. The church lobbied successfully against bills introduced in 1850 and 1851 by Melgund which proscribed all teaching of religion. Relations between the Free and UP supporters deteriorated after Lord Advocate James Moncrieff, a loyal adherent of the Free Church, introduced a new education bill late in 1853 which contrived to bypass the religious instruction difficulty by leaving such teaching in the school curriculum, but allowing parents who objected to withdraw their children from these classes. Moncrieff believed that this provision would accommodate the scruples of Voluntaries, but the bill provided that the cost of religious instruction would be part of the general school expenses, and so would be funded by ratepayers, regardless of religion.

The bitterness felt among UP adherents at this measure led to fierce denunciations of the role of the Free Church. A Voluntary newspaper argued that 'he must be rather defective in mental vision that [sic] does not see that the whole movement is in the direction of Free Church interest and Free Church principles.'[18] The UPs' outrage was almost certainly heightened because until then they had sensed that the Free Church had been moving steadily towards Voluntaryism. The bill was rejected in the Commons, thanks to a rare combination of English Dissenter MPs and defenders of the establishment principle, both in Scotland and in England. Moncrieff tried again in 1855 with a bill which dropped the requirement that religious instruction be provided for no extra charge. But great exception was taken by UPs to a clause added on the floor of the Commons permitting Episcopalian and Roman Catholic schools to stay outside the national scheme, yet still receive full government grants. The Free Church was charged with double standards, having previously agitated against grants to Maynooth, but were now complicit in the state subsidising the teaching of Catholicism. Hence, Moncrieff's bill was voted down by the same alliance which had destroyed his previous bill.

The consequences of this dispute between the Free and UP churches were serious. The rift opened up in 1854–5 postponed any attempt to unite the two for almost a decade. This left the Church of Scotland with the breathing space to rebuild, which it took eagerly, as illustrated in Chapter 5. A further result was the breakdown of the political alliance between the Free and Voluntary churches, fatal cracks in which were revealed in the 1857 election, at which the schools question often predominated. At Paisley, where a Free Church Liberal fought a Voluntary, a local paper reported that 'The Lord Advocate's bill has been made the test-point of this election.'[19] Almost all the constituencies held by the alliance were lost, as in Dundee, where a staunch Whiggish supporter of the state church defeated a Voluntary. Similar trends occurred in Glasgow and Aberdeen, and although in a few seats sitting representatives of the alliance clung on, by 1859 more losses were sustained. As well as the contentious education issue, by 1857 the impact of the Maynooth grant was diminished as a political issue, and to many voters it had now become an index of bigotry. With the Free–UP coalition in smithereens, the urban Whigs were restored to power.

ENTREPRENEURIAL RADICALISM

But religious Radicalism was not the sole challenge to Scottish Whiggery, for there was also a grouping of 'Entrepreneurial Radicals' operating in the 1850s. Led by John Bright and Richard Cobden, they advocated measures to promote the interests of business by reducing government expenditure in wasteful areas, such as colonial acquisitions, military expenditure and foreign wars. They fervently opposed state extravagance and incompetence, especially patronage and the lack of competition for public appointments and contracts. Reforms in these fields would permit the reduction of direct taxation, which acted as a brake on business profitability and entrepreneurship. They also pressed for wider free trade arrangements, simplification of commercial law, notably in shipping and company legislation, and were emphatically not in favour of legislation to protect the rights of labour. This package of business-friendly policies had a deeper long-term strategy, for they were conceived as the next step following the abolition of the Corn Laws in the long march to curtail the economic, social and political power of the landed elite. Several Scots, both in parliament and outside, were prominent members of the pressure group: for instance, Samuel Laing, William Ewart, R. A. MacFie and Duncan MacLaren. Some, of course, were also involved in religious Radicalism, the most prominent being MacLaren.

The Entrepreneurial Radicals launched a series of movements to promote these goals, but none were very successful in Scotland – or, indeed, elsewhere. The most promising of these bodies was the Administrative Reform Association, which focused on the British failures in the early phase of the Crimean War. The association argued the blunders were the result of incompetent aristocratic leadership in both the government and the military, so that only the removal of these boobies and the installation of an efficient administration firmly grounded in sound commercial practices could address the difficulties. There was a degree of interest in Scotland in the programme of the association, but the movement foundered as the war turned in Britain's favour, and its failure opened up far-reaching discords in the Radical movement. Some in the Administrative Reform Association believed that peace, not war, was better for commerce and prosperity, and Duncan MacLaren had organised a Peace Conference in Edinburgh in October 1853 to promote this case. The conference was almost universally denounced in the Scottish press, including Radical organs, and McLaren's influence was diminished for a period. Others in the Administrative Reform Association, however, such as W. E. Baxter, the Dundee textile manufacturer, wanted the war to be won, and believed that greater efficiency would achieve that goal.

By the end of the Crimean War in 1856, the broad movement of entrepreneurial radicalism was therefore divided. Palmerston replaced Aberdeen as premier in early 1855 and his successful prosecution of the war, leading a cabinet full of members of the landed class, with Fox Maule (now Lord Panmure) playing a crucial role as Secretary for War, undermined the argument that the aristocracy were all congenitally unfit to govern. A clear signal of the eclipse of entrepreneurial radicalism was posted in the 1857 election. This contest occurred after an alliance of Tories and Radicals defeated the government in a division censuring Palmerston's aggressive policy towards China. The prime minister received fulsome messages of support from bodies in Dundee and Glasgow representing Far East traders. The local backlash against dissident radicals was so strong that the MPs for Aberdeen and Greenock announced their retiral from parliament because of their China votes – although in the latter, the MP subsequently recanted and was re-elected.

Furthermore, Palmerston's vigorous approach to foreign affairs persuaded many radicals that the goal of free trade required a strong naval force to break sea blockades. Colonies were now viewed less as draining resources from Britain, and more as potential markets and sources of supply for raw material. Samuel Laing argued this in 1864, robustly denouncing the simplistic view that free trade theory was inherently hostile to imperialism. Palmerston's assiduous wooing of industrialists in the later 1850s made him very popular among the middle-class grassroots, and this was confirmed by his election in 1863 as rector of Glasgow University. His easy triumphs in the general elections of 1857 and 1859 reinforced the widespread approval of his handling of political matters. Hereafter, attempts to resuscitate broad reform bodies met with very limited support. MacLaren was at the head of the Scottish wing of Bright's Parliamentary Reform Association, started in 1858, which met with barely any support and soon folded.

Most Entrepreneurial Radicals thereafter turned from over-arching campaigns to specific single-issue causes: William Ewart, MP for Dumfries, concentrated on his hobby-horse of metrication of weights and measures, while many businessmen put their energies into securing the assimilation of the commercial laws of Scotland and England. Cobden's death in 1865 marked the terminus of the concept of entrepreneurial radicalism as a form of class warfare. A further sign of a changing political climate came with the conferment of a deputy lord-lieutenantship for Angus on W. E. Baxter, while Laing accepted an appointment as a junior Treasury minister in 1859, and in 1860 he moved on to sit on the Council of India. The consequence of these processes was that by the start of the 1860s, the Whigs had survived the various challenges to their hegemony, and therefore seemed set for a long period of pursuing moderate centralist policies.

SCOTTISH CHARTISM

Scotland played a key role in triggering the start of Chartism. The majority of Scottish working-class men were excluded from the franchise as defined by the Reform Act, and for much of the 1830s they were less involved in politics than in the run-up to 1832. Instead, workers turned to such activities as trade unionism and co-operative ventures. But towards the end of the decade, an economic downturn resulted in high levels of unemployment and a fall in wages, which intensified the plight of handloom weavers. By 1840, it was stated that there were 15,000 unemployed in Paisley, a city whose total population was around 50,000. The severity of the sentences imposed on the leaders of the Glasgow cotton-spinners' union in 1838 after their conviction for acts of violence against strike-breakers galvanised working-class reformers across Britain. The trial convinced many that the state was hostile to working-class institutions, and was unresponsive to demands for change. In Scotland, the rift within middle-class radicals between the religious and the purely political wings indicated that independent working-class political action was necessary. Because of the great swell of UK-wide support for the cotton-spinners, the mass meeting to launch the British-wide Chartist campaign took place in Glasgow, on 21 May 1838. Seventy trade unions sent deputations, and veteran radicals from earlier episodes, including James Turner of Thrushgrove, attended.

Scottish Chartism began very successfully; within two years, there were 169 branches, well ahead of the Anti-Corn Law League's 35, and often with high membership levels – Tillicoultry's 1,000 supporters came from a total population of around 4,000. Although most branches were in Lowland towns and villages, there were also far-flung outposts, such as Wick. The movement was well organised, especially compared to England and Wales: it boasted a central body, with a paid secretary, and about ten regional associations which co-ordinated national and branch activities. By 1840, there were five Scottish Chartist newspapers, all with healthy circulations – at its peak, Glasgow's *Chartist Circular* had 20,000 readers – and English titles, particularly the *Northern Star*, were also widely read. The first national petition to parliament in June 1839 attracted many signatories – 79,000 in Glasgow alone (19,000 more than the city's 1833 petition against the Corn Laws), and proportionately more Scots than English subscribed. In most towns and villages, touring Chartist speakers attracted large audiences, and there were in addition regular local meetings and rallies.

The movement drew support from a broad spectrum of occupations, both declining and thriving. Textile centres were very active, with branches spread across the central belt from Ayrshire to Angus, with two sets of declining crafts – handloom weavers and male spinners – particularly involved. The other substantial source of support was in larger towns, where both skilled workers and unskilled labourers became involved in the movement. Glasgow, for instance, had joiners and engineers like Malcolm Macfarlane and William Pattison, but also many labourers, frequently of Irish origin. In the four major cities, there was a strong core of shopkeepers, tradesmen and small employers present, often providing leadership, as instanced in Glasgow by James Moir, a tea dealer, and George Ross, a wholesale shoemaker. There were few Chartist organisations in agricultural districts, and mining areas were on the whole initially not very active, unless close to weaving villages, as in Clackmannanshire. This changed in 1842, when Chartists became involved in a Lanarkshire miners' strike, thus succeeding in welding the economic grievances of the latter with the former's political programme.

A notable aspect of the Scottish movement was the involvement of women, which was the first time this had occurred at a sustained level in working-class politics. There were at least twenty female Chartist associations, not just in large towns, but also in smaller places like Alva, Kirriemuir and Sinclairtown, near Kirkcaldy. Elsewhere, they joined the local association; in Tillicoultry a third of the members – 300 – were females. Women took a full part in branch activities; they attended meetings, marched in rallies and signed petitions beside men. This last was somewhat unusual, as in middle-class reform bodies like the Anti-Corn Law and Anti-Slavery societies, women frequently signed separate petitions. Furthermore, they participated in electioneering, there were female speakers, mostly at local events, and several had letters and articles published in Chartist papers. On the other hand, only a few men advocated female suffrage, because most seem to have defined masculinity as integral to citizenship. By 1850, men believed that politics was a male province, as they were the sole breadwinners for their women and children, and the vote was a reward for property in skill and for economic responsibility. So, after Chartism sank, there was little further engagement by working-class women in politics for nearly a quarter of a century.

Although subscribing fully to the Six Points of the Charter, Scottish Chartism differed markedly from the English and Welsh varieties in several crucial areas. Firstly, it had a shorter effective lifespan, for by late 1842 the movement was almost extinguished, whereas elsewhere it survived longer. In 1840, there were 127 local branches, but three years later only 39 existed, and by 1848 membership in Dundee had dwindled from a peak of several thousand to barely 100. The five Scottish Chartist papers had all disappeared by the end of 1843. Developments in 1848 in England – a mass rally at Kensington Common and revived activity in general – were not mirrored in Scotland: fifty-one meetings that year were reported in England, against only two in Scotland. There was a violent street disturbance in Glasgow in March that year, at which seven people were shot, but the consensus was that this was only vestigially Chartist in nature, and more a looting riot by the unemployed and poor. Behind this divergence lay other factors: Scotland had little appetite for using violence to achieve the Charter, there was a greater readiness to

> **The Six Points of the Chartists**
>
> These were set out in the People's Charter, issued by the London Working Men's Association on 8 May 1838. They were: (1) universal adult male suffrage; (2) voting by secret ballot; (3) equal constituency electorates; (4) annual parliaments (at the time, the maximum duration was seven years); (5) abolition of the property qualification for MPs (at the time, this was an annual income of £600 for county and £300 for burgh members); (6) payment of MPs. This programme reflected widespread disenchantment among the working classes at the operation of the 1832 Reform Act, and it presented a scheme designed to entrench the benefits of mass enfranchisement against erosion by various devices. So, the secret ballot would protect voters from undue influence or outright intimidation by, for example, landowners or employers. Equal electorates would both end the gerrymandering of constituency sizes and give the same weight to voters in cities as in small towns. Annual parliaments were seen as the means to ensure that an MP kept his election pledges and responded to his constituents' demands. The abolition of the MPs' property qualification, along with payment of MPs, would, of course, make it possible for workingmen to enter parliament.

co-operate with middle-class radicals, and there was as much focus on moral, intellectual and social self-improvement as on direct political agitation.

By 1842, mounting unease in Scotland at the proclivity elsewhere to pursue a strategy based on physical force seems to have played a part in Chartism's loss of momentum. There was no real participation in England's 'sacred month' campaign (i.e. a general strike) in 1839, and the Newport Rising in November 1839, in which twenty-four Chartists were killed by the authorities, attracted only limited support. Fewer Scots signed the second national petition in 1842 than the first in 1839, because many objected to its militant tone and contents, whereas in England it attracted more signatories. The Plug Plot of August 1842 in the north of England, a plan to immobilise industry by strike action, drew no significant involvement in Scotland, apart from a minor skirmish in the Dundee area. In good part, Scottish reluctance to be drawn into potentially violent projects stemmed from the experience of previous such events dating back to the 1790s and continuing up to the cotton-spinners' trial. In all such episodes, the treatment meted out to the radicals by the authorities had been very severe, and far harsher than in similar English cases. So, in a survey of branch opinion taken in 1839 regarding support for violent action, Scotland was overwhelmingly against, unlike the rest of Britain – although

THE AGE OF THE FIRST REFORM ACT 263

it should be noted that most Scots were not opposed in principle to physical force, but only contemplated it as a very last resort, and with thorough planning in advance.

Scottish Chartism was much more than a purely political movement; it was also concerned with wider concerns, often searching for alternatives to conventional practices and wisdom. There were high levels of class unity and a rejection of middle-class interference, as seen in the distinctive religious, educational and moral organisations which Scottish Chartists developed in the period. There was widespread dissatisfaction with mainstream religion: apart from Patrick Brewster, the minister of Paisley Abbey, few Presbyterian divines championed the cause. Chartists argued that the churches were too comfortable with the prevailing social order, and had forgotten Christ's sympathy for the poor and powerless. Non-Intrusionists were singled out for their hypocrisy, since they championed the case for democracy in choosing ministers, but denied it for workingmen at parliamentary elections. But Christianity itself was not rejected – indeed the independent Glasgow Universalist Church had exerted great influence in the 1820s and 1830s on a number of leading Chartists, notably John Fraser – and prayers were frequently said before Chartist meetings. More formally, Chartists churches were set up, with at least twenty-nine established in a range of places, which was on a larger scale than in England and Wales. The ministers were frequently well-known local activists, but as part of the general decay of Chartism, a scant three churches were known to be functioning by 1848.

Temperance, too, was a central element in Chartism; the first Scottish Chartist Convention, held in 1838, took place in a Temperance Coffee House. The Chartists set up an organisation quite distinct from the middle-class Scottish Temperance League, with many local leaders enrolled. After the 1840s, several ex-Chartists switched their energies to advocating Temperance as the key to working-class self-improvement; one former member, Robert Cranston, established a chain of tea-rooms in an attempt to counter the lure of the pub. Education, too, was a preoccupation for Chartists, as it was deemed an essential prerequisite for the elevation of working people. Scottish schooling provision was in general very inadequate, while church schools purveyed unwelcome religious messages, so Chartist schools at once filled a gap and passed on the ideals and ethos of the movement. For adults, the road to improvement was offered through lectures on a range of topics and evening classes, where practical instruction was given, particularly in technology and science. Chartists played a central role in helping found co-operative stores, which simultaneously undercut private retailers, provided better-quality food and developed a sense among workers of gaining control over their lives. Around twenty societies were formed under Chartist auspices, with Hawick probably the most successful. Social events were another area explored by Chartists: there were tea parties held for women, excursions for families, activities for children and debating societies for adults.

Set in this broader picture of the culture of Scottish Chartism, the dissonance with the physical force element is comprehensible. From as early as 1839, there had been secessions by those who felt the extreme wing was too ascendant in the British-wide movement, but this did not mean the abandonment of agitation for political change. Most of these people co-operated with middle-class radicals in the Complete Suffrage Union (CSU), a body set up in Birmingham to forge a middle way between Chartism and the one-issue Anti-Corn Law League. At its peak there were some fifty branches of the CSU in Britain, of which twenty were in Scotland. Glasgow and Paisley reformers were very active in the CSU, including ex-Chartists such as William Pattison and Malcolm MacFarlane, two early stalwarts of the movement, as well as Patrick Brewster. This willingness to join middle-class reformers was also seen in the good relations which Scottish Chartists enjoyed with opponents of the Corn Laws. Although Chartists frequently disrupted league meetings in the early 1840s, this was essentially both an argument over tactics and a bid to get public attention, since most Scottish Chartists supported repeal, but contended that franchise reform should come first, as that would ensure the abolition of protectionism.

This differentiation between Scottish and English Chartism arose in some degree because of divergent experiences in the 1830s. The latter was fuelled by working-class resentment at what was perceived as a betrayal by the middle class of the cross-class consensus which had existed during the campaign for parliamentary reform. The assumption had been that while workingmen would not be enfranchised, the middle class who did get the vote would ensure that policies of common interest would be pursued. However, deep grievances were fostered by middle-class support for the New Poor Law and resistance to Factory Reform legislation, which both bore very harshly on working people. Neither of these questions had such a strong impact in Scotland, so the strong feelings of class antagonism prevalent in England were much less pronounced in Scotland. Rather, as the links with the CSU and Corn Law repealers indicate, there was a greater tendency in Scottish Chartism to characterise the landowning aristocracy as the major social force inimical to universal progress and prosperity.

The decline in Scottish Chartism from 1842 was not necessarily because of an upturn in the economy: Paisley was just then entering into a profound economic and social crisis with the worst conditions anywhere in Britain, provoking cabinet-level discussions and government-led initiatives to alleviate the situation. Some have argued that Chartism failed because the Tory government introduced measures to demonstrate that the state was not inflexibly opposed to working-class interests, but these actions had barely begun when Chartism closed down in Scotland.[20] The aftermath of the Chartist decline in the mid-1840s left working-class politics in a hiatus. There were splutterings of post-Chartist radicalism in the early 1850s, while others moved towards seeking positions in local government, with a view to improving working-class conditions by municipal action. James Moir in Glasgow and David Lewis in Edinburgh were two instances of this strategy, while Samuel Bennett became provost of Dumbarton in 1874. But an essential change occurred during the 1850s: most working-class political demands dropped the universalism contained in Chartism's call for full male suffrage. Instead, different, more utilitarian reasons were deployed in arguing for extending the franchise to workingmen.

NOTES

1. M. Dyer, *Men of Property and Intelligence: The Scottish Electoral System Prior to 1884* (1996), 41 (Table 3.2).
2. Durham University Archives, Earl Grey MSS, GRE/B37/3/28/1–3, F. Jeffrey to Lord Grey, 30 August 1831.
3. NRS, Clerk MSS, GD 18/3350, J. Brown to Sir G. Clerk, 23 December 1834.
4. See pp. 83–4.
5. BL, Peel MSS, Add. MS 40318, ff. 49–52, Sir J. Graham to Peel, 11 December 1836.
6. NRS, Dalhousie MSS, GD 45/14/646, P. M. Stewart to F. Maule, 31 December 1839, 9 January 1840.
7. BL, Peel MSS, Add. MS 40616, ff. 214–15, Graham to F. R. Bonham, 29 July 1841.
8. See pp. 128–34 for a full account of this.
9. See p. 131 for an extended discussion of this.
10. BL, Peel MSS, Add. MS 40422, ff. 221–2, Sir J. Graham to Sir R. Peel, 25 November 1837.
11. See pp. 131–4.
12. BL, Peel MSS, Add. MS 40318, ff. 261–2, R. Lamond to Sir J. Graham, 21 June 1841.
13. Ibid., Add. MS 40485, ff. 79–80, J. Campbell to Peel, 7 July 1841.
14. G. Douglas and G. D. Ramsay (eds), *The Panmure Papers* (1908), Vol. I, 12, 23.
15. NLS, Minto MSS, MS 12340, ff. 46–7, J. Haldane to Lord Melgund, 10 May 1847.
16. *Scottish Congregational Magazine* (1846), unpaginated, 'Address by the Scottish Board of Dissenters'.

17. NRS, Clerk MSS, GD 18/3926, Sir J. Graham to Sir G. Clerk, 16 May 1854.
18. *Glasgow Chronicle*, 15 March 1854.
19. *Paisley Herald*, 4 April 1857.
20. G. S. Jones, *Languages of Class: Studies in English Working Class History, 1832–1982* (1983), 18–21, 168–78.

CHAPTER 10

Inching towards Democracy: Politics, c. 1865–1880

THE CAMPAIGN FOR THE SECOND REFORM ACT

Although the specific details of the Scottish Second Reform Act of 1868 were to a considerable degree shaped by 'high politics' conducted within the confines of Westminster, the movement of opinion outside parliament contributed significantly to the outcome. As with the campaign for the first Reform Act, the demand in Scotland for a wider franchise brought together middle- and working-class opinion. But for both classes, this involved important shifts from previous perspectives. Also, this time the organisational pressure for change came almost exclusively from workingmen, while the middle class was less directly engaged.

In the light of the setbacks of the later 1850s, outlined in the previous chapter, middle-class Radicals shifted their strategy in the early 1860s. Until then, they had displayed no great appetite for franchise extension; rather, they contended that parliamentary reform should concentrate on taking seats away from small-town constituencies and giving them to larger under-represented urban areas. This policy was perceived as the most effective means of ending the aristocratic domination of the Commons. It was assumed that greater representation of large towns and cities would enfranchise substantial numbers of taxpayers who would approve of cutting wasteful government expenditure. This had particular appeal in Scotland, where most burgh constituencies consisted of groups of four or five often quite sizeable towns, while the counties returned a far higher proportion of MPs than in England.

This approach contained no provision to extend significantly the vote to the working class, because many Radicals feared that workingmen would support policies out of self-interest, rather than the wider national interest (which, of course, middle- and upper-class voters invariably did). Samuel Laing, the MP for the Wick Burghs, articulated these concerns, warning that workers might opt to jettison free trade for protectionism in order to preserve their jobs. Instead, there was a preference for 'fancy franchises', which would give extra votes to middle-class men, such as university graduates, or income-tax-payers at a stated level. But gradually, developments led these middle-class radicals to embrace the view that giving the vote to some workingmen would not be dangerous, but instead could be beneficial to their agenda. As noted in Chapter 9, Bright's 1858 reform campaign, based on redistribution and the ballot, failed to attract significant support in Scotland, after which most middle-class radicals accepted that the most likely means of securing their goal was to link it to an extension of the vote to some working-class men. By this time, moreover, these bourgeois reformers perceived the upper echelons of the working class as no longer posing a threat to economic, social and political stability. It was relatively straightforward to make this adjustment in Scotland, since Scottish Chartism had been less militant than elsewhere in Britain. There were three broad reasons for the reappraisal by middle-class Radicals: namely, the growth of a shared viewpoint on foreign affairs; the character of the development of working-class institutions through the 1850s; and the moderation of working-class political programmes.

There was pronounced working-class sympathy throughout the 1850s for suppressed European nationalities, sustaining a tradition which originated in the French revolutionary era. Karl Blind and Louis Kossuth, who toured Scotland to champion the aspirations of, respectively, Poland and Hungary, drew enthusiastic responses. Italy, however, evoked the greatest interest; Mazzini made several visits in the early 1850s, and later Garibaldi was ecstatically received. Edinburgh and Glasgow jointly contributed one-quarter of the total British funds raised to support the latter's Red Shirts, and a troop of 500 Scottish volunteers, mostly Glasgow artisans, fought in 1860–1 in the Risorgimento. Scottish workingmen hoped that the rights of labour would be better protected by democratic nation-states, and it is revealing that the formation in 1864 of the Dundee workingmen's franchise reform movement was due to the initiative of factory-based Garibaldi committees.

The other international cause of freedom espoused by the working class of Scotland in this period was support for the North in the American Civil War. From the outset, commitment to emancipation was widespread, as radicals from Hawick to Aberdeen championed Lincoln against the Confederates. The loss of the supply of Southern raw cotton caused serious hardship to textile workers in the west of Scotland, but did not materially dent support for the North. Many workingmen believed that the advance of freedom in America would accelerate franchise reform in Scotland.

Middle-class reformers seized on this evidence of working-class commitment to the abstract causes of justice, liberty and nationhood as a favourable portent, since many of them were also enthusiastic backers of European national movements, both for liberal internationalist values of civil and religious liberty, and for the desire to establish free trade relations with these countries. For bourgeois radicals, support for the North in the American Civil War was unquestioning, since it was the culmination of well over half-a-century of sustained campaigning against slavery everywhere. Sharing platforms at rallies gave them a sense of common purpose with the politically engaged working class, and also suggested that extending the vote to these men, who were mostly artisans, far from presenting any threat to the political system, would rather boost the radicals' electoral prospects against the landed Tory and Whig ruling elites.

The new trade unions of the 1850s, spearheaded by the Amalgamated Society of Engineers, were normally reluctant to strike except as a last resort, and acknowledged the right of employers to make profits, provided union members were fairly rewarded. As noted in Chapter 3, the formation in 1853 of the Edinburgh Trades Council, followed by the establishment of the Glasgow United Trades Council in 1858, heralded a new departure by creating a city-wide forum for the discussion of matters of mutual interest and the development of a common stance on trade-related issues. The representative structure of the trades councils indicated that workingmen had embraced a key feature of democratic institutions. They voiced the views of skilled men, effectively the only unionised workers in this era. The trades councils tended to be moderate and often, as in Edinburgh, had a 'no-politics' rule – a far remove from the unions in the 1820s and 1830s, and so reassuring to middle-class reformers. Moreover, in these councils, a younger cadre of working-class leadership came forward, holding different positions on industrial, social and political topics from the more militant earlier generations.

Evidence of a strong British patriotic spirit among Scottish workingmen was highlighted in 1859, when alarm caused by the threat of a French invasion led to the revival of the Volunteer movement across Britain. By 1862, Scottish enrolment, at 5 per cent of 15–49-year-olds, was almost double England's 3 per cent. Middle-class men joined in healthy numbers, but more significant was the high levels of Scottish working-class enthusiasm for the movement: workingmen made up half of all recruits in the north-east, while the employees in a Lanarkshire ironworks petitioned the managers to assist in forming a factory corps. Almost all the workmen Volunteers were artisans, with several of their corps explicitly rejecting enrolment by unskilled labourers.

Another comforting shift for middle-class reformers was the mellowing of formerly militant working-class political leaders and the dilution of their political agenda from the mid-1840s. Prominent ex-Chartists who entered local government transmuted into relatively moderate, sensible figures who worked within the system to further goals often shared by their fellow councillors.[1] By the start of the 1860s, then, the political demands of working-class reformers had retreated substantially from the long tradition originating in the decade of the French Revolution and persisting into the Chartist era. Indeed, as discussed above,[2] during the 1850s there was only very limited interest in pushing for franchise reform among non-voters, as attempts, usually by ex-Chartists, to agitate for reform failed to attract any significant support. Interest was so low that in 1863, a prominent Glasgow reformer decided that, in despair at the lack of interest in political change among the city's workers, he would instead campaign for the city council to provide public baths.

The moderation of the new generation was displayed in the Scottish National Reform League, formed in Glasgow on 17 September 1866 to campaign for an extension of the vote to workingmen. The organising force was the league's secretary, George Jackson, a journeyman watchmaker and jeweller, while the former Chartist James Moir was the figurehead president. The league was an instant success: within four months of its inception, it achieved a relative level of support which it had taken the English Reform League two years to reach, and it continued to recruit proportionately more members. The league's Glasgow demonstration on 16 October 1866 – only one month after its formation – was the largest seen in Scotland since 1832. Around 38,000 marchers from some 50 unions and workplaces took part, and on all sides there was consensus that good order was maintained throughout the proceedings. The league enjoyed positive links with the middle-class radicals, mainly through the person of John Bright, who was hero-worshipped by league supporters and was presented with an address from admirers at the October rally. Nevertheless, the league was run by and for the working class, with no significant middle-class involvement.

These cross-class bridges were facilitated by the important change in the goals of the league from those generally espoused by earlier working-class radical movements. The league demanded franchise reform less as a universal human right or as a prerequisite for destroying Old Corruption than for other reasons. One was instrumental: trade unions came to realise that legislative action was necessary to redress workplace grievances. The most pressing issue was to amend the Master and Servant Act, which was denounced as being heavily weighted towards the employer, and from 1863 to 1866, Glasgow Trades Council led the British-wide campaign against the measure. The second case for conferring the vote on workingmen was one of status. They had adopted many of the attributes of respectability and self-improvement which had been urged on them by middle-class moralists, and they felt entitled to be rewarded by admission to full citizenship. In 1865, an Edinburgh artisan clinched his argument for enfranchising workingmen thus: 'I appeal to the success of the Volunteer movement, and if there is one class more patriotic than the other, it is the working class.'[3] From this standpoint, universal manhood suffrage, while desirable, was no longer an essential desideratum; instead the league acquiesced in household suffrage as an acceptable 'instalment'.

In the face of these developments among the working class, most Scottish Liberal MPs were prepared to go along with the Reform League's franchise demands, albeit some, notably James Moncrieff, did so reluctantly and only after a last-minute change of mind. At most seven Scottish Liberal members joined the party's internal opponents of reform – the Adullamites – an appreciably lower percentage than English Liberals. Gladstonian Liberalism provided a large tent which encompassed the party's diverse strands. Gladstone's leadership was virtually unchallenged, since his endorsement in 1864 of franchise reform was widely believed to have initiated the campaign which culminated in the Second Reform Act. The central principles which he expounded were that the Liberal party was a national party, representing all classes, and was in favour of social reform. It stood for ethics and morality in government, both at home and abroad, and put personal freedom and individual civil liberties before aristocratic and feudalistic privilege. Retrenchment in state expenditure was essential to promote these goals, as it would eliminate corruption and patronage, instead encouraging governmental efficiency. These were objectives to which all sectors of Scottish Liberalism could subscribe, at least initially, although differences of nuance and emphasis were quite soon to emerge.

THE SCOTTISH SECOND REFORM ACT

The Scottish Second Reform Act of 1868 was carried by the Conservatives, led by Disraeli, who exploited discord within the Liberal party as to the exact extent of enfranchisement. But Disraeli also strove to insert a number of devices designed to restrict the democratising implications of household suffrage. The number of Scottish voters rose by 120 per cent, and although this was greater than England's increase of 93 per cent, the proportion of enfranchised Scots (1:3.5 of adult males) still lagged behind the English ratio of 1:2.5.

This discrepancy may be partly caused by the persistence of the difference in income and wealth between the two countries which had been present in 1832. There were, however, other reasons why at least one-third of urban adult males in Scotland were voteless. One was the requirement that the householder personally paid local rates. While this was quite commonplace in England, the normal practice in Scotland was that in the case of property valued below £4, the landlord paid the rates, and recouped this by adding the cost to the rent. The Glasgow electoral registration officer stated in 1880 that just over one-quarter of Glasgow householders (28,000 of 107,000) did not pay their rates personally. In addition, the qualification for the household vote on property worth over £10 was six months' residence, but for occupancy of a property worth under £10, one year's residence in the same house was required. Because of the peculiarities of leasing practice in Scotland, outlined in Chapter 4, this effectively meant that a voter in the latter category had to have occupied the property for almost eighteen months, but there was a high degree of residential mobility prevalent in Scottish towns and cities. Thus, Glasgow's registration officer noted that around one-third of the city's population moved annually, and one calculation indicated that one-half of personal ratepayers in Glasgow were disqualified because of this.

> **The franchise system under the Second Reform Act of 1868**
>
> In burgh constituencies, the vote was given to all male householders, whether owners or tenants, with no minimum house value. But it was required, firstly, that they had been in the property for twelve months; secondly, that they had not been in receipt of poor relief in the previous twelve months; and, thirdly, that they had paid poor rates for the current year. A male lodger franchise was introduced, set at a rent of £10 per annum. In county seats, the vote for owners of property was reduced from a valuation of £10 to £5, while all tenants paying an annual rent of £14 or more were enfranchised. These provisions were very close to those in England and Wales, except that the Scottish tenants' qualification of £14 was £2 higher.

Nevertheless, the transformation in the social composition of the electorate flowing from the act was significant; in Glasgow, manual workers grew from 35 per cent of voters in 1867 to 66 per cent by 1868. The vast bulk of the new electorate, however, was located among the lower-middle and skilled working classes, rather than being dominated by legions of poor, unskilled voters, which had been the nightmare conjured up by opponents of the measure.

As in 1832, the redistribution aspect of the Second Reform Act mitigated many of the radical democratic tendencies embedded in the expanded franchise, with the objective of weakening the Liberals and protecting the Tories. The creation of the Border Burghs meant that these towns, widely regarded as hotbeds of Liberalism, were withdrawn from their county constituencies, leaving the two shire seats of Peebles & Selkirk and Roxburgh more likely to be Conservative. The boundary lines of the three extra county seats were drawn in such a way as to give the Tories a chance to avoid being swamped by a larger Liberal vote. Thus, in Lanarkshire, the Northern seat, which contained almost

> **The redistribution of constituencies, 1868**
>
> Scotland was allocated five additional seats (against eight in 1832), making a total of fifty-eight. Three of these went to the large counties of Aberdeen, Ayr and Lanark, but Peebles and Selkirk were conjoined into one seat. Among burghs, Dundee was given a second MP, and Glasgow gained a third member. A new seat consisting of Hawick, Galashiels and Selkirk – usually called the Border Burghs – was formed. The upshot was that there were 32 county and 26 burgh MPs, with 79 burghs now directly represented. England returned 258 borough and 170 county MPs. In addition, two constituencies were created for graduates of Scottish universities to return MPs: Edinburgh and St Andrews formed one seat, Aberdeen and Glasgow the other. In England, five MPs were returned for three universities (Cambridge, London and Oxford), while in Ireland, two MPs represented one university (Trinity College, Dublin). There were 2,175 voters for each MP in the English Universities seats; in the Scottish seats, there were 4,623.

all of the industrial areas, had 5,458 voters – double the 2,871 in the more agricultural Southern seat. The addition of a third member for Glasgow was intended to be a hidden means of reducing the net strength of the city's Liberal representation. Voters in the city were restricted to two votes each, although three MPs were to be returned. The Tories' calculation was that it would be well-nigh impossible to organise Liberal voters to distribute their votes evenly, so letting a Tory slip in as the third MP, thereby reducing Glasgow's net Liberal tally from two to one.

As an additional restraint on galloping democracy, the act had a differential impact on the burgh and county electorates. The average burgh seat had 5,943 voters per MP, while the county figure was 2,401, whereas in 1865, the respective figures were 2,414 and 1,652, so the disparity in favour of counties had widened significantly, with burgh electorates moving from being 50 per cent to 150 per cent greater than counties. These averages, of course, concealed very wide inequalities: Sutherland had 358 voters in 1868, while Glasgow had 45 times as many voters per MP, which was actually a slight increase from the ratio between these two in 1832. The over-representation enshrined in the First Reform Act of the mainly agricultural regions in the north and south of the country persisted. The Highlands returned eight MPs, although on the basis of the number of voters, the figure should have been 2.5, and comparable figures for the Borders were 9.2 actual MPs against 4.3 based on voter numbers. Glasgow's electorate entitled the city to twelve MPs, but it had only three.

WOMEN AND THE FRANCHISE

The Second Reform Act raised the issue of women's role in politics in several ways. In Aberdeen, the electoral registration officer, J. D. Milne, a prominent advocate of women's rights, interpreted the act as allowing suitably qualified females to be enrolled as voters, contending that it did not stipulate that only males had the right to vote. As a result, above 1,000 women were included with just over 8,300 male voters, but his decision was contested in the courts, which determined that women were clearly not intended to receive the vote. Nevertheless, this episode reflected the steady growth in the case for female enfranchisement. Earlier signs of a heightened political presence for women were evident in their roles in popular movements of the post-1832 period. Middle-class women took a central part in the Anti-Corn Law League. They attended meetings, took petitions round houses for signatures and organised fund-raising ventures, the biggest of which was the 1845 Edinburgh Bazaar. As noted earlier, this activity came in the wake of the agitation for the abolition of slavery, and drew in veterans of that campaign. The rise in the scope and scale of women's education at the same time gave women confidence, and also led to serious questioning of their subordinate social position and their exclusion from the franchise. In 1843, Margaret Reid's *A Plea for Women* was published, making an impassioned case for women to enjoy a greater public presence, and its impact has already been discussed.[4] And indeed, women were more visible in civil society. As seen above, the Presbyterian churches turned increasingly to women to assist in a range of church activities, both in Scotland and in oversees missionary endeavours. Likewise, many urban voluntary associations relied on substantial input from women.[5] Hence, a major proponent of women's political rights was the Scottish Women's Temperance Association (SWTA), which had legions of active members. Unlike its English counterpart, the SWTA was wholeheartedly committed to female suffrage, which it saw as intimately associated with religion, social reform and philanthropy.

The Second Reform Act marked a further stage in the political engagement of women. In some cases, this meant voicing their views in public, frequently in unflattering language. At polling day in Rothesay in 1868, female millworkers turned up to heckle the Conservative candidate. It does not yet seem to have been accepted that women would undertake canvassing and registration work, these only developing in the final decade or so of the century. However, it is instructive that perhaps the most eloquent passage in Gladstone's Midlothian campaign speeches was given in Dalkeith to an audience which included women, among whom were 'the factory girls of the place'.[6]

The British-wide National Society for Women's Suffrage (NSWS) started in 1867, and Edinburgh was one of the three founding branches.

The issue of women's right of access to higher education was a current topic of debate and litigation in the city, which may help explain Edinburgh's early commitment. The refusal of the courts to sanction the Aberdeen registrar's decision mobilised opinion in Scotland, and in the early 1870s, a wider audience was reached by the use of an itinerant speaker, Jane Taylor, who toured various towns and cities to advocate the case. By 1874, twenty-four branches had been founded in Scotland. The membership of the NSWS branches included, along of course with numerous women, a range of male civic leaders, such as MPs, councillors, university professors and clergymen. The society contended that as property was the basis for enfranchisement, women who met that criterion should have the vote, and this partly explains why most of the female leadership appears to have been middle class in background, although some working-class women attended meetings. The activities of the NWSS primarily focused on petitioning parliament and holding public meetings.

At the sub-parliamentary level, women's involvement in elections to public bodies was somewhat chequered. Whereas in England, suitably qualified women were eligible to vote in municipal contests from 1869, this right did not apply in Scotland until 1882. Scotswomen could vote in parochial council and in certain police commission elections, but they could not stand as candidates until 1894 for parochial councils, 1907 for burgh councils and 1914 for county councils. However, from the outset – in 1873 – they could not only vote but also run for office in school board elections, and quite quickly a number of women were elected, the first being Jane Arthur in Paisley in 1873.

LIBERAL TRIUMPHS AND TENSIONS

The 1868 general election was held in the aftermath of the euphoria engendered by the campaign to broaden the franchise. The Liberal party made major advances, reducing the Tories from just over one-quarter of MPs in 1865 to rather less than one-eighth, but equally pertinent was the amity existing between middle-class radicals and working-class political leaders. The Scottish National Reform League had long been determined to have some representatives in parliament, but made little headway in the election, apart from Glasgow. Here, thanks to an arrangement with the two sitting MPs, the third seat was allocated to the league's chosen candidate, in return for co-operation in a scheme to allocate votes equally between all three Liberals, thereby thwarting Tory hopes. Elsewhere, the league either endorsed existing MPs, as in Aberdeen, or was too slow in choosing a candidate, which was the case in Dundee and Edinburgh.

The league also had a very limited impact at sub-parliamentary elections. Its secretary, George Jackson, lost in a working-class ward in the 1869 Glasgow municipal election, and while seven league candidates won in the Dundee council election of 1868, by 1870 they had been absorbed into a sort of ratepayers' alliance, and only three were then elected. Edinburgh underwent a similar process to Dundee. At the 1873 school board elections, the league's candidates did poorly almost everywhere. This pattern underlined the essential unity forged by Gladstonian Liberalism. The comfortable absorption of the new voters into the Liberal fold was manifested in the 1868 Kilmarnock election. The Reform League's secretary visited the constituency to support the candidacy of the social reformer, Edwin Chadwick, against the Whiggish sitting MP, who was the son of an English earl. Despite the league's approval – and John Stuart Mill's public endorsement – Chadwick lost heavily.

But the relative harmony of 1868 unravelled at the 1874 general election, and came less from the newly enfranchised working class than from urban middle-class radicals, who differed in policy and strategy from the earlier generation of reformers. The 1874 contest resulted in the emergence of a number of MPs supporting a militant evangelical platform, most of them winning burgh seats – notably Glasgow, Aberdeen, Dundee and Kilmarnock – by defeating rival Whiggish candidates, including sitting MPs. This momentum continued through the rest of the decade, with triumphs against moderate Liberals in Greenock in 1878, and in 1880 at Aberdeen, plus a second gain in Glasgow. These advances laid the groundwork for the mighty internal struggle for power between 1880 and 1886 which convulsed the Scottish Liberal party in the years preceding the Irish Home Rule crisis.

The new Radicals were less interested than their mid-Victorian predecessors in economic liberalism and political assaults on an inefficient aristocratic governing class. Such issues were, by and large, now regarded as satisfactorily settled, with perhaps the significant exception of the need to apply free trade principles to ownership of land. Instead, they redirected their focus to advocating social, moral and ecclesiastical reforms, pre-eminently the disestablishment of the Church of Scotland, Temperance legislation and the repeal of the Contagious Diseases Acts. A complex interconnected set of factors lay behind the advent of this movement. Firstly, changed circumstances facilitated a revival of the political alliance between the Free Church and the United Presbyterians (UPs), which had disintegrated in the later 1850s. The collapse in 1873 of negotiations to merge the two churches ended the attempt to undermine the state church by creating a single Presbyterian body which would comfortably outnumber it.[7] Very quickly after the breakdown, meetings were held to proclaim the shared desire of the Free and Voluntary churches to mount a political campaign for Scottish disestablishment.

But this new middle-class radicalism had wider and deeper sources than frustration at the failure of church union. From the later 1860s, its proponents were concerned with rethinking approaches to irreligion and related moral and social problems, which all seemed resistant to existing strategies, as is discussed in Chapter 5. The enfranchisement of working-class men in 1868 accelerated this reconsideration, as the implications of an electorate with at best only limited connections with organised Christianity called for an urgent response. Now it was contended that church-building and urban mission work by themselves would not succeed, unless accompanied by wider social reforms. An influential Glasgow charity formed in 1871, with the telling title of the Association for the Religious and Social Improvement of the City, listed the key barriers to Christianisation in a significantly new order, namely, lack of education, intemperance and poor housing, with want of church accommodation placed below these. The movers behind this body were evangelical clergy and laymen, primarily drawn from the Free and UP churches. They included individuals like J. C. White, a chemical manufacturer, who was instrumental in securing the return of a radical over the sitting Whig MP at Kilmarnock in 1874. Many of these sorts of men gave crucial support in the Glasgow 1874 election to Dr Charles Cameron, the successful radical candidate. Cameron was owner-editor of the *North British Daily Mail*, which had carried many surveys of social problems in the city, almost certainly written with input from evangelical reformers.

Having established a correlation between social problems and irreligion, evangelicals had advanced from regarding the principles of laissez-faire and voluntary action as adequate means to address the crisis. Legislation was necessary because only central government could impose statutory uniform moral standards, and this required more MPs with an evangelical background who were committed to pushing for such measures. The Contagious Diseases Acts were a prime target for the new radicals: 'The Act in itself is positively immoral, a masterpiece of class legislation and a cowardly outrage upon weak and defenceless women.'[8] Cameron's most enthusiastic backer, William Quarrier, urged Christian voters to elect MPs 'who value Moral Legislation as a first consideration'.[9] The obstacles placed by local authorities in the way of social reform projects, such Glasgow Council's relaxed policy on alcohol licensing, drew many into municipal politics, particularly William Collins, another leading supporter of Cameron. In Dundee, F. Y. Henderson, a city MP from 1880, entered the local council for similar reasons.

The clearest sign of a change from seeking to effect moral and social reform by reliance on exhortation and persuasion to legislative diktat was shown in the Temperance movement. For some thirty years from its inception in 1829 – in, quite naturally, Greenock – the Scottish Temperance League generally pursued a policy of moral suasion. But progress along these lines proved very slow, and

The Contagious Diseases question

In the early 1860s, the military authorities became exercised by the extent of venereal disease prevalent among men in the armed services; one medical expert suggested that at least 10 per cent were affected. There were grave concerns that the effectiveness of British military forces would be seriously undermined unless drastic action was taken. The government's response was to introduce two acts, in 1864 and 1866, rather coyly named the Contagious Diseases Acts, which applied to thirteen garrison towns and naval ports. The acts empowered local Justices of the Peace to order women whom the police suspected of being prostitutes to undergo a medical inspection, which was both brutal and humiliating. The women could only continue to ply their trade if they were pronounced clean by doctors, but if infected, they were normally confined to a lock hospital for up to three months until cured. A third piece of legislation was enacted in 1869, which extended the inspection regime to a further six towns. The act additionally increased the maximum duration of internment in a lock hospital to nine months.

This last act provoked a great outcry, with the leading objections being raised by three groups. Supporters of women's rights contended the act was grossly discriminatory, as only the women had to submit to a highly intrusive examination. The men, who were the direct causes of the spread of such sexually transmitted diseases, were not required to submit to any equivalent inspection. A second focus of opposition came from those who argued that the civil liberties enshrined in the British constitution were being breached by these arbitrary arrests. They also objected both to instances of the harsh treatment and harassment by the police of women suspects, as well as the use of plain-clothes officers. The third body of opposition was drawn from evangelical Christians, who found the acts to be a deplorable breach of moral standards. They complained that the consequence of the acts was that the state was condoning prostitution, whereas the correct approach, they claimed, was to stamp it out entirely.

Opposition in Scotland to the acts was strong. Josephine Butler, the leader of the repeal movement, commented on the warm reception which she invariably received at meetings in Scotland. By 1873, the three main Presbyterian churches had expressed their hostility, and in 1875 Glasgow Trades Council also denounced the acts. Scotswomen engaged in agitations for suffrage reform and for Temperance were prominent in the agitation against the legislation. Of the Liberal MPs who voted for House of Commons motions in 1873 and 1876 to repeal the legislation, a disproportionately high number held Scottish seats. The abolition of the acts was eventually achieved in 1886. The incidence of venereal diseases among the armed forces subsequently declined.

There are two interesting Scottish aspects to the campaign. Firstly, the acts did not apply to any locality in Scotland. Secondly, the Glasgow Police Act of 1866 gave powers to the city's authorities to control prostitutes which were nearly as draconian as the Contagious Diseases legislation, yet there was little demurral at their application. Public solicitation by women was prohibited, and the police and the city magistrates acted jointly to compel women defined as prostitutes to choose between leaving Glasgow or entering a local Magdalene Institution, which was a charitable body dedicated to training prostitutes to find 'respectable' employment as housemaids or laundresses, etc. The regime in the Magdalene was very strict: women had to stay for two years; outside contacts were prohibited; the working day lasted for ten hours. Good behaviour was rewarded with money and extra food, but indiscipline was dealt with by beatings or solitary confinement. If both these options were rejected, the authorities would assign women to confinement in the city's lock hospital, which operated a disciplinary procedure akin to incarceration in a prison. This 'Glasgow System', mediated by the police, the councillors, doctors and philanthropists, maintained the moral order of the city by stigmatising prostitutes through fines and arrests in a manner which closely paralleled that carried out elsewhere through the mechanism of the Contagious Diseases Acts.

in 1858 the Scottish Permissive Bill Association (SPBA) was formed to promote a more interventionist and *dirigiste* solution to the liquor problem, stressing that 'Prohibitive Legislation alone can be effective against the public sources of intemperance.'[10] The SPBA advocated Local Veto legislation, which would permit local communities to vote to ban the sale of alcoholic products in their areas. At first, the association had little impact on parliamentary elections, but at the 1874 election, a transformation occurred, and the influence of the association was widely acknowledged as significant, if not crucial, in securing radical victories in Dundee, Glasgow and Leith, while the victor in the 1878 Greenock by-election was a vice-president of the SPBA.

There were several causes for this breakthrough in the fortunes of the Local Veto campaign. The anti-drink movements both grew rapidly and co-operated more closely than previously. Two new Temperance bodies – the Band of Hope and the Independent Order of Good Templars – emerged soon after the 1868 election, attracting young people and working-class women. By 1876, the Templars, after only six years' presence in Scotland, had 80 branches with over 62,000 enrolled members. Moreover, the coolness which had existed between the SPBA and the older Scottish Temperance League dissolved with the appointment of William Collins as president of the latter in 1872. Collins enjoyed good relations with the SPBA officials, and soon there was an overlap of personnel between the two bodies, with five men serving as directors of both. The league and the SPBA also worked closely with the Good Templars, so the unity among Temperance societies now presented a formidable united front, with greater financial strength: in 1875–6 the SPBA's annual income was triple that of 1865–6.

The SPBA led the politicisation of Temperance when it moved in the later 1860s from propaganda and educational work to electoral action, initially in municipal contests. In 1872, the association remarked: 'The great truth should ever be kept in view that all temperance efforts should culminate at the ballot box. Moral suasion is a great principle, but it does not meet all the wants of this particular question.'[11] An early harbinger of the movement's impact came in June 1872, when a radical defeated a local Whig in an Aberdeen by-election. It was reported that over 1,000 Temperance supporters voted for the victor, who won by 1,777. After parliament rejected a Local Veto petition, the SPBA developed its political machinery in the run-up to the 1874 election, conducting a canvass of electors, registering eligible supporters and, above all, seeking the selection of sympathetic candidates. This last was seen as decisive, as the prohibitionists' journal stressed shortly before polling:

> Hitherto we have in no small way begun at the end. We first voted for men hostile to the Permissive Bill and then petitioned them to pass the bill. We propose to alter all that. The temperance question being of all questions the most momentous; we urge that it shall have the first place.[12]

Perhaps the most graphic evidence of the role of Temperance activists came in Glasgow, where great numbers of them contributed to Cameron's victory by canvassing and distributing literature on a grand scale: around 100 teetotallers delivered 53,000 leaflets and 4,000 letters to voters in one day; there were just over 54,000 on the electoral register. The most regular presences on the platform at Cameron's public meetings were men associated with the Temperance cause. But the influence of the teetotallers was not confined to urban Scotland. In semi-feudal Roxburghshire, the Liberal candidate, the ultra-Whig Arthur Elliot, a son of Lord Minto, was warned in 1879 that the local SPBA activists were restive:

> I have just seen a leader of the Temperance party in the county from whom I have ascertained that they are organising for fear of an election . . . [I]t is of the greatest importance that the [Temperance] party be appeased as they have considerable voting power in the county [and] . . . as they are capital workers and nearly all good sound Liberals.[13]

Elliot duly met the anti-drink faction and pledged his support for the Local Veto. In the general election held in 1880, he captured the seat from the Tory incumbent by just ten votes, in a poll of 1,708.

This rising tide of middle-class radicalism in Scottish burghs had apparent similarities to the contemporaneous emergence of radical politics in major English cities, with Birmingham under the leadership of Joseph Chamberlain as the archetype. But there were profound differences. Birmingham's civic gospel was influenced less by evangelicalism pure and simple than by a broader social reform approach, derived in part from the influence of the Rev. H. W. Crosskey, Chamberlain's chaplain. Crosskey had been the Unitarian minister in Glasgow in the 1850s, but he and his successors had only minimal influence on the city's Liberal politicians. Scottish radicalism operated on a narrower front, concentrating primarily on religion-related social and political issues. Thus, whereas Chamberlain made championing the rights of organised labour a central plank in his political manifesto, on this topic middle-class Scottish radicals were still imbued with laissez-faire ideology, so that there were scarcely any equivalents of the English 'new model employers', of whom the most prominent was A. J. Mundella. Apart from Dundee and Leith, radical candidates were preponderantly averse to supporting trade union rights. Dr Cameron commented that as an employer, '[a]ll I contend is for justice and I say if union men have a right to fight against offices, offices have a right to fight against union men (cheers).'[14]

For much of the 1870s, Scottish working-class organisations felt badly let down both by the official Liberal policy on labour laws and by the hostile response of local radicals, such as Duncan MacLaren, to the demands of organised labour. The Criminal Law Amendment Act of 1871 was particularly resented in Scotland. So great was the bitterness felt towards these Liberal MPs who supported the measure that the Edinburgh Trades Council organised an alliance of advanced Liberals to oppose MacLaren in the 1874 general election. This discontent broadened into a general critique of the radicals' caucus system of politics as a breach of personal freedom and a manipulation of democracy. Liberal disunity in Greenock at a by-election in 1878 mainly arose because of workingmen's rejection of a candidate supported by the local radical caucus who was opposed to enhancing the rights of unions, while in 1879, a strong push was launched by workingmen Liberals in Edinburgh to put forward a candidate at the next election. This restricted vision evinced by Scottish middle-class radicals with regard to labour questions may very well have contributed to the rise of a separate labour political organisation in the later 1880s, somewhat ahead of the same process in England. Indeed, a precursor of conflict between unions and laissez-faire Liberalism had emerged in 1868, when several unions and trades councils had backed the efforts of Lord Elcho, the High Tory MP for East Lothian, to rescind the Master and Servant Act in the teeth of opposition from orthodox Liberal politicians.

The Criminal Law Amendment Act, 1871

Legislation in 1825 had removed a number of the disabilities under which trade unions had operated, the most important change being that strikes were no longer outlawed. Across the next forty years, trade unions grew both in numbers and in membership. However, in the later 1860s, legal decisions struck at certain rights which unions had long assumed they enjoyed. Firstly, in 1867, union picketing during a strike was ruled to be illegal, and the penalty imposed was imprisonment. Secondly, in the case of **Hornby v. Close** (1867), it was determined that union funds were not protected from malversation by officials, in contradistinction to Friendly Societies, whose assets were protected. This decision was interpreted by trade unionists as indicating that they occupied an inferior status in common law compared to other organisations, and they launched a campaign to redress these grievances.

The outcome of this agitation was the Criminal Law Amendment Act of 1871, which gave full protection to union funds. But in the course of its passage through parliament, backbenchers introduced clauses which effectively maintained picketing as an illegal criminal act, with a mandatory sentence of three months' hard labour. The union movement was incensed at this, for two reasons. Firstly, it was discriminatory, as union coercion by picketing was an offence, whereas intimidatory action by employers – most prominently, blacklisting union activists – went unpunished. Secondly, unions claimed this was class legislation directed wholly at them, and they insisted instead that cases of violent picketing should be covered by the general criminal laws of the land. Thus, the act of 1871 was viewed by the unions as a challenge to the identity and status of workingmen as both producers and as citizens.

Opposition to the act escalated as severe sentences were handed down for picketing, the most notorious being the imprisonment of the female relatives of striking London gas-workers for intimidating strike-breakers. In Scotland, there was barely a handful cases under the act, and the sentences imposed were milder than in England. Nevertheless, the organised agitation throughout Britain which demanded the measure's withdrawal was led by the Glasgow Trades Council. In 1873, 18,000 workers in Glasgow and 15,000 in Edinburgh signed petitions against the act, and the climax of the national campaign came with two huge rallies held in Edinburgh in August and in Glasgow in November 1873. In England, the unions' campaign for equal treatment under the law was supported by progressive Liberal employers, such as Joseph Chamberlain, A. J. Mundella and J. S. Colman. But few Scottish captains of industry took up this cause, while Duncan MacLaren,

> the most prominent Scottish middle-class Radical MP, strenuously resisted lobbying by unions against the act, and he was joined in this stance by most fellow Radicals. As noted, this contributed to tensions within the Scottish party.
>
> The act was replaced in 1875 by two acts, which conferred corporate immunity and repealed the restrictions on picketing.

The 1874 general election results posed two challenges to mainstream Scottish Liberals; namely, the loss of twelve seats to the Conservatives, and the potential stresses on internal unity arising from the growth of the radicals. The rest of the decade saw a struggle between the factions in the party, which were resolved for the time being by Gladstone's Midlothian campaign of 1879–80. The 1874 election demonstrated that the party's organisation was in a poor condition and utterly inadequate to cope with contemporary electioneering conditions, especially after the introduction of the secret ballot in 1872. The decline in Tory activity in the 1850s and 1860s meant that Liberal organisation had frequently petrified: in Roxburghshire, where no Conservative stood after 1841, the Liberal Registration Committee had dwindled by 1868 to a mere four subscribers. Few seats had a permanent party structure, the majority relying instead on legal agents to handle registration and run election campaigns. Spurred on by W. P. Adam, Liberal chief whip from 1874 until 1880, improvements began to be implemented after the 1874 setback, often accompanying the advent of a new MP or candidate. Dundee and Edinburgh already had Liberal committees, and the advantages of formal organisation produced a steady spread of Liberal associations elsewhere.

Scottish disestablishment had not been a prominent issue in the 1868 and 1874 elections. The added ingredient to the long-running anti-state church campaign was the adhesion of the Free Church, which created the Scottish Disestablishment Association in 1874. This association collaborated fully with the long-established Liberation Society, which was closely identified with the Voluntaries. For about three years, however, the campaign seemed becalmed, and Church (of Scotland) Liberals were not particularly concerned: the *Scotsman*'s editor told the rising star of Scottish Whiggery, Lord Rosebery, early in 1875 that 'the public remains apathetic', hence 'the rather cool reception of the agitation'.[15] A sea-change in attitudes was precipitated at the end of 1877 when Lord Hartington, Gladstone's successor as Liberal leader, publicly endorsed Scottish disestablishment. The radicals could now assert that the leadership backed their stance, and redoubled their efforts to win over both party and public opinion. Moves were made in several seats to have a committed disestablisher selected as candidate, but in the 1880 election, the disestablishment lobby enjoyed very limited success, as only eight Scottish Liberal candidates were unqualified advocates of the cause.

THE RECRUDESCENCE OF CENTRIST LIBERALISM

The advance of the disestablishers was contained – and Liberal unity thereby maintained – for the remaining years of the 1870s in three ways. The first was a renaissance of aristocratic Whiggery across the decade, after a quarter-century of relative inactivity. A wave of younger men (most were born between 1839 and 1851) emerged, fully committed to the Whig tradition; seventeen members of eleven titled Whig families stood at elections between 1868 and 1880. Indeed, there were, briefly, more Liberal than Tory Scottish dukes.[16] One analysis of Scottish Liberal MPs in 1878 indicates that there were twelve Radicals, eight traditional Whigs and ten 'Young Whigs', with the comparable English totals being seventy-two Radicals, thirty-seven traditional Whigs and forty-nine young Whigs, suggesting that Scotland was less radical and more Whiggish than England.[17] At the forefront of these aristocrats was Lord Rosebery, whose powerful oratory and wide-ranging cultural and social interests established him by the later 1870s as the leading Scottish Liberal. Additionally, W. P. Adam was the descendant of the Whig party's great manager in the 1790s, reinforcing the sense of a continuing historic link. The moderate policies pursued by Palmerston may well have encouraged Whigs to re-enter Scottish Liberal politics, after the bruising internal struggles of the preceding two decades. Also, Gladstone gave peers favourable treatment: for instance, members of the noble houses of Aberdeen, Breadalbane, Elgin, Argyll and Minto were given plum colonial posts. Gladstone's careful adoption of a relatively centrist position on most controversial questions confronting the party reassured Whigs that he was, *au fond*, one of them.

The second check on radicalism came as working-class Liberal organisations colluded with urban Whigs in constituency associations to thwart the Radical caucuses from exercising full control over the choice of candidates, as in Greenock in 1878 and Glasgow in 1879. In the latter case, the very wealthy Whiggish chemical manufacturer, Sir Charles Tennant, was endorsed by the Glasgow Workmen's Liberal Electoral Union in preference to a radical who was politically very close to Cameron and his moral reform backers. Tennant was elected as the city's MP. Usually in such instances, the drive to maintain Liberal unity prevailed over factional gain, as all sides were aware that, whereas in the recent past, disputes over candidates could be resolved at the polls in a popular plebiscite, the performance of the Conservatives in 1874 indicated that open divisions could constitute electoral suicide. Liberal versus Liberal contests at general elections occurred in thirteen seats in 1868 and nine in 1874, but only two in 1880.

The final obstacle to rampant radicalism was Gladstone's return to active politics in the very late 1870s. An early instance of his influence concerned the potentially explosive question of Scottish disestablishment. Here Gladstone displayed his characteristic adroitness in issuing ambiguous messages which served simultaneously to assuage the anxieties of some in the party yet also sustained the expectations of others. He delighted the Free Church leader, Robert Rainy, by informing him in 1879 that the topic would be confronted once Scottish opinion had clearly declared its position, but did not explain how this could be expressed. Six months later, Gladstone gave assurances which successfully placated a worried Church of Scotland Liberal. As the intermediary who transmitted his message reported back: 'I think his mind is easier in consequence and his condition altogether happier.'[18] The outcome was that by 1881, disestablishment seemed to have slipped down the menu of political priorities. In that year, at the first meeting of the Scottish Liberal Association, formed by a merger of the two regional associations, the chair noted that the issue of the status of the national church had been replaced as a top priority by topics like land tenure, landlord–tenant relations and the reform of House of Commons procedure.

Figure 10.1 Gladstone at West Calder, 1879. © The Scotsman Publications. Licensor: www.scran.ac.uk

But it was Gladstone's 1879–80 election campaign in Midlothian, and especially his first speaking tour in November and December 1879, which had the greatest impact in smoothing over internal party dissension in Scotland. His oratorical stump was remarkable for several reasons. Firstly, he drew very large audiences: a highly sympathetic observer claimed that across 14 days of speechifying, perhaps 250,000 attended his meetings, and on at least one occasion, it was claimed that he addressed around 75,000 people.[19] Not all who heard him were voters; some were women, others were unenfranchised males, such as agricultural workers and miners. Yet the wider resonances of his speeches in shaping political opinion in the whole community must have been huge. Moreover, he did not confine his oratory within Midlothian's boundaries. Gladstone spoke in several places through the Borders and the central Lowlands, including Glasgow, Motherwell and Perth, and no doubt many from nearby places would have come to hear the greatest political orator of the age: quite conceivably voters in at least twenty constituencies could have heard him. Gladstone's speeches dampened the Scottish Liberal party's schismatic propensities by devoting the bulk of all ten speeches to attacking the record of Disraeli's government. He excoriated the frivolous and reckless foreign policy pursued by the Tories, especially waging needless wars in Afghanistan, the Balkans and South Africa, and he denounced Disraeli's handling of domestic economic and fiscal questions as incompetent and responsible for the depressed state of trade. He pilloried the government for failing to address electoral abuses, in particular the creation of fictitious votes. On the contentious issues afflicting Liberal unity in Scotland, he was less than expansive. Temperance, disestablishment and the land question each got one terse passage in a single speech, and only anodyne generalities were offered. The upshot was that Gladstone succeeded triumphantly in unifying his party against the Conservatives, so that the 1880 election in Scotland was one of the most overwhelming Liberal victories since 1832. The wobbles of the 1870s seemed put to bed.

THE CONSERVATIVES' DILEMMAS:
(I) RURAL DIFFICULTIES

In England, the Conservatives' recovery from the mid-Victorian slough began with the 1865 general election, their best result since 1852, and continued steadily thereafter. In 1874, the party enjoyed its best performance since the First Reform Act, holding just over three-fifths of the total, and while in 1880 it fell back, it still had nearly as many MPs as in 1865 and 1868. Borough constituencies remained profitable for the Tories, with a very strong presence in Lancashire cotton towns.

Table 10.1 Scottish and English Conservative MPs, 1865–80

Election	Scotland		England	
	Seats	%	Seats	%
1865	11	20.4	212	47.9
1868	7	12.0	211	46.4
1874	18	31.1	280	62.1
1880	6	10.4	196	43.5

In sharp contrast, the number of Scottish Tory MPs returned in 1865 was the lowest since the disastrous 1832 contest. But worse was to come in 1868, when, despite the careful scheme of redistribution, constructed to countermand prospective Liberal advantage in a widened electorate, the party held fewer seats than in 1832, even although the actual number of Scottish MPs was 15 per cent greater. The Tory triumph in England in 1874 was emphatically not emulated in Scotland, which had only the fifth best result out of the eleven elections held since the First Reform Act, and in percentage terms was comfortably below the worst English performance in the entire period. The 1880 election pushed the modest advance of Scottish Conservatism in 1874 decisively into retreat, with an even poorer performance than the nadir of 1868. In sum, the share of seats won in Scotland ranged between one-half (1865, 1874) and one-quarter (1868, 1880) of the English tally.

The electoral problems facing the party in Scotland were twofold. Firstly, there was the long-standing difficulty that urban constituencies remained unbreachably Liberal. Secondly, there was a significant erosion of the Conservatives' solid strength in county seats, which began in the 1865 election and continued in 1868, when there were seven shire Tory MPs, against fourteen in 1859, despite there being two more county seats in Scotland. The recovery to fourteen victories in 1874 merely restored the 1859 position, which itself had been the poorest result for counties since 1832. In 1880, the party fell back to the dire 1868 level for these seats. This record had no parallel in England, where county representation held steady. The difficulty in Scotland arose from deeply felt grievances entertained by tenant-farmers towards their landlords, which was in great contrast to England, where landowner–tenant relations were as a rule reasonably harmonious, while in Scotland, these were on an almost purely commercial footing, with little stress on the agrarian romanticism which characterised the views of many in England.

Scottish farmers had two major complaints. The first was the operation of the Game Laws as they applied to ground game, i.e. hares, rabbits and deer. Proprietors in the 1860s started to appreciate the potential profits which ground game hunting offered: 'Of late years more especially, hunting has been so very much in fashion among the rich classes as to have made the reservation of low country game a source of considerable income to needy and greedy landlords.'[20] In law, farmers were forbidden to kill ground game, although these animals were highly destructive of crops, impacting not solely on arable growers, but also on pastoralists, as root vegetables were indispensable for feeding overwintered livestock. The steady growth in deer forests led to these animals invading winter feed fields, a particular issue in areas such as Aberdeenshire. This was all starkly different from England, where tenants enjoyed clear legal rights to exterminate ground game on their property. Hence, Scottish farmers argued, game legislation was 'hurtful to the best interest of Rural Society; an Obstacle to the Progress of Agriculture and the development of the productive resources of the Country.'[21]

The second source of dispute was the landlord's right of hypothec. Hypothec afforded greater protection to landowners than the right of distress in England, as it gave security for rent over the tenant's crops, livestock, implements, machinery and household furnishings. Moreover, it conferred preferential creditor ranking for landlords in bankruptcy proceedings against a tenant. Tenants argued that hypothec encouraged high rental levels, as landlords knew they were safe from loss if tenants defaulted, but steep rents reduced farmers' income available for expenditure on agricultural improvements. Furthermore, an 1864 court judgment ruled that the landlord's right under hypothec extended to a tenant's produce which had been sold to a third party, such as a butcher, auctioneer or grain merchant, while the landlord's preferential status above general creditors adversely affected suppliers of goods and services, including financial advances. This implied that the wider rural economy was imperilled, and consequently many rural businesses and tradesmen sided with the tenants to oppose it. So, at a protest meeting in Tain in 1873, a local bank manager strenuously protested against the evils of hypothec.

The vigour with which tenants pursued their objections was not simply due to the sudden emergence of these grievances, but also because of a growing sense of class-consciousness and solidarity among Scottish farmers. As we have seen in Chapter 1, these men were prosperous, enterprising and the great innovators in agricultural practice, yet felt condescended to by lairds, who were often regarded as ineffectual and ill-informed on farming matters – these perceptions pulse through William Alexander's *Johnny Gibb of Gushetneuk*, which, although set in 1840s rural Aberdeenshire, was published in serial form in 1869–70. In 1865, an article in the farmers' journal argued that after the emancipation of trade and then of slaves, there now was needed 'the emancipation of the tenant-farmer from that craven spirit of subservience which has too long characterised the majority of us'.[22] A significant stage in this process occurred with the publication in 1847 of the *North British Agriculturist*. This weekly paper fostered a sense of unity among a geographically discrete community and thus became the mouthpiece for farmers. Two institutions founded in 1864 underscored the emergence of an assertive tenant-farmer identity. One was the Chamber of Agriculture – a clear analogue to the chambers of commerce, which acted to advance the interests of business – which strove to raise matters of general concern to farmers. The other was the Scottish Farmers' Club, sited in Edinburgh, which provided a social meeting place for the tenantry.

Political subordination by tenant-farmers to their social superiors was called into question by these developments, for it was alleged that landowner MPs were unlikely to air the grievances of their tenantry in parliament, and indeed might suppress evidence hostile to the interests of lairds. A Kincardineshire tenant complained to the Tory candidate in the 1865 election that the evidence presented to a recent House of Commons Select Committee on Hypothec had been so one-sided that the committee concluded that the system had only very minor imperfections: 'Na, na, they took guid care to seek nane o' my class (laughter and applause).'[23] The conclusion was that only the return of men closer to the farmers could effect the necessary legislative changes. Thus, the victorious farmers' champion in the Angus by-election of 1872 pointedly did not visit the great houses in the county, which customarily were the first ports of call for all candidates. The 1872 Ballot Act removed any risk of vindictive action by landlords, so that the age of deference had truly passed, as a Cromarty farmer expatiated in 1873:

> The day is gone by when the so-called farmers' friends, when soliciting our votes, would pat us on the back and call us a set of jolly fellows, highly intelligent and that sort of thing, and then when subjects affecting our interests came in before Parliament would vote dead against us, and explain their conduct away by saying that we were a set of clod-hoppers who hardly knew the difference between a cow and a pig, and rudely add that we should mind our clods, and not meddle with politics . . . We have now got power if we care to use it.[24]

The upshot of these trends was that in a range of counties, tenant-farmers rejected candidates who would not accede to their demands for reform. The first dramatic instance of the changed political weather came in the 1865 Kincardineshire contest. Won by the Tories in 1832, no Liberal stood again until 1865, when the party's candidate campaigned almost exclusively on farmers' grievances. The Tory, Sir John Gladstone (the elder brother of William), was a laird with a reputation as a harsh enforcer of the Game Laws against his own tenants. The farmers heckled him at meetings and canvassed for the Liberal, who won with almost two-thirds of the vote. In 1868, proponents of tenants' rights won in six counties, while elsewhere, for example, East Lothian, defenders of the landlords' interest saw their majorities sharply reduced. One Tory candidate lamented that 'one thing is clear, that the political power of the County [Perthshire] is – for this Election at least – wholly in the hands of the farmers'.[25]

In the 1874 election, Conservative gains in seats like Perthshire, South Ayrshire and Inverness-shire were largely due to their candidates highlighting the failure of the Liberal government to assuage the tenant-farmers' demands. Thus, in Roxburghshire, local farmers complained that 'nor can they forget that the questions of game and hypothec are no further advanced toward a settlement than they were in 1868'.[26] But, in addition, electioneering practice shifted drastically, as several Conservative candidates sought to retrieve the situation by meeting with and listening to the tenants, which seems to have been quite an innovation. The Perthshire Tory newspaper outlined this new strategy:

> The Perthshire election of 1874 will have failed to achieve the goal which it ought to achieve if it does not have upon the minds of the lairds of Perthshire a deep and strong conviction that the best interests of the county require, not only at the moment of a contest, but at all times, that they and their tenants should make common cause.[27]

The conflict was finally resolved with the passage in 1880 of two acts, one completely abolishing hypothec on agricultural property and the other allowing tenants to destroy ground game on their farms. But the fifteen-year upheaval in county seats carried two serious consequences for the Tories. Firstly, the party not unnaturally felt obliged to concentrate its efforts after 1865 in restoring its dominance in county seats, and as a consequence, urban Toryism was downgraded as a priority. Secondly, the negative image of the landowning class which many urban middle-class Scots already had was reinforced, and this critical attitude was highly influential during the crofters' agitation of the mid-1880s.

The Conservatives' poor Scottish election results in 1868 and 1874 led to a reappraisal of party organisation, whose bedraggled condition was shown in the numbers of uncontested seats. In 1868, the party put up candidates in only just over one-third of seats (twenty out of fifty-eight), against almost three-quarters in England; in 1874 Tory candidates stood in 59 per cent of Scottish seats, still lagging far behind England's 85 per cent. Meanwhile, in 1868, the

Liberals put candidates up in fifty-five Scottish seats (95 per cent). A report commissioned by Disraeli in 1876 concluded that among the general populace the party was perceived to consist almost exclusively of lairds, their factors and lawyers. Organisation was noted as virtually non-existent; in West Lothian, it consisted of around ten landowners whose role did not go much beyond meeting before elections to select a candidate. From the mid-1860s, however, Conservative Associations looked to recruit farmers to both constituency and local parish committees. To encourage participation by tenants, subscription fees were frequently set at very low levels – 10p a year in West Kilbride – or not charged at all, as in Stirlingshire.

A second development was the adoption of a more professional and permanent approach in lieu of amateurism and informal structures. Perthshire epitomised the new format: a central committee was set up to maintain continuous activity, while local agents were appointed to lead activists in registration work, distributing literature and canvassing voters. But these developments were mostly confined to the central and southern Lowlands. In the north-east and the Highlands, organisation remained structurally rudimentary and socially fossilised, and these were the two areas where the party had the least electoral success: together, they returned only one of the fourteen county seats won in 1874, although they contained ten of the thirty-two shire constituencies.

Establishing links between Scottish landed and urban Tories proved very difficult. In England, the National Union was formed in 1867 to bring country and town Conservatives together, but an effective Scottish counterpart was not established until 1882. Unlike the National Union, the Scottish National Constitutional Association, also formed in 1867, had no representative system involving local associations; membership was open only to individuals, and these were overwhelmingly drawn from landowners and Edinburgh lawyers: in 1872 it had 321 members, 164 of whom were landowners; 101 members lived in Edinburgh, and a mere nine in Glasgow.

The association focused more on county seats than burghs, especially those in the western Lowlands, as was apparent when it acted to support newspapers in an effort to spread the party's message and counter the dominant influence in most places of Liberal titles. In 1872, the association assisted in the founding of Conservative-supporting journals in Aberdeen and Inverness, which were funded and managed by lairds and Edinburgh lawyers. It was left to businessmen in the west, notably James Baird, to provide most of the £50,000 which was required to launch a Glasgow daily – the *Glasgow News* – in 1873, with minimal input from landowners. In 1879, the *Glasgow News* required additional capital, but several leading Tory country gentry refused to help, objecting to the tone of the paper, and so a Clydeside shipbuilder, William Pearce, came to the rescue by injecting a generous sum.

THE CONSERVATIVES' DILEMMAS: (2) URBAN OBSTACLES

The party's weakness in burghs remained intractable, because most urban voters rejected the Conservatives' message on key issues of central concern in Scotland. The almost complete antipathy displayed by adherents of the Free and United Presbyterian churches towards the Tories was a near-fatal incubus, for three broad reasons. Firstly, the members of these churches together outnumbered those of the Church of Scotland in many towns and cities. Secondly, they were both exceptionally well-represented among not just the solid middle class, but also the lower-middle classes, who were precisely the social layers into which the English Conservatives were making substantial inroads. Thirdly, the intransigent hostility of these two sects was more or less solid: in the 1868 general election for the two Scottish university seats, 1,081 Free and UP church ministers voted Liberal and a mere 34 voted Conservative.

A sign that the party was completely unattuned to the sensitivities of the Free Church came in 1874. One of the earliest acts passed by Disraeli's government was the abolition of lay patronage in the Church of Scotland, the core issue behind the Disruption of 1843. The measure was designed to woo back into the state church those Free Churchmen who had opposed the merger negotiations with the UPs.[28] Moreover, the highly successful coalition between the Free Church and established church members who stood for the Use and Wont party in the school board elections in 1873 – especially in towns and cities, where they were the largest group in Aberdeen, Edinburgh, Glasgow and Perth – suggested that there was a sizeable body of Free Church laymen who might re-join the Church of Scotland. Disraeli was assured by influential Scottish Tories, notably his lord advocate, E. S. Gordon, that the reform would yield positive ecclesiastical and political benefits.

This was a crude and crass misreading of the mood in the Free Church. It was indignantly rejected by all but a small handful, even among those who had opposed the abortive Free–UP merger, such as William Kidston, an important Glasgow Tory – and a close relative of the future Conservative prime minister, Andrew Bonar Law. Tory Free Churchmen were deeply offended because there was neither a formal acknowledgement of the justice of the Free Church's position in 1843 nor any reference to the hardships endured by their church after the Disruption. A Tory-voting Glasgow businessman reflected a widely held opinion:

> I cannot join the Establishment . . . But for the existence and prosperity of the Free Church she would never have got rid of patronage and the State has never acknowledged the wrong she did to the party who left in 1843.[29]

The mishandling of this issue had deeper consequences. Many in the Free Church, more especially in its urban Lowland strongholds, who had wished for union with the United Presbyterians now felt impelled to support disestablishment. On the very day in 1874 that the Church of Scotland General Assembly approved of the bill to abolish patronage, the Free Church General Assembly for the first time voted for disestablishment, and later in the year the church formed the Scottish Disestablishment Association. Hence, the Tories, rather than buttressing the Church of Scotland, ironically kick-started a very serious attempt to weaken the power of that church, while simultaneously leaving themselves even more politically bereft in burgh constituencies. Their strategy thus proved completely counterproductive.

To compound the obstacles facing the Conservatives, the state church in Scotland was not, as in England, 'the Tory party at prayer'. The two great leaders of the Church of Scotland in the 1870s were Principals John Caird of Glasgow University and John Tulloch of St Andrews University, and both were committed Liberals. 'Church Liberals' were also widespread among lay supporters of the state church: for example, Charles Tennant, the great chemical manufacturer, and R. V. Campbell, an Edinburgh advocate.

Despite their ineptitude and ignorance of the social complexities of burgh life, the Tories could find glimmers of hope in their performance in urban constituencies in the 1874 election. Their poll in some places rose by 60 per cent or more, and Conservative Associations had been founded in several larger towns, including Dundee, Edinburgh and Glasgow – where in the last there were 2,800 members in 1874. Disraeli's discernment of 'The Angel in the Marble', i.e. the existence of a substantial working-class element sympathetic to Conservatism, is sometimes seen as a key facet of the party's success, which was fostered by a range of social reform legislation enacted by the 1874–80 administration. But several of these measures, especially in housing and sanitary reform, did not apply to Scotland, so there was little political dividend for the party. Lord Elcho's championing in the mid-1860s of the reform of the Master and Servant Act in order to make it less oppressive for workers had pointed to a possible avenue to reach Scottish workingmen. Despite Elcho's success in forming links with sections of the west of Scotland labour movement, there was no follow-up. Five candidates stood for the party in Glasgow over the elections of 1868, 1874 and 1880, and only one referred to social reform in his election address. The *Glasgow News* was consistently opposed to any modification of the labour laws.

A different approach to winning working-class votes, namely, appealing to popular Protestantism – which seemed to have been successful in industrial Lancashire – was adopted in parts of the west of Scotland which had a considerable Irish Catholic presence, especially where native Scottish antipathies to these immigrants were reinforced by the many Ulster Protestants also settled there. The results of the first school board elections in 1873 promised substantial benefits for the Conservative party, especially as local leadership cadres emerged from the contests, and existing leaders reached out to a new constituency, so broadening the party's bases. James N. Cuthbertson, the chair of the Glasgow School Board, stood as a Conservative at Kilmarnock in 1880. In the 1874 election, 'the Bible in the school' was a Tory vote-winner in several constituencies, for instance Ayr Burghs, where both Liberal and Conservative local papers agreed that it was the crucial factor in the Tory gain.

The Orange Order was the main organisation in Scotland which championed popular Protestantism.[30] The movement explicitly identified itself as Conservative in political outlook, as the head of the order in Glasgow observed in 1874:

> They had returned a Conservative member for Glasgow . . . They had got a good sound solid Conservative government (cheers) in place of a mixty-maxty government of Churchmen, Ritualists, Quakers, Jews, Infidels, Papists . . . Every sound Orangeman was a Conservative and if there were any Radicals in their ranks they were as rare as black swans.[31]

But there were two disadvantages in seeking to enlist this section of society. Firstly, the school board electorate was significantly wider than that for parliamentary elections (in Glasgow in 1873, the respective electorates were 101,871 and 53,111), and it soon became evident that many who voted for Use and Wont candidates were ineligible to vote in the latter. Secondly, aligning the party so explicitly with working-class Orangeism tended to alienate the urban middle classes, the social category which the Tories in England had so successfully yoked to their ideology. In Scotland, many of these people, alert to the sophisticated theological currents of the time, rejected the uncompromising fundamentalism of popular Protestantism. Also, committed to law and order, they were profoundly embarrassed and antagonised by the tumult and street violence too often prevalent at Orange demonstrations, which confirmed the middle-class perception that the disorder associated with the movement was an unwelcome importation of Irish political activities, and quite alien to the Scottish tradition. Instead, the Freemasons, a less overtly sectarian organisation with a broad historical background and which included Whiggish and Radical members – including Robert Burns – provided a more acceptable locus for staunchly Protestant members of the landed and commercial elite, as well as respectable artisans. In 1879, there were around 70,000 Freemasons in Scotland, rather more than twice the number of Orangemen.

The political influence of the Orange Order within the Conservative party varied from place to place. But in most seats, the primary objective of the Tories was to reach out to moderate Liberals and centrists, which meant side-lining any hints of Orangeism. So, when James Bain, a Conservative candidate for

Glasgow in 1880, claimed the endorsement of the Orange Order, middle-class Conservatives became uneasy. An eminent local businessman, who was initially pencilled in as Bain's running-mate, withdrew, evidently because of distaste for his potential partner's pronouncements. Bain and his running-mate were soundly defeated, as was Cuthbertson at Kilmarnock. The rightward movement of the Scottish solid bourgeoisie was thus postponed – at least until the Irish Home Rule question reshaped the political terrain.

NOTES

1. See p. 265.
2. See p. 265.
3. *Scotsman*, 28 June 1865.
4. See p. 73.
5. For more on these various developments, see Chapter 3.
6. W. E. Gladstone, *Political Speeches in Scotland, November and December 1879* (1879), 88–94.
7. See pp. 140–1.
8. *Reformer*, 28 May 1870, also 25 June 1870.
9. *Glasgow Herald*, 4 February 1874.
10. SPBA, *Address to the Electors and Ratepayers of Scotland* (1861), 9.
11. SPBA, *14th Annual Report* (1871–2), 3; cf. G. L. Hayter, *The Prohibition Movement* (1897), 266–7.
12. *Social Reformer*, 8 (December 1873), 136.
13. NLS, A. R. D. Elliot MSS, MS 49485, ff. 70–1, J. Anderson to A. R. D. Elliot, 9 January 1878 [*recte* 1879?] (stresses in original).
14. *North British Daily Mail*, 2 February 1874.
15. NLS, Rosebery MSS, MS 10074, ff. 146–7, A. Russel to Rosebery, 17 February 1875.
16. Liberal dukes: Argyll, Hamilton, Roxburghe, Sutherland; Conservative: Atholl, Buccleuch, Montrose.
17. T. A. Jenkins, *Gladstone, Whiggery and the Liberal Party, 1874–86* (1988), App. II, 300–6.
18. BL, Gladstone MSS, Add. MS 41461, ff. 245–6, 265–6, C. Tennant to Gladstone, 15, 19 December 1879.
19. W. E. Gladstone, *Political Speeches in Scotland, November and December 1879* (1879), 214. The claim is made by the anonymous compiler-editor of Gladstone's speeches.
20. *The Present Position, Prospects and Duties of the Scotch Farmer Viewed in Relation to the Landlord's Right of Hypothec, the Operation of the Game Laws . . . and the New Reform Bill* (1866), 5.
21. NRS, Lord Advocates' MSS, AD 56/10, Petition enclosed in A. McCracken to Lord Advocate, 11 March 1870.
22. *North British Agriculturist*, 28 June 1865.

23. Ibid., 5 April 1865.
24. *Inverness Advertiser*, 2 September 1873.
25. GCA, Stirling of Keir MSS, T-SK 29/22/477, W. Stirling-Maxwell to W. Smythe, 12 August 1872 (copy).
26. *Kelso Chronicle*, 20 February 1874.
27. *Perthshire Journal*, 16 February 1874.
28. See pp. 140–1 for this episode.
29. J. C. Gibson, *The Diary of Sir Michael Connal, 1835–91* (1895), 161 (22 May 1876); cf. 151, 152 (5 June, 12 August 1874).
30. See pp. 88–90, 170–3 for a fuller discussion.
31. *Glasgow Herald*, 13 July 1874.

Conclusion: Approaching Niagara?

For both parties, the outcome of the 1880 general election heralded a return to the status quo. The Conservatives' aim to build on the advances achieved in the 1874 general election by securing more gains in urban constituencies was comprehensively defeated. Moreover, they were now acutely aware that shire seats were no longer reliably safe. Additionally, there was the looming prospect, realised in the Third Reform Act of 1884–5, of an enlarged county electorate created by the enfranchisement of the rural working class on the same footing as the Second Reform Act had established for urban workers. Tories fretted that the new voters, whether farm-workers or miners, would be more inclined to support the Liberals.

By contrast, the Liberals felt reassured on several fronts by the 1880 results. The so-called 'leap in the dark' represented by the Second Reform Act had resulted in a safe landing, since workingmen almost everywhere had been assimilated into the broad Liberal camp. Furthermore, after the internal tensions during the decade after 1868, Gladstone's barnstorming Midlothian campaign had triumphantly restored party unity based on traditional mid-Victorian tenets.

But over the two decades after the 1880 contest, what had originally been viewed as hairline fissures in Scottish Liberalism became gaping crevasses, so that the party's triumph became less of a climax and more of a climacteric, ushering in its long-term decline. There were several contributory components to this embryonic existential crisis, with an underlying seismic shift in political consciousness at play on both the right and the left of the spectrum.

Gladstone's introduction of an Irish Home Rule bill in 1885 was the first factor. The measure was rejected by a broad spectrum of the party, which broke away to form the Liberal Unionists, and this opposition was particularly marked in Scotland. The split was horizontal, rather than lateral. Seceders included many titled landowners, such as the Duke of Argyll and Lord Minto, yet others, notably Lords Rosebery and Elgin, remained in the Gladstonian camp. Again, while a number of centrist Liberals decamped, others – for example, Henry Campbell-Bannerman and R. B. Haldane – did not. Most of those in the radical camp stayed loyally with Gladstone, yet there were two highly significant figures who joined the Liberal Unionists, namely the veteran rebel, Duncan MacLaren, and C. Fraser Mackintosh, the foremost champion of the crofters' cause. But the most influential social stratum in Liberal Unionism comprised the urban solid middle class. This encompassed prominent businessmen, professionals and academics – the great scientist, Sir William Thomson, afterwards Lord Kelvin, was President for some six years of the West of Scotland Liberal Unionists.

The significance of this last cadre was that it comprised a crucial social category which Sottish Conservatives had failed to reach. Moreover, they provided both a corps of highly efficient political organisers and also a substantial funding resource for the new party. In addition, the support given to Liberal Unionism by the adhesion of the two most influential Scottish newspapers, the *Glasgow Herald* and the *Scotsman*, boosted the party's credibility.

Scottish Liberal Unionists were exercised by a disparate range of issues. The possible economic threat posed by Protectionism – which many Irish nationalists championed – to the extensive trade and business links between Scotland and Ireland was a major factor, particularly in the west of Scotland. Also, Gladstone's plan for a government buy-out of Irish landowners drew objections on the one hand from those who believed in the inviolable rights of property, and on the other, from Scots who contrasted the favourable treatment of the Irish peasantry with the harsh policy shown (at that point in time) towards the Scottish crofters.

The consequent electoral co-operation between the Liberal Unionists and the Conservatives re-cast the political landscape, for it simultaneously reinforced the Unionist support in counties and prised open urban constituencies hitherto deaf to the blandishments of Toryism. Liberal Unionist parliamentary candidates were heavily drawn from business and professional men, while Conservatives still tended to be recruited from landowners. The presence of Scottish Liberal Unionists MPs was appreciably higher than in England. In the latter, Liberal Unionists formed only 12–15 per cent of all Unionist MPs in the four general elections held between 1886 and 1900. But in Scotland, in 1886, Liberal Unionists won seventeen of the twenty-seven Unionist victories, and subsequently held just under half of all seats. The shift in allegiance was vividly illustrated in the general election of 1900, when for the first time since 1832, the Liberals did not have a majority of MPs; and in Glasgow, where in 1885 the Liberals held all of the city's seven constituencies, the Unionist alliance now in 1900 enjoyed a clean sweep.

But while Liberal Unionism represented essentially a realignment on the right, there were also signs of shifting trends on the left. By the end of the

1880s, several trades unions and trades councils had become increasingly disenchanted with the Liberals' preoccupation with issues like disestablishment and temperance, in preference to addressing workers' grievances. In addition, socialist movements emerged in this decade, and their emphasis on the social and economic problems of capitalism drew support from organised labour, as the formation of the Scottish Labour Party in 1888 showed.

It was, then, apparent that the traditional values of the Liberal party in Scotland, such as laissez-faire, constitutional reform, fiscal austerity and moral improvement, were losing their appeal as politics moved to a more class-based foundation. At the same time, the prevailing economic and social ideologies of classic Liberalism was being increasingly challenged on many fronts. The implications of these processes would be worked out over subsequent generations.

Guide to Further Reading

GENERAL

For a long-term perspective on the history of Scotland, M. Lynch, *Scotland: A New History* (1991), is the most scholarly study. T. M. Devine, *The Scottish Nation: A Modern History* (2012), is the authoritative work on the modern period. Useful surveys of the period covered here include J. F. McCaffrey, *Scotland in the Nineteenth Century* (1998); G. Morton, *Ourselves and Others: Scotland, 1832–1914* (2012); and B. Lenman, *Enlightenment and Change: Scotland, 1736–1832* (2009). Three expert collective surveys are M. Lynch (ed.), *The Oxford Companion to Scottish History* (2001); T. M. Devine and J. Wormald (eds), *The Oxford Handbook to Modern Scottish History* (2012); and R. A. Houston and W. Knox (eds), *The New Penguin History of Scotland* (2001). C. Harvie, *Scotland and Nationalism: Scottish Society and Politics, 1707 to the Present* (2004), fizzes with ideas and is full of illuminating details. L. Abrams et al. (eds), *Gender in Scottish History since 1700* (2006), is a wide-ranging treatment of the role of women in all aspects of Scottish history. Two cities have excellent scholarly histories: for Aberdeen, see E. P. Dennison et al. (eds), *Aberdeen before 1800: A New History* (2002), and W. H. Fraser and C. H. Lee (eds), *Aberdeen, 1800–2000: A New History* (2000). For Glasgow there is, firstly, T. M. Devine and G. Jackson (eds), *Glasgow, Volume I: Beginnings to 1830* (1995), and secondly, W. H. Fraser and I. Maver (eds), *Glasgow, Volume II: 1830 to 1912* (1996).

CHAPTER 1

For Lowland agriculture, T. M. Devine, *The Transformation of Scotland: Social Change and the Agrarian Economy, 1660–1815* (1994), is a careful study based on estates spread across the country. I. Carter, *Farm Life in North-east Scotland, 1840–1914: The Poor Man's Country* (1979), charts developments in the north-east, in a splendid example of the blending of the historical and sociological disciplines, and T. M. Devine (ed.), *Farm Servants and Labour in Lowland Scotland, 1770–1914* (1984), offers a comprehensive treatment of the topic. For the Highlands, the reader needs to triangulate between three major historians: J. Hunter, *The Making of the Crofting Community* (new edn, 2010), is a trenchant critique of the landowning class and a stout champion of the crofters; E. Richards, *The Highland Clearances* (2000), offers a nuanced interpretation which points to the dilemmas faced by lairds; and T. M. Devine, *Clanship to Crofters' War: The Social Transformation of the Scottish Highlands* (1994), stresses the pressure of economic trends. See also E. Richards, *Debating the Highland Clearances* (2007).

CHAPTER 2

The first chapters in T. M. Devine et al. (eds), *The Transformation of Scotland: The Economy since 1700* (2005), offer the most recent overview of Scotland's economic development in the nineteenth century. C. A. Whatley, *The Industrial Revolution in Scotland* (1997), is a brisk, thoughtful review of the topic, while R. H. Campbell, *The Rise and Fall of Scottish Industry* (1980), has many acute observations on industrial strengths and weaknesses. A. Cooke, *The Rise and Fall of the Scottish Cotton Industry, 1778–1914* (2010), is the main work on the industry, as is A. J. Durie, *The Scottish Linen Industry in the Eighteenth Century* (1979), for linen. There are no in-depth histories of the components of the Scottish heavy industry sector. Banking is covered by S. G. Checkland, *Scottish Banking: A History, 1695–1973* (1975), and railways by C. J. A. Robertson, *The Origins of the Scottish Railway System, 1722–1844* (1983).

CHAPTER 3

C. A. Whatley, *Scottish Society, 1707–1830: Beyond Jacobitism, towards Industrialisation* (2000), is excellent for the earlier period. There are helpful essays in both T. M. Devine and R. M. Mitchison (eds), *People and Society in Scotland, Volume I: 1760–1830* (1988), and W. H. Fraser and R. J. Morris (eds), *People and Society in Scotland, Volume II: 1830–1914* (1990). The two-volume histories of both Aberdeen and Glasgow listed in the General section above have invaluable chapters. The structure and values of the solid middle class are handled brilliantly in E. Gordon and G. Mair, *Public Lives: Women, Family and Society in Victorian Britain* (2003), a close study of a part of Glasgow's west end; and G. Morton's *Unionist-Nationalism: Governing Urban Scotland, 1830–60* (1999), based on Edinburgh, is equally insightful. A useful survey of the working classes is given in W. Knox, *Industrial Nation: Work, Culture and Society in Scotland, 1800 to the Present* (1999). E. Gordon, *Women and the Labour Movement in Scotland, 1850–1914* (1991), demonstrates the independence and power of organised women workers.

CHAPTER 4

M. W. Flinn et al., *Scottish Population History from the Seventeenth Century to the 1930s* (1977), guides us through the Scottish health data. The relevant chapters in the histories of Aberdeen and Glasgow listed in the General section have invaluable material on urban living conditions in these cities. The opening chapter in R. Rodger (ed.), *Scottish Housing in the Twentieth Century* (1989), is a masterly exposition of the central components of the working-class housing crisis in the Victorian era. The ideological and practical aspects of poor relief policy in Scotland are discussed in R. Mitchison, *The Old Poor Law in Scotland: The Experience of Poverty, 1574–1845* (2000). I. Levitt (ed.), *Government and Social Conditions in Scotland, 1845–1919* (1988), offers a broad range of contemporary evidence on social problems.

CHAPTER 5

C. G. Brown, *Religion and Society in Scotland since 1707* (1997), is the standard work: comprehensive, subtle and always alert to the wider social context. S. J. Brown, *Thomas Chalmers and the Godly Commonwealth* (1984), provides an incisive and systematic treatment of Chalmers's achievements in both religious and secular affairs. S. J. Brown and M. Fry (eds), *Scotland in the Age of the Disruption* (1993), uses a range of commentators to review the causes of the split and its long-term ramifications. A. C. Cheyne, *The Transforming of the Kirk: Victorian Scotlands* [sic] *Religious Revolution* (1983) presents a lucid, well-marshalled explanation of post-Disruption currents in Scottish Presbyterianism. L. MacDonald, *A Unique and Glorious Mission: Women and Presbyterianism in Scotland, 1830–1930* (2000), provides an interesting account of the role of women in church life.

CHAPTER 6

R. D. Anderson is the unchallenged authority on Scottish education, as demonstrated in *Education and the Scottish People, 1750–1918* (1995), and he has co-edited *The Edinburgh History of Education in Scotland* (2015). J. McDermid,

The Education of Scottish Working-Class Girls in Victorian Scotland: Gender, Education and Identity (2005), is a compelling account. G. Morton, *Unionist-Nationalism: Governing Urban Scotland, 1830–1860* (1999), discusses an important phase in Scottish attitudes to the Union, and his *William Wallace: A National Life* (2014), is a deft study of Wallace's reputation which illuminates the complexity of national identity. The changing perception of Highlanders is illuminated by R. Clyde, *From Rebel to Hero: The Image of the Highlander, 1745–1830* (1995), while C. J. W. Withers, *Urban Highlanders: Highland–Lowland Migration and Urban Gaelic Culture, 1700–1900* (1998), provides a sobering appraisal of the fairly unproblematic assimilation of Highlanders into Lowland society. D. MacMillan, *Scottish Art, 1460–2000* (2004), is a sweeping panorama of Scottish painting, while J. Morrison, *Painting the Nation: Identity and Nationalism in Scottish Painting, 1800–1920* (2003), exposes the attempts by artists to depict Scottish nationality. M. Glendinning et al. (eds), *The History of Scottish Architecture from the Renaissance to the Present Day* (1996), traces the emergence of a distinctive Scottish architectural style in the nineteenth century. The literary scene is covered in S. Manning (ed.), *The Edinburgh History of Scottish Literature, Volume II: Enlightenment, Britain and Empire (1707–1918)* (2007). The importance to Scots of the British Empire is dealt with in T. M. Devine, *Scotland's Empire: The Origins of the Scottish Diaspora* (2003), and M. Fry, *Scottish Empire* (2001). S. K. Kehoe, *Creating a Scottish Church: Catholicism, Gender and Ethnicity in Nineteenth Century Scotland* (2010), is a stimulating account of the experiences encountered by Irish Catholic immigrants seeking to integrate with mainstream Scottish society. M. Mitchell, *The Irish in the West of Scotland, 1797–1848* (1998), is a useful corrective to the view that the Irish were peripheral to working-class political, social and economic movements in the first half of the nineteenth century. E. W. McFarland deals with Orangeism in *Protestants First: Orangeism in 19th Century Scotland* (1990).

CHAPTER 7

The impact of the French Revolution on Scotland is explored in B. Harris (ed.), *Scotland in the Age of the French Revolution* (2005); and Harris, *The Scottish People and the French Revolution* (2008), also looks at the social background of the period. R. M. Sunter, *Patronage and Politics in Scotland, 1707–1832* (1986), is a thoughtful, well-informed study of electoral politics, which has been rather unjustly neglected. M. Fry, *Patronage and Principle: A Political History of Modern Scotland* (1987), is a brisk political survey, and his follow-up work, *The Dundas Despotism* (1992), makes a fair attempt to rehabilitate the reputation of Henry Dundas.

CHAPTER 8

As discussed in the previous section, Sunter's and Fry's two books are highly relevant here. G. Pentland, *The Spirit of the Union: Popular Politics in Scotland, 1815–21* (2011), is an exciting and innovative dissection of the immediate post-war working-class radical movements. W. H. Fraser, *Scottish Popular Politics from Radicalism to Labour* (2000), is a thoughtful examination of extra-parliamentary movements by the doyen of Scottish labour history. Pentland's earlier study, *Radicalism, Reform and National Identity in Scotland, 1820–33* (2008), deals with the lead-up to the First Reform Act in an exemplary piece of research.

CHAPTERS 9 AND 10

Fraser, Fry (*Patronage and Principle*), and Pentland (*Radicalism, Reform and National Identity*), all listed in the further reading for Chapter 8, remain highly relevant. I. G. C. Hutchison, *A Political History of Scotland, 1832–1924: Parties, Elections and Issues* (1986), like its author, is now somewhat creaky. W. H. Fraser, *Chartism in Scotland* (2010), is a comprehensive account of the movement, and is an appropriate monument to Fraser's lifelong contribution to the historiography of the Scottish working classes.

Bibliography

BOOKS

L. Abrams, *The Orphan Country: Children of Scotland's Broken Homes from 1845 to the Present Day* (1998).
L. Abrams et al. (eds), *Gender in Scottish History since 1700* (2006).
R. J. Adam (ed.), *Sutherland Estate Management, 1802–16* (2 vols, 1972).
D. Allan, *Virtue, Learning and the Scottish Enlightenment* (1993).
R. D. Anderson, *Education and Opportunity in Victorian Scotland* (1983).
R. D. Anderson, *Education and the Scottish People, 1750–1918* (1996).
R. D. Anderson et al. (eds), *The Edinburgh History of Education in Scotland* (2015).
K. Barclay and D. Simonton (eds), *Women in Eighteenth Century Scotland: Intimate, Intellectual and Public Lives* (2013).
D. G. Barrie, *Police in the Age of the Enlightenment: Police Development and the Civic Tradition in Scotland, 1775–1865* (2008).
A. Benchimol, *Intellectual Politics and Cultural Conflict in the Romantic Period: Scottish Whigs, English Radicals and the Making of the British Public Sphere* (2010).
P. Bolin-Hort, *Work, Family and the State: Child Labour and the Organisation of Production in the British Cotton Industry, 1780–1920* (1989).
B. D. Bonnyman, *The Third Duke of Buccleuch and Adam Smith: Estate Management and Improvement in Enlightenment Scotland* (2014).
J. I. Brash (ed.), *Scottish Electoral Politics, 1832–54* (1974).
E. Breitenbach and E. Gordon (eds), *Out of Bounds: Women in Scottish Society, 1800–1945* (1992).
E. Breitenbach et al. (eds), *Scottish Women: A Documentary History, 1780–1914* (2013).
J. H. F. Brotherston, *Observations on the Early Public Health Movement in Scotland* (1952).

T. Brotherstone (ed.), *Covenant, Charter and Party: Traditions of Revolt and Protest in Modern Scottish History* (1989).
T. Brotherstone and D. J. Withrington (eds), *The City and Its Worlds: Aspects of Aberdeen's History since 1794* (1996).
C. G. Brown, *Religion and Society in Scotland since 1707* (1987).
S. J. Brown, *Thomas Chalmers and the Godly Commonwealth* (1982).
S. J. Brown, *The National Churches of England, Ireland and Scotland, 1801–46* (2001).
S. J. Brown, *Providence and Empire: Religion, Politics and Society in the United Kingdom, 1815–1914* (2008).
S. J. Brown and M. Fry (eds), *Scotland in the Age of the Disruption* (1993).
J. Burnett, *Riot, Revelry and Rout: Sport in Lowland Scotland before 1860* (2000).
R. A. Cage, *The Scottish Poor Law, 1750–1845* (1981).
R. A. Cage (ed.), *The Working Class in Glasgow, 1750–1914* (1987).
A. B. Campbell, *The Lanarkshire Miners: A Social History of Their Trade Unions, 1775–1874* (1979).
R. H. Campbell, *The Rise and Fall of Scottish Industry, 1707–1939* (1980).
R. H. Campbell, *Owners and Occupiers: Changes in Rural Society in South-West Scotland before 1914* (1991).
I. Carter, *Farm Life in North East Scotland, 1840–1914: The Poor Man's Country* (1979).
V. Chancellor, *The Political Life of Joseph Hume, 1777–1855* (1986).
M. Chase, *1820: Disorder and Stability in the United Kingdom* (2013).
O. Checkland, *Philanthropy in Victorian Scotland: Social Welfare and the Voluntary Principle* (1980).
S. G. Checkland, *Scottish Banking, 1695–1975* (1975).
S. G. Checkland, *The Elgins, 1766–1917: A Tale of Aristocratic Proconsuls and Their Wives* (1988).
A. C. Cheyne, *The Transforming of the Kirk: Victorian Scotland's Religious Revolution* (1983).
A. C. Cheyne (ed.), *The Practical and the Pious: Essays on Thomas Chalmers, 1780–1847* (1985).
R. A. Church, *The History of the British Coal Industry, Volume III: 1830–1913 – Victorian Pre-eminence* (1986).
A. Clark, *The Struggle for the Breeches: Gender and the Making of the British Working Class* (1995).
J. Clive, *Scotch Reviewers: The Edinburgh Review, 1802–15* (1951).
L. Colley, *Britons: Forging the Nation, 1707–1837* (1992).
S. Collini, *That Noble Science of Politics: A Study in Nineteenth Century Intellectual History* (1983).
S. Conway, *The British Isles and the War of American Independence* (2000).

A. Cooke, *The Rise and Fall of the Scottish Cotton Industry, 1778–1914* (2010).
A. Cooke et al. (eds), *Modern Scottish History* (1998).
J. E. Cookson, *The British Armed Nation, 1793–1815* (1997).
A. A. Cormack, *Teinds and Agriculture* (1930).
E. J. Cowan and R. J. Finlay (eds), *Scottish History: The Power of the Past* (2002).
R. M. W. Cowan, *The Newspaper in Scotland: A Study of Its First Expansion, 1815–60* (1946).
A. Cox, *Empire, Industry and Class: The Imperial Nexus of Jute, 1840–1940* (2013).
A. J. G. Cummings and T. M. Devine (eds), *Industry, Business and Society in Scotland since 1700* (1994).
M. Curthoys, *Governments, Labour and the Law in Mid-Victorian Britain: The Trade Union Legislation of the 1870s* (2004).
M. Daunton, *House and Home in the Victorian City: Working-Class Housing, 1850–1914* (1983).
N. Davidson, *The Origins of Scottish Nationhood* (2000).
M. Demata and D. Wu (eds), *British Romanticism and the Edinburgh Review: Bicentenary Essays* (2002).
T. M. Devine (ed.), *Scottish Farm Servants and Labour in Lowland Scotland, 1770–1914* (1984).
T. M. Devine, *The Great Highland Famine: Hunger, Emigration and the Scottish Highlands in the Nineteenth Century* (1988).
T. M. Devine (ed.), *Conflict and Stability in Scottish Society, 1700–1850* (1990).
T. M. Devine (ed.), *Irish Immigration and Scottish Society in the Nineteenth and Twentieth Centuries* (1991).
T. M. Devine, *Clanship to Crofters' War: The Social Transformation of the Scottish Highlands* (1994).
T. M. Devine (ed.), *Scottish Elites* (1994).
T. M. Devine, *The Transformation of Rural Scotland: Social Change and the Agrarian Economy, 1660–1815* (1994).
T. M. Devine, *Exploring the Scottish Past* (1995).
T. M. Devine, *Scotland's Empire, 1600–1815* (2003).
T. M. Devine, *The Scottish Nation: A Modern History* (2010).
T. M. Devine and G. Jackson (eds), *Glasgow, Volume I: Beginnings to 1830* (1995).
T. M. Devine and R. Mitchison (eds), *People and Society in Scotland, Volume I: 1760–1830* (1988).
T. M. Devine and J. R. Young (eds), *Eighteenth Century Scotland: New Perspectives* (1999).
T. M. Devine et al. (eds), *The Transformation of Scotland: The Economy since 1700* (2005).

T. Dickson (ed.), *Scottish Capitalism: Class, State, and Nation from before the Union to the Present* (1980).
T. Dickson (ed.), *Capital and Class in Scotland* (1982).
R. K. Donovan, *No Popery and Radicalism: Opposition to Roman Catholic Relief in Scotland, 1778–82* (1987).
M. Durey, *Transatlantic Radicals and the Early American Republic* (1997).
A. J. Durie, *The Scottish Linen Industry in the Eighteenth Century* (1979).
M. Dyer, *Men of Property and Intelligence: The Scottish Electoral System Prior to 1884* (1996).
R. Emerson, *Academic Patronage in the Scottish Enlightenment: Glasgow, Edinburgh and St Andrews Universities* (2008).
D. Englander, *Landlord and Tenant in Urban Britain, 1838–1918* (1983).
D. Englander, *Poverty and Poor Law Reform in Nineteenth Century Britain, 1830–1914* (1998).
J. Evans, *The Gentleman Usher: The Life and Times of George Dempster (1732–1818), Member of Parliament and Laird of Dunnichen and Skibo* (2005).
T. Ferguson, *The Dawn of Scottish Social Welfare: A Survey from Medieval Times to 1863* (1948).
T. Ferguson, *Scottish Social Welfare, 1864–1914* (1958).
J. Fergusson, *Letters of George Dempster to Sir Alexander Fergusson, 1756–1813* (1934).
D. R. Fisher (ed.), *The History of Parliament: The House of Commons, 1820–32* (2009).
M. W. Flinn, *The History of the British Coal Industry, Volume II: 1700–1832, the Industrial Revolution* (1984).
M. W. Flinn et al., *Scottish Population History* (1977).
R. Floud et al., *Height, Health and History: Nutritional Status in the United Kingdom, 1750–1980* (1990).
B. Fontana, *Rethinking the Politics of Commercial Society: The Edinburgh Review, 1802–32* (1985).
W. H. Fraser, *Conflict and Class: Scottish Workers, 1700–1838* (1988).
W. H. Fraser, *Scottish Popular Politics: From Radicalism to Labour* (2000).
W. H. Fraser, *Chartism in Scotland* (2010).
W. H. Fraser and C. Lee (eds), *Aberdeen, 1800–2000: A New History* (2000).
W. H. Fraser and I. Maver (eds), *Glasgow, Volume II: 1830–1912* (1996).
W. H. Fraser and R. J. Morris (eds), *People and Society in Scotland, Volume II: 1830–1914* (1990).
M. Fry, *Patronage and Principle: A Political History of Modern Scotland* (1987).
M. Fry, *The Scottish Empire* (2001).
M. Fry, *The Dundas Despotism* (2nd edn, 2004).
M. Fry, *Wild Scots: Four Hundred Years of Scottish History* (2005).

J. Fyfe (ed.), *The Autobiography of John MacAdam (1806–83), with Selected Letters* (1980).
E. Gauldie, *The Dundee Textile Industry, 1790–1885, from the Papers of Peter Carmichael of Arthurstone* (1969).
E. Gauldie, *Cruel Habitations: A History of Working-Class Housing, 1780–1918* (1974).
E. Gauldie, *One Artful and Ambitious Individual: Alexander Riddoch (1745–1822)* (1989).
A. Gee, *The British Volunteer Movement, 1794–1814* (2003).
D. E. Ginter (ed.), *Whig Organisation in the General Election of 1790: Selections from the Blair Adam Papers* (1967).
M. Glendinning and S. W. Marland, *Buildings of the Land: Scotland's Farms, 1750–2000* (2008).
M. Glendinning et al., *A History of Scottish Architecture: From the Renaissance to the Present Day* (1996).
A. Goodwin, *The Friends of Liberty: The English Democratic Movement in the Age of the French Revolution* (1979).
E. Gordon, *Women and the Labour Movement in Scotland, 1850–1914* (1991).
E. Gordon and G. Mair, *Public Lives: Women, Family and Society in Victorian Britain* (2003).
G. Gordon (ed.), *Perspectives of the Scottish City* (1985).
G. Gordon and B. Dicks (eds), *Scottish Urban History* (1983).
W. M. Gordon, *Mill Girls and Strangers: Single Women's Independent Migration in England, Scotland and the United States, 1850–81* (2002).
R. Q. Gray, *The Labour Aristocracy in Victorian Edinburgh* (1976).
T. Griffiths and G. Morton (eds), *A History of Everyday Life in Nineteenth Century Scotland* (2009).
C. Gulvin, *The Scottish Hosiery and Knitwear Industry, 1680–1980* (1984).
C. Hamlin, *Public Health and Social Justice in the Age of Chadwick: Britain, 1800–54* (1998).
M. Harper, *Emigration from North-East Scotland, Volume I: Willing Exiles* (1988); *Volume II: Beyond the Broad Atlantic* (1988).
B. Harris (ed.), *Scotland in the Age of the French Revolution* (2005).
B. Harris, *The Scottish People and the French Revolution* (2008).
B. Harris and C. MacKean, *Scottish Towns in the Age of the Enlightenment, 1740–1820* (2014).
J. Harris, *The British Iron Industry, 1700–1850* (1988).
C. Harvie, *Scotland and Nationalism: Scottish Politics and Society, 1707 to the Present* (2004).
P. Hillis, *The Barony of Glasgow* (2007).
R. A. Houston and I. D. Whyte (eds), *Scottish Society, 1500–1800* (1989).

R. K. Huch and P. R. Ziegler, *Joseph Hume, the People's M.P.* (1985).
J. Hunter, *The Making of the Crofting Community* (2nd edn, 2010).
C. K. Hyde, *Technological Change and the British Iron Industry, 1700–1870* (1977).
D. T. Jenkins and K. G. Ponting, *The British Wool Textile Industry, 1770–1914* (1982).
T. A. Jenkins, *Gladstone, Whiggery and the Liberal Party, 1874–86* (1988).
G. S. Jones, *Languages of Class: Studies in English Working Class History, 1832–1982* (1983).
P. M. Jones, *Agricultural Enlightenment: Knowledge, Technology and Nature, 1750–1840* (2016).
P. Jupp, *British Politics in the Era of Reform: The Duke of Wellington's Administration, 1828–30* (1990).
M. J. M. Kedslie, *Firm Foundations: The Development of Professional Accounting in Scotland, 1850–1900* (1990).
S. K. Kehoe, *Creating a Scottish Church: Catholicism, Gender and Ethnicity in Nineteenth Century Scotland* (2010).
C. Kidd, *Subverting Scotland's Past: Scottish Whig Historians and the Creation of an Anglo-British Identity, 1689–c.1830* (1993).
C. Kidd, *Union and Unionists: Political Thought in Scotland, 1500–2000* (2008).
J. Kirk (ed.), *The Church in the Highlands* (1998).
W. Knox, *Hanging by a Thread: The Scottish Cotton Industry, c.1850–1914* (1995).
W. Knox, *Industrial Nation: Work, Culture and Society in Scotland, 1800 to the Present* (1999).
P. Laxton and R. Rodger, *Insanitary City: Henry Littlejohn and the Condition of Edinburgh* (2014).
W. C. Lehman, *John Millar of Glasgow* (1960).
L. Leneman, *A Guid Cause: The Women's Suffrage Movement in Scotland* (1991).
B. P. Lenman, *Enlightenment and Change: Scotland, 1746–1832* (2nd edn, 2009).
B. Lenman et al., *Dundee and Its Jute Industry, 1850–1914* (1969).
I. Levitt (ed.), *Government and Social Conditions in Scotland, 1845–1918* (1988).
I. Levitt and T. C. Smout, *The State of the Scottish Working Class in 1843* (1979).
D. G. Lockhart (ed.), *Scottish Planned Villages* (2002).
F. Lyall, *Of Presbyters and Kings: Church and State in the Law of Scotland* (1980).
T. McBride, *The Experience of Irish Migrants to Scotland, 1836–91: A New Way of Being Irish* (2006).

M. McCahill, *Order and Equipoise: The Peerage and the House of Lords, 1783–1806* (1978).
A. W. MacColl, *Land, Faith and the Crofting Community, 1843–93* (2006).
I. McCraw, *Victorian Dundee at Worship* (2002).
J. McDermid, *The Education of Working-Class Girls in Victorian Scotland: Gender, Education and Equality* (2005).
L. O. MacDonald, *A Unique and Glorious Mission: Women and Presbyterianism in Scotland, 1830–1930* (2000).
I. MacDougall (ed.), *Minutes of Edinburgh Trades Council, 1859–73* (1968).
E. W. McFarland, *Protestants First: Orangeism in 19th Century Scotland* (1990).
E. W. McFarland, *Ireland and Scotland in the Age of Revolution* (1994).
E. W. McFarland, *John Ferguson, 1836–1906: Irish Issues in Scottish Politics* (2003).
G. K. McGilvary, *East India Patronage and the British State: The Scottish Elite and Politics in the Eighteenth Century* (2008).
P. McHugh, *Prostitution and Victorian Social Reform* (1980).
J. R. MacIntosh, *Church and Theology in Enlightenment Scotland: The Popular Party, 1740–1800* (1998).
A. MacKillop, *'More Fruitful than the Soil': Army, Empire and the Scottish Highlands, 1715–1815* (2000).
A. A. MacLaren, *Religion and Social Class: The Disruption Years in Aberdeen* (1974).
A. A. MacLaren (ed.), *Social Class in Scotland: Past and Present* (n.d.).
D. MacMillan, *Scottish Painting, 1460–2000* (2000).
G. MacPherson, *Dugald Stewart: The Pride and Ornament of Scotland* (2003).
D. McRoberts (ed.), *Modern Scottish Catholicism* (1979).
S. Manning (ed.), *The Edinburgh History of Scottish Literature, Volume II: Enlightenment, Britain and Empire (1707–1918)* (2007).
R. Marsden and C. Smith, *Engineering Empire: A Cultural History of Technology in Nineteenth Century Britain* (2005).
D. Mays (ed.), *The Architecture of Scottish Cities: Essays in Honour of David Walker* (1997).
M. Michie, *An Enlightenment Tory in Victorian Scotland: The Career of Sir Archibald Alison* (1997).
C. Midgely, *Women against Slavery: The British Campaign, 1780–1870* (1992).
L. Miskell et al. (eds), *Victorian Dundee: Image and Realities* (2000).
J. Mitchell, *Governing Scotland: The Invention of Administrative Devolution* (2003).
M. J. Mitchell, *The Irish in the West of Scotland, 1798–1848: Trade Unions, Strikes and Political Movements* (1998).
M. J. Mitchell (ed.), *New Perspectives on the Irish in Scotland* (2008).

R. Mitchison, *The Old Poor Law in Scotland: The Experience of Poverty, 1574–1845* (2000).
J. Morrison, *Painting the Nation: Identity and Nationalism in Scottish Painting, 1800–1920* (2000).
G. Morton, *Unionist Nationalism: Governing Urban Scotland, 1830–60* (1999).
G. Morton, *William Wallace: Man and Myth* (2001).
G. Morton, *Ourselves and Others: Scotland, 1832–1914* (2012).
I. Mowat, *Easter Ross, 1750–1850: The Double Frontier* (1981).
C. W. Munn, *The Scottish Provincial Banking Companies, 1747–1864* (1981).
J. F. Munro, *Maritime Enterprise and Empire: Sir William MacKinnon and His Business Network, 1823–93* (2003).
A. Murdoch, *British History, 1660–1832: National Identity and Local Culture* (1998).
A. Murdoch (ed.), *The Scottish Nation: Identity and History* (2007).
N. L. Murray, *The Scottish Handloom Weavers, 1790–1850: A Social History* (1978).
S. Nenadic, *Lairds and Luxury: The Highland Gentry in Eighteenth-Century Scotland* (2007).
M. S. Ó Cathain, *Republicanism in Scotland, 1858–1916: Fenians in Exile* (2007).
P. O'Leary, *Sir James Mackintosh: The Whig Cicero* (1989).
W. Orr, *Deer Forests, Landlords and Crofters: The Western Highlands in Victorian and Edwardian Times* (1982).
C. S. Orwin and E. H. Whetham, *A History of British Agriculture, 1846–1918* (1964).
L. Paterson, *The Autonomy of Modern Scotland* (1994).
D. Paton, *The Clergy and the Clearances: The Church and the Highland Crisis, 1790–1850* (2006).
P. L. Payne, *Colvilles and the Scottish Steel Industry* (1979).
P. L. Payne, *Growth and Contraction: Scottish Industry, c.1860–1990* (1992).
G. Pentland, *Radicalism, Reform and National Identity in Scotland, 1820–33* (2008).
G. Pentland, *The Spirit of the Union: Popular Politics in Scotland, 1815–20* (2011).
N. T. Phillipson, *The Scottish Whigs and the Reform of the Court of Session, 1785–1830* (1990).
W. Pickard, *Member for Scotland: A Life of Duncan MacLaren* (2011).
P. A. Pickering and A. Tyrell, *The People's Bread: A History of the Anti-Corn Law League* (2000).
A. Plassart, *The Scottish Enlightenment and the French Revolution* (2015).
S. Pollard and P. Robertson, *The British Shipbuilding Industry, 1870–1914* (1979).
R. Pope (ed.), *Religion and National Identity: Wales and Scotland, 1700–1900* (2001).

K. D. Reynolds, *Aristocratic Women and Political Society in Victorian Britain* (1998).
E. Richards, *The Leviathan of Wealth: The Sutherland Fortune in the Industrial Revolution* (1973).
E. Richards, *A History of the Highland Clearances, Volume II: Agrarian Transformation and the Evictions, 1746–1886* (1982); *Volume II: Emigration, Protest, Reasons* (1985).
E. Richards, *Patrick Sellar and the Highland Clearances: Homicide, Eviction and the Price of Progress* (1999).
E. Richards, *The Highland Clearances: People, Landlords and Rural Turmoil* (2000).
C. J. A. Robertson, *The Origins of the Scottish Railway System, 1722–1844* (1983).
E. Robertson, *Glasgow's Doctor: James Burn Russell, MOH, 1837–1904* (1998).
Lord Rodger of Earlsferry, *The Courts, the Church and the Constitutional Aspects of the Disruption of 1843* (2008).
R. Rodger (ed.), *Scottish Housing in the Twentieth Century* (1989).
R. Rodger, *The Transformation of Edinburgh: Land, Property and Institutions in the Nineteenth Century* (2001).
M. St John, *The Demands of the People: Dundee Radicalism, 1850–70* (1997).
L. J. Saunders, *Scottish Democracy, 1815–40* (1950).
R. Saville, *Bank of Scotland: A History, 1695–1995* (1996).
G. Searle, *Entrepreneurial Politics in Mid-Victorian Britain* (1993).
J. S. Shaw, *The Political History of Eighteenth Century Scotland* (1999).
A. Slaven, *The Development of the West of Scotland, 1750–1960* (1975).
A. Slaven and D. H. Aldcroft (eds), *Business, Banking and Urban History* (1982).
A. Slaven and S. Checkland (eds), *Dictionary of Scottish Business Biography, Volume I: The Staple Industries* (1986); *Volume II: Processing, Distribution, Service* (1990).
D. C. Smith, *Passive Obedience and Prophetic Protest: Social Criticism in the Scottish Church, 1830–1945* (1987).
M. Smitley, *The Feminine Public Sphere: Middle-Class Women in Civic Life in Scotland, 1870–1914* (2009).
R. M. Sunter, *Patronage and Politics in Scotland, 1707–1832* (1986).
D. B. Swinfen, *Moncrieff: The Life and Career of James Wellwood Moncrieff, 1st Baron Moncrieff of Tullibole* (2015).
S. Szreter, *Health and Wealth: Studies in History and Policy* (2005).
J. Tomlinson et al., *The Decline of Jute: Managing Industrial Change* (2011).
R. G. Thorne (ed.), *The History of Parliament: The House of Commons, 1790–1820* (1986).
A. Tindley, *The Sutherland Estate, 1850–1920: Aristocratic Decline, Estate Management and Land Reform* (2010).

D. Turnock, *The Making of the Scottish Rural Landscape* (1995).
G. Vaughan, *The 'Local' Irish in the West of Scotland, 1851–1921* (2013).
D. M. Walker, *A Legal History of Scotland, Volume VI: The Nineteenth Century* (2001).
J. R. Walkowitz, *Prostitution and Victorian Society: Women, Class and the State* (1980).
C. A. Whatley, *The Industrial Revolution in Scotland* (1997).
C. A. Whatley, *Scottish Society, 1707–1830: Beyond Jacobitism, towards Industrialisation* (2000).
A. E. Whetstone, *Scottish County Government in the Eighteenth and Nineteenth Centuries* (1981).
I. D. Whyte, *Scotland and the Abolition of Black Slavery, 1756–1838* (2001).
C. W. J. Withers, *Gaelic Scotland: The Transformation of a Culture Region* (1988).
C. W. J. Withers, *Urban Highlanders: Highland–Lowland Migration and Urban Gaelic Culture, 1700–1900* (1998).
A. S. Wohl, *Endangered Lives: Public Health in Victorian Britain* (1983).
A. L. Wold (ed.), *Scotland and the French Revolutionary War, 1792–1802* (2015).

ARTICLES, ETC.

L. Abrams, 'Families of the Imagination: Myths of Scottish Family Life in Scottish Child Welfare Policy', *Scottish Tradition*, 27 (2002).
G. G. Acheson et al., 'Organisational Flexibility and Governance in a Civil-Law Regime: Scottish Partnership Banks during the Industrial Revolution', *Business History*, 53 (2011).
C. M. Allan, 'The Genesis of British Urban Development, with Special Reference to Glasgow', *Economic History Review*, 18 (1965–6).
A. Anderson, 'The Poor Law in Nineteenth Century Scotland', in D. Fraser (ed.), *The New Poor Law in the Nineteenth Century* (1976).
M. Anderson, 'Population Growth and Population Restriction in Nineteenth Century Rural Scotland', in T. Bengtsson and O. Saito (eds), *Population and Economy from Hunger to Modern Economic Growth* (2000).
R. D. Anderson, 'In Search of "the Lad of Parts": The Mythical History of Scottish Education', *History Workshop*, 19 (1983).
R. D. Anderson, 'Scottish University Professors, 1800–1939: Profile of an Elite', *SESH*, 7 (1987).
R. D. Anderson, 'Scottish History and National Identity', *SHR*, 92 (2012).
D. B. A. Ansdell, 'The 1843 Disruption of the Church of Scotland in the Isle of Lewis', *RSCHS*, 24 (1990–2).

D. Ansdell, 'Disruptions and Controversies in the Highland Church', in J. Kirk (ed.), *The Church in the Highlands* (1998).
B. Aspinwall, 'The Formation of the Catholic Community in the West of Scotland', *Innes Review*, 33 (1982).
B. Aspinwall, 'Popery in Scotland, 1820–1920: Image and Reality', *RSCHS*, 22 (1984–6).
B. Aspinwall, 'The Welfare State within the State: The St Vincent de Paul Society in Glasgow, 1848–1920', in W. J. Shiels and D. Wood (eds), *Voluntary Religion* (1986).
B. Aspinwall, '"Children of the Dead End": The Formation of the Archdiocese of Glasgow, 1815–1914', *Innes Review*, 43 (1992).
B. Aspinwall, 'The Formation of a British Identity within Scottish Catholicism, 1830–1914', in R. Pope (ed.), *Religion and National Identity: Wales and Scotland, 1700–1900* (2001).
B. Aspinwall, 'The Reverend Alessandro Gavazzi (1808–89) and Scottish Identity: A Chapter in Nineteenth-Century Anti-Catholicism', *Recusant History*, 28 (2006–7).
B. Aspinwall, 'Catholic Devotion in Victorian Scotland', in M. J. Mitchell (ed.), *New Perspectives on the Irish in Scotland* (2008).
B. Aspinwall and J. McCaffrey, 'A Comparative View of the Irish in Edinburgh in the Nineteenth Century', in R. Swift and S. Gilley (eds), *The Irish in the Victorian City* (1985).
C. M. Atherton, 'The Development of the Middle-Class Suburb: The West End of Glasgow', *SESH*, 11 (1991).
E. Bachin, 'Brothers of Liberty: Garibaldi's British Legion', *Historical Journal*, 58 (2015).
N. Ballantyne, 'The Lanarkshire Puddlers: A Case Study of Work and Wages in the Malleable Iron Industry, 1870–1900', *SLHSJ*, 36 (2001).
M. Bangor-Jones, 'Sheep Farming in Eighteenth Century Sutherland', *Agricultural History Review*, 50 (2002).
D. G. Barrie, '"Epoch-making" Beginnings to Lingering Death: The Struggle for Control of the Glasgow Police Commission, 1833–46', *SHR*, 86 (2007).
D. G. Barrie, 'Police in Civil Society: Police, Enlightenment and Civil Society in Urban Scotland, 1780–1833', *Urban History*, 37 (2010).
D. G. Barrie, 'A Typology of British Police: Locating the Scottish Municipal Police Model in Its British Context, 1800–35', *British Journal of Criminology*, 50 (2010).
D. G. Barrie and S. Broomhall, 'Policing Bodies in Urban Scotland, 1780–1850', in S. Broomhall and J. van Gent (eds), *Governing Masculinities in the Early Modern Period: Regulating Selves and Others* (2011).
S. Blackden, 'The Board of Supervision and the Scottish Parochial Medical Service, 1845–90', *Medical History*, 30 (1986).

P. Bolin-Hort, 'Managerial Strategies and Worker Responses: A New Perspective on the Decline of the Scottish Cotton Industry', *SLHSJ*, 29 (1994).
C. B. Bow, 'In Defence of the Scottish Enlightenment: Dugald Stewart's Role in the 1805 John Leslie Affair', *SHR*, 92 (2015).
G. R. Boyer and T. J. Hatton, 'Wage Trends in the Regions of the United Kingdom, 1850–1913', in S. J. Connolly (ed.), *Kingdoms United? Great Britain and Ireland since 1850: Integration and Diversity* (1999).
J. I. Brash, 'The New Scottish County Electors in 1832: An Occupational Analysis', *Parliamentary History*, 15 (1996).
P. Brett, 'Political Dinners in Early Nineteenth Century Britain: Platform, Meeting-Place and Battleground', *History*, 81 (1996).
J. Brims, 'The Covenanting Tradition and Scottish Radicalism in the 1790s', in T. Brotherstone (ed.), *Covenant, Charter and Party* (1989).
J. Brims, 'From Reformers to "Jacobins": The Scottish Association of the Friends of the People', in T. M. Devine (ed.), *Conflict and Stability in Scottish Society, 1700–1850* (1990).
R. Britton, 'Wealthy Scots, 1876–1913', *Bulletin of the Institute of Historical Research*, 58 (1985).
D. Brookes, 'Gladstone and MidLothian: The Background to the First Campaign', *SHR*, 64 (1985).
C. G. Brown, 'The Sunday School Movement in Scotland, 1780–1914', *RSCHS*, 21 (1981–3).
C. G. Brown, 'Protest in the Pews: Interpreting Presbyterianism and Society in Fracture during the Scottish Industrial Revolution', in T. M. Devine (ed.), *Conflict and Stability in Scottish Society, 1700–1850* (1990).
C. G. Brown, '"To Be Aglow with Civic Ardour": The "Godly Commonwealth" in Glasgow, 1843–1914', *RSCHS*, 26 (1996).
D. Brown, 'The Government of Scotland under Henry Dundas and William Pitt', *History*, 83 (1998).
D. Brown, 'Scotland and the Ministry of All the Talents, 1806–7', in A. Murdoch (ed.), *The Scottish Nation: Identity and History* (2007).
M. Brown, 'Dugald Brown and the Problem of Teaching Politics in the 1790s', *Journal of Irish & Scottish Studies*, 1 (2007).
S. J. Brown, 'Religion and the Rise of Liberalism: The First Disestablishment Campaign in Scotland, 1829–43', *Journal of Ecclesiastical History*, 48 (1997).
D. Brunton, 'Policy, Powers and Practice: The Public Response to Public Health in the Scottish City', in D. Sturdy (ed.), *Medicine, Health and the Public Sphere in Britain, 1600–2000* (2002).
D. Brunton, '"Evil Necessities and Abominable Erections": Public Conveniences and Private Interests in the Scottish City, 1830–70', *Social History of Medicine*, 18 (2005).

D. Brunton, 'Health, Comfort and Convenience: Public Health and the Scottish Police Commissioners, 1800–70', *Scottish Archives*, 17 (2011).
K. Burgess, 'Authority Relations and the Division of Labour in British Industry, with Special Reference to Clydeside, c1860–1930', *Social History*, 11 (1986).
J. Butt, 'Capital and Enterprise in the Scottish Iron Industry, 1780–1840', in J. Butt and J. T. Ward (eds), *Scottish Themes* (1976).
J. Butt, 'Labour and Industrial Relations in the Scottish Cotton Industry during the Industrial Revolution', in J. Butt and K. Ponting (eds), *Scottish Textile History* (1987).
T. J. Byres, 'Entrepreneurship in the Scottish Heavy Industries, 1870–1900', in P. L. Payne (ed.), *Studies in Scottish Business History* (1967).
A. K. Cairncross and J. B. K. Hunter, 'The Early Growth of Messrs J. & P. Coats, 1830–83', *Business History*, 29 (1985).
K. J. Cameron, 'William Weir and the Origins of the "Manchester League" in Scotland, 1833–9', *SHR*, 58 (1979).
A. B. Campbell, 'Honourable Man and Degraded Slaves: A Comparative Study of Trade Unionism in Two Lanarkshire Mining Communities, c.1830–74', in R. Harrison (ed.), *Independent Collier: The Coal Miner as Archetypal Proletarian Reconsidered* (1978).
A. B. Campbell and F. Reid, 'The Independent Collier in Scotland', in R. Harrison (ed.), *Independent Collier: The Coal Miner as Archetypal Proletarian Reconsidered* (1978).
R. H. Campbell, 'Inter-County Migration in Scotland: The Experience of the South-West in the Nineteenth Century', *SESH*, 4 (1984).
R. H. Campbell, 'The Making of the Industrial City', in T. M. Devine and G. Jackson (eds), *Glasgow, Volume II: Beginnings to 1830* (1995).
I. Carter, 'Class and Culture among Farm Servants in the North-East', in A. A. MacLaren (ed.), *Social Class in Scotland: Past and Present* (n.d.).
R. A. Chandler, 'Questions of Ethics and Etiquette in the Society of Accountants in Edinburgh, 1853–1951', *Accounting History*, 22 (2017).
O. Checkland, 'Chalmers and William Pultney Alison: A Conflict in Scottish Social Policy', in A. C. Cheyne (ed.), *The Practical and the Pious: Essays on Thomas Chalmers, 1780–1847* (1985).
J. Christadolou, 'The Glasgow Universalist Church and Scottish Radicalism from the French Revolution to Chartism: A Theology of Liberation', *Journal of Ecclesiastical History*, 43 (1992).
P. Clapham, 'Agricultural Change and Its Impact on Tenancies: The Evidence of Angus Rentals and Tacks, 1760–1850', in A. J. G. Cummings and T. M. Devine (eds), *Industry, Business and Society in Scotland since 1700* (1994).
T. Clarke, 'Early Chartism in Scotland: A Moral Force Movement?', in T. M. Devine (ed.), *Conflict and Stability in Scottish Society, 1700–1850* (1990).

J. E. Cookson, 'The Napoleonic Wars, Military Scotland and Tory Highlandism in the Early Nineteenth Century', *SHR*, 78 (1999).

R. D. Corrins, 'The Great Hot-Blast Affair', *Industrial Archaeology*, 6 (1970).

R. D. Corrins, 'The Scottish Business Elite in the Nineteenth Century: The Case of William Baird & Co.', in A. J. G. Cummings and T. M. Devine (eds), *Industry, Business and Society in Scotland since 1700* (1994).

E. J. Cowan, 'The Covenanting Tradition in Scottish History', in E. J. Cowan and R. J. Finlay (eds), *Scottish History: The Power of the Past* (2002).

M. Cragoe, 'The Great Reform Act and the Modernisation of British Politics: The Impact of Conservative Associations, 1835–41', *Journal of British Studies*, 47 (2008).

B. L. Crapster, 'Scotland and the Conservative Party in 1876', *Journal of Modern History*, 29 (1957).

N. Davidson, 'Class Consciousness and National Consciousness: The Scottish General Strike of 1820', in K. Flett and D. Renton (eds), *New Approaches to Socialist History* (2003).

N. Davidson, 'The Scottish Path to Capitalist Agriculture, 2: The Capitalist Offensive, 1747–1815; 3: The Enlightenment as the Theory and Practice of Improvement', *Journal of Agrarian Change*, 4/5 (2004–5).

M. T. Davis, 'Prosecution and Radical Discourse during the 1790s: The Case of the Scottish Sedition Trials', *International Journal of the Sociology of Law*, 33 (2005).

T. Day, 'The Construction of Aberdeenshire's First Turnpike Roads', *Journal of Transport History*, 24 (2003).

N. Denny, 'Temperance and the Scottish Churches, 1870–1914', *RSCHS*, 23 (1988).

T. M. Devine, 'An Eighteenth-Century Business Elite: Glasgow West India Merchants, c.1750–1815', *SHR*, 57 (1978).

T. M. Devine, 'The Failure of Radical Reform in Scotland in the Later Eighteenth Century: The Social and Economic Context', in T. M. Devine (ed.), *Conflict and Stability in Scottish Society, 1700–1850* (1990).

T. M. Devine, 'The Making of a Farming Elite? Lowland Scotland, 1750–1850', in T. M. Devine (ed.), *Scottish Elites* (1994).

T. M. Devine, 'The Urban Crisis', in T. M. Devine and G. Jackson, *Glasgow, Volume I: Beginnings to 1830* (1995).

T. M. Devine, 'Industrialisation', and 'The Transformation of Agriculture: Cultivation and Clearance', in T. M. Devine et al. (eds), *The Transformation of Scotland: The Economy since 1700* (2005).

B. Dicks, 'Choice and Constraint: Further Perspectives on Socio-Residential Segregation in Nineteenth-Century Glasgow, with Particular Reference to Its West End', in G. Gordon (ed.), *Perspectives of the Scottish City* (1985).

T. Dickson and W. Spiers, 'Changes in the Class Structure in Paisley, 1750–1845', *SHR*, 60 (1981).

G. M. Ditchfield, 'The Scottish Representative Peers and Parliamentary Politics, 1787–93', *SHR*, 60 (1981).
F. K. Donnelly, 'The Scottish Rising of 1820: A Reinterpretation', *Scottish Tradition*, 6 (1976).
R. K. Donovan, 'The Popular Party of the Church of Scotland and the American Revolution', in R. B. Sher and J. R. Smithers (eds), *Scotland and America in the Age of Revolution* (1990).
M. Duffy, 'Pitt and the Origins of the Loyalist Association Movement of 1792', *Historical Journal*, 39 (1996).
R. Duncan, 'Artisans and Proletarians: Chartism and Working-Class Allegiance in Aberdeen, 1838–42', *Northern Scotland*, 4 (1981).
A. Durie, 'Market Forces and Intervention: The Spectacular Growth of the Linen Industry in Eighteenth Century Scotland', *Scotia*, 15 (1991).
M. Dyer, '"Mere Detail and Machinery": The Great Reform Act and the Effects of Redistribution on Scottish Representation, 1832–68', *SHR*, 62 (1983).
D. Englander, 'Wages Arrestment in Victorian Scotland', *SHR*, 62 (1983).
W. Ferguson, 'The Reform Act (Scotland) of 1832: Intention and Effect', *SHR*, 45 (1966).
W. Ferguson, 'The Electoral System in the Scottish Counties before 1832', in W. D. Sellar (ed.), *The Stair Society Miscellany*, 2 (1984).
R. J. Finlay, 'Queen Victoria and the Cult of the Scottish Monarchy', in E. J. Cowan and R. J. Finlay (eds), *Scottish History: The Power of the Past* (2002).
M. W. Flinn, 'Malthus, Emigration and Potatoes in the Scottish North-West, 1770–1870', in L. M. Cullen and T. C. Smout (eds), *Comparative Aspects of Scottish and Irish Economic and Social History, 1600–1900* (1978).
N. Forsyth, 'Presbyterian Historians and the Scottish Invention of British Liberty', *RSCHS*, 34 (2004).
J. Foster et al., 'Irish Immigrants in Scotland's Shipyards and Coalfields: Employment Relations, Sectarianism and Social Class', *Historical Research*, 84 (2011).
C. Frank, 'The Sheriff Court or the Company Store: Truck, the Arrestment of Wages and Working-Class Consumption in Scotland, 1870–71', *Labour History Review*, 79 (2014).
W. H. Fraser, 'Trade Unions, Reform and the Election of 1868 in Scotland', *SHR*, 50 (1971).
W. H. Fraser, 'Developments in Leisure', in W. H. Fraser and I. Maver (eds), *Glasgow, Volume II: 1830–1912* (1996).
W. H. Fraser, 'The Chartist Press in Scotland', in J. Allen and O. R. Ashton (eds), *Papers for the People: A Study of the Chartist Press* (2005).
W. H. Fraser and I. Maver, 'The Social Problems of the City', and 'Tackling the Problems', in W. H. Fraser and I. Maver (eds), *Glasgow, Volume II: 1830–1912* (1996).

M. T. Furgol, 'Chalmers and Poor Relief: An Incidental Sideline?', in A. C. Cheyne (ed.), *The Practical and the Pious: Essays on Thomas Chalmers, 1780–1847* (1985).

J. Fyfe, 'The *North British Review*: Advocate of Italian Independence', *Scottish Tradition*, 6 (1976).

J. Fyfe, 'Scottish Volunteers with Garibaldi', *SHR*, 57 (1978).

E. Gauldie, 'The Dundee Jute Industry', in J. Butt and K. G. Ponting (eds), *Scottish Textile History* (1985).

A. Gestrich and J. Stewart, 'Unemployment and Poor Relief in the West of Scotland, 1870–1900', in S. King and J. Stewart (eds), *Welfare Perspectives* (2007).

A. Gibb, 'Industrialization and Demographic Change: A Case Study of Glasgow, 1801–1914', in R. Lawton and R. Lee (eds), *Population and Society in West European Port-Cities, c.1650–1939* (2002).

S. D. Girvin, 'Nineteenth Century Reforms in Scottish Legal Education: The Universities and the Bar', *Journal of Legal History*, 14 (1993).

M. Goldie, 'The Scottish Catholic Enlightenment', *Journal of British Studies*, 30 (1991).

E. Gordon and G. Mair, 'Middle-Class Family Structure in Nineteenth-century Glasgow', *Journal of Family History*, 24 (1999).

W. M. Gordon, 'Highland Daughters, Lowland Wages: The Migration of Single Women from the Scottish Highlands to Abbey Parish, Paisley, c. 1851', *SLHSJ*, 32 (1997).

W. M. Gordon, 'The Demographics of Scottish Poverty: Paisley Applicants for Relief, 1861 and 1871', *JSHS*, 30 (2010).

W. M. Gordon, 'The Obligation to Support the Widow: Settlement, the New Poor Law and the Scottish Local State', *JSHS*, 35 (2015).

M. Gray, 'Migration in the Rural Lowlands of Scotland, 1750–1800', in T. M. Devine and D. Dickson (eds), *Ireland and Scotland, 1600–1850: Parallels and Contrasts in Economic and Social Development* (1983).

M. Gray, 'The Processes of Agricultural Change in the North-East, 1790–1870', in L. Leneman (ed.), *Perspectives in Scottish Social History* (1988).

M. Gray, 'North East Agriculture and the Labour Force, 1790–1875', in A. A. Maclaren (ed.), *Social Class in Scotland: Past and Present* (n.d.).

R. Q. Gray, 'Styles of Life, the "Labour Aristocracy" and Class Relations in Later Nineteenth Century Edinburgh', *International Review of Social History*, 18 (1973).

R. Q. Gray, 'Thrift and Working-Class Mobility in Victorian Edinburgh', in A. A. MacLaren (ed.), *Social Class in Scotland: Past and Present* (n.d.).

W. W. Groves, 'The New Poor Law in Nineteenth Century Scotland, with Special Reference to Lanarkshire', *Scottish Archives*, 8 (2002).

C. Gulvin, 'The Rise and Decline of Dickson & Lang, Hosiery Tweed Manufacturers, 1802–1908', *Transactions of the Hawick Archaeological Society* (1975).
C. Hamlin, 'Environmental Sensibility in Edinburgh, 1839–40: The "Fetid Irrigation" Controversy', *Journal of Urban History*, 20 (1994).
H. J. Hanham, 'Religion and Nationality in the Mid-Victorian Army', in M. R. D. Foot (ed.), *War and Society* (1973).
B. Harris, 'Scotland's Newspapers, the French Revolution and Domestic Radicalism (*c*.1789–1794)', *SHR*, 84 (2005).
B. Harris, 'Scottish–English Connections in British Radicalism of the 1790s', in T. C. Smout, *Anglo-Scottish Relations from 1603 to 1900* (2005).
B. Harris, 'Towns, Improvement and Cultural Change in Georgian Scotland: The Evidence of the Angus Burghs, 1760–1820', *Urban History*, 33 (2006).
B. Harris, 'Parliamentary Legislation, Lobbying and the Press in Eighteenth Century Scotland', *Parliamentary History*, 26 (2007).
B. Harris, 'Popular Politics in Angus and Perthshire in the Seventeen-Nineties', *Historical Research*, 80 (2007).
B. Harris, 'The Enlightenment, Towns and Urban Society in Scotland, *c*.1760–1820', *English Historical Review*, 126 (2011).
W. O. Henderson, 'The Cotton Famine in Scotland and the Relief of Distress, 1862–4', *SHR*, 30 (1951).
P. Hillis, 'Presbyterianism and Social Class in Mid-Victorian Glasgow: A Study of Nine Churches', *Journal of Ecclesiastical History*, 32 (1981).
P. Hillis, 'Education and Evangelisation: Presbyterian Missions in Mid-Nineteenth Century Glasgow', *SHR*, 66 (1987).
P. Hillis, 'Working-Class Membership of the Presbyterian Churches of Scotland, 1840–80', *SLHSJ*, 33 (1998).
P. Hillis, 'The Social Composition of the Cathedral Church of St Mungo in Late Nineteenth Century Glasgow', *JSHS*, 31 (2011).
P. L. M. Hillis, 'The Sociology of the Disruption', in S. J. Brown and M. Fry (eds), *Scotland in the Age of the Disruption* (1993).
J. C. Holley, 'The Two Family Economies of Industrialisation: Factory Workers in Victorian Scotland', *Journal of Family History*, 6 (1981).
V. Honeyman, '"A Very Dangerous Place": Radicalism in Perth in the 1790s', *SHR*, 87 (2008).
G. Houston, 'Labour Relations in Scottish Agriculture before 1870', *Agricultural History Review*, 6 (1958).
C. K. Hyde, 'The Adoption of the Hot Blast by the British Iron Industry', *Explorations in Economic History*, 10 (1973).
J. L. Innes, 'Landuse Changes in the Scottish Highlands in the Nineteenth Century: The Role of Pasture Degeneration', *SGM*, 99 (1983).

G. Jackson, 'The Trial for Treason of James Wilson, July, 1820', *Juridical Review* (1994).
M. Johnstone, 'Farm Rents and Improvement: East Lothian and Lanarkshire, 1670–1830', *Agricultural History Review*, 57 (2009).
B. A. Jones, 'The American Revolution, Glasgow and the Making of the Second City of Empire', in S. P. Newman (ed.), *Europe's American Revolution* (2006).
D. Jones, 'Women and Chartism', *History*, 68 (1983).
S. K. Kehoe, 'Irish Migrants and the Recruitment of Catholic Sisters in Glasgow, 1847–78', in F. Fergus and J. McConnel (eds), *Ireland and Scotland in the Nineteenth Century* (2009).
C. Kidd, 'Teutonist Ethnology and Scottish Nationalist Inhibition, 1780–1880', *SHR*, 74 (1995).
C. Kidd, 'Sentiment, Race and Revival: Scottish Identities in the Aftermath of Enlightenment', in L. Brockliss and D. Eastwood (eds), *A Union of Multiple Identities: The British Isles, c.1750–c.1850* (1997).
C. Kidd, 'Conditional Britons: The Scottish Covenanting Tradition and the Eighteenth Century British State', *English Historical Review*, 117 (2002).
C. Kidd, 'The Ideological Uses of the Picts, 1707–c.1900', in E. J. Cowan and R. J. Finlay (eds), *Scottish History: The Power of the Past* (2002).
C. Kidd, 'Race, Empire and the Limits of Nineteenth Century Scottish Nationhood', *Historical Review*, 46 (2003).
E. King, 'Popular Culture in Glasgow', in R. A. Cage (ed.), *The Working Class in Glasgow, 1780–1914* (1987).
K. Kinninmonth, 'Weber's Protestant Work Ethic: A Case Study of Scottish Entrepreneurs, the Coats Family of Paisley', *Business History*, 58 (2016).
W. Knox, 'Whatever Happened to Radical Scotland? The Economic and Social Origins of the Mid-Victorian Political Consensus in Scotland', in N. MacDougall and R. A. Mason (eds), *People and Power in Scotland* (1992).
W. Knox, 'Technology and Toil in Nineteenth Century Scotland: An Overview', *Études Écossaises*, 12 (2009).
M. Leask, 'Thomas Muir and *The Telegraph*: Radical Cosmopolitanism in 1790s Scotland', *History Workshop Journal*, 63 (2007).
I. Levitt, 'Welfare, Government and the Working Class: Scotland, 1845–1914', in D. McCrone et al. (eds), *The Making of Scotland: Nation, Culture and Social Change* (1989).
I. Levitt, 'Henry Littlejohn and Scottish Health Policy, 1859–1908', *Scottish Archives*, 2 (1996).
F. Lyall, 'The Case of the Ross and Cromarty Rangers (and the Aberdeen Riot)', *Juridical Review* (1995).
J. MacAskill, 'The Highland Kelp Proprietors and the Struggle over the Salt and Barilla Duties, 1817–31', *JSHS*, 26 (2006).

T. McBride, 'The Secular and the Radical in Irish Associational Culture in Mid-Victorian Glasgow', *Immigrants & Minorities*, 28 (2010).
J. McCaffrey, 'Thomas Chalmers and Social Change', *SHR*, 60 (1981).
J. F. McCaffrey, 'Roman Catholics in Scotland in the Nineteenth and Twentieth Centuries', *RSCHS*, 21 (1981–3).
M. W. McCahill, 'The Scottish Peerage and the House of Lords in the Late Eighteenth Century', in C. Jones and D. L. Jones (eds), *Peers, Politics and Power: The House of Lords, 1603–1911* (1986).
R. B. McCready, 'St Patrick's Day in Dundee, c 1850–1900: A Contested Irish Institution in a Scottish Context', in F. Fergus and J. McConnel (eds), *Ireland and Scotland in the Nineteenth Century* (2009).
J. McDermid, 'What to Do with Our Girls? The Schooling of Working-Class Girls in Scotland, 1872–1900', *History of Education Researcher*, 71 (2003).
J. McDermid, 'Handmaid to a Patriarchal Tradition: The Schoolmistress in Victorian Scotland', *Études Écossaises*, 9 (2003–4).
C. M. M. MacDonald, 'Abandoned and Beastly? The Queen Caroline Affair in Scotland', in Y. G. Brown and R. Ferguson (eds), *Twisted Sisters: Women, Crime and Deviance in Scotland since 1400* (2002).
C. M. M. MacDonald, '"Their Laurels Wither'd, and Their Name Forgot": Women and the Scottish Radical Tradition', in E. J. Cowan and R. J. Finlay (eds), *Scottish History: The Power of the Past* (2002).
H. MacDonald, 'Boarding-Out and the Scottish Poor Law, 1845–1914', *SHR*, 75 (1996).
E. W. McFarland, 'A Reality and Yet Impalpable: The Fenian Panic in Mid-Victorian Scotland', *SHR*, 77 (1998).
E. W. McFarland, 'Scottish Radicalism in the Later Eighteenth Century: "The Thistle and the Shamrock"', in T. M. Devine and J. R. Young (eds), *Eighteenth Century Scotland: New Perspectives* (1999).
G. I. T. Machin, 'The Disruption and British Politics, 1834–43', *SHR*, 51 (1972).
I. F. MacIver, 'The Evangelical Party and the Eldership in the General Assemblies, 1820–43', *RSCHS*, 20 (1978–80).
I. F. MacIver, 'Chalmers as a "Manager" of the Church, 1831–40', in A. C. Cheyne (ed.), *The Practical and the Pious: Thomas Chalmers, 1780–1847* (1985).
I. F. MacIver, 'Unfinished Business? The Highland Churches Scheme and the Government of Scotland, 1811–35', *RSCHS*, 25 (1993–5).
I. F. MacIver, 'Moderates and Wild Men: Religion, Politics and Party Division in the Church of Scotland, 1800–43', in A. Murdoch (ed.), *The Scottish Nation: Identity and History* (2007).
J. M. MacKenzie, 'Essay and Reflection: On Scotland and the Empire', *International History Review*, 15 (1993).

J. M. MacKenzie, 'Empire and National Identity: The Case of Scotland', *Transactions of the Royal Historical Society*, 6th ser., 8 (1998).
J. M. MacKenzie, 'Presbyterianism and Scottish Identity in Global Context', *Britain and the World*, 10 (2017).
F. MacKichan, 'A Burgh's Response to the Problems of Urban Growth: Stirling, 1780–1880', *SHR*, 57 (1978).
F. MacKichan, 'Lord Seaforth and Highland Estate Management in the First Phase of Clearance (1783–1815)', *SHR*, 86 (2007).
F. MacKichan, 'Lord Seaforth (1754–1815): The Lifestyle of a Highland Proprietor and Clan Chief', *Northern Scotland*, n.s., 5 (2014).
A. MacKillop, 'Community Coercion and Myth: The Recruitment of the Highland Regiments in the Late Eighteenth Century', *IRSS*, 26 (2001).
A. MacKillop, 'For King, Country and Regiment? Motive and Identity in Highland Soldiers, 1746–1815', in S. Murdoch and A. MacKillop (eds), *Fighting for Identity: The Scottish Military Experience, c 1500–1900* (2002).
A. MacKillop, 'The Political Culture of the Scottish Highlands from Culloden to Waterloo', *Historical Journal*, 46 (2003).
A. MacKillop, 'Riots and Reform: Burgh Authority, the Language of Civic Reform and the Aberdeen Riot of 1785', *Urban History*, 44 (2017).
S. McKinstry and Y. Y. Ding, 'Alex Cowan & Sons Ltd, Papermakers, Penicuik: A Scottish Case of Weber's Protestant Ethic', *Business History*, 55 (2013).
A. A. MacLaren, 'Presbyterianism and the Working-Class in a Mid-Nineteenth Century City', *SHR*, 46 (1967).
A. A. MacLaren, 'Class Formation and Class Fractions: The Aberdeen Bourgeoisie, 1830–50', in G. Gordon and B. Dicks (eds), *Scottish Urban History* (1983).
A. A. MacLaren, 'Patronage and Professionalism: The "Forgotten Middle Class", 1760–1860', in D. McCrone et al. (eds), *The Making of Scotland: Nation, Culture and Social Class* (1989).
A. A. MacLaren, 'Privilege, Patronage and the Professions: Aberdeen and Its Universities, 1760–1860', in J. J. Carter and D. J. Withrington (eds), *Scottish Universities: Distinctiveness and Diversity* (1992).
B. MacLellan, 'The Response of the Dundee Churches to the Coming of State Education', *RSCHS*, 29 (1999).
E. V. MacLeod, 'A City Invincible? Edinburgh and the War against Revolutionary France', *British Journal of Eighteenth Century Studies*, 23 (2000).
E. V. MacLeod, 'Scottish Responses to the Irish Rebellion, 1798', in T. Brotherstone et al. (eds), *These Fissured Isles: Irish, Scottish and British History, 1798–1848* (2005).
N. Mansfield, 'Radical Banners as Sites of Memory', in P. Pickering and A. Tyrell (eds), *Contested Sites: Commemoration, Memorial and Popular Politics in Nineteenth Century Britain* (2004).

B. Marsden, 'Ranking Rankine: W. J. M. Rankine (1820–1872) and the Making of "Engineering Science" Revisited', *History of Science*, 51 (2013).
W. M. Mathew, 'The Origins and Occupations of Glasgow Students, 1740–1839', *Past & Present*, 33 (1966).
I. Maver, 'Politics and Power in the Scottish City: Glasgow Town Council in the Nineteenth Century', in T. M. Devine (ed.), *Scottish Elites* (1994).
I. Maver, 'The Guardianship of the Community: Civic Authority Prior to 1833', in T. M. Devine and G. Jackson (eds), *Glasgow, Volume I: Beginnings to 1830* (1995).
I. Maver, 'Glasgow's Civic Government', in W. H. Fraser and I. Maver (eds), *Glasgow, Volume II: 1830–1912* (1996).
I. Maver, 'Leisure and Culture in the Nineteenth Century', in W. H. Fraser and C. H. Lee (eds), *Aberdeen, 1800–2000: A New History* (2000).
D. E. Meek, 'The Gaelic Bible, Revival and Mission: The Spiritual Rebirth of the Nineteenth Century Highlands', in J. Kirk (ed.), *The Church in the Highlands* (1998).
J. Melling, 'Employers, Industrial Housing and the Evolution of Company Welfare Policies in Britain's Heavy Industry in the West of Scotland, 1870–1920', *International Review of Social History*, 26 (1981).
I. Meredith, 'Irish Migrants in the Scottish Episcopal Church in the Nineteenth Century', in M. J. Mitchell (ed.), *New Perspectives on the Irish in Scotland* (2008).
R. C. Michie, 'Trade and Transport and the Economic Development of North-Eastern Scotland in the Nineteenth Century', *SESH*, 3 (1983).
G. F. Millar, 'Maynooth and Scottish Politics: The Role of the Maynooth Grant Issue, 1845–57', *RSCHS*, 27 (1997).
G. F. Millar, 'The Conservative Split in the Scottish Counties, 1841–7 [*recte*, 1841–57]', *SHR*, 81 (2001).
D. C. Miller, 'Of Patents, Principles and the Construction of Heroic Invention: The Case of Neilson's Hot-Blast in Iron Production', *Proceedings of the American Philosophical Society*, 160 (2016).
M. Milne, 'Archibald Alison: Conservative Controversialist', *Albion*, 27 (1995).
L. Miskell, 'Civic Leadership and the Manufacturing Elite: Dundee, 1820–70', in L. Miskell et al. (eds), *Victorian Dundee: Images and Realities* (2000).
L. Miskell, 'From Conflict to Co-operation in Urban Improvement: The Case of Dundee, 1790–1850', *Urban History*, 29 (2002).
L. Miskell and C. A. Whatley, '"Juteopolis" in the Making: Linen and the Industrial Transformation of Dundee, c. 1820–50', *Textile History*, 30 (1999).
M. J. Mitchell, 'The Catholic Irish and Chartism in the West of Scotland', in T. Brotherstone et al. (eds), *These Fissured Isles: Ireland, Scotland and British History, 1798–1848* (2005).

M. J. Mitchell, 'Irish Catholics in the West of Scotland in the Nineteenth Century: Despised by Scottish Workers and Controlled by the Church?', in M. J. Mitchell (ed.), *New Perspectives on the Irish in Scotland* (2008).
F. Montgomery, 'The Unstamped Press: The Contribution of Glasgow, 1831–6', *SHR*, 59 (1980).
F. Montgomery, 'Glasgow and the Struggle for Parliamentary Reform, 1830–32', *SHR*, 61 (1982).
L. R. Moore, 'The Aberdeen Ladies Educational Association, 1877–83', *Northern Scotland*, 3 (1977–80).
L. Moore, 'Invisible Scholars: Girls Learning Latin and Mathematics in the Elementary Public Schools of Scotland before 1872', *History of Education*, 13 (1984).
L. Moore, 'Educating for the "Woman's Sphere": Domestic Training versus Intellectual Discipline', in E. Breitenbach and E. Gordon (eds), *Out of Bounds: Women in Scottish Society, 1800–1945* (1992).
L. Moore, 'The Scottish Universities and Women Students, 1862–92', in J. J. Carter and D. J. Withrington (eds), *Scottish Universities: Distinctiveness and Diversity* (1992).
L. Moore, 'Young Ladies' Institutions and the Development of Secondary Schools for Girls in Scotland, 1833–c.1870', *History of Education*, 32 (2003).
J. Mori, 'Responses to Revolution: The November Crisis of 1792', *Historical Research*, 69 (1996).
J. B. Morrell, 'The Leslie Affair: Careers, Kirk and Politics in Edinburgh, 1805', *SHR*, 54 (1975).
R. J. Morris, 'Urban Associations in England and Scotland, 1750–1914: The Formation of the Middle Class or the Formation of Civil Society?', in G. Morton et al. (eds), *Civil Society Associations and Urban Places* (2006).
G. Morton, 'Civil Society, Municipal Government and the State: Enshrinement, Empowerment and Legitimacy in Scotland, 1800–1929', *Urban History*, 25 (1998).
G. Morton, '"The Most Efficacious Patriot": The Legacy of William Wallace in Nineteenth Century Scotland', *SHR*, 77 (1998).
G. Morton, 'Scotland is British: The Union and Unionist-Nationalism, 1807–1907', *Journal of Irish & Scottish Studies*, 1 (2007).
I. A. Muirhead, 'Churchmen and the Problem of Prostitution in Nineteenth Century Scotland', *RSCHS*, 18 (1972–4).
I. A. Muirhead, 'Catholic Emancipation in Scotland: [1] The Scottish Reaction; [2] The Debate and the Aftermath', *Innes Review*, 24 (1973).
C. W. Munn, 'Scottish Provincial Banking Companies: An Assessment', *Business History*, 23 (1981).

C. W. Munn, 'The Development of Joint-Stock Banking in Scotland, 1810–45', in A. Slaven and D. H. Aldcroft (eds), *Business, Banking and Urban History* (1982).
C. W. Munn, 'Aspects of Bank Finance for Industry in Scotland, 1845–1914', in R. Mitchison and P. Roebuck (eds), *Economy and Society in Scotland and Ireland, 1500–1939* (1988).
A. Murdoch, 'Scotland and the Idea of Britain in the Eighteenth Century', in T. M. Devine and R. J. Young (eds), *Eighteenth Century Scotland: New Perspectives* (1999).
A. Mutch, 'A Contested Eighteenth-Century Election: Banffshire, 1795', *Northern Scotland*, n.s., 2 (2011).
S. Nenadic, 'Political Reform and the "Ordering" of Middle Class Protest', in T. M. Devine (ed.), *Conflict and Stability in Scottish Society, 1700–1850* (1990).
S. Nenadic, 'The Small Family Firm in Victorian Britain', *Business History*, 35 (1993).
S. Nenadic, 'The Middle Ranks and Modernisation', in T. M. Devine and G. Jackson (eds), *Glasgow, Volume II: Beginnings to 1830* (1995).
S. Nenadic, 'The Victorian Middle Classes', in W. H. Fraser and I. Maver (eds), *Glasgow, Volume II: 1830–1912* (1996).
S. Nenadic, 'Experience and Expectation: The Transformation of the Highland Gentlewoman 1680–1820', *SHR*, 80 (2001).
S. Nenadic, 'The Impact of the Military Profession on Highland Gentry Families, 1730–1830', *SHR*, 85 (2006).
S. Nenadic, 'Gender and the Rhetoric of Business Success: The Impact on Women Entrepreneurs and the "New Woman" in Late Nineteenth Century Edinburgh', in N. Goose (ed.), *Women's Work in Industrial England: Regional and Local Perspectives* (2007).
A. G. Newby, 'Land and the "Crofter Question" in Nineteenth Century Scotland', *IRSS*, 35 (2010).
M. Nicolson and I. Donnachie, 'The New Lanark Highlanders: Migration, Community and Language', *Family & Community History*, 6 (2003).
S. M. Nisbet, 'The Making of Scotland's First Industrial Region: The Early Cotton Industry in Renfrewshire', *JSHS*, 29 (2009).
M. Nixon et al., 'The Material Culture of Scottish Reform Politics, c.1820–c.1884', *JSHS*, 32 (2012).
A. Noble, 'Urbane Silence: Scottish Writing and the Nineteenth Century City', in G. Gordon (ed.), *Perspectives of the Scottish City* (1985).
A. O'Reilly, '"All Irishmen of Good Character": The Hibernian Society of Glasgow, 1792–1824', in F. Fergus and J. O'Connel (eds), *Ireland and Scotland in the Nineteenth Century* (2009).

T. E. Orme, 'Toasting Fox: The Fox Dinners in Edinburgh and Glasgow, 1801–25', *History*, 99 (2014).
B. D. Osborne, 'Dumbarton Shipbuilding and Workers' Housing, 1850–1900', *Scottish Industrial History*, 3 (1980).
J. Patrick, 'The 1806 Election in Aberdeenshire', *Northern Scotland*, 1 (1972–3).
P. Payne, 'The Savings Bank of Glasgow, 1836–1914', in P. L. Payne (ed.), *Studies in Scottish Business History* (1967).
H. B. Peebles, 'A Study in Failure: J. & G. Thomson and Shipbuilding at Clydebank, 1871–90', *SHR*, 69 (1990).
G. Pentland, 'Patriotism, Universalism and the Scottish Conventions, 1792–4', *History*, 89 (2004).
G. Pentland, 'Scotland and the Creation of a National Reform Movement, 1820–32', *Historical Journal*, 48 (2005).
G. Pentland, 'The Debate on Scottish Parliamentary Reform, 1830–32', *SHR*, 85 (2006).
G. Pentland, 'The French Revolution, Radicalism and the "People Who Were Called Jacobins"', in U. Broich et al. (eds), *Reactions to Revolutions in the 1790s and Their Aftermath* (2007).
G. Pentland, '"Betrayed by Infamous Spies"? The Commemoration of Scotland's "Radical War"', *Past & Present*, 201 (2008).
G. Pentland, 'Radical Returns in the Age of Revolutions', *Études Écossaises*, 13 (2010).
L. Peters, 'The Scottish Borders and the American Civil War', *Northern History*, 39 (2002).
L. J. Philip, 'The Creation of Settlements in Rural Scotland: Planned Villages in Dumfries and Galloway', *SGM*, 119 (2003).
M. Pittock and C. A. Whatley, 'Poems and Festivals, Art and Artefact and the Commemoration of Robert Burns, c.1844–c.1896', *SHR*, 93 (2014).
A. Plassart, 'Scottish Perspectives on War and Patriotism in the 1790s', *Historical Journal*, 57 (2014).
G. D. Pollock, 'Saints and Sinners: Church Members in Glasgow's East End, 1873–85', *IRSS*, 31 (2006).
C. Pulsifer, 'Nationality, Social Background and Wealth in a Mid-Victorian Highland Regiment: The Officer Corps of the 78th Highland Regiment, 1868–71', *Scottish Tradition*, 23 (1998).
J. Rendall, '"Women That Would Plague Us With Rational Conversation": Aspiring Women and Scottish Whigs, 1790–1830', in S. Knott and B. Taylor (eds), *Women, Gender and Enlightenment* (2005).
P. Richard, 'The State and Early Industrial Capitalism: The Case of the Handloom Weavers', *Past & Present*, 83 (1979).
E. Richards, 'Highland Emigration in the Age of Malthus: Scourie, 1841–51', *Northern Scotland*, n.s., 2 (2011).

P. Riggs, 'The Standard of Living in Scotland, 1800–50', in J. Kolmos (ed.), *Stature, Living Standards and Economic Development* (1994).
A. J. Robertson, 'The Decline of the Scottish Cotton Industry, 1860–1914', *Business History*, 12 (1970).
P. Robertson, 'Scottish Universities and Industry, 1860–1914', *SESH*, 4 (1984).
M. Robson, 'The Borders Farm Workers', in T. M. Devine (ed.), *Scottish Farm Servants and Labour in Lowland Scotland, 1750–1914* (1984).
R. Rodger, 'The Law and Urban Change: Some Nineteenth Century Scottish Evidence', *Urban History Yearbook* (1979).
R. Rodger, 'Speculative Builders and the Structure of the Scottish Building Industry, 1860–1914', *Business History*, 21 (1979).
R. Rodger, 'Employment, Wages and Poverty in the Scottish Cities', in G. Gordon (ed.), *Perspectives of the Scottish City* (1985).
R. Rodger, 'The Victorian Building Industry and the Housing of the Scottish Working Class', in M. Doughty (ed.), *Building the Industrial City* (1986).
R. Rodger, 'Working Class Housing Problems in Britain, 1850–1914', *International Review of Social History*, 36 (1987).
R. Rodger, 'Concentration and Fragmentation: Capital, Labor and the Structure of Mid-Victorian Scottish Industry', *Journal of Urban History*, 14 (1988).
W. D. Rubinstein, 'New Men of Wealth and the Purchase of Land in Nineteenth Century England', *Past & Present*, 92 (1981).
B. Schmidt, 'Dugald Stewart, "Conjectural History" and the Decline of Enlightenment Historical Writing in the 1790s', in U. Broich (ed.), *Reactions to Revolution in the 1790s, and Their Aftermath* (2007).
I. J. Shaw, 'John Paton and Urban Mission in Nineteenth Century Glasgow', *RSCHS*, 35 (2005).
J. S. Shaw, 'Land, People and Nation: Historicist Voices and the Highland Land Campaign, c.1850–83', in E. Biagini (ed.), *Citizenship and Community: Liberals, Radicals and Collective Identities in the British Isles, 1865–1931* (1996).
A. Sheps, 'The Edinburgh Reform Convention of 1793 and the American Revolution', *Scottish Tradition*, 5 (1975).
R. Sher and A. Murdoch, 'Patronage and Party in the Church of Scotland, 1750–1800', in N. MacDougall (ed.), *Church, Politics and Society in Scotland, 1400–1929* (1983).
M. Simpson, 'Urban Transport and the Development of Glasgow's West End, 1830–1914', *Journal of Transport History*, n.s., 1 (1972–3).
M. Simpson, 'The West End of Glasgow, 1830–1914', in M. Simpson and T. H. Lloyd (eds), *Middle Class Housing in Britain* (1977).
M. Skinnider, 'Catholic Elementary Education in Glasgow, 1818–1918', in T. R. Bone (ed.), *Studies in the History of Scottish Education, 1872–1939* (1967).

A. Slaven, 'Entrepreneurs and Business Success and Business Failure in Scotland', in D. H. Alcroft and A. Slaven (eds), *Enterprise and Management: Essays in Honour of Peter L. Payne* (1995).
W. Sloan, 'Employment Opportunities and Migrant Group Assimilation: The Highlanders and Irish in Glasgow, 1840–60', in A. J. G. Cummings and T. M. Devine (eds), *Industry, Business and Society in Scotland since 1700* (1994).
C. Smith, 'Witnessing Power: John Elder and the Making of the Marine Compound Engine, 1850–58', *Technology & Culture*, 55 (2014).
J. A. Smith, 'The Free Church Constitutionalists and the Establishment Principle', *Northern Scotland*, 22 (2002).
J. H. Smith, 'The Cattle Trade of Aberdeenshire in the Nineteenth Century', *Agricultural History Review*, 3 (1955).
P. J. Smith, 'The Foul Burns of Edinburgh: Public Health Attitudes and Environmental Change', *SGM*, 91 (1975).
P. J. Smith, 'The Legislated Control of River Pollution in Victorian Scotland', *SGM*, 98 (1982).
P. J. Smith, 'The Rehousing/Relocation Issue in an Early Slum Clearance Scheme: Edinburgh, 1865–85', *Urban Studies*, 26 (1989).
P. J. Smith, 'Slum Clearance as an Instrument of Sanitary Reform: The Flawed Vision of Edinburgh's First Slum Clearance Scheme', *Planning Perspectives*, 9 (1994).
S. S. Smith, 'Retaking the Register: Women's Higher Education in Glasgow and beyond, c. 1796–1845', *Gender & History*, 12 (2000).
T. C. Smout, 'Where Had the Scottish Economy Got to by the Third Quarter of the Eighteenth Century?', in I. Hont and M. Ignatieff (eds), *Wealth and Virtue: The Shaping of Political Economy in the Scottish Enlightenment* (1983).
T. C. Smout, 'A New Look at the Scottish Improvers', *SHR*, 91 (2012).
J. Smyth, 'Thomas Chalmers, the "Godly Commonwealth" and Contemporary Welfare Reform in Great Britain and the USA', *Historical Journal*, 57 (2014).
L. Soltow, 'Inequality of Wealth in Land in Scotland in the Eighteenth Century', *SESH*, 10 (1990).
E. Spiers, 'Highland Soldier: Imperial Impact and Image', *Northern Scotland*, n.s., 1 (2010)
H. Strachan, 'Scotland's Military Identity', *SHR*, 85 (2006).
W. W. Straka, 'The Law of Combination in Scotland Reconsidered', *SHR*, 64 (1985).
R. M. Sunter, 'The Problems of Recruitment for Scottish Line Regiments during the Napoleonic Wars', *Scottish Tradition*, 26 (2001).
C. Swan, 'Female Investors within the Scottish Investment Trust Movement in the 1870s', in A. Lawrence et al. (eds), *Women and Their Money, 1700–1950* (2009).

F. Szasz, 'Scotland, Abraham Lincoln and the American Civil War', *Northern Scotland*, 16 (1996).
M. Townsley, '"Store Their Minds with Much Valuable Knowledge": Agricultural Improvement at the Selkirk Subscription Library, 1799–1814', *British Journal of 18th Century Studies*, 38 (2015).
R. H. Trainor, 'The Elite', in W. H. Fraser and I. Maver (eds), *Glasgow, Volume II: 1830–1912* (1996).
N. L. Tranter, 'Popular Sports and the Industrial Revolution in Scotland: The Evidence of the Statistical Accounts', *International Journal of the History of Sport*, 4 (1987).
N. L. Tranter, 'The Social and Occupational Structure of Organised Sport in Central Scotland during the 19th Century', *International Journal of the History of Sport*, 4 (1987).
N. L. Tranter, 'Organised Sport and the Middle-Class Woman in Nineteenth Century Scotland', *International Journal of the History of Sport*, 6 (1989).
N. L. Tranter, 'The Chronology of Organised Sport in Nineteenth Century Scotland: A Regional Study – I: Patterns; II: Causes', *International Journal of the History of Sport*, 6 (1990).
N. L. Tranter, 'Women and Sport in Nineteenth Century Scotland', in G. Jarvie and J. Burnett (eds), *Sport, Scotland and the Scots* (2000).
J. H. Treble, 'The Development of Roman Catholic Education in Scotland, 1878–1978', in D. McRoberts (ed.), *Modern Scottish Catholicism* (1979).
M. Turnbull, 'Bishop Geddes and Robert Burns', *Innes Review*, 67 (2016).
W. H. K. Turner, 'Flax Weaving in Scotland in the Early Nineteenth Century', *SGM*, 99 (1983).
A. Tyrell, 'Political Economy, Whiggism and the Education of Working-Class Adults in Scotland, 1817–40', *SHR*, 48 (1969).
A. Tyrell, 'Paternalism, Public Memory and National Identity in Early Victorian Scotland: The Robert Burns Festival at Ayr in 1844', *History*, 90 (2005).
A. Tyrell, 'The Earl of Eglinton, Scottish Conservatism and the National Association for the Vindication of Scottish Rights', *Historical Journal*, 53 (2010).
A. Tyrell and M. T. Davis, 'Bearding the Tories: The Commemoration of the Scottish Political Martyrs of 1793–4', in P. Pickering and A. Tyrell (eds), *Contested Sites: Commemoration, Memorial and Popular Politics in Nineteenth Century Britain* (2004).
R. E. Tyson, 'The City of Glasgow Bank in the Crisis of 1857', in D. H. Aldcroft and A. Slaven (eds), *Enterprise and Management: Essays in Honour of Peter L. Payne* (1995).
R. Tyzack, '"No Mean City"? The Growth of Civic Consciousness in Aberdeen with Particular to the Work of the Police Commissioners', in T. Brotherstone

and D. J. Withrington (eds), *The City and Its Works: Aspects of Aberdeen's History since 1794* (1996).

W. Vamplew, 'Railways and the Iron Industry: A Study of Their Relationship in Scotland', in M. C. Reed (ed.), *Railways in the Victorian Economy* (1969).

W. Vamplew, 'Railways and the Transformation of the Scottish Economy', *Economic History Review*, 24 (1971).

E. Vincent, 'The Responses of Scottish Churchmen to the French Revolution', *SHR*, 73 (1994).

F. Voges, 'Moderate and Evangelical Thinking in the Later Eighteenth Century: Differences and Shared Attitudes', *RSCHS*, 22 (1984–6).

E. M. Wainwright, 'Dundee's Jute Mills and Factories: Spaces of Production, Surveillance and Discipline', *SGM*, 121 (2005).

D. M. Walker, 'Legal Studies and Scholarship in the Age of David Murray, 1842–1928', *Juridical Review* (1993).

F. Walker, 'National Romanticism and the Architecture of the City', in G. Gordon (ed.), *Perspectives of the Scottish City* (1985).

J. T. Ward, 'The Factory Reform Movement in Scotland', *SHR*, 41 (1962).

J. T. Ward, 'Textile Trade Unionism in Nineteenth Century Scotland', in J. Butt and K. G. Ponting (eds), *Scottish Textile History* (1985).

A. Watson and E. Allan, 'Depopulation by Clearance and Non-enforced Emigration in the North-East Highlands', *Northern Scotland*, 10 (1990).

R. K. Webb, 'Literacy among the Working Classes in Nineteenth Century Scotland', *SHR*, 33 (1954).

P. W. Werth, 'Through the Prism of Prostitution: State, Society and Power', *Social History*, 19 (1994).

C. A. Whatley, 'Royal Day, People's Day: The Monarch's Birthday in Scotland, c.1660–1860', in R. A. Mason and N. MacDougall (eds), *People and Power in Scotland* (1992).

C. A. Whatley, 'Women and the Economic Transformation of Scotland, c.1740–1880', *SESH*, 14 (1994).

C. A. Whatley, 'Labour in the Industrialising City, c.1660–1830', in T. M. Devine and G. Jackson (eds), *Glasgow, Volume II: Beginnings to 1830* (1995).

C. A. Whatley, 'Custom, Commerce and Lord Meadowbank: The Management of the Meal Market in Scotland, c.1740–c.1820', *JSHS*, 32 (2012).

I. D. Whyte, 'Urbanization in Early Modern Scotland: A Preliminary Analysis', *SESH*, 9 (1989).

C. W. J. Withers, 'Class, Culture and Migrant Identity: Gaelic Highlanders in Urban Scotland', in G. K. Kearns and C. W. J. Withers (eds), *Urbanising Britain: Essays on Class and Community in the Nineteenth Century* (1991).

D. J. Withrington, 'The 1851 Census of Religious Worship and Education, with a Note on Church Accommodation in Mid-Nineteenth Century Scotland', *RSCHS*, 18 (1972–4).

D. J. Withrington, 'The Making of the Veto Act, 1832–4', *RSCHS*, 28 (1998).
A. S. Wold, 'Loyalism in Scotland in the 1790s', in U. Broich et al. (eds), *Reactions to Revolutions in the 1790s and Their Aftermath* (2007).
C. Young, 'The Economic Characteristics of Small Craft Businesses in Rural Perthshire, c. 1830–1900', *Business History*, 36 (1994).
C. Young, 'Rural Artisan Production in the East-Central Lowlands of Scotland, c. 1600–1850', *SESH*, 16 (1996).

Index

Abbotsford, 167
Abercromby, James, 165, 218, 218–19, 223, 226
Aberdeen, 12, 13, 47, 55, 64, 65, 67, 69, 70, 73, 78, 91, 100, 102, 113, 130, 135, 136, 138, 144, 150, 169, 184, 185, 187, 190, 220, 268, 292
Aberdeen, 4th earl of, 133, 250, 250–1, 258; 1st marquess of, 284
Aberdeen Banking Co., 50
Aberdeenshire, 13, 15–16, 17, 49, 123, 129, 170, 288
Aberlour Orphanage, 120
Acharn, 26
Adam, Robert, 167
Adam, Wm, 189, 198, 207, 210
Adam, Wm Patrick, 283, 284
Addington, Henry, 208
Administrative Reform Association, 257
Admiralty, 45, 59–60
Advocates, Faculty of, 66, 209
Afghanistan, 286
Africa, 159
  South, 62, 160, 286
Agnew, Sir Andrew, 244
Aikey Brae Fair, 21
Airdrie, 95, 180
Alexander, Wm, 288
Alford, 7
Alison, Prof. Wm P., 145
Alison, Sheriff Sir Archibald, 232, 240, 242, 243
Allan Shipping Line, 62

Alloa, 16
Almond river, 103
Althorp, Lord, 216
Alva, 39, 156, 161
Amalgamated Society of Engineers, 269
America
  Latin/South, 10, 18, 51, 57, 61, 62, 225
  North, 1, 51, 57, 61
  see also Canada; United States of America
Anderson, Adam, 164
Andersonian Institute, 53
Angus, 15, 39, 46, 190, 214, 222, 259
Anstruther East, 186
Anstruther, Sir John, 210
anti-Catholicism, 170–3, 251; see also sectarianism
Anti-Corn Law League, 248–50, 249, 260, 261, 264, 274
Arbroath, 102, 224
Archiestown, 19
architecture, 167
Ardrossan, 16, 43
Ardtornish, 26
Argyll, duke of, 7th, 33–4; 8th, 246–7, 250–1, 297
Argyllshire, 22, 24, 26, 30, 135, 155, 170, 190
Arkwright, Richard, 38
Army recruitment, 28, 29–30, 155–6, 199–200, 203
Arnott & Co., 77
Arrol, Sir Wm, 45

INDEX 335

art, 166–7, 168
Arthur, Jane, 275
Assynt, 25
athletics, 87
Atholl, duke of
    4th, 204, 205, 216
    6th, 247
Auchterarder, 130, 134
Auckland, Lady, 233; *see also* Elliot, Gilbert
Australia, 34, 61, 140, 160
Ayr, 102, 222
Ayrshire, 9, 16, 22, 37, 42, 43, 49, 50, 58, 59, 68, 95, 169, 172, 181, 190, 191, 195, 215, 260

Baillie, Peter, 210
Bain, Andrew G., 160
Bain, James, 294–5
Baird, James, 55, 68, 249, 291
Baird, John, ironmaster, 68
Baird, John, radical, 215
Baird, Wm, 68, 249
Baird, Wm, & Co., 42, 50, 54, 58, 60, 61
Balkans, 286
Ballater, 237
Ballot Act (1872), 289
Balmoral Castle, 34, 154, 167
Balzac, Honoré de, 166
Band of Hope, 279
Banffshire, 15, 170
Baptists, 123
Barcaldine Castle, 31
Barra, Isle of, 33
Bathgate, 27
battles
    Balaclava (1854), 155, 286
    Camperdown (1797), 158
    Corunna (1809), 158
    Culloden (1746), 2, 166
    Jemappe (1792), 192
Baxter Brothers & Co., 39, 55, 57
Baxter Park, 68
Baxter, W. E., 68, 258, 259
Beardmore, Wm & Co., 45–6
Beardmore, Wm, Junior, 53

Begg, Rev. James, 140, 145, 162
Bellenden, 5th baron, 206–7
Bengal, 2
Bennett, Samuel, 265
Berlioz, Hector, 166
Bettyhill, 25
Binning, Lord, 226
Birmingham, 281
Bizet, Georges, 166
Black, Adam, 68–9, 256
Black, Prof. Joseph, 16, 53
Blackie, Lord Provost John, 114
Blackie, Prof. John Stuart, 157
Blackwood's Magazine, 226–7, 227–8, 231–2, 234, 243, 244
Blind, Karl, 162, 268
boarding-out, 120
Bonnybridge, 215
Borders, 25, 38, 39, 48, 80, 81
bowls, 87
Bowring, Sir John, 253
Brahan Castle, 32
Braxfield, Lord, 188
Breadalbane, marquess of
    1st, 204
    1st [new creation], 284
    2nd, 247
Brechin, 130
Brewster, Principal Sir David, 255–6
Brewster, Rev. Patrick, 145, 263, 264
bridges, 15
Bridgewater, duke of, 24
Bright, John, 160, 257, 259, 268, 270
Bristol, 231
British Convention of the Friends of the People, 194
Brodie of Brodie, James, 204
Brontë, Charlotte, 166
Brontë, Emily, 166
Brora, 25
Brougham, Henry, 216, 221, 222
Bruce, King Robert, 153, 161–2
Brunel, Isambard K., 46
Buccleuch, duchess of, 5th, 173
Buccleuch, duke of, 3rd, 9, 14, 15, 204; 5th, 226, 247, 250
Buchanan, George, 151, 153

burgh reform movement, 64–5, 184–7, 189, 193, 219–20, 229
Burke, Edmund, 185–6, 192, 201, 221, 231
Burma, 62
Burns, George, 54
Burns, Robert, 86, 165, 171, 190, 204, 294
Burns, Wm, 162
Burton, J. Hill, 154
Bute
  earl of, 3rd, 157, 190
  marquess of, 1st, 198
  marquess of, 3rd, 173, 240
Bute, Isle of, 37
Butler, Josephine, 278
by-elections
  Aberdeen (1872), 280
  Angus (1872), 289
  Ayrshire (1829), 234
  Edinburgh (1839), 254
  Glasgow (1837), 254; (1879), 284
  Greenock (1878), 276, 279, 281, 284
  Paisley (1836), 253
  Perthshire (1840), 133, 246

Cadder Iron Co., 41
Caird, Principal Rev. John, 293
Cairns, Rev. John, 137
Caithness, 250
Calabar, 159
Caledonian canal, 46
Caledonian Railway Co., 49
Callander, James T., 191
Calvinism, 54
Cameron, Dr Charles, 277, 280, 281, 284
Campbell of Barcaldine, Sir Duncan, 31–2
Campbell, Richard Vary, 293
Campbell-Bannerman, Henry 297–8
Campbeltown, 58
Camperdown Mills, 41
Canada, 2, 24, 62, 120, 158–60, 172;
  see also America, North
canals, 46–7
Candlish, Rev. Robert, 134
Canning, George, 223, 225, 226, 227, 228
Canonbie, 7
Captain Swing disturbances, 20, 231
Carmichael, Peter, 55
Caroline, Queen, 221, 222, 224, 233–4

Carron, 159
Carron Iron Co., 45, 60, 203, 215
Cart river, 103
Cartwright, Major John, 213–14, 215
Celtic Magazine, 156
Celtic societies, urban, 35
Celts, 156
Chadwick, Edwin, 102, 276
Chalmers, Rev. Thomas, 71, 114, 116–18, 120, 126–7, 129, 133–4, 142, 145, 159, 171, 221
Chamber of Agriculture, 289
Chamberlain, Joseph, 281, 282
Chambers, Robert, 138
Chambers, Wm, 255–6
Chambers of Commerce, 219–20
Charles X, king, of France, 230
Chartism, 78, 90, 145, 174, 179, 215–16, 259–65, 269–70
child labour, 83–4, 143, 144–5
China, 61, 62, 230, 258–9
Church of England, 122, 132, 145, 246
Church of Scotland, 2, 4, 35–6, 64–5, 66, 77, 88, 116–18, 122–39, 140–1, 145–6, 171, 183–4, 196, 197, 225, 228, 244, 255–7, 276, 292–3
  Disruption, 127–34, 245–6
  Evangelicals, 66, 125–32, 133–5, 198, 221, 228, 244–7
  Moderates, 23, 35, 66, 125–8, 130–1, 134, 157, 171, 183–4, 197, 221, 245
  politics, 131–5, 245–7, 255–7, 283–4, 285
  see also Free Church of Scotland; United Presbyterian Church; Voluntary Presbyterian Churches
Church Liberals, 283, 285, 293
Church Service Society, 138
City of Glasgow Bank, 51–3, 107
Clackmannanshire, 16, 25, 38, 207, 251
Claim of Right, 131–2
Clanranald see MacDonald of
Clark, J. & J., & Co., 57, 61
Clerk, Sir George, 6th baronet, 225–6, 227
Clyde Iron Works, 41
Clyde river, 37, 43, 49, 103
Clydesdale Bank, 51
Coatbridge, 42, 169
Coats, J. & P., & Co., 38, 50–1, 57, 60

INDEX 337

Coats, Thomas, 123
Cobbett, Wm, 8
Cobden, Richard, 160, 257, 259
Cockburn, Henry, 133, 164, 183, 216, 217, 221, 223, 226
Coigach, 34
Coll, Isle of, 30
Collins, Wm, Junior, 247, 277, 279–80
Collins, Wm, Senior, 129, 246
Colman, J. S., 282
Colquhoun, A. Campbell, 164
Colville, David, 51, 58
Combination Laws, Repeal of, 90, 215, 225
Commercial Bank of Scotland, 51
Complete Suffrage Union, 78, 264
Condie, John, 56
Condorcet, marquis de, 198
Congregationalists, 123
Conservative party (including Tories), 4–5, 22, 66, 132–3, 200–7, 209–10, 224–8, 231–2, 239, 240–51, 259, 272–3, 275, 283, 286–99
constituencies
    Aberdeen (post-1832), 237, 242, 252, 253, 255, 257, 259, 275, 276, 280
    Aberdeen Burghs (pre-1832), 224, 233
    Aberdeen & Glasgow Universities, 273, 292
    Aberdeenshire, 204, 250–1, 273
    Angus, 205, 289
    Argyllshire, 250–1
    Ayr Burghs, 294
    Ayrshire, 187, 188, 234, 247, 250, 251, 273
    Ayrshire South, 290
    Banffshire, 187–8, 204
    Border Burghs, 272, 273
    Buteshire, 240, 274
    Cromarty-shire, 187, 233
    Dunbartonshire, 205, 247, 252, 277
    Dundee, 242, 253, 255, 257, 275, 276, 279, 281, 283
    East Lothian, 22, 248–9, 281, 290
    Edinburgh, 205, 237, 252, 253, 254, 255, 275, 281, 283
    Edinburgh & Saint Andrews Universities, 273, 293
    Elgin Burghs, 204
    Falkirk Burghs, 242, 245, 249, 253
    Fife-shire, 232, 248
    Glasgow, 237, 245, 247, 253, 254, 255, 257, 273, 274, 275, 276, 277, 279, 280, 284, 293, 295, 298
    Greenock, 242, 245, 253, 259, 276, 279, 281, 284
    Haddington Burghs, 242, 245, 254
    Inverness Burghs, 237, 242
    Inverness-shire, 188, 226, 234, 290
    Kilmarnock Burghs, 242, 245, 253, 276, 294, 295
    Kincardineshire, 233
    Kinross-shire, 289–90
    Kirkcudbrightshire, 187, 224
    Lanarkshire, 234, 251
    Lanarkshire North, 273–4
    Lanarkshire South, 273–4
    Leith Burghs, 239, 253, 279, 281
    Midlothian-shire, 5, 160, 161, 226, 239, 241, 274, 283, 286, 297
    Morayshire, 204
    Nairn-shire, 204
    Paisley, 242, 253, 255, 257
    Peebles-shire & Selkirkshire, 272
    Perth, 255
    Perthshire, 204, 205, 210, 246, 247, 290, 291
    Renfrewshire, 224, 234, 245, 253
    Ross-shire & Cromarty, 232, 247
    Roxburgh-shire, 237, 247, 250, 272, 280–1, 283, 290
    Saint Andrews Burghs, 247
    Selkirkshire, 250
    Stirling Burghs, 255
    Stirlingshire, 187, 188, 204, 205, 233, 291
    Sutherlandshire, 188, 233, 273
    West Lothian, 291
    Wick (Northern) Burghs, 232
    Wigtown Burghs, 240
    Wigtownshire, 242, 244
Contagious Diseases Acts, 276, 277–9
Co-operative movement, 76–7, 93, 263–4
Corgarff, 13
corn laws, 5, 191, 219, 228–9, 230, 248–51, 253, 258
Corruption, Old, 270
cottars, 7, 14, 19

county franchise reform movement, 187–8, 191, 193
Court of Session
  decisions, 90, 115–16, 130
  reform of, 189, 209, 233, 235
Covenanters, 144, 165–6, 167
Cowan, Charles, 162, 246
Cox Brothers & Co., 40–1, 60, 68
Cranston, Robert, 263
cricket, 87
Crieff, 49
Crimean War, 40–1, 258–9
Crinan canal, 41
Crofters' War, 35, 36
Cromarty, 289
Crosskey, Rev. Henry W., 281
Cullen, 26
Cullen, Prof. Wm, 16
Culrain, 34, 35
Cults, 69
Culzean Castle, 167
Cunard line, 44, 54, 59
Cunninghame district, 13
Cupar, 102, 220, 243
curling, 87
Cuthbertson, John Neilson, 294

Daer, Lord, 193
Dale, David, 38, 123
Dalglish, Robert, 179
Dalhousie, 10th earl of, 160, 250; *see also* Maule, Fox
Dalkeith, 274
Dalkeith, Lord, 252
Dalrymple, John, 138, 223, 252; *see also* Stair, Lord
Darwinism, 138
Davitt, Michael, 174, 178
Declaration of Rights (1689), 217
Deed of Separation, 132
Deer Forests, 34
deference, 242
Dempster, George, 38, 183, 192
Denny, Wm & Co., 44, 80
Derby, 251
Dick & Laing, 51
Dickens, Charles, 68, 166, 167
Diseases

bronchitis, 96
cholera, 96, 97, 108, 112
smallpox, 96
tuberculosis, 96
typhoid, 108
typhus, 96, 96–7, 108, 112
zymotic, 96
see also Health
Disraeli, Benjamin, 160, 164, 167, 243, 271, 286, 291
Disestablishment, 140, 141, 253, 276, 283–4, 285, 292–3, 299; *see also* Free Church of Scotland; Liberal party; Voluntary Presbyterian Churches
Disruption, 5, 65, 127–35, 154, 245–6
Dixon, Wm, 56
docks, 39, 49
Donaldson Line, 62
Donizetti, Gaetano, 166
Dubs, Henry, 45
Duff, Alexander, 159
Dumas, Alexandre, the elder, 166
Dumbarton, 44, 80, 185, 265
Dumfries, 102, 227, 243, 253
Dumfries-shire, 22
Dunbartonshire, 91, 95
Duncan, Admiral Adam, 158
Duncan, Thomas, 167
Dundas, Henry, later 1st viscount Melville, 2, 4, 66, 189, 195–8, 201–7, 207–8, 209, 210, 233
Dundas, Robert, later 2nd viscount Melville, 207, 210, 224, 226
Dundas, Sir Thomas, later 1st baron Dundas, 207
Dundas of Arniston, Robert, 226
Dundee, 39, 40, 47, 49, 50, 55, 57, 61, 64, 73, 78, 79, 84, 85, 90–1, 99, 102, 111, 112, 113, 135, 138, 143, 156, 169, 171–2, 174, 176, 178, 179, 183, 212, 213–14, 220, 222, 229, 231, 249, 259, 261, 262, 268, 276, 277
Dundonald, 9th earl of, 16
Dunfermline, 39, 119, 185
Durness, 23

East India Co., 2, 158, 159, 202–3, 204–5
East Lothian, 8, 10, 17

economy
 agriculture, 1, 7–22, 248–9, 287–90
 banking, 49–53, 67
 brewing, 25, 46
 brickmaking, 27
 coal mining, 3, 19, 25, 37, 39, 41, 42–3, 46–7, 48, 50, 58, 59, 60, 61–2, 79, 80–1, 103, 107, 158, 189
 cotton manufacture, 37–8, 50, 52, 55, 56–7, 60, 61, 84–5, 152, 219, 268
 fishing, 25, 27
 heavy engineering, 3, 43–6, 50, 53, 54, 61, 79, 89, 106–7, 160, 168
 iron manufacturing, 3, 41–2, 43, 44, 45, 46, 47–8, 57–8, 61–2, 79, 106, 158
 jute manufacture, 40–1, 56–7, 61, 85, 158
 linen manufacturing, 1, 38–9, 55–6, 61, 79, 84–5, 189
 locomotive building, 45, 47–8, 61, 62
 shipbuilding, 3, 13, 43–5, 59–60, 62, 79, 158
 steel production, 44, 51, 58
 transport, 13–14, 46–9
 wool manufacturing, 13, 23, 24–5, 26, 34, 38–9, 48, 51, 57, 60, 79, 81
Edinburgh, 2, 14, 28, 43, 46–7, 48, 55, 56, 61, 64, 67, 68–9, 73, 77, 78, 88, 89, 92–3, 90–1, 100, 101, 102, 103, 105, 107, 108, 110, 113, 114, 117, 124, 132, 135, 136, 150, 165, 167, 169, 176–7
 politics, post-1832, 243, 249, 251, 258, 259, 268, 269, 274, 281, 282, 291, 292, 293
 politics, pre-1832, 186, 187, 191, 192, 194, 197, 199, 200, 213, 221, 222, 223, 225, 227, 228, 229, 230, 233, 234
education, 53–4, 65, 74, 75–6, 84, 88, 92–3, 118, 122, 127, 136, 143–4, 148–53, 160, 164, 165, 177, 179–81, 255–7, 263, 275; see also universities
Education Act (1872), 74, 86, 143, 149, 164, 177, 180
Educational Institute of Scotland, 67
Eglinton, 13th earl of, 162, 204, 250

Elcho, Lord, later 10th earl of Wemyss, 281, 293
Elder, John, 44, 59
elections, general
 1784, 206
 1790, 189, 206
 1796, 206
 1802, 208
 1806, 208
 1807, 209
 1812, 210
 1818, 224
 1820, 224
 1826, 224
 1830, 224,
 1831, 224, 230
 1832, 240, 253, 287
 1835, 240, 253
 1837, 240, 244, 245, 246, 253
 1841, 240, 245, 246–7, 253, 254
 1847, 240, 247, 248, 250, 252, 253, 255
 1852, 240, 250, 256, 286
 1857, 240, 252, 257, 258–9
 1859, 240, 252, 257
 1865, 286, 287, 289–90
 1868, 275, 283, 284–5, 286, 287, 290, 290–1, 293
 1874, 276, 283, 284–5, 286, 287, 290, 290–1, 291, 293, 294, 297
 1880, 276, 281, 284, 284–5, 286, 287, 293, 297–8
 1886, 298
electorate, 187, 237, 271–2, 273
Elgin, 204
Elgin, earl of, 7th, 11, 15; 8th, 160; 9th, 284, 297
Elibank, 7th Lady, 233
Eliot, George, 167
Ellice, Edward, 32
Elliot, Arthur R. D., 280–1
Elliot, Gilbert, later 1st earl of Minto, 184, 192, 207; see also Auckland, Lady (Eliot's sister)
Elphinstone, 12th Lady, 233
Elphinstone, 12th Lord, 204, 205
Emigration, 24, 160
Empire, 157–61
Encyclopedia Britannica, 171

England, 58, 59–60, 61, 65, 68, 73, 83, 84, 97, 104–7, 115, 119, 120, 122, 123–4, 132, 136, 138, 142, 145, 148, 149, 151, 152, 153, 158, 160–1, 163, 165, 167, 169, 171, 177
   politics, post-1832, 237, 238, 239–40, 240–1, 242, 243–4, 245, 248, 250, 251, 252, 259, 260–4, 267, 269, 271, 273, 275, 281, 282, 284, 286–7, 288, 290–1, 293, 294, 298
   politics, pre-1832, 187, 189, 191, 193, 194, 195, 196, 197, 198, 199, 200–1, 202, 206, 214–15, 215–16, 218, 224, 226, 227, 228, 230, 231–2
Enlightenment, Scottish, 2, 5, 14, 55, 71, 149, 152–3, 171, 183, 216–18, 234; *see also* Ferguson, Adam; Hume, David; Millar, Prof. John; Smith, Adam; Stewart, Prof. Dugald
entrepreneurship, 53–62
Episcopalian Church of Scotland, 2, 123–4
Ericht river, 15
Erskine, Henry, 189, 191, 192–3, 198, 207, 209–10
Esk river, 103
Evangelical Union Church, 123
Ewart, Wm, 258, 259
Ewing, James, 229
Eyre, Archbishop Charles, 174, 177

factory reform, 145, 244
Fairfield Shipbuilding & Engineering Co., 59
Falkirk, 45, 57, 203, 215
famine, 8
   Great Highland, 23, 32–3, 36, 154
   Irish, 169–70, 172, 177, 179
Farmers' Clubs, 16
Farr parish, 35, 135
Federation of Celtic Societies, 157
feeing fairs, 21
Female Industrial Schools, 149
Fenianism, 177
Fenton Barns, 10, 26, 248
Fergus, Dr Andrew, 108
Ferguson, Adam, 71, 157
Ferguson, John, 177–9
Fergusson, Ronald C., 224

Fergusson, Sir James, 6th baronet, 164–5
feudal system, 104, 187
Fife, county of, 12, 46, 68, 126, 195
Fife, 2nd earl of, 15, 39, 187–8, 204, 205, 233
Findlater, 7th earl of, 204
Finlay, Kirkman, 28, 179, 232
Fletcher, Archibald, 220
football, 87
Forfar, 48, 186
Forfeited Estates, 156
Forrest, James, 247
Fort William, 123
Forth & Clyde canal, 46
Fortrose, 185
Fox, Charles James, 198–9, 207, 208, 232
Fox Dinners, 222–3, 227, 234
France, 1, 184
   war with, 192, 193, 195
   see also Revolutions, French
Fraser, John, 263
Fraserburgh, 185, 186
Free Church of Scotland, 4, 33, 35–6, 63, 123, 132–41, 143, 144–5, 154, 159, 220, 226, 227, 243, 244, 247, 249, 251, 252–8, 260, 261, 289, 291
   Disruption, 127–35, 154
   political involvement, 5, 141, 247, 254–7, 276, 283–4, 285, 292–3
   relations with Voluntaries, 5, 140–1, 254–7, 276
   see also Church of Scotland; United Presbyterian Church; Voluntary Presbyterian Churches
Free Colliers, 89–90
Free Trade, 5, 78, 217, 219, 220, 230, 249, 258, 259, 269, 276
Free Presbyterian Church of Scotland, 138
Freemasons, 294
Friendly Societies, 88
Friends of the People (English), 189, 192; *see also* Scottish Friends of the People

Gaelic, 135–6, 153, 155, 156–7
Gaelic Society of Inverness, 156
Gainsborough, Thomas, 54

Gairloch, 23
Galashiels, 273
Galloway, earl of, 7th, 207; 8th, 15; 9th, 240, 242
Galloway region, 49, 115–16
Galt, John, 168
Game Laws, 248–9, 287–8, 289–90
Garibaldi, Giuseppe, 162, 268
Gartsherrie, 42, 54
Gaskell, Mrs, 167
Geddes, Bishop John, 171
geology, 138
George III, king, 213
George IV, king, 220–3, 224
Gerrard, J., 194
Gibbon, Lewis Grassic, 18
Gillon, Wm D., 244
Girvan, 215
Gladstone, Sir John, 289–90
Gladstone, Wm Ewart, 5, 78, 160, 250, 271, 283, 284–5, 297, 298
Glasgow, 3–4, 14, 28, 37–8, 43, 44, 45, 47, 48, 49, 52–3, 55, 56, 60, 62, 64, 67, 69–70, 72, 73, 74, 75, 77, 80, 82–3, 84–5, 88, 89, 90, 91, 94, 95, 96, 97, 98, 99, 100, 102, 103, 105, 107, 111, 112, 116–18, 124, 136, 139, 144, 145, 146, 150, 152–3, 155, 157, 158, 168, 169, 172, 174, 175, 176–7, 179–80
  politics, post-1832, 243, 244–5, 247, 249, 250, 251, 260, 261, 263, 264, 268, 269, 270, 277, 278, 279, 282, 284, 286, 291, 292, 294
  politics, pre-1832, 184, 186, 191, 193, 199, 213, 214, 220, 221, 222, 226, 230, 231, 233
Glenelg, 32, 115
Glengarry, 29, 32
Glenquoich, 32
Goderich, Viscount, 228
Goethe, J. W. von, 166
golf, 87, 88
Gordon, Captain John, 32
Gordon, Edward S., 292
Gordon, 4th duchess of, 233
Gordon, 4th duke of, 15, 204, 209
government, Scottish, 162–5, 218
Grace, Dr W. G., 87

Graham, Sir James, 245
Grant, Charles, 225–6
Grant, General James, 188
Grant, James, 162
Grant, James P., 8, 28–9
Grant, John, 162
Grant, Sir Archibald, 19
Grant of Grant, Sir James, 8th baronet, 204
Great Eastern, 46
Greenock, 33, 44, 48, 72, 101, 102, 103, 135, 154, 155, 170, 172, 204, 277
Grenville, George, 208–9, 232

Hadden, Gavin, 65
Hadden, James, 65
Haldane, James, 123
Haldane, Richard B., 297
Haldane, Robert, 123
Hamilton, 59, 180
Hamilton, duke of, 9th, 8, 216; 11th, 252
Hamilton, 11th duchess of, 173
Hamilton, Gavin, 166
Hamilton, Lord Archibald, 216–17
Hardie, Andrew, 215
Hardie, James Keir, 144
Harris, Isle of, 23, 32
Harry, Blind, 161
Hartington, marquess of, 283
Harvey, Sir George, 168
Hawick, 60, 263–4
health, 3–4, 95–7, 100–3, 108–13; *see also* diseases
height, 97
Helmsdale, 25
Henderson, F. Y., 277
Hertfordshire, 8
Higher Criticism, 138, 139
Highland & Agricultural Society, 16
Highlands, 3, 4, 37, 41, 116, 120, 170, 199–200
  Clearances, 22–36, 123, 128, 135–6, 138, 140–1, 150, 152–7, 166, 168, 178, 191–2, 225
Highlander, 156
Hill, Rev. George, 126, 197
Hillfoots, 38
Hogarth, Wm, 54

Hogg, James, 227
Hope, George, 247, 249
Hornby v. Close (1867), 282
Horner, Francis, 216
housing, 4, 92, 97–107, 113–14
Howden, James, 44
Hugo, Victor, 166
Hume, David, 157
Hume, Joseph, 224, 230, 233
Hungary, 163, 268
Huskisson, Wm, 223, 225, 227, 228
Hutton, James, 138
Hydepark Locomotive works, 45
hypothec, 107, 288–90

identity, national
   British, 4, 157–63, 269, 270
   Irish, 173
   Scottish, 4, 148–56, 157–8, 158–61
Ilay, Lord, 2
Importance of a National Church, The, 127
Independent Friends, 189
Independent Order of Good Templars, 279–80
India, 2, 57, 61, 62, 75, 158, 160, 203, 230
Indies, West, 61, 62, 159
industrial relations,
   Criminal Law Amendment Act, 281–3
   Master & Servant Act, 20, 270, 293
   strikes, 80, 85, 89, 90, 215, 261, 262
   trade unions, 80, 85, 89, 90–3, 229, 260, 261, 269–71, 281–3
   trades councils, 88, 90, 91, 92–3, 262, 269, 270, 278, 281, 282
   see also working classes
infant mortality, 97
Institute of Bankers of Scotland, 67
Institute of Chartered Accountants of Scotland, 67
Institute of Engineers & Shipbuilders in Scotland, 54, 67
Inverness, 47, 100, 220, 291
Inverness-shire, 22, 24, 135, 170, 200
Inverurie, 186
Ireland, 32–3, 89–90, 124, 154, 156, 168, 172–3, 175, 177, 178, 195, 198, 215, 398
Irish Home Government Association, 177
Irish Home Rule, 6, 162, 276, 295, 297

Irish immigrants, 89–90, 154, 168–73, 192
   politics, 89, 174–9, 260–1
Irish Land League, 36
Isla river, 15
Italy, 268

Jackson, George, 270, 276
Jacobites, 2, 152, 153, 157, 166, 228
Jedburgh, 112, 183
Jeffrey, Francis, 133, 164, 215, 216, 218–19, 221, 223, 234
Jenner's store, 77
Jesuits, 173, 180
Jex-Blake, Sophia, 75
jingoism, 160
Johnny Gibb of Gushetneuk, 288

Kailyard, 168
Kames, Lord, 10, 16
kelp, 23, 30–1
Kelso, 13
Kelso river, 103
Kelvin, Lord, 54, 298
Kelvin river, 103
Kennedy, Thomas F., 216, 221, 226, 228, 230
Kerr, Wm, 14
Kidston, Wm, 292
Kilbarchan, 54
Kildonan, 25, 34
Kilmany, 126
Kilmarnock, 227, 243
Kincaldrum, 68
Kincardine Moss, 10
Kincardineshire, 68
Kingsley, Charles, 167
Kinnoull, 11th earl of, 130
Kirk, Alexr C., 44
Kirkcaldy, 40, 249, 261
Kirkcudbrightshire, 22, 210
Kirkintilloch, 47, 128
Kirriemuir, 267
Knoydart, 32, 68
Kolkata, 57, 159
Kossuth, Louis, 162

Labour party, 144
Laing, Samuel, 258, 259, 267–8

Lanark, 102
Lanarkshire, 8, 37, 41, 42–3, 48, 58, 59, 83, 95, 115–16, 169, 171–2, 180, 215, 261, 269
Lancashire, 67, 68, 84–5
Lancefield Forge, 45
Land Question
  Irish, 177
  Scottish, 177
landowners, 3, 14–15, 19–20, 22, 23, 27–34, 36, 128, 135, 152, 155, 161, 178, 187–8, 189, 200, 204, 219, 227, 232, 233, 240, 242, 244, 247, 249, 288, 291, 297–8
Langholm, 192
Lansdowne, 3rd marquess of, 226, 228
Lauder, Robert S., 166
Lauderdale, 8th earl of, 208–9, 217
Lavery, Sir John, 88
Law, Andrew Bonar, 292
Lawson, George, 160
Lee, Rev. Robert, 137–8
Leeds, 57
Leith, 110, 113, 136
Leochel Cushnie, 64
Leslie Case, 65–6
Leslie, John, 65–6
Lesmahagow, 59
Lewis, David, 265
Lewis, Isle of, 23
Liberal party, 4, 5, 22, 78, 141, 161, 239, 247, 251–3, 271–3, 275–86, 290–1, 292, 293, 297–9; *see also* radicalism; Whig party
Liberal Unionists, 297–8
Liberation Society, 283
Lincoln, President Abraham, 268
Lipton, Sir Thomas, 77
literature, 165–6, 167–8
Littlejohn, Dr Henry, 67, 108, 109–10
Liverpool, 30, 42, 49, 61, 169
Liverpool, Lord, 225
Livingstone, David, 151, 159
Local Veto, 280
Loch, James, 24, 25, 153
Lochs
  Goil, 103
  Katrine, 102

Long, 103
  Thom, 102
Lochinver, 25
Lochmaben, 186
Lockhart, A. E., 250
Lockhart, J. G., 227
London, 13, 44, 47, 48
London Corresponding Society, 191, 192, 194
Lord Advocates, 163–5
Lothian, marquesses of, 173
Lothians, the, 12, 15, 17, 18, 21, 45, 48, 59
Lovat, 12th Lord, 173
loyalism, 4, 196–201, 207, 224
Lucknow, siege of (1857), 155
Lyell, Charles, 138

MacAulay, Thomas Babington, 254
MacColl, Rev. Dugald, 171
MacCombie, Wm, of Aberdeen, 64
MacCombie, Wm, of Tillyfour, 12
MacCulloch, Horatio, 161, 166
MacCulloch, James, 160
MacDonald, Alexander, 88, 90, 92
MacDonald, Sir John A., 160
MacDonald of Clanranald, Ranald, 32
MacDonald of Sleat, 2nd baron, 27
MacDonnell of Glengarry, 32
MacFarlane, Malcolm, 261, 264
MacFie, Robert A., 258
MacGonagoll, Wm, 86
MacHugh, Edward, 178
MacIntosh, Charles, 53
MacKenzie, Alexander, 160
MacKenzie, Dr John, 23
MacKenzie, Francis, 23
MacKenzie, Rev. David, 35, 135
MacKenzie, Sir Kenneth, 23
MacKenzie of Applecross, Thomas, 247
MacKenzie Stewart, Mrs, 232
MacKinnon, Wm, 62
MacKintosh, C. Fraser, 298
Mackintosh, Sir James, 221
MacLaren, Duncan, 68–9, 250, 258, 259, 281, 282–3, 298
Macleod, Rev. Norman, 137
MacLeod of Harris, 24

MacLeod of MacLeod, Norman, 31, 188, 191
MacNeil of Barra, Roderick, 30–1
MacNeill, Malcolm, 110
MacNeill, Sir John, 110
Magdalene Institutes, 71, 279
Magna Carta, 213, 215
Maine, Sir Henry, 156
Maitland, Frederick W., 156
Manchester, 38, 56, 84, 100, 214
Mansfield, 3rd earl of, 200
Margarot, Maurice, 194, 213
Marist Brothers, 177
Marlborough, 232
Marshall, Rev. A., 120
martyrs, radical, 199
Marx, Karl, 166
Matheson, Sir James, 33, 247
Mauchline, 215
Maule, Fox, later Lord Panmure, then 11th earl of Dalhousie, 134, 164–5, 216, 247, 252, 258
Maxwell, Lady, 234
Maxwell, Sir John, 8th baronet, 224, 234, 244
Maynooth College, 251, 254, 257
Mazzini, Giuseppe, 268
Mechanics Institutes, 88
Medical Act (1858), 66
Medical Officers of Health, 67, 109–10, 111
Meikle, Andrew, 11
Melbourne, Lord, 131, 133, 164–5, 246
Melgund, Lord, later 3rd earl of Minto, 255, 256
Melville
  1st viscount *see* Dundas, Henry
  2nd viscount *see* Dundas, Robert
Men, The, 135–6
Mendelssohn, Felix, 166
Methil, 43
Methodists, 123
middle classes, 3, 35, 49–50, 54, 69–76, 100, 102, 104–5, 106, 107, 112, 119, 150, 151, 154–5, 161
  occupations, 2, 48–9, 60, 64, 65–8, 74, 76–7, 122, 160, 181, 204
  politics, post-1832, 5–6, 68–9, 77–8, 111–12, 114, 237, 241, 242–3, 244–5,
246–7, 249, 252–3, 257–9, 260, 264, 267–71, 272, 274–81, 290, 292, 294–5, 298–9
  politics, pre-1832, 5, 184–7, 192, 197, 198, 199, 214, 215–16, 217–23, 224–5, 228–32
  religion, 65, 70–2, 74–5, 77, 124–5, 128, 129, 136, 137–8, 142, 144, 155–6, 176–7, 275–9
Middle Party, 132, 134, 135
Midlothian, 56
Militia, 199
Militia Act (1797), 195–6, 199–200
Mill, John Stuart, 276
Millar, Prof. John, 152, 183, 191, 193, 198, 216
Miller, J. F., 168
Milne, J. Duguid, 274
Milton, Lord, 252
Mines Act (1842), 84
Ministry of All the Talents, 208–9
Mintlaw, 237
Minto, earl of
  1st, 233
  2nd, 228
  3rd, 252, 255–6
Mirrlees, Watson & Co., 45
missions, Protestant
  home, 141–4
  overseas, 159
Moffat, Robert, 159
Moir, James, 261, 265, 270
Moira, Lord, 209
Moncrieff, James, 164, 221, 256–7, 271
Moncrieff, Rev. Sir Henry Wellwood, 221
Monkland, 59, 119–20
Monkland canal, 46
Monkland Friendly Society, 190
Monkland Iron Co., 51
Monteith, James, 38
Monteith, Robert, 173
Montrose, 101, 220, 243
Montrose, 3rd duke of, 188, 204, 205, 233
Moore, Sir John, 158
Moray, 115–16
Morvern, 26
Motherwell, 95, 286
Muir, Thomas, 192, 193, 198

Mundella, A. J., 281, 282
Municipal Corporations Act (1835), 252
Munro, James, 160
Murdoch, John, 156
Murray, Alexander, 151
Murray, John A., 133, 216
Murray, Patrick, 210
Mushet, 41
Musselburgh, 199, 239

Napier, Robert, 44, 59
Nasmyth, Alexander, 168
National Association for the Vindication of Scottish Rights, 162–3, 165
National Bank of Scotland, 51
National Brotherhood of St Patrick, 178
National Convention of the Scottish Friends of the People
  First (1792), 192
  Second (1793), 193
  Third (1793), 193–4
National Education Association of Scotland, 255–6
National Society for Women's Suffrage, 274–5
National Union of Conservative and Constitutional Associations, 291
nationalism, European, 268–9
Neilson, James Beaumont, 41, 47, 51, 53
Neilson, Walter, 45
New Hebrides, 159
New Lanark, 37, 38, 83–4
New Pitsligo, 237
New Statistical Account [*NSA*], 20, 36
New Zealand, 34, 61, 160
Newcastle-upon-Tyne, 100
Newport Rising, 262
newspapers, 35, 134, 154, 160, 176–7, 184, 196–7, 220, 242–3, 251, 252–3
  Bee, 197
  Edinburgh Gazetteer, 196
  Edinburgh Observer, 165
  Glasgow Constitutional, 243, 251
  Glasgow Courier, 226
  Glasgow Free Press, 176–7
  Glasgow Herald, 226, 298
  Glasgow News, 291, 293
  Glasgow Saturday Evening Post, 244
  Glasgow Sentinel, (1809–11), 213; (1850–77), 213
  Inverness Advertiser, 154
  North British Daily Mail, 154, 277
  Northern Ensign, 154
  Northern Star, 260
  Scotsman, 160, 176–7, 220, 251, 283, 298
  Witness, 134, 154
Newtyle, 47
Nicolson, John, 123
Non-Intrusionists, 130–4, 246–7, 249, 263
North British Australian Co., 159
North British Banking Co., 49
North British Locomotive Co., 45
Nottingham, 131

Oban, 23
O'Brien, Bronterre, 179
Ochiltree, 54
O'Connell, Daniel, 230
O'Connor, Feargus, 179
Old Deer, 21
Old Monkland, 47
Old Statistical Account [*OSA*], 7, 20
Orange Order, 89–90, 171–3, 294–5
Orbiston, 93
Orders in Council, 219, 221
Oswald, Alexr H., 250
Otago, 160
Owen, Robert, 38, 83–4, 93
Owenite Co-operation, 93

Pacific Islands, 151
Paine, Thomas, 190–1, 196, 197, 215
Paisley, 37, 54, 55, 66, 72, 75, 100, 124, 170, 172, 195, 220, 222, 230–1, 260, 264, 275
Paisley canal, 46
Palgrave, Francis T., 26
Palmer, Rev T. F., 193
Palmerston, Lord, 5, 250, 251, 258, 259, 284
Panmure, Lord *see* Maule, Fox
Papal aggression, 171, 176, 251
Parkhead Forge, 45
Parliamentary Reform Association, 259
Parnell, Charles Stuart, 174, 177
Parsons, C. A., & Co., 60

Paton, John, 159
patronage
  Church of Scotland, 125, 129–30, 152, 203, 205, 246
  political, 202–5, 224, 225
Patronage Abolition Act (1874), 293–4
Patronage Act (1712), 129–30
Pattison, Wm, 261, 264
Peace Conference, 258
Pearce, Wm, 291
Peel, Sir Robert, 23, 225, 226, 227, 244–5, 246–7
Peelites, 250–1
peers, Scottish, elections, 206
penal reform, 225
periodicals, 154, 227–8, 252–3
  Blackwood's Magazine, 226–7, 227–8, 231–2, 234, 243, 244
  Celtic Magazine, 156
  Edinburgh Review, 5, 55, 71, 154, 209, 216, 217, 218, 221, 227–8, 234, 252–3
  Farmers' Magazine, 16
  Highlander, 156
  North British Agriculturist, 289
  North British Review, 252
Perth, 87, 100, 154, 155, 186, 189, 191, 214, 222, 243, 286, 292
Perthshire, 20, 22, 30, 190, 195, 200
Peterhead, 200
Peterloo, 214, 219
Picts, 152–3
piping, 156
Pitt Club dinners, 227, 228
Pitt, Wm, the Younger, 188, 189, 197, 207–8
Plea for Women, A, 75, 274
Plug Plot, 262
Poland, 268
Police Commissions, 72–4, 108, 110–11, 163, 220, 229
Police Scotland Act (1833), 253
Pollock, Sir Frederick, 156
Pollokshaws, 234
pollution, 4, 102–3, 112
Pollution Act (1876), 108
Poor Laws, 4, 33, 71, 84, 107, 115–20, 122, 136, 137, 144, 145, 175, 221, 242, 243–4, 264
  Board of Supervision, 102, 108–10, 119

Popular Protestantism, 293–5
population, 1, 22–3, 61, 95, 96
Port Glasgow, 204
Port Gordon, 15
Portland, 4th duke of, 207, 209
Portobello, 239
Portsoy, 190, 237
Post Office Savings Bank, 88
Presbyterian Dissenters *see* Voluntary Presbyterians
Present Happiness of Great Britain, The, 197
professions, 65–8
prostitution, 278–9
Protectionism, 62, 219, 228, 230, 248–9, 250–1, 267, 298
Public Health, 108–13

Quakers, 196, 197
Quarrier, Wm, 123, 277
Quarrier's Homes, 120
Queensberry, 7th marquess of, 250

'Radical Rising', 5, 90, 214–16
radicalism, 5, 198, 222, 259, 267
  entrepreneurial, 257–9
  middle-class, 74, 78, 162, 170, 210, 221, 252–4, 260, 265, 267–8, 269, 270, 275–84, 298
  Tory, 243–4
  working-class, 90, 92, 162, 190, 194–6, 198–9, 212–16, 218–19, 221, 229, 260, 265, 267–76
  see also Chartism; Conservative party; Liberal party; Whig party
Rae, Sir Wm, 164, 225, 226
railways, 3, 47–9
Rainy, Rev. Robert, 138, 285
Rankine, Prof. W. J. M., 54
redistribution, constituencies, 238–40, 267, 272–3
Reflections on the Revolution in France, 192
Reform Act
  First (1832), 228–31, 237–40
  Second (1868), 267–71, 271–3
  Third (1884–5), 297
Reformation, Scottish, 148–9, 151, 152
Reid, George, 168
Reid, Margaret, 75, 274

Relief Church, 128; *see also* United Presbyterian Church; United Secession Church; Voluntary Presbyterian Churches
Renfrewshire, 13, 37, 72, 95, 169, 215, 230–1
Revolt of the Field, 20
Revolutions
   American, 157–8, 184–5
   French (1789), 4–5, 182–3, 184, 189–90, 192, 196
   French (1830), 230, 232
   'Glorious', 152, 213
Reynolds, Sir Joshua, 54
Rights of Man, The, 190–1
Risorgimento, 268
roads, 8, 13, 15, 47
Robertson, Rev. Wm, 152
Rogan, Patrick, 176
Roman Catholic Church, 2, 122, 151, 170–81, 196, 251, 257, 293–4
   Emancipation, 128, 171, 189, 210, 224, 226–7, 228
Rosebery, 5th earl of, 283, 284
Ross, George, 261
Ross & Cromarty, 12, 22, 34, 156–8, 200
Rossini, Gioacchino, 166
Rosslyn, 2nd earl of, 217
Rothesay, 190
Rotomohama, 44
Roxburgh, Wm, 160
Roxburghshire, 200
rugby, 87
Russell, Dr John B., 67, 103
Russell, Lord John, 216
Rutherfurd, Andrew, 133

Sabbath School Union of Scotland, 143
Saint Andrews, 88
Saint Fillans, 156
Saint Kilda, 24
Saint Vincent de Paul Society, 175, 176, 178–9
sanitation, 100
School Boards, 144, 276, 293, 294–5
'Scots Wha Hae', 162
Scott, David, 203, 205
Scott, Sir Walter, 165–7, 222, 227, 228
Scottish Baronial style, 167

Scottish Central Board of Dissenters, 131, 253–5
Scottish Coal & Iron Miners' Association, 90
Scottish Disestablishment Association, 283, 293
Scottish Farmers' Club, 289
Scottish Friends of the People, 191–7
Scottish Home Rule Association, 178
Scottish Institute of Engineers & Shipbuilders, 54, 67
Scottish Labour party, 178, 299
Scottish Liberal Association, 285
Scottish National Constitutional Association, 291
Scottish National Reform League, 179, 270–1, 275–6
Scottish Permissive Bill Association, 279–81
Scottish Public Health Acts (1867, 1875), 109
Scottish Temperance League, 263, 277, 279
Scottish Trades Union Congress, 91
Scottish Women's Temperance Association, 75, 274
Seafield estate, 14
Seaforth, 1st baron, 23, 27–8, 30, 31, 32, 207, 232
Secession churches, 152; *see also* Relief Church; United Presbyterian Church; Voluntary Presbyterian Churches
Sectarianism, 89–90, 170–3, 294–5; *see also* anti-Catholicism
Self Help, 92
Selkirk, 16
Selkirk, 5th earl of, 217
Selkirkshire, 250
Sellar, Alexr C. 26
Sellar, Patrick, 23–7, 153
Sellar, Wm, 26
Service, James, 161
Sheridan, Robert Brinsley, 189
Shetland, 123, 250
Shotts Iron Co., 41–2
Simon, Sir John, 110
Sinclair, Sir John, 210
Sinclairtown, 261

Sites Question, 247
Six Acts, 214
Skene, 64
Skirving, Wm, 194
Skye, Isle of, 27
Slammanan, 48
slaughterhouses, 101
slavery, abolition of, 159, 171, 221, 223, 230, 234, 261, 269, 274
Sleat, 27
Slessor, Mary, 159
Small, James, 11
Smiles, Samuel, 92
Smith, Adam, 14, 217–18, 219, 249
Smith, Alexander, 103, 168
Smith, James, 138
Smith, Wm Robertson, 138
Smollett, Alexander, 250
Smyllum Orphanage, 175
Smythe, Wm, 110
Somerville, Rev. Thomas, 183, 192
Sons of the Rock Society, 72
Southampton, 242
Spenceans, the, 215
Spencer, 2nd earl of, 208–9
Spinningdale, 25
Spiritual Independence, 130–1, 246
sport, 86, 87–8
Stafford, Lord *see* Sutherland, 1st duke of
Staffordshire, 62
Stair, 8th earl of, 223; *see also* Dalrymple, John
Stanley, 37
Stanley, Caleb, 168
steamboats, 13
Stendhal, 166
Stewart, Prof. Dugald, 55, 183, 198, 216
Stewarton, 130
Stirling, 72, 78, 96, 100–1, 102, 108, 111, 112, 161, 186, 187
Stirlingshire, 24, 37, 48, 87, 172, 200
Stoke-on-Trent, 242
Stormont, Lord, 87
Stornoway, 23
Story, Rev. Robert H., 137
Strathaven, 215
Strathnaver, 25, 26, 34, 135
strikes *see* industrial relations

Stubbs, George, 54
suburbs, 69–70
Suez canal, 57
sugar-milling machinery, 45
Sunday Schools, 143
Sunset Song, 18
Sutherland, countess of, later 1st duchess of, 24, 232
Sutherland, duke of, 1st, 24, 27; 2nd, 33, 36
Sutherland estate, 24–7, 35
Sutherlandshire, 22, 24–7, 33, 34, 153, 200

Tain, 183
Tarland, 126
Tavistock, Lord, 252
Tay Rail Bridge, 45
Taylor, Jane, 275
teinds, 122
Telford, Thomas, 66
Temperance, 71, 75, 88, 114, 146, 173, 176, 196, 263, 274, 276, 277, 279–81, 285
tenant-farmers, 15–16, 287–90
Tennant, Charles (1768–1838), 53
Tennant, Charles & Co., 103, 284
Tennant, Sir Charles (1823–1906), 54, 58, 68, 293
tennis, 88
Tennyson, Alfred, Lord, 26
Test Acts, Repeal of, 191, 225
Teutonism, 152–3, 155
theatres, 70, 76, 91–2
Thomson, Alexander, of Banchory, 244
Thomson, J. & G., & Co., 44, 59, 60
Thrushgrove, 151, 161, 213–14
Tillicoultry, 261
Tiree, Isle of, 33–4
tithes, 122
tobacco trade, 1
Tod & MacGregor, 44
Tolpuddle Martyrs, 89
Tolstoy, Count Leo, 166
Tories *see* Conservative party
Toryism, Liberal, 223, 225–6
trade, overseas, 1, 37–8, 43, 57, 61–2, 106–7, 158–9, 184, 219, 225, 230, 249, 259
trade unions *see* industrial relations
Trades Councils *see* industrial relations
Trades Union Congress, 91

Tranent, 195
trials, state, 192, 193, 194, 196–9, 214, 218
Troon, 69
Tulloch, Principal Rev. John, 293
Turgenev, Ivan, 166
Turner, J. M. W., 54
Turner, James, of Thrushgrove, 260
Turriff, 21
Tweeddale, marquess of
  7th, 207
  8th, 226

Ulster, 123, 169–70, 172, 293–4
unemployment, 80, 83, 84, 96–7, 106–7, 115–16, 260
Union, Treaty of (1707), 152, 157, 161–2, 165, 186, 189, 209, 230, 231
Union Bank of Scotland, 51
Union canal, 46
Unitarians, 196, 197
United Free Church of Scotland, 141
United Irishmen, 198
United Presbyterian Church of Scotland, 251, 276, 293; *see also* Relief Church; Secession Churches; United Secession Church; Voluntary Presbyterian Churches
United Scotsmen, 194, 214
United Secession Church, 128, 256; *see also* Relief Church; Secession Churches; United Presbyterian Church; Voluntary Presbyterian Churches
United States of America, 2, 61, 62, 157, 159, 184–5, 198
  Civil War, 39, 41, 268–9
  see also America, North
United Trades of Glasgow, 90–1
universities, 148–51, 203–4
  Aberdeen, 55, 66, 148, 151, 203
  Cambridge, 151
  Edinburgh, 16, 26, 53, 55, 65–6, 75–6, 129, 151, 157, 183, 198, 203–4, 256
  Glasgow, 16, 54, 55, 56, 88, 184–5, 198, 203, 220, 244, 245, 259
  Oxford, 26, 151
  Saint Andrews, 66, 197, 203

urban improvement schemes, 113–14
urbanisation, 73, 95
Use & Wont, 144, 294

Verdi, Giuseppe, 68
Vestiges of Creation, The, 138
Veto Act (1834), 129–30
Victoria, Queen, 34, 103, 154, 178
villages
  planned, 19–20
  commuter, 69–70
Voluntary Presbyterian Churches, 65, 124–31, 137–41, 146, 152, 196, 244–6, 249, 254–7
  Disestablishment, 283
  political involvement, 131–4, 141, 245–7, 254–7, 276, 283–4, 292–3
  relations with Free Church, 140–1, 254–7
  see also Relief Church; Secession Churches; United Presbyterian Church; United Secession Church
voluntary organisations, 71–2, 74–5, 78
Volunteers, 199–200, 215, 218, 267, 270
votes, fictitious, 187–8, 238–9

wages, 60, 74, 83, 85–6, 106, 212, 214, 229
Wallace, Wm, 153, 161–2
Wallace National Monument, 161, 167
Water of Leith, 110
water supply, 102
Watson, Hugh, 12
Watt, James, 53
Watt, Robert, 194
Wellington, 1st duke of, 226, 228
Wemyss, 8th earl of, 250
Wesley, John, 123
West Lothian, 59
West of Scotland Liberal Unionist Association, 298
Western Bank, 51–3
Westminster Confession, 125, 138
Whig Club of Dundee, 183
Whig party, 4, 5, 66, 131–3, 154, 165, 171, 183, 184, 188–93, 200–1, 204, 206, 207–10, 216–24, 228–30, 241, 244, 245–7, 250–9, 269, 276, 280, 283, 284–5; *see also* Liberal party; radicalism

White, John C., 277
Wick, 109, 154, 253, 260
Wigtownshire, 22
Wild Men, the, 132, 134
Wilkes, John, 157
Wilkie, David, 166
Wilson, John, 215
women, 25, 29, 35, 74–5, 85–6, 116, 145–6, 169, 173, 174, 177, 185–6, 261, 279
   education, 74, 75–6, 93, 149–50, 181, 274
   politics, 71, 222, 232–4, 261–4, 274–5, 278, 286
   work, 1, 17–19, 25, 56, 74, 76, 79, 83–5, 116, 145, 181
working classes, 9, 41, 104–5, 107, 117–18, 126–7, 136, 138–9, 141–4, 149–50, 151, 155
   occupations, 2, 16, 28, 42, 45–6, 48, 49, 78–86, 106–7, 113–14, 116, 168–9, 170, 260
   politics, post-1832, 5, 22, 112, 174, 178, 179, 243–4, 245, 249, 259–65, 267–72, 275–6, 281–3, 286, 293–5, 297, 298–9
   politics, pre-1832, 5, 151, 161, 179, 190–1, 192, 195–6, 199–200, 212–18, 229–31, 213–14
   see also industrial relations; unemployment; wages
Wyvill, Rev. Christopher, 187, 188

Yorkshire, 25
Yorkshire Association, 187, 188
Young, Wm, 24–5
Young Ireland, 177
Young Ladies' Institutes, 150

EU representative:
Easy Access System Europe
Mustamäe tee 50, 10621 Tallinn, Estonia
Gpsr.requests@easproject.com